A DREAM WITHIN A DREAM

THE LIFE OF

EDGAR ALLAN POE

A DREAM WITHIN A DREAM

THE LIFE OF EDGAR ALLAN POE

NIGEL BARNES

PETER OWEN PUBLISHERS
LONDON AND CHESTER SPRINGS, PA, USA

PETER OWEN PUBLISHERS
73 Kenway Road, London SW5 0RE

Peter Owen books are distributed in the USA by
Dufour Editions Inc., Chester Springs, PA 19425-0007

First published in Great Britain 2009

ISBN 978-0-7206-1322-3

A catalogue record for this book is available from the British Library.

Printed and bound in Great Britain by
Windsor Print Production Ltd, Tonbridge

For my sister Sharon

A Dream Within a Dream

Take this kiss upon the brow!
And, in parting from you now,
Thus much let me avow –
You are not wrong, who deem
That my days have been a dream;
Yet if hope has flown away
In a night, or in a day,
In a vision, or in none,
Is it therefore the less gone?
All that we see or seem
Is but a dream within a dream.

I stand amid the roar
Of a surf-tormented shore,
And I hold within my hand
Grains of the golden sand –
How few! yet how they creep
Through my fingers to the deep,
While I weep – while I weep!
O God! can I not grasp
Them with a tighter clasp?
O God! can I not save
One from the pitiless wave?
Is *all* that we see or seem
But a dream within a dream?

Edgar Allan Poe

CONTENTS

ILLUSTRATIONS

Between pages 192 and 193

I

THE FEVER CALLED 'LIVING'

In the depths of the English winter of 1795, a small, cold little girl huddled up to her mother and stared wide-eyed at the huge ship that lay before her. This was the first time she had ever seen a ship, let alone one that was about to take her away from her native land forever. It was the biggest thing she had ever seen, and she must have felt a thrill of adventure as she stared at the *Outram*, gently bobbing in the water as they queued to board her. Among the passengers huddled near the gangplank she would have known two others: Miss Green, who had worked with her mother, and an enigmatic figure called Charles Tubbs, who either was, or was soon to be, her father.

Of course, Tubbs was not to be her real father.[1] Her natural father had died six years before. The little girl would have remembered him as part of her small family, but she had only been six years old when he passed away. She knew his name was Henry Arnold, but she would transmit nothing more about him to posterity. In the future, few people would know anything else: maybe a relative had been the great composer Samuel Arnold – and maybe not. Perhaps Henry Arnold had written a play; perhaps he had been an actor. This phantom of a man had appeared from the mist, married Elizabeth Smith in 1784, given her a daughter and then just as mysteriously disappeared. And he remains shrouded in the mists of the late eighteenth century.

Elizabeth had acting in her blood. Her father, William Smith, had trod the boards at the Theatre Royal in Drury Lane, in London's West End, and his daughter would follow. It is possible that friends and relatives of Smith's may have looked after the girl and got her work in the same theatre. She first walked on to that famous stage in 1781, playing a small part in the comic opera *The Woodman*. From that time on, an actress she would remain – and it was to this actress that Arnold was drawn. After a short, passionate romance they became engaged, and they married in St George's Church, Hanover Square, in 1784. Their daughter arrived three years later.

For the next few years the family was settled and in no hardship. Elizabeth was now under her husband's protection and had a steady job in the Drury Lane Theatre, appearing regularly in most of their productions. The little girl, who had been named after her mother, must have found the play-acting and the lights, the backstage and the greasepaint exciting.[2] It became her life, and she soon grew accustomed to the happy-go-lucky ambience of the theatre.

The first tragedy, one of many, that befell little Elizabeth was the death of her father in about 1793; after this it was left to her mother to look after them both, which she did with her acting. With only one wage coming in, life was much harder for the two Elizabeths. The young girl was still too small to go on stage, although she may have appeared in some tiny non-speaking roles that required an infant. The warmth of the theatre company, her life as it was and the friends she had made in the purlieus of London Town were all she knew; but soon all of this was to change. Her mother had met a man who seemed to have a lot of plans for her future. He was Mr Charles Tubbs.

'Charley' was a forceful man and not without graces of his own. He was an actor and a musician, especially noted for his piano-playing; and he had a natural way of talking to people and of ingratiating himself. He began to go out with Elizabeth Arnold, and finally she agreed to marry him. But Charley's plans went beyond marriage.

It is likely that Tubbs saw Elizabeth as a glittering ornament on the American stage. She herself would have been well aware of the current trend – since the end of the American Revolutionary War in 1783 – for actors to travel to the United States and make their name there. Tubbs was as enthusiastic about this as he was about everything, and at last they wrote to Charles Powell of the Boston Federal Street Theater explaining their background. The manager was only too happy to employ them, so the Elizabeths said farewell to Drury Lane and, in the cold winter of 1795–6, made their preparations to leave the country of their birth.

On 3 January 1796 the *Outram* safely arrived in Boston Harbor, and the small family disembarked. Almost as soon as their feet touched American soil the press reported their arrival, although this was quite probably ochestrated by Tubbs to ensure publicity. On the fifth of the month the *Massachusetts Mercury* announced: 'On Sunday arrived in the Port . . . Mrs Arnold and her daughter from the Theatre Royal, Covent Garden, and Miss Green. Both engaged by Mr Powell for the Boston Theater.'[3]

Almost before the family had settled into their new home they took to the stage. In those days there was only one stage in Boston, the Federal Street Theater, and this is where they would stay for at least the next nine months. Mrs Tubbs had taught Elizabeth several songs that she could sing, and that is how she was introduced to the public in June of that year. The audiences were enchanted by the slim, curly-haired young girl, as well as by her mother, and the critics were kind.

It seemed to Mrs Tubbs that all was going well in her adopted country, but her husband was not satisfied with working for a living, and filling the pockets of a theatre owner. He decided he would start his own company, and his silver tongue soon persuaded some of his fellow actors to join him. It was a reckless and hopeless venture, as Tubbs had little management experience and no financial backing. The project went ahead on the strength of his enthusiasm, and by November of the same year he was ready to open the new Portland Theater in Maine. The small family moved house and arrived in Portland, learned roles and prepared for their début performance. Charley must have felt a warm pride when he first opened his playhouse to the public.

His success did not match his optimism; not even the charm of Elizabeth Tubbs and her daughter could keep the venture afloat. The press reviews were good, and the *Eastern Herald and Gazette* said with regard to the nine-year-old, 'her powers as an actress would do credit to any of her sex of maturer age', as well as reporting that 'Mrs Tubbs and her daughter . . . received and certainly deserved the warmest marks of approbation'.[4] But praise does not pay bills, and lack of managerial skill and capital meant that the theatre project began to creak at the seams. The outcome was obvious within a few weeks. Tubbs had no choice but to fold the new company, and because he had estranged himself from the Boston theatre he had to look for work elsewhere. His family must have felt ill at ease in this uncertain and irregular way of life. Perhaps Tubbs explained that this was how things were in the USA; no doubt he soothed them by telling them that theatrical companies abounded in America and that within a few days they would be in work again.

Working in the theatre was a precarious occupation in the USA, and throughout the Revolution all playhouses were closed by order of the Continental Congress. As late as 1794 the author Timothy Dwight wrote, 'to indulge a taste for playgoing means nothing more or less than the loss of that most valuable treasure: the immortal soul'.[5] Apart from puritanical prejudices, actors were thought of as ne'er-do-wells and actresses, often, as little better than prostitutes. Theatres were inevitably cold and poorly lit; companies often had to make do with whatever room or venue they could find. Although towns normally boasted a theatre, there was usually only one, and more often that not that its success rose and fell in tune with the fancies of a fickle public. Actors were poorly paid and were forced to keep working every night to earn enough on which to subsist. They were constantly on the run from zealous campaigners and epidemics of disease, one of the most feared being 'yellow jack' or yellow fever. A thespian life was far from comfortable. All of which made Tubbs's efforts the more remarkable and the outcome less so.

So began the weary schedule of travelling, playing and moving on. For a brief period the family joined Harper's Company, but then they were lured by a big name in theatrical circles at the time – John Sollee. With Sollee's company the family seemed quite settled, and they went to New York to open a season there. But hardly had they arrived when they were forced to flee yellow fever. To escape the disease they played in Charleston, where things went well enough until once more Tubbs got the lust for independence and led an attempt to form a splinter group called the Charleston Comedians. As might be expected, Sollee did not take kindly to this betrayal, as he saw it, and among other things he called Tubbs 'vermin'.

This time Tubbs had learned from his mistake, and the group lasted somewhat longer than had the ill-fated Portland Theater in Maine. But the new arrangement was not beneficial for his wife; the next year, 1798, the company visited Philadelphia, and while they were there this city, too, was hit by an outbreak of the dreaded yellow fever. From that time, 26-year-old Elizabeth Tubbs vanishes from the records; she must have died, almost certainly of yellow jack. The company fled. The eleven-year-old daughter was now motherless and in strange surroundings, relying solely on her stepfather for support. Tubbs did not renege on his obligations, and the girl was put under the protection of himself and a woman in the company, a Miss Snowden. Life had to go on, and hardly had Elizabeth had time to mourn the passing of her mother than she was back on stage, singing and acting for her bread.

Once the pestilence had left Philadelphia they returned for a season, but they had lost one of their star actresses and things looked bleak. The company once again disbanded. By May 1799, while looking for a theatrical troupe with which to work, they came into contact with well-known impresario Thomas Wignell and affiliated themselves to his Philadelphia Company. While this meant a wage it also meant a commitment to hard work. Once again scripts were conned, and off they went on the road, touring several towns before settling back in Philadelphia. Here another actor joined the troupe – Mr Charles Hopkins. Then in August 1800 the company was offered a plum job – the inauguration of the new theatre in Washington.

On their return once more to Philadelphia, Elizabeth suffered another disaster: Charles Tubbs died – or at least nothing more was ever heard of him. Miss Snowden married a fellow company member, Mr Usher, and the group amalgamated with the Chestnut Theater Company. Once again, hardly recovered from her latest tragedy, the little girl had to learn lines and move on, always travelling, always trudging around the country to earn her living. Only thirteen, and under the protection of the Ushers, Elizabeth must have found life gruelling. But she grew into an attractive young girl, with curly dark hair and large expressive eyes; moreover, she began to rise through the acting ranks. She realized that her only option was to work, and to earn well she had to play well.

The company toured Baltimore and then returned to Philadelphia for a season in 1801. Here Elizabeth took on the toughest challenge she had yet faced – the part of Ophelia, at the age of fourteen. Such a difficult role reflects how well the company thought of her talents, and to judge by her future roles she did not let them down. Sadly, no critical review remains of this performance; perhaps her recent bereavement came to her as she mourned for Polonius. She was later to play several other Shakespearan parts, and the critical acclaim that survives suggests she was an adequate and at times a good actress.

By 1802, when Charles Hopkins had been with the company for just over two years, he had developed a strong affection for Elizabeth; and he proposed to her. She had had plenty of time to gauge her feelings and, at the age of fifteen, she accepted him. They married in July of that year and after a very short time were back on the stage. But at least Elizabeth could now feel slightly more secure; she had a protector and someone who could take care of her in the sometimes unsavoury places in which they had to stay as they travelled around.

The wedding must have been a blessing for her. Although they returned to the stage, it was not to act with their old company; instead, they made a completely new start and joined Green's Virginia Company. Their life was no easier, but at least they had each other's companionship, and that was something. They moved to Norfolk and played there in 1803; the next year they went to Richmond. During this time actors came and went; but in July 1804 an actor arrived at Green's who was to have a huge impact on the short life remaining to Elizabeth Hopkins. His name was David Poe, and he was a dark, handsome man who had run away from his home and his job to take to the stage. To find out exactly where he came from, we must leave Green's at Richmond and travel back in time.

The Italian branch of the Poe family fled from Italy and thence from France to escape the crusade against the Albigensian heretics – the slaughter was wholesale, and many innocents died along with the accused. The fugitive family finally holed up in Scotland, where they found themselves embroiled in yet another religious conflict, this time involving the Covenantors, who fought against the Stuart kings' insistence that they were the spiritual heads of the Church. After the Pentland Rising of 1666 these Poes fled to Ireland; and one of them, David, had a son called John who in turn called his child David, and he became a tenant farmer. With David Poe the farmer we enter the land of hard fact – in the sleepy village of Dring, County Cavan, at the start of the eighteenth century. Little is known about him, apart from the fact that he had a son called John. John married well to a Jane McBride, whose brother became an admiral; they had a son called David, and all we know of the family is that they emigrated to America in about 1750. Here we encounter a problem in telling the story of this family; the Poe predilection for the name 'David'.

Their son, David, is in many ways a towering branch on the Poe family tree. A no-nonsense, proud man, fiercely patriotic, David was a wheelwright who married a girl called Elizabeth Cairnes. When the Revolutionary War broke out he joined up and fought with courage against the British. So well respected was he that by 1779 he had reached the rank of major and was Assistant Deputy Quartermaster General; by this time he had become a local celebrity, admired by all his family and neighbours, who knew him affectionately as 'General Poe'. When Lafayette passed through Baltimore Poe spent $500 on fitting out his troops, and his wife made 500 pairs of pantaloons for them. After his death Lafayette was said to have visited his grave and said, *'Ici repose un cœur noble!'* ('Here rests a noble heart!'). In 1814 he took part in the Battle of North Point at the age of seventy-one.[6] General Poe had five sons – John, William, George Washington, David and Samuel – and two girls – Maria (later to marry a William Clemm) and Elizabeth. David Jr was destined for law, studying under William Glynn, barrister, but he loved acting, setting up the 'Thespian Club' with friends. The story was that, sent on legal business, he travelled to Norfolk and saw Elizabeth Arnold (Elizabeth Hopkins's stage name) on stage: love-struck, he followed her to Charleston. Whatever the reason, he gave up law, to his family's disgust, to take up acting as a profession.

In 1803 he made his début with the Charleston Theater as an officer in a pantomime.[7] By June 1804 he had joined Green's Company and had met Elizabeth Hopkins; had he really been so besotted with her he must have been bitterly disappointed to see the wedding band on her finger. The first time he had the opportunity of acting with Elizabeth was later that month in a production of *Speed the Plough*.[8] It seems that in some ways Elizabeth's husband resembled her stepfather; in July, Hopkins led a revolt against the management and as a result found himself in charge of the company. For a while all went well; and next year, 1805, they briefly visited Baltimore before returning to Richmond. At this point, we can see that life was at least bearable for the teenage actress and her manager-husband; it must have been a rare period when her only worries were to learn her lines and to act – everything else could be left to Charles Hopkins. But she was jolted from her sense of security in October when Hopkins died. The cause of his death is unknown, but it is not difficult to guess the reaction of his widow.

At eighteen years of age Elizabeth had lost her father, mother, stepfather and now her first husband. But she was not to remain uncomforted; David Poe had been watching from the wings, and one can imagine how afflicted he was by the pain of the girl he had grown to admire so much. He no doubt stayed with her and comforted her through the lonely weeks ahead, after the funeral and when she had to face acting again. And within six months Poe had proposed to her.

It is crucial to understand the situation in which Elizabeth found herself. As a child actress she was protected by adults, but as a grown-up she was vulnerable and needed to be under a man's protection. Actresses were anyway looked down upon in some echelons of society, but a girl on her own would certainly make tongues wag.

She had already been friends with Poe since 1804. She may already have felt an attraction for the young man, and he must undoubtedly have made an eloquent plea on his own behalf. One can readily imagine his protestations of affection and of his desire to care for her and how desperately he was saddened by her anguish. But in practical terms Elizabeth had little choice, for the sake of her respectability and her future; she accepted his proposal, and they were married in April 1806.

They had little time to waste. They played at the New Theater in Philadelphia before visiting New York; then they returned to join the Boston Federal Street Theater. It must have been a strange experience for Elizabeth to revisit one of the first places she had known when she arrived in America a long decade ago. A great deal had happened since then, but soon she would experience something else for the first time – the thrill of motherhood. They had their first child, William Henry, on 30 January 1807, but so great was their need for money that Elizabeth was back on stage by 25 February. It is thought that their son may have been sent to live with Grandfather Poe, but that is not certain; what is sure is that as the weeks went by their situation grew increasingly difficult. Acting was always a precarious profession, and the Poes were soon in serious financial trouble. Audiences were dropping fast and as a result so were wages. One can only imagine how tough it was for these actors to give their all to dwindling houses just to earn enough for food. Sometimes failing audiences would cause the premature termination of a season; sometimes the theatres could not open. All they could do was rely on the advertising posters and hope people wanted to see them. All too often not enough did.

Occasionally there was a ray of hope when one of the great actors toured the provinces, bringing with him or her the promise of bigger profits. One of these highlights occurred in January and February 1808, when Elizabeth played Ophelia and Cordelia to the Hamlet and Lear of the acclaimed actor Thomas A. Cooper, but that did not relieve their financial plight. When the season ended, the Poes were desperate; only desperation could have forced them to visit Richmond between seasons and to cobble together 'an entertainment' in an effort to raise cash. Poe would have counted on the lack of rivals to ensure a modest audience, but it is unknown how much they earned. In the off season Elizabeth proved that she was not only an accomplished actress, but was interested in other arts; she painted a picture called *Boston Harbor: Morning 1808*.

In the following season, October, another great actor came to Boston – the tragedian James Fennell. To his King Lear the Poes played Edmund and Cordelia. Then on 19 January 1809 Elizabeth gave birth to her second son, Edgar. It is thought that the little newcomer went to live with his grandfather General Poe until the end of the Boston season, when he was collected. On the back of her painting, Elizabeth wrote: 'For my little son Edgar, who should ever love Boston, the place of his birth, and where his mother found her best and most sympathetic friends.'

Money was so short that David Poe made a trip south in an attempt to borrow from his family. He wrote to George Poe, son of his Uncle George:

> You promised me on your honor to meet me at the Mansion House on the 23rd – I promise you on my word of honor that if you will lend me 30, 20, 15 or even 10$ I will remit it to you immediately on my arrival in Baltimore . . . Your answer by the bearer will prove whether I yet have 'favor in your eyes' or whether I am to be despised by (as I understand) a rich relation when a wild boy I join'd a profession which I then thought and now think an honorable one. But which I would most willingly quit if it gave satisfaction to your family provided I could do any thing else that would give bread to mine. Your politeness will no doubt enduce you to answer this note from Yours &c., D. Poe Jr.[9]

The company had at least met with some measure of success in their ploy of inviting top-name actors to play with them. In April 1809 the celebrated John H. Payne joined them to play Romeo and Hamlet; and in May Cooper took them to New York, to play at the Park Theater. This was as fine a theatre as any; a little later a contemporary actor wrote of it as 'of the horseshoe form, with three tiers of boxes; it is handsome, and in all respects as well appointed as any theatre out of London'.[10] But trouble was brewing between the Poes. David had joined the profession in a burst of optimism and defiance, a young man ready to take on the whole world. Things had not worked out as he envisaged. Over the months he had faced deprivation and disillusionment. To make matters worse, he wasn't a great actor. A major problem seemed to be his pronunciation, which had been commented on in previous reviews; but now the press hounded him, ridiculing his every performance.[11] It is not known whether Poe was a heavy drinker before this time, but now, thanks to financial worries and the bad press, he took to the bottle and failed to appear in at least one production. By October a newcomer, Edmund Simpson, had taken over his roles.

The Park Theater closed early in 1810 owing to bad business but opened again when Payne revisited; Elizabeth played the roles of Regan, Ophelia and Juliet, which once again reflects her abilities. But fate had not finished with her yet. Towards the end of the year her second husband died or at least he vanished from the scene; no further record of him exists. One story tells that he died from tuberculosis, and that seems the most likely explanation. So once again Elizabeth was left on her own, albeit pregnant.

The company visited Richmond in August, and around 20 December Rosalie, her only daughter, was born. It is all but impossible to understand how Elizabeth kept going. The only answer is, of course, that she had no choice; she had small mouths to feed besides her own. So she looked after her children and her baby as well as learning her lines and appearing on the stage every night. What is more, another spectre haunted her. She was ill.

In January 1811 she joined Placide's Company of Charleston, and after the season they visited Norfolk, arriving in Richmond during August. Here Payne once again joined them. But Elizabeth was failing fast. She had a lung condition that was almost certainly tuberculosis, possibly contracted from her late husband. But there could be no rest. Three hungry children forced her to tread the boards every night, to sing and dance for the entertainment of the crowds. While the other actors lived in a tavern, she lived in a room in a neighbouring milliner's shop. It is likely that she gave what she had to her offspring while she did without herself. Still, she fought on and performed until she could physically act no more; on 9 October she was given a benefit, and then she took to her bed.

It must have been heartbreaking for her to see her children at the bedside and be unable to do anything for them. Little Edgar was not quite three, too young to take in what was happening; Rosalie was little more than a baby. Perhaps William Henry was there, too. Shocked by what he saw, Payne agreed to stay an extra night and a second benefit was performed, and news of her predicament found its way to the press. On 29 November the *Richmond Enquirer* wrote,

> TO THE HUMANE HEART:
> Mrs Poe, lingering on the bed of disease and surrounded by her children, asks your assistance and *asks it perhaps for the last time.*[12]

She died on 8 December 1811 and was buried on Church Hill in Richmond's St John's Churchyard. She had lived a tough life: she had married twice, had three children and played over 200 roles in her twenty-four years. As an actress she was generally given light criticism but more often praise, sometimes fulsome; she seems to have had a flexible, disarmingly natural approach to her art, and she excelled in light comical, flirtatious roles. Many spectators enthused over her sweet singing voice, and she sang many modern songs to some of the best theatrical orchestras. Two days after her death the following notice appeared in the *Enquirer*:

> Dead – On Sunday last, Mrs Poe, one of the actresses of the company at present playing on the Richmond Boards. By the death of this Lady the Stage has been deprived of one of its chief ornaments. And to say the least of her, she was an interesting Actress, and never failed to catch the applause, and command the admiration, of the beholder.[13]

Two weeks and two days later the Richmond Theater burned down.

2

YOURS AFFECTIONATELY

Irvine is a small harbour town in Ayrshire, Scotland. At the end of the eighteenth century it was even smaller, with a population of just over 3,000. Although the sea accounted for most of the work done here, there existed a unification of trade guilds – the 'Incorporated Trades' – which consisted of 'hammermen, weavers, tailors, cordiners, skinners, wrights, squaremen and coopers'.[1] The abundance of such trades produced goods of varied types which gave opportunities for enterprising businessmen. In 1775 one of Irvine's merchants, William Galt, decided that there were opportunities for trade in America, so he left for Richmond in search of his fortune, arriving just at the outbreak of the American Revolutionary War. Galt soon settled down in Richmond, Virginia, and started up a general business. He had an acute commercial sense and soon began to prosper; then in 1780, after a notorious decree by the traitor Benedict Arnold, the town was set ablaze. Richmond recovered quickly, but stores and supplies were in great demand. Galt must have found himself very busy in that period; and when hostilities ended the aftermath of the war gave rise to even more opportunities. After a few years he became a wealthy man and a well-known, prominent and respected member of Virginian society. In 1795 he became a naturalized American citizen and was able to expand even further. By 1800 he was looking for clerks to work in his offices, and he gave one of the jobs to his nephew, John Allan, and the other to Charles Ellis.

The Allans were another Scottish family and were also of Irvine stock; John Allan's father was a shipmaster (for those looking for coincidences in Poe's life, he had a ship in his fleet called *Tamerlane*). Having had no more than a standard education, at the age of fifteen Allan accepted his Uncle William's offer and was sent off to the New

World to join him as a clerk. His father must have appreciated the potential in such an offer; good prospects and a steady wage.

John Allan joined his co-worker Ellis, and the two worked hard. Allan had an incentive to be industrious; he wanted to earn money and he wanted to get an insight into the machinery of barter and trade. Each day he watched the orders coming in, the suppliers, the clients and exactly who they were until he had a thorough grasp of Richmond business. Staying with his Uncle William may also have given him a chance to learn how the wealthy man had accrued his fortune. Allan had discussions about their future and what their plans might be; Ellis wanted them at some stage to begin a business of their own, and as the months and years went by they saved enough capital for a modest enterprise. Allan had to learn how to manage his personal accounts, how to conserve money and how to live within a tight budget.

By the time he was twenty he and Ellis were ready to launch their own merchant business, so after a search around the town they found an acceptable location at Main and Thirteenth Street and registered their company under the title Ellis & Allan. Thanks to their past experience, the project was a success. When it came to business, Allan had a mind for dollars and cents and was careful and prudent with money, whether it was the company's or his own. He wasn't mean; he just wanted value for money and did not wish to spend it unnecessarily. This attitude towards cash flow, the need to have everything written down and checked, to control and husband money has very important repercussions later in this story. Allan had no time for waste or overindulgence. However, he did like comfort.

He also liked women. They were his greatest weakness and would remain so throughout his life. He had a strong physique, dark hair with sideburns, a slightly long nose and a square jaw; women seemed to be as attracted to him as he was to them. He was twenty-three when he met two sisters, Ann ('Nancy') and Frances 'Fanny' Keeling Valentine; he wooed Fanny, and in 1804 he married her. Fanny was a slightly mousy but pretty girl with an expressive face and curly dark hair.

As there was plenty of room above the business the couple moved in above the premises. Fanny's sister moved with them and would stay with them in the future. John Allan had already done a lot in his short life, but, interestingly, he had a secret ambition; to be an author. For classical literature he had the greatest regard, if not so much for popular fiction. In a telling letter written later to a friend (and relative of Fanny), James Nimmo, he says of Shakespeare, 'Gods! What would I not give, if I had his talent for writing! And what use would I not make of the raw material at my command!'

As well as continuing to run the business, the Allans were making friends and acquaintances around town, including people in 'the merchant set'. Of course, John would have being cultivating such friendships since he first went into business to ensure goodwill; but now there was another reason. Allan was making his name in the town of Richmond, and it was important that he was well respected. Richmond was very conservative in its outlook and still had a strong sense of class, so he had to win recognition in society. Breeding was important, of course, but so was wealth – even 'new money'; this he was starting to accrue, and now his greatest desire was to be thought of as a Southern gentleman. He succeeded very well and began to make influential acquaintances, such as William Wirt, candidate for the Virginia Presidency, and Judge Marshall, who had sworn him in as a new American subject. He also got on well with his neighbours, William and Jane McKenzie, who had two children, John and Mary.

There remained one thing to make Allan's life complete – children, a family of his own and an heir to whom he could pass on his share of the business. This was not his desire alone – Fanny was also very fond of children and longed for them. But there was to be no child born to her, now or ever. It was not that Allan wasn't virile; after a few years he had his first (and not his last) illegitimate child, and that would mark the beginning of a string of love affairs which continued through most of his married life. Frances Allan must at times have felt inadequate and hurt. The only solution, she would have felt, would have been to have a child of her own.

Fanny got along very well with Mrs McKenzie, and it seems that they became very close friends. Fanny doubtless spent many hours visiting the McKenzies and would have been saddened at the sight of the family that she so much desired for herself. Perhaps she confided her fears and hopes to Jane as their friendship grew. Such was the state of affairs when the Placide Theater Company hit town, and Jane and Fanny first read about the dying actress Elizabeth Poe. Her death was announced soon after, and talk began. What was to become of the poor children Elizabeth had left behind? William Henry was to stay with General Poe, but by now the General and his wife were too old to take on more, so they would have to start looking for foster-guardians. The idea may have made Fanny's heart jump. A child! Just what was needed to make their house a real home! Perhaps it would even stop her husband's extramarital affairs.

Allan and Fanny were still young, and Allan may still have been hoping for a legitimate child of his own. He would also have been apprehensive about taking in a stray from the none-too-respectable background of acting. How would this affect his hard-won acceptance among the rather snobbish Richmond community? Besides, he already had one child to look after, and did he really wish to be saddled with more responsibility without getting closer to an heir? The couple must have had many words about it, and Allan would not have felt quite the same about taking in Elizabeth Poe's orphan son as Fanny did. He seemed to be opposed to adopting the child as his own son, but perhaps his wife's entreaties hit a raw nerve after all; maybe a child would be a blessing to the house. So, not without misgivings, he relented and agreed to take on one of the children; Mrs McKenzie took the other. The Allans took Edgar, and the confused mite was bundled from the players' lodgings to the house of perfect strangers. Although John Allan was not to play a positive role in Edgar Poe's life, he was no Murdstone. He treated the little boy kindly and in the first years acted just as a real father might have done. Fanny, of course, was delighted with the lad, and he became quite the pet of the house. But although John Allan was willing to step into the role of a father, he was acutely aware that Edgar was not his real son, and his mercenary side would always see him as an object of charity. Perhaps he still expected that one day he would have a son of his own.

There are few memories of Poe's early childhood; but stories suggest he was a handsome boy and that he would entertain guests by reciting poetry, once reading from *The Lay of the Last Minstrel*.[2] At five Edgar began school; he was first taught by Dr Clotilda Fisher and then for a short time he attended Mr William Ewing's school. At that time he seems to have settled in very well, mixing easily with the other children. In infancy, class or caste have no part in friendship, and children just want to communicate with each other. There is nothing to suggest that Edgar was anything but a contented child – in fact he seems to have been quite popular with all the children, a particular friend being Catherine W. Poitiaux.

In 1818 Allan wrote to Mr Ewing describing Edgar as 'a fine Boy and I have no reason to complain of his progress'. During some summers the family would visit the Virginia Sulphur Springs, and once they stayed at the holiday home of a friend called Whitty, in Buffalo Springs.

As a young clerk Allan had learned many important lessons about business, including the reason his uncle William Galt emigrated in the first place. In fact, Galt was a good role model; someone who had seen the opportunities and followed them up, someone who could coldly weigh the risk incurred against the possibility of success. Allan was at this time keeping a close eye on matters in Britain and the state of the Napoleonic Wars.[3] Sensing that hostilities may be nearing an end, he talked to his partner about the possibility of branching out to London. Timing was critical, and just as Galt had arrived in a time of want and made a profit before and after the Revolutionary War, so could they emulate his example. They almost certainly discussed the matter with his uncle.

In June 1815 the family set sail for England to inaugurate a new business branch, not of Ellis & Allan but of Allan & Ellis. John Allan was not going to travel to Britain and miss the opportunity of visiting his relatives in his home town, so the family travelled north to Irvine. It was a proud man who stepped along the streets of his home town, a successful thirty-year-old businessman who, fifteen years earlier, had left those shores an inexperienced lad. After family meetings and some business, they said their farewells and made their way south to London.

The Allans (Edgar was now known as Edgar Allan) settled in at 47 Southampton Row.[4] It was only a walk away from the Theatre Royal, where his grandmother had performed so many times, and the lanes and alleys his mother would have known so well. Soon letters from home began to arrive, and one proves Edgar's popularity; Catherine Poitiaux wrote: 'Tell him I want to see him very much . . . Tell him Josephine and all the children want to see him very much.'

Edgar attended a school in Sloane Street run by the Misses Dubourg until he was old enough to attend the Manor House School in the village of Stoke Newington. It must have been daunting for the child to have been shuttled from country to country, from school to school, but he seems to have settled into the routine. In Stoke Newington he would have seen an archetypal English village in archetypal English countryside complete with country lanes.

Although his biographers have often said that Manor House School had little effect on Poe, it certainly remained in his memory long enough to inspire the school in his story 'William Wilson'; the headmaster, Dr Bransby, is even mentioned by name.[5] Bransby later claimed to recall Poe, but his recollection was vague and his statement that the boy was given an extravagant amount of pocket money by Allan seems unlikely. Poe later described the school itself. His description does not match the building exactly, and most commentators argue that he used the real school as a model and romanticized it. Whether he did so deliberately is uncertain.

The boy stayed at the school only for two years. Things had gone badly for John Allan: his wife was thoroughly miserable and sick in Britain, and his business venture had foundered. At one point he found he only had $100 to his name. So now he had to choose between saving his pride or facing economic facts, and he knew that his only recourse was to admit defeat and to go home. They packed up all their belongings, and Edgar was taken away from school. Although this must have been a bitter disappointment to Allan, he was at heart a realist as well as a businessman; some time before he had written to Ellis: 'I am not one of those much addicted to suffer by unavailing regrets.'

They arrived back in July 1820, and once again Edgar had to adjust to life in Richmond. Their first concern was somewhere to live, as they now had little money and could not afford to buy a home. Charles Ellis was happy for the family to live with him while they sorted themselves out, and so the two families lived together for about a year. It says much about Allan that after this time he had already saved enough money to be able to afford a house of their own, in Fifth Street.

Edgar resumed his education in the school of Joseph H. Clarke, which was taken over by William Burke on his retirement in 1823; there he studied Latin, French and classics. But it seems that Allan had made a firm decision about his foster-son; he did not wish to adopt him fully and legally. To mark this decision, Edgar was once again known as Edgar Poe. The reason is unclear. Perhaps his recent brush with poverty had brought home to Allan the extent of his own responsibilities; and bills for the education of his illegitimate child, Edward Collier, were also coming in. In England, perhaps, where they were unknown, the boy's name was relatively unimportant, but now they were back among folk they knew and to accept the boy as part of their true family would have been a significant step. Allan was acutely aware that the child was the orphan of a strolling player; to adopt him would be in some way associating with his background, which Allan could never do. It was one thing to gain the respect of his neighbours by entirely taking in a waif as an act of charity; it was another to accept him publicly as his own.

This was an important issue. In the early nineteenth century Virginia was a focal point in the Old South, and it was proud of its ancestry. In the surrounding country, and especially around the James River, plantations had a history stretching back 200 years and more; and the first slaves had arrived there as 'indentured servants' in 1619. For over 100 years cotton had been a major crop, and the system of slavery became entrenched. In this prosperous county Richmond became the industrial nerve-centre, and the citizens became aristocratic in their outlook and customs. It was the norm for a family to have black domestic servants – Allan himself had at least two.[6]

Of Edgar's school days in Richmond little is known for certain, and reminiscences are not wholly reliable. Some describe him sitting on a fence with his friends, others testify to his influence on his elders, while still others remember his athletic feats. Colonel John T.L. Preston recalls Poe as 'self-willed, capricious, inclined to be imperious, and though of generous impulses, not steadily kind, or even amiable'.[7] He also remembers that he joined a debating society and wrote satirical verses about its members; he also joined the Thespian Society. Poe himself only mentions 'the sad experience' of this time. While he took part in sports such as boxing, achieved local fame by swimming six miles up the James River against the tide, and was a good scholar, it was also well known that he was an object of charity – a waif taken in by a local household.

An awareness of class would never, until now, have entered Poe's mind. He had played with these children as an infant and had been their equal. Even in the boarding school in England he was seen as an equal – if an alien one. Suddenly to become aware of class prejudice directed at him, and even more keenly his background, must have deeply injured him. The children around here would be well off, from good ancestry, and may not have taken to the little orphan boy from a disreputable theatrical background; he would be seen as belonging to a lower class altogether. Added to this his memories of disruption and loss would not make for a happy boy. A picture emerges of a slightly melancholy, aloof child who, as children will, pitted himself against any challenge set him. Two of his friends at this time were Robert Stanard and Robert Sully, nephew of the artist Thomas Sully.

Perhaps the most basic need, and one that was to haunt his entire life, was the need for love. Although he stated that he did not remember his real mother, it is possible that he kept some deep memory within him; in his tales his heroines are invariably pallid, sick and on the point of death. The bond with his foster-mother was strong and enduring. As he entered adolescence it is hardly surprising that his first infatuation should be with a mother-figure.

Poe's first taste of love was to be an obsession with Mrs Jane Stanard, mother of Robert. For Poe, this feeling surpassed any passion he had known; at their first meeting she captivated him so much that for a time he was speechless and (according to his own account) almost fainted. Although Mrs Stanard was mentally unstable, Poe idolized her and called her 'Ma' (as he did Mrs McKenzie). He watched with increasing desperation as she slowly deteriorated, and perhaps there were faint stirrings of memory as she began to sink to her death bed.[8] When she died he was grief-stricken, and although many scorn the tale that he paid nightly visits to her grave this would not have been out of character. The effect on Edgar must have been terrible, for death would seem to haunt those he loved. However, there was a small consolation; she was the inspiration for the later poem 'To Helen', whose second stanza runs:

> On desperate seas long wont to roam,
>   Thy hyacinth hair, thy classic face,
> Thy Naiad airs have brought me home
>   To the glory that was Greece
> And the grandeur that was Rome.

There was also something else that was upsetting for Edgar Poe. The fact that his foster-father was indulging in love affairs around Richmond was common knowledge and would have come to his ears, perhaps as a spiteful remark by one of his schoolmates. His strong affection for Fanny would have made him resent John Allan's behaviour. Friction was appearing between the two, father and son, which would increase as the years went by. It was not eased by the fact that Allan constantly reminded him he was an object of charity. In Allan's mind Poe should be eternally grateful for the pains he had been at to look after him, and he often reminded him of that, too.

These factors did not make for a contented teenager. Edgar slowly sank into depression and spent his time moping about the house. At one point his elder brother William Henry wrote, asking why he had not replied to his last letter; Allan read it and asked Edgar about it. It seems that Edgar's answer was not what Allan wanted to hear, and there were obviously cross words, at least from Allan. There is considerable agitation in the letter when Allan himself writes to William Henry:

> I have just seen your letter of the 25th ult. to Edgar and am much afflicted, that he has not written to you. He has had little else to do for me he does nothing & seems quite miserable, sulky & ill-tempered to all the Family. How we have acted to produce this is beyond my conception – why I have put up so long with his conduct is little less wonderful. The boy possesses not a Spark of affection for us not a particle of gratitude for all my care and kindness towards him. I have given a much superior Education than ever I received myself. If Rosalie has to relie on any affection from him God in his mercy preserve her – I fear his associates have led him to adopt a line of thinking & acting very contrary to what he possessed when in England . . .
>
> At least She is half your sister & God forbid my dear Henry that We should visit upon the living the Errors & frailties of the dead . . .

Within this letter there is an open suggestion that Rosalie was illegitimate. There are no grounds for supporting the idea that David Poe was not the father of Rosalie, although there had obviously been rumours. Perhaps Allan did not want to be thought of as responsible for Poe's sister as well as him. In fact, Rosalie was an undeveloped girl whose mental age would remain that of a twelve-year-old.

There was a reason why John Allan may have been short-tempered at this time: financially, disaster was following disaster. Bad luck seemed to have followed him from London to Richmond, and his main business venture began to look shaky. In fact things were so bad that in 1824 the firm of Ellis & Allan was dissolved. The family was now in great difficulties, and Allan was forced to approach Galt for more help. Galt had an empty house at Fourteenth Street and Tobacco Alley, and he gave it to them to live in, so at least they had a roof above their heads, if little else.

While at school Poe, along with many others, joined the Richmond Junior Volunteers, otherwise known as the Junior Morgan Riflemen, Poe in the rank of lieutenant. When the great diplomat and general Lafayette visited the town in 1824, Edgar was a member of the guard of honour that acted as his escort. It is easy to imagine the excitement the boys felt, wielding real artillery and acting as real soldiers.

Poe had already begun to write poetry. Here is the only fragment that remains from this time:

> Last night, with many cares & toils oppres'd,
> Weary, I laid me on a couch to rest.

The Allan family were by now in further need of money, and even the business-honed mind of John Allan could make nothing out of nothing. Things must have been desperate when in March 1825 a sad event relieved Allan of all his troubles. His uncle William Galt died and left him a rich man. The first thing Allan did was to move to more salubrious surroundings; he bought a large house on the corner of Main and Fifth Streets for $14,950. William Henry Poe came to visit his brother that year, too.

Edgar again fell in love, this time with someone closer to his own age; Sarah Elmira Royster, whose family lived opposite and whose likeness he drew. They even plighted their troth, but her father was not altogether keen on the relationship, probably because of Poe's background. They carried on a love affair by letters until Edgar left for university, and from this time on Elmira's father held on to all his letters, only giving them back after she was married to a man called Shelton. Poe did not brood on these things for long, however, because changes were happening in his life. He came to the end of his schooling, and now his future had to be considered. He was lucky that Allan's windfall came when it did.

Edgar was sent to the University of Virginia in Charlottesville. As a gentleman – and a wealthy one – of Richmond, it would have been John Allan's social if not legal obligation to allow his foster-son a decent education, and so he was sent to this modern establishment, founded and designed by Thomas Jefferson himself and popularly known as Jefferson's University; Jefferson lived on site for over a year until his death. Edgar enrolled in its second year, in the schools of ancient and modern languages, and would have met the ex-President. The university's code of conduct was modern, too, with a stress on self-government, although a Board of Censors was supposed to hear minor charges. This was Jefferson's cherished dream, embodying his belief in the sanctity of democracy. Like many other worthwhile doctrines, it worked better on paper than in practice; in fact it became an unmitigated disaster. The experiment ended in riots and fights as well as a dissipated lifestyle, and more stringent rules had to be put in place, including the appointment of 'sheriffs' and a Grand Jury to hear disciplinary charges; judicial powers reverted to the faculty.

Poe matriculated with 135 others on Valentine's Day, 1826. In his letters home he was obviously excited at being at university and living away from home – for the first time feeling like an adult. The atmosphere of freedom and rebellion surprised him, and the rioting was a source of great excitement, although he seems never to have joined in. He recognized that he was there to learn, and that is what he did, proving that he was an excellent scholar. The new student forbore from writing to his family until he received his new clothes from Allan, with which he was well pleased. When he did write, he expressed awed amazement at the rioting that was still going on:

> You have heard no doubt of the disturbances in College. Soon after you left here the Grand Jury met and put the Students in a terrible fright – so much so that the lectures were unattended – and those whose names were upon the Sheriff's list travelled off into the woods & mountains, taking their beds & provisions along with them. There were about 50 on the list, so you may suppose the College was very well thinn'd. This was the first day of the fright – the second day, 'a proclamation' was issued by the faculty forbidding 'any student under pain of a major punishment to leave his dormitory between the hours of 8 & 10 A M (at which time the Sheriffs would be about) or in any way to resist the lawful authority of the Sheriffs.' This order however was very little attended to, as the fear of the Faculty could not counterbalance that of the Grand Jury. Most of the 'indicted' ran off a second time into the woods and upon an examination the next morning by the Faculty, some were reprimanded, some suspended and one expelled . . .
>
> Dixon made a physical attack upon Arthur Smith, one of Blow's Norfolk friends, and a 'very fine fellow' – he struck him with a large stone on one side of his head, whereupon Smith drew a pistol (which are all the fashion here) and had it not miss'd fire, would have put an end to the controversy.

It would be interesting to assess the kind of person Poe was while at the university. Unfortunately, many of the reminiscences that have come down to us were given long after his death and are in the main unreliable, as everyone wanted people to know that they were in some way acquainted with the author. They were also written after Poe's name had been blackened and were made to fit in with the opinion then current about him. None the less some of these memories, particularly of his close colleagues, bear examination. Thomas Bolling remembered a constant melancholy expression and that Poe filled the walls of his room at 13 West Grange with sketches. The sadness and feeling of loneliness do ring true, given his recent experiences. But it would be a mistake to paint a one-sided picture of Poe. It is true that he found his school days sad but, on the other hand, he joined in the athletics, boxed and swam in the river. And just as Bolling often found him depressed, there were certainly times when he felt sociable and joined in the extramural activities of the other students; for example, he held a post in the University Debating Society. However, Poe's was not exactly a normal temperament, in that he experienced bouts of melancholy, and this disorder would dog him throughout his life.

By way of exercise he loved to walk in the surrounding mountains, sometimes in the company of a local dog; these walks later gave him the idea for 'A Tale of the Ragged Mountains'. For the rest of his time on earth – only another twenty-three years – he had a love of the country, and wherever he lived, if he could, he would walk down rural lanes or find some object of natural beauty. Perhaps this side of him came from his travels in Britain, admiring the Scottish countryside and even the country lanes of Stoke Newington. These were the years when Poe seemed at his happiest, so he may have taken a nostalgic pleasure in immersing himself in natural beauty.

As well as nature, Poe was drawn to celestial beauty – the stars and planets. Many children are, but Allan's house boasted a telescope through which Poe would have observed for himself the wonders of the universe. Space and extraterrestrial bodies also interested him for the rest of his life.

Did Poe drink at university? This question seems to be of great moment. Other writers' and artists' love of drink is often waved away or even interpreted in a positive sense, as high spirits and a *joie de vivre*. Hemingway's reputation suffers little from his legendary Cuban drinking bouts. But in Poe's case the question takes on a more sombre meaning, and among famous writers he is most often pilloried by those who campaign against the evils of liquor: his drinking is always seen in a negative light, and few people seem to sympathize with the man himself. In fact Poe hated alcohol, and he was disastrously incapable of holding his drink when he did indulge. As for his drinking at university, no one really knows. The memoirs of his colleagues were compiled long after the event. It seems very likely that he did drink, and if he did it was because he couldn't not do so. To lose sight of that is to ignore the niceties and expectations of Richmond hospitality. Drinking was expected; to refuse a drink was the basest of bad manners; and to be a little tipsy was considered a lovable foible. Alcoholism was a different matter, of course, but everyone was expected to drink a relative's or a friend's health. Teetotallers were rare and looked on as being rather odd – even cranks. If Poe was offered a drink it would have been the poorest of manners and etiquette to refuse and that was the last thing Poe wanted. Having suffered so many social indignities at school, he did not want to go through the same at university. Interestingly, an account talks of him 'gulping' his wine in one mouthful, suggesting that he disliked it even at that stage. If Poe did drink, it never interfered with his studies, and he was never reported for any indiscretions.

Even after a few months the university's crackdown had not completely quelled the boisterous behaviour of some students. In September, Poe wrote the following short letter to Allan:

> We have had a great many fights up here lately. The faculty expelled Wickliffe last night for general bad conduct, but more especially for biting one of the student's arms with whom he was fighting. I saw the whole affair – it took place before my door. Wickliffe was much the strongest but not content with that, after getting the other completely in his power, he began to bite – I saw the arm afterwards, and it was really a serious matter. It was bitten from the shoulder to the elbow and it is likely that pieces of flesh as large as my hand will be obliged to be cut out. He is from Kentucky – the same one that was in suspension when you were up here some time ago.

Poe's words are friendly enough, but his life at university was not without problems, not least financial difficulties stemming from John Allan's parsimony. Having sent his foster-son to the best university around, he drew the line at supporting him adequately. It is hardly credible that a man of Allan's business and financial sense would have failed to appreciate the cost of a university course; and even if he had Poe would soon have reminded him. But Allan sent Poe off to the university at Charlottesville with hardly enough money to cover his board and lodgings. According to Poe, Allan had sent him a mere $110, whereas $50 were needed for board and $60 for two professors, let alone anything else; this meant that Poe was forced to get books on credit and ran into debt for his lodgings, which was against the rules of the establishment. Allan had insisted that Poe attend the lectures of three professors, but Poe could only afford two, and he chose Long and Blaettermann.[9] Hiring a servant was not a matter of choice but obligatory. It is hardly surprising that Poe was seen 'in the light of a beggar' and this, of course, was the last thing he wanted; desiring equality in the eyes of Virginia's elite, he was again looked down upon. That must have been galling.

Sheer need drove Poe to apply to a relative of William Galt, James, but he was not prepared to help. There was only one alternative, fraught with terrible risks; the gambling table. Cards were very popular in the university, and joining a card school was very simple, indeed it was a good way of showing your respectable and wealthy background. To Poe it also offered a lifeline, if he was successful. He must have felt his pulse race as the first cards were dealt to him, and he began to play, gambling everything on his playing ability. Unfortunately, he was cursed with very little in the way of good fortune throughout his life. He proved to be a poor card player and soon ran up large debts. As he could never hold his drink his colleagues may well have taken advantage of him, and it was perhaps at these card nights that he downed glasses of 'peach and honey'. To get out of trouble, he took the worst possible decision – he borrowed, always hoping that the next night would save him, but that night never came. If he did make the odd small win, there were more often large losses and in the end he was in debt to the tune of $2,000, with no possible way of repaying it. By his own account, he stopped gambling in September, but by that time the damage had been done. Despite his financial worries, he did well in his examinations, especially in French and Latin; but these small successes were probably dwarfed by the worry of his crushing debts. He discussed them on one of his last nights at the university, when librarian William Wertenbaker visited him; Poe was depressed, saying that he was honour bound to repay them all.

Poe returned to Richmond, and a story has it that he walked over to see Elmira Royster and found himself in the midst of her marriage party. This seems to be confirmed by Poe's early poem, 'To —', which begins: 'I saw thee on thy wedding day . . .' However, as this was published before Elmira's marriage, the party he gatecrashed may have been an engagement party. Another story suggests he did not find out that she had married until 1829.

Allan inevitably discovered that Poe had run up the huge debts, and he refused to honour them; he also refused to pay any further university fees. Gambling debts would have been anathema to someone as careful and parsimonious as Allan, and the total sum of Poe's debts must have left Allan reeling.

The antagonism between the two men reached a head, and although Poe could not answer the charges Allan levelled against him, he must have been afraid of the consequences both of what he had done and what Allan had threatened. Should one of his creditors so decide, he could put Poe in very hot water indeed. There was legislation to protect the creditor, and debtors could face a summons to pay up or go to gaol. Perhaps Allan might not have let matters go that far – but his recent words would have suggested that he might.

One night, after taking a drink, Allan again scolded the young man, touching on the subject of Poe's birth and his mother. To hear her talked of so derogatively by Allan drove Poe into a rage. Allan's words were especially intolerable given his own infidelities, which were so upsetting to his beloved foster-mother. There was a huge row. Enraged beyond measure and driven to desperation, Poe made up his mind never to put up with such treatment again. His heart ached for Fanny Allan, whom he genuinely loved and respected, but he could no longer stay under the same roof as someone who had not only insulted his family but also his own wife.

Both men went to bed seething with rage. When they met again the next morning Allan again started to rail at Poe. Another row broke out, and Allan went as far as to wish the young man dead before turning on his heel, leaving Poe shaking with fury.

When Allan returned he found that Poe had gone. He had made his way to the Court House Tavern, intending to travel to Boston to see if he could make a living there. However, he soon realized that he had nothing to live on. Still fuming, he sent Allan the following salvo:

> March 19th 1827. Richmond Monday
> Sir, After my treatment on yesterday and what passed between us this morning, I can hardly think you will be surprised at the contents of this letter. My determination is at length taken, to leave your house and indeavor to find some place in this wide world, where I will be treated – not as you have treated me.

This is not a hurried determination, but one on which I have long considered, and having so considered my resolution is unalterable. You may perhaps think that I have flown off in a passion, & that I am already wishing to return; But not so. I will give you the reasons which have actuated me, and then judge.

Since I have been able to think on any subject, my thoughts have aspired, and they have been taught by *you* to aspire, to eminence in public life – this cannot be attained without a good Education, such a one I cannot obtain at a Primary school. A collegiate Education therefore was what I most ardently desired, and I had been led to expect that it would at some future time be granted – but in a moment of caprice you have blasted my hope because forsooth I disagreed with you in an opinion, which opinion I was forced to express.

Again, I have heard you say (when you little thought I was listening and therefore must have said it in earnest) that you had no affection for me.

You have moreover ordered me to quit your house, and are continually upbraiding me with eating the bread of Idleness, when you yourself were the only person to remedy the evil by placing me to some business.

You take delight in exposing me before those whom you think likely to advance my interest in this world.

You suffer me to be subjected to the whims & caprice, not only of your white family, but the complete authority of the blacks. These grievances I could not submit to; and I am gone. I request that you will send me my trunk containing my clothes & books, and if you still have the least affection for me, – as the last call I shall make on your bounty – to prevent the fulfillment of the Prediction you this morning expressed, send me as much money as will defray the expences [*sic*] of my passage to some of the Northern cities & then support me for one month, by which time I shall be enabled to place myself in some situation where I may not only obtain a livelihood, but lay by a sum which one day or another will support me at the University. Send my trunk &c to the Court-house Tavern, send me I entreat you some money immediately, as I am in the greatest necessity. If you fail to comply with my request, I tremble for the consequence.

Yours &c
Edgar A. Poe

It depends upon yourself if hereafter you see or hear from me.

The letter, like many others that Poe wrote, was composed in anger and, in this case, teenage angst. How many other teenagers have argued and threatened to run away from home? But Edgar had many issues with his guardian: he was a very introverted and dependent boy and had not left home for more than a day when he began to wish for paternal protection once again. Too proud to beg, he (as he would again) reverted to an attempt to elicit pity from Allan:

> Dear Sir,
> Be so good as to send me my trunk with my clothes – I wrote to you on yesterday explaining my reasons for leaving. I suppose by my not receiving either my trunk, or an answer to my letter, that you did not receive it. I am in the greatest necessity, not having tasted food since Yesterday morning. I have no where to sleep at night, but roam about the Streets – I am nearly exhausted. I beseech you as you wish not your prediction concerning me to be fulfilled, to send me without delay my trunk containing my clothes, and to lend if you will not give me as much money as will defray the expence of my passage to Boston ($12) and a little to support me there until I shall be enabled to engage in some business. I sail on Saturday – a letter will be received by me at the Court House Tavern, where be so good as to send my trunk.
>
> I have not one cent in the world to provide any food.

Allan did make a reply by return of post. The injuries he felt are still obviously fresh as in places the letter seethes with savage irony. Perhaps he was glad to be relieved of responsibility for Edgar; perhaps he was pleased that he would be able to continue his affairs undisturbed by his foster-son's attention. But there is more to his reply. He was still angry, but his anger was to some extent softened by his feelings of guilt; some of what Poe had written hit home, and Allan felt the need to defend himself:

> Sir,
> Your letter of Monday was received this morning, I am not at all surprised at any step you may take, at any thing you can say, or any thing you may do, you are a much better judge of the propriety of your own conduct and general treatment of those who have had the charge of your infancy & have watched with parental solicitude & affection over your tender years affording you such means of instruction as was in

> their power & which was performed with pleasure until you became a much better judge of your own conduct, rights & privileges than they, it is true I taught you to aspire, even to eminence in Public Life, but I never expected that Don Quixotte, Gil Blas, Jo: Miller & such works were calculated to promote the end.
>
> It is true and you will not deny it, that the charge of eating the Bread of idleness, was to urge you to perseverance & industry in receiving the classics, in presenting yourself in the mathematics, mastering the French &c. &c. how far I succeeded in this you can best tell, but for one who had conceived so good an opinion of himself & his future intentions I hesitate not to say, that you have not evinced the smallest disposition to comply with my wishes, it is only on this subject I wish to be understood, your Heart will tell you if it is not made of marble whether I have not had good reason to fear for you, in more ways than one. I should have been justly chargeable, in reprimanding you for faults had I had any other object than to correct them.
>
> Your list of grievances require no answer the world will reply to them – & now that you have shaken off your dependence & declared for your own Independence – & after such a list of Black charges – you Tremble for the consequences unless I send you a supply of money.

So in March 1827 Poe fled from Richmond. No one knows where he found the money to do so. As he left he missed a letter from a university colleague, one of his creditors asking for repayment. Interestingly, it seems that at the time Poe was using a pseudonym – Henri Le Rennet.[10] Without money or prospects, he launched himself into a one-sided battle with the world.

3

I AM AT PRESENT A SOLDIER

While at university Poe had been trying his hand at verse – just what Allan would have called 'eating the bread of idleness'. He had produced a dozen or so poems which he thought decent enough, and his ambition was to find a publisher for them. The idea of becoming a poet had been with him for some time now, even before his infatuation with his first 'Helen', Mrs Stanard. But although he had a folder of poems under his arm he had no way of selling them.

The next few weeks must have been difficult for Poe, and money must have been scarce. Why he went to Boston is not clear, unless he was impressed by the words his mother had written on the back of her painting. There may also have been more prosaic reasons. Boston, the City upon a Hill, had been central during the Revolution and had been the scene of many important events, such as the Boston Tea Party and the Siege and Battle of Boston.[1] When the war was over Boston prospered, and at the time Poe travelled there it was one of America's – even the world's – major trading ports. Allan would have used it for some of his business ventures.

It is a great surprise to find that almost as soon as Poe landed in the city he managed to get a book published. He visited a publisher, Calvin F.S. Thomas, who was so impressed by the eighteen-year-old's efforts that he agreed to print a number of copies. To win the respect of the people in the area he decided to entitle the work *Tamerlane and Other Poems, by a Bostonian*. The volume is today exceptionally rare and exceptionally valuable – but that was not the case when the thin volume appeared in 1827. It made no profit and brought in no food.

The main poem, of over 400 lines, was 'Tamerlane', a Byronic epic which Poe improved and revised as the years went by. Tamerlane (a historic character from the family of one of Genghis Khan's ministers) is here portrayed as a poor shepherd's son who is besotted with Ada; he plights his troth, promising to make her a queen upon his return from seeking his fortune in the world, but she dies (Poe's heroines never survive). Alongside 'Tamerlane' there are nine short 'fugitive pieces', including 'Dreams', 'Visit of the Dead', 'The Lake' and 'Untitled' ('The Happiest Hour').

At this time Poe was most influenced by the Romantic poets. The Romantic movement began in Britain around 1790, led by such illuminati as Blake, Coleridge and Wordsworth; later poets of the genre, who embraced metaphysical subjects, included Byron, Keats and Shelley. Wordsworth defined the style as 'the spontaneous overflow of powerful feelings', while Coleridge saw their poetry as 'the mediatress between, and reconciler of nature and man'. The movement developed as a reaction to political change at the time of the Napoleonic wars, increased industrialization and a revolution in philosophical and religious ideas. Although Romanticism was a new style, it had evolved naturally from the Gothic movement, which embodied dark fears, ghosts and terror in general. Poe was especially impressed by Byron and his one-time friend and literary executor Tom Moore. The style of 'Tamerlane' owes much to Byron and has a similar feel to his 'The Deformed Transformed'. One line in particular, 'The sound of revelry by night', is uncomfortably close to 'There was a sound of revelry by night' from Byron's 'The Eve of Waterloo'.

Little is known for sure about this period in Poe's life, but he must have found it difficult to eat and live. It is hardly likely, although possible, that Allan may begrudgingly have sent something. Perhaps the young man did find some odd jobs. But however he managed to survive, it soon became imperative that he find a permanent position or at least some constant income. The solution must have been born of desperation; he joined the army.

Two things may have persuaded him to do this. The first was his family history. His grandfather, General Poe, had been a towering figure in the family, and had been hugely admired and respected. The whole family had been proud of his efforts during the Revolution. What better role model could there be? Edgar will also have remembered one of the proudest moments of his life – how, with John Lyle and others, he had formed a guard of honour for General Lafayette.

He often chose to be known by a name other than his own, perhaps in the hope that he could leave behind the one that had given him so much shame. In May 1827 he enrolled at Boston Harbor, giving his name as Edgar A. Perry, his age as twenty-two (although he was only eighteen) and his occupation as clerk. Private Perry joined Battery H of the First Artillery, and was based at Fort Independence, Castle Island, which lies in the harbour. Castle Island was so named because the fort was locally known as the Castle; it had been destroyed during hostilities with the British and was repaired under the directions of Paul Revere. The Castle was one of a string of forts hurriedly put up in the 1770s to repel the advances of the British.

Poe stayed in Fort Independence only for five months; after this his company were moved to Fort Moultrie on Sullivan's Island, in Charleston Harbor. This was another fort with a long history, which again suffered during the Revolutionary War. In fact, the fort that Poe arrived at was the third and most lasting model. It was Colonel Moultrie who held off a British attack here in 1776 and after whom the fort was renamed, although the British were to take control of it soon after. The fort was rebuilt to strengthen fortifications in the harbour, but it was subsequently hit by a hurricane. In 1809 the third fort was built, this time of enduring brick. Sullivan's Island impressed Poe, and later he would use the location as the setting for one of his most celebrated stories, 'The Gold Bug'.

He performed his duties well, was never on report and seems to have settled into military life as a model soldier. He made few friends socially but did make the acquaintance of Colonel William Thaydon, a connection that was to last beyond his military career. But as time passed by he began to tire of army life and longed to be free again – perhaps to return to his beloved literature. Of course he could not simply walk out of the army; on the other hand, he had no idea what to do. He turned for advice to another acquaintance he had made in the battalion – Lieutenant J. Howard. Howard had introduced him to Colonel James House, so they all got together to discuss Poe's future plans, and they explained the rules governing how to leave the army. It was all very straightforward. To begin with, he needed permission – which could only be given if a letter from his guardian were sent to his superior officers. After that, the matter would be simple enough; he needed to find a substitute soldier for himself and then he would be free.

A letter from his guardian? Poe's heart must have sunk when he heard those words. Weakly he replied that it would not provide an obstacle and that the two were reconciled, but he dreaded trying to persuade Allan to act on his behalf. The echoes of their last huge argument were still ringing in his ears. All he could do was to cross his fingers and give his foster-father's address in the hope that he would help; after all, he was asking very little, just a letter confirming that he wished Poe to leave the army. It would take no effort at all.

A reply soon came from Allan, who was not in a forgiving mood. He did not agree that leaving the army was the best thing for Poe; he suggested instead that it might be better if Poe were to stay until the end of his term – five years. When Poe was told of the reply he was disappointed but perhaps not surprised. If he was going to escape the military he had to persuade Allan to change his mind. On 1 December he took up his pen to address Allan for the first time in over twenty months.

As usual with Poe's letters to his foster-father, there is much that is pitiable about it. He claims to be a changed man and that he is no longer an aimless or directionless boy. He seeks Allan's forgiveness. He is prudent with his money now and needs no assistance in that respect. But he needs Allan's help in getting free from his present situation, in which the best years of his life would be wasted. He even hints at suicide if he is forced to languish in the army:

> I could not help thinking that you believed me degraded & disgraced, and that any thing were preferable to my returning home & entailing on yourself a portion of my infamy: But, at no period of my life, have I regarded myself with a deeper Satisfaction – or did my heart swell with more honourable pride – The time may come (if at all it will come speedily) when much that appears of a doubtful nature will be explained away, and I shall have no hesitation in appearing among my former connexions – at the present I have no such intention, and nothing, short of your absolute commands, should deter me from my purpose . . .
>
> The period of an Enlistment is five years – the prime of my life would be wasted – I shall be driven to more decided measures if you refuse to assist me . . .
>
> A letter addressed to Lieut: J. Howard assuring him of your reconciliation with myself (which you have never yet refused) & desiring my discharge would be all that is necessary . . .

Soon after this Poe's battery, under the command of Colonel House, moved to Fort Monroe, Old Point Comfort. Old Point Comfort is in Virginia, about twelve miles from Norfolk, and the fort was a new one, having only been garrisoned five years earlier. Here Poe once again took up his duties, awaiting Allan's reply, but none came. By 22 December he still had received nothing, so he sent another letter, recapitulating what he had said earlier, and went on to say:

> There is that within my heart which has no connection with degradation – I can walk among infection & be uncontaminated. There never was any period of my life when my bosom swelled with a deeper satisfaction, of myself and (except in the injury which I may have done to your feelings) of my conduct. My father, do not throw me aside as degraded, I will be an honour to your name.

Should Allan still turn him adrift:

> Here take farewell – neglected, I will be doubly ambitious, & the world shall hear of the son whom you have thought unworthy of your notice. But if you let the love you bear me outweigh the offence which I have given, then write me my father, quickly . . .

Allan was still in no mood to involve himself in Poe's affairs and was not even willing to answer his letters. He was not convinced by Poe's protestations that he was a changed man, and he thought it better that the young man stay where he was; he was not yet twenty years old, and the life of a soldier might continue to mould him. If Poe was being truthful about the change army life had wrought in him, that was all the more reason to leave him where he was.

Allan was probably right. As far as it went, Poe's army career had been successful, and as if to underline that fact on New Year's Day 1829 he was promoted to sergeant major. His problem was not that he was a poor soldier but that the life was not for him, and he wanted to move in other directions. Hadn't he already had a book published; and what heights could he reach if he pursued the career of a writer with all his effort? He had just finished a long poem – the longest he had ever written – and he was proud of it. In fact, despite the critics he would remain fond of it until the end of his life.

The new poem was called 'Al Aaraaf', the title of Sura 7 of the Koran. The meaning of the phrase had been a matter of some deliberation, and it was the popular view that it meant a kind of Islamic limbo. This is the interpretation taken up by Poe, and he places it in a nova discovered by Tycho Brahe. In fact *al aaraaf*, more properly transcribed as *al a'raaf*, is the plural of *'arf* , meaning a high place. The people on the high places are about to enter Paradise, and they look down on sinners who cannot aspire to such *al a'raaf*.[2] Although it certainly does not refer to any kind of limbo as described by Poe, this does not detract from the poem itself.

God's message is conveyed to the world by seraphs doing the angel Ligeia's bidding, but Michelangelo and Ianthe fail to respond, leading to their barring from the gates of Heaven. Here is the part in which Ligeia first makes her entrance (note the nod to Coleridge):

> Ligeia! Ligeia!
>   My beautiful one!
> Whose harshest idea
>   Will to melody run,
> O! is it thy will
>   On the breezes to toss?
> Or, capriciously still,
>   Like the lone Albatross,
> Incumbent on night
>   (As she on the air)
> To keep watch with delight
>   On the harmony there?

So pleased was Poe with the poem that he imagined it would be responsible for his big breakthrough into the world of poetry. Hence the need he felt to leave the army and make strenuous efforts to interest people in his new work.

Allan was being stubborn, so Poe had to change his plans. He knew Allan would never accept his wish to make a career from writing, so he had to come up with something else. He hit upon a compromise. Allan did not want Poe to leave the military life, but he might be persuaded to let him continue army life in a different guise. Perhaps his recent promotion had again stirred some pride in himself and memories of General Poe. If he must remain in the army, at least he, too, could make a name for himself; which would mean becoming a commissioned officer. He could do that if he were to join the Military Academy at West Point. Once again Poe's mind begin to spin, and his imagination pieced together a great new start as a cadet. Should he gain a commission he could cast off for ever the stigma of being the son of lowly actors; he would become an officer as well as a gentleman.

He began his new campaign by contacting an intermediary, his neighbour's son, John McKenzie. This came to nothing, so on 4 February he tackled his guardian again. He wrote of his gratitude for past services – a good start – and he also told of his desire to go to West Point and pursue a worthwhile career. But he made two blunders: first, he asked for money, and, second, he brought up the unhealed wound of his behaviour at university and the argument between them, albeit he accepted the blame now and admitted fault – to some degree.

Again there was no answer. There was more on Allan's mind than just Poe's future. Fanny was sick and failing fast, and Allan's attention was focused on her. She had been ill for some time, but now, in the latest stages of her illness, she was in great pain. Poe's letters had been no more than a minor irritant, and doubtless Allan thought that Poe was settled enough in a career as it was and so paid little heed to his pleas. The doctors spoke gravely of Fanny's condition, and Allan began to despair. Soon it became apparent that she was not going to pull through, and she took to her bed for the last time. Although Allan had had his share of extramarital associations, he had been devoted to his wife; this must have been a time of great anguish for him. However, during their last conversations Fanny begged Allan to forgive the boy and to help him – and he agreed to her last request; he promised to forgive Poe and to take care of him.

On 20 February the *Richmond Whig* announced: 'Died on Saturday morning last, after a lingering and painful illness, Mrs Frances K. Allan, consort of Mr John Allan, aged 47 years.'[3] News was sent to Poe's battery, and it must have hit him hard; of all the people he had known, she was the most beloved. Fanny Allan had interceded between her husband and him, had shown her love for him in so many ways, had treated him as a son. His real mother had died and left him a vulnerable small child, and now his foster-mother had fallen sick and died, too. Poe was distraught, and hurriedly asked for compassionate leave. It was granted, and he rushed back to Richmond as fast as he could. He was too late. Frances Keeling Allan's body had been laid to rest the day before. Poe was sorely distressed and set off to visit her grave. When he looked down at the fresh earth and the flowers, he was so overcome with grief in the graveyard that he had to be helped out.

The first meeting between Poe and his guardian since he left Richmond must have been difficult. Allan did not want Poe at home, writing poems and leading a life of idleness. At first sight, the idea of going to

West Point was sound enough, but what guarantee was there that he would be accepted? Poe explained the esteem in which he was held by senior officers in his battery – Colonel Drayton, for instance – and how, with their recommendations, the passage would be easy.

As usual, Poe had the utmost confidence in himself and saw his entrance to the Military Academy as a foregone conclusion. After his interview with Allan he returned to Fort Monroe in high spirits. He visited Colonel Drayton, but found he had gone off to visit the President-Elect, so he set about preparing for the entrance examination. He then wrote to Allan suggesting that letters from important family friends in the judicial and military worlds might help him.

Next he set about getting his discharge from the army. This was dependent upon Poe finding a replacement for himself; but things did not go according to plan. He had discussed the matter with both Colonel House and Lieutenant Howard, and they both agreed that, at their own discretion, they would enlist the first recruit and pass him off as the substitute, and in that case all Poe would have to pay would be a nominal 'bounty' sum of $12. As luck would have it (in Poe's words) both officers were absent when the substitute was arranged, so he was forced to pay a lump sum for the replacement. Taking Poe's place was Sergeant Samuel Graves, known good-naturedly as 'Bully Graves', who agreed to act as substitute for the sum of $75. Poe little suspected how such a small matter would later come back to haunt him. He paid Graves $25, leaving him a credit note for the other $50.

At last Edgar A. Poe, alias Edgar A. Perry, left the US Army in April 1829. The first thing he did was to ask various people in positions of authority to write character references for him. This they did, which suggests that he was a well-liked and capable soldier. Lieutenant Howard stated that 'his habits are good and entirely free from drinking'; Captain Griswold stated that he 'is highly worthy of confidence'; Lieutenant-Colonel Worth 'unhesitatingly' recommended him; while Congressman (and family friend) James P. Preston wrote that 'he is a young gentleman of genius and talents'.

Poe had returned to his old home in Richmond. He determined, perhaps at Allan's instigation, to go to Washington as soon as possible and arrange a meeting with the Secretary of War, Major Eaton. For his own part, Allan wrote a cold letter, reflecting the fact that it was not his own idea: 'Frankly, Sir, do I declare that he is no relation to me whatever; that I have many in whom I have taken an active interest to promote theirs; with no other feeling than that, every man is my care, if he be in distress.' Perhaps this was meant for Poe's eyes as well as for those at the War Office.

Poe took his references and visited Major Eaton in his office in Washington, where all seemed to go well. Eaton would have remembered his grandfather's fame, and doubtless his name was mentioned at their meeting. Poe would also have described his military career to date, his rise to the rank of sergeant major and his aspirations with regard to the Military Academy.

He did not return to Richmond immediately. Allan had advised him to find out all he could about General Poe's actions in the Revolutionary War, as this might help him in his attempt to enter West Point, so he went off to Baltimore where some members of his family were still living, including his father's sister, Maria Clemm, and the Herrings – particularly his cousin Elizabeth who was the daughter of Poe's Aunt Elizabeth. But Poe had other intentions besides visiting his grandfather's home town; in fact, he felt that General Poe was so well known that he didn't need to substantiate anything. His main purpose was in trying to get 'Al Aaraaf' published. He sought to enlist the help of family friends, and sent a copy of the poem to William Wirt, Attorney General of the USA (he had been offered the Presidency of the University of Virginia) and author of *The Letters of a British Spy*.

Wirt was somewhat bemused by the poem but wrote a friendly enough reply, stating that he had never written any poetry himself and so felt he was not a competent judge. However, 'it will, I know, please modern readers – but to deal candidly with you (as I am bound to do) I should doubt whether the poem will take with old-fashioned readers like myself. But this will be of little consequence – provided it be popular with modern readers.' He went on to suggest that Poe contact someone more fitted to helping him on his way – such as Mr Walsh of the *American Quarterly Review*.

Allan was unaware as yet of Poe's attempts to break into the field of literature. In the only other letter we have of his to Poe, sent on 18 May, he concentrated on Poe's attempt to get to West Point and forwarded $100 to provide lodgings and food for his sojourn in Baltimore. He wrote in his typical blunt manner: 'I cover a Bank check of Virginia, on the Union Bank of Maryland (this date) of Baltimore for one Hundred Dollars payable to your order. Be prudent and careful.' To which came the dutiful reply:

> Dear Pa,
> I received your letter this morning enclosing a draft for $100 for which liberal allowance you will be sure that I feel grateful . . .
>
> I have succeeded in finding Grandmother & my relations – but the fact of my Grandfather's having been Quarter Master General of the whole US Army during the Revolutionary war is clearly established – but its being a well known fact at Washington, obviates the necessity of obtaining the certificates you mentioned.
>
> Not presuming upon Mr Wirt's former acquaintance, I introduced myself personally & for a first attempt at self introduction succeeded wonderfully. He treated me with great politeness, and invited me to call & see him frequently while I stay in Baltimore – I have called upon him several times.
>
> I have been introduced to many gentlemen of high standing in the city, who were formerly acquainted with my grandfather, & have altogether been treated very handsomely.

While this was going on, Poe was secretly attempting to find a publisher for his work. Quick to take up Wirt's suggestion, he travelled to Philadelphia, staying at Heiskill's Indian Queen Hotel. Unfortunately, when Poe went to visit Mr Walsh of the *American Quarterly Review* he discovered that he had left town. This was something of a blow, as he had hoped for a letter of introduction to the publishers Lea & Carey. He decided that while he was there he might as well approach them anyhow, so in an attempt to impress he wrote to them in a literary style, including a quote from de León's 'Vida Retirada', enclosed some of 'Al Aaraaf' and told of his hopes of getting his poems published. He ended with: 'I cannot refrain from adding that Mr Wirt's voice is in my favor.'

He did finally get to see Walsh, and they discussed the poem and its content – presumably Poe had sent him a copy after Wirt's suggestion. It would seem that Walsh's opinion of Poe's work was favourable, and indeed he agreed to give it notice in the *Review* if it were to get into print. But therein lay the rub – it was very difficult for a poet to be published in America at that time. When Poe mentioned his approach to Lea & Carey he was warned not to build up his hopes. Isaac Lea might be prepared to publish the work – but only if there was a safety net. He would almost certainly not consider publishing at his own risk – especially not an unpublished writer.

Poe had to face the fact that he needed a backer or the project would soon founder. The cost of publishing the book would run to about $100 at that time – and Poe had nowhere near that sort of cash. There was one person and one person only to whom he could turn – and that would be very tricky indeed. Allan had already made it quite clear that wasting time on poems and the like was to chew the bread of idleness, and Poe probably could foresee his guardian's reaction. But it was his only option. He must have taken a deep breath as he lifted his pen and wrote to his 'dear pa':

> The request I have to make is this: that you will give me a letter to Mssrs Carey, Lea, & Carey saying that if in publishing the poem 'Al Aaraaf' they shall incur any loss, you will make it good to them.
>
> The cost of publishing the work, in a style equal to any of our American publications, will at the extent be $100 – this then, of course, must be the limit of any loss supposing not a single copy of the work to be sold. It is more than probable that the work will be profitable & that I may gain instead of lose, even in a pecuniary way.
>
> I would remark, in conclusion that I have long given up Byron as a model – for which, I think, I deserve some credit . . .

Allan's doubtless icy response does not survive. He did write on the back of the letter: 'Replied to Monday, 8th June 1829 strongly censuring his conduct – and refusing any aid.' There was a further exchange of letters (now lost) until Poe wrote again, in a conciliatory tone, agreeing to withdraw the manuscript if Allan so desired.

He was now out of money again and had to ask for more. Allan was losing his temper. He had agreed to help Poe out of the army on one condition and one condition only – that he exert every effort to get into West Point. He had gone to Baltimore to visit family and to drum up more support for his application. He had written once before, predicting that Poe never would obey his advice, and now he was proved correct; instead of conscientiously gathering materials and references he was messing about with publishers and poetry. Allan was not willing to put up with such behaviour, and Poe had better come to his senses, forget about poems and come back down to earth.

Worse was to follow. Having sent Poe $100 just over five weeks earlier, he did not expect a request for more quite so soon. To explain his predicament, Poe had to confess to the substitution of Samuel Graves for himself and how he owed Graves $50. It had been sheer bad luck; had either Colonel House or Lieutenant Howard been there he would only have needed to pay $12. On top of this, he had been robbed while staying at Beltzhoover's Hotel by none other than a cousin of his, Edward Mosher Poe. He recovered $10 by going through Mosher's pockets, but the rest had gone. He threatened to expose the thief, but his cousin begged him not to do so on account of his wife. So he had not done so, but he was now sorely pushed for money.

Allan may or may not have believed Poe's story, but if he did believe it (and it sounds too outlandish to be fiction) he must have wondered how so much misfortune could befall one man. To lose such a sum of money would have been scandalous to someone of Allan's temperament, and, probably because he did not want to act in the heat of the moment, he did not reply. Suspecting Allan's annoyance, Poe wrote to smooth things over. He also mentioned that he had heard the rumour that his maternal grandfather was the traitor Benedict Arnold.

> Since I have been in Baltimore I have learnt something concerning my descent which would have, I am afraid, no very favourable effect if known to the War Dept: viz: that I am the grandson of General Benedict Arnold – but this there will be no necessity of telling.

By the time another three weeks had passed Poe was getting desperate. He had visited General Poe's widow, but she was in no state to put him up – and because he had to live in boarding houses he was running up large bills. He wrote another application for help, and added:

> I sometimes am afraid that you are angry & perhaps you have reason to be – but if you will but put a little more confidence in me, I will endeavor to deserve it.
>
> I am sure no one can be more anxious, or would do more towards helping myself than I would, if I had any means of doing it – without your assistance, I have none. I am anxious to abide by your directions, if I knew what they were.
>
> You would relieve me from a great deal of anxiety by writing me soon. I think I have already had my share of trouble for one so young.

A reply eventually came from Allan and in no friendly tone. He wanted to know more about all the losses of which Poe had written. He wanted to know exactly what had happened before he could consider writing them off. Why had Poe never mentioned anything about the cost of the substitute until now? He was disparaging about the theft incident and wanted proof of what had happened. Begrudgingly, however, he did send some cash, with a gibe that rankled Poe, who replied that he was 'truly thankful for the money which you sent me, notwithstanding the taunt with which it was given "that men of genius ought not to apply to your aid". It is too often their necessity to want that little timely assistance which would prevent such applications.'

To get on the right side of Allan, he decided to go to Washington on his way home and try to expedite things. Once again he was received by the Secretary of War, Major Eaton, who explained how matters stood. The September intake was full, and on the surplus list there were forty-six applicants, all of whom had dropped out or been rejected apart from ten. Poe was next on the list, which made his entry into West Point that year unlikely, although still feasible. Otherwise, he would have to wait until June 1830, at which time his entry would be guaranteed. Poe explained all this in his next letter to Allan, as well as the Graves and Mosher incidents. He had agreed not to expose Mosher on the condition that he admitted the theft in a letter; this was in Poe's possession and he was willing to show it to Allan as proof that the theft took place.

However, there was one other thing in Allan's letter which both puzzled and confounded Poe. Allan had mentioned that he was not really anxious to see Poe, which made him wonder why. It seemed that Allan had not forgiven him for his past misdemeanours. He had tried to explain everything to Allan but was confused about their present relationship. Did Allan's aversion to seeing him mean that he was cutting him off once again? If so, why did he send a reply and cash?

In fact, Allan did not want Poe around because he was in the midst of one of his amours; the presence of his foster-son could be embarrassing and create difficulties. They had already had one major argument on the subject, and Allan did not wish to involve Poe in his private life. Better to pay him to stay away – as long, that is, as he did not go on losing and squandering the money.

Things were not going well for Poe. Lea & Carey had refused to publish his work. He did not want to antagonize a possible future publisher, so he wrote to them thanking them for their advice; at a meeting with Isaac Lea, the latter had expressed his opinion that the small collection would not sell well and that Poe's best option was to approach one of the magazines, such as the *Souvenir*. This was the first time the idea of becoming a magazine contributor had been mooted, and Poe was quite taken with the idea. That he was reading them is apparent in a cutting remark he made about John Neal, the critic, who had written disparagingly of the journal and whom he now described as one 'who now & then hitting, thro' sheer impudence, upon a correct judgement in matters of authorship, is most unenviably ridiculous whenever he touches the fine arts'. This, the first criticism from Poe's pen, became a sort of prototype for the future.

Poe also asserted that he had 'made a better disposition of my poems than I had any right to expect'. This may have been bluster; on the other hand, he had been in talks with another publisher, Hatch & Dunning, who had apparently shown some interest. Nobody could accuse Poe of indolence at this point of his life. Also, whatever may have been Allan's suspicions, Poe was also genuinely making an effort to secure a place at West Point. In fact he now blamed Allan for risking a delay because after their reconciliation, when Poe returned to Old Point Comfort, he was under the impression that Allan himself was making efforts to get him into West Point. It had taken two months for his release to come through, and if Allan had been making the initial enquiries his place in the September intake would have been assured. As it was, when he returned home he had five bare months to make all the arrangements, which was not enough time because a waiting list had already grown. So, reasoned Poe, if he did not make the next intake Allan only had himself to blame.

But there was still an obstinate silence on Allan's part. It is easy to imagine the frustration Poe must have felt – told he was unwanted, not knowing what to do next and unaware of the true reason. His next letter betrays a note of agitation:

> Dear Sir,
> I am unable to account for your not answering. If you are offended with me, I repeat that I have done nothing to deserve your displeasure . . .
>
> . . . If you have not forgiven me for my former conduct, that is a different thing – but you told me that you had. I am however aware that I have many enemies at home who fancy it their interest to injure me in your estimation.
>
> By your last letter I understood that it was not your wish that I should return home – I am anxious to do so, but if you think that I should not, I only wish to know what course I shall pursue.
>
> If you are determined to do nothing more in my behalf, you will at least do me the common justice to tell me so. I am almost sure of

> getting the appt in Sepr & certain at any rate of getting it in June – if I could manage until that time I would be no longer a trouble to you.
>
> I think it no more than right that you should answer my letter.
>
> Perhaps the time may come when you will find that I have not deserved half the misfortunes which have happened to me & that you suspected me unworthily.

In the meantime Poe decided to look up his family and hunted out his father's sister, Maria, who had married a William Clemm but was now widowed. She was in many ways a remarkable woman. Broad and slightly masculine, since her husband's death she had learned how to subsist on very little and soon became mistress of that craft. She was resourceful and industrious, would wash, darn or take in lodgers – anything that might bring money to the household. She was also adept at writing begging letters when her industry failed to provide enough for basic necessities.

She was living in Mechanics Row, Wilks Street, with a motley collection of relatives. There was her daughter Virginia, a plump little girl of eight years, and a son called Henry. Edgar's elder brother, William Henry, was living there, too, along with General Poe's widow, who had suffered a stroke, leaving her incapacitated. She had been awarded a small pension, and this sum was like gold dust to the poor family circle. By the time Poe visited them they were in a financial crisis.

William Henry Poe's story was a sad one that was slowly coming to an end. It seems that while William Henry (or Henry as he was called) lived with General Poe as a child, the Allans discouraged his meeting Edgar because Fanny was afraid the Poes may want Edgar back. It has been said that Allan's reference to Rosalie's dubious background may have veiled a hidden threat to expose the family skeleton, but that seems unlikely. On the death of General Poe, Henry's guardian, he was looked after by an old friend of his father's, Henry Didier, who had studied law along with him. When Henry had grown to an appropriate age, Didier employed him in his counting-house. Eventually Henry joined the Clemm household, and around this time he signed up with the merchant navy. On one of the few occasions Edgar met Henry he introduced him to his sweetheart Sarah Elmira Royster, who remembered the uniform. At one point Henry sailed with the ship the USS *Caledonia,* and while at sea he visited Montevideo in Uruguay and various other countries; from 1827 on he wrote articles about his travels for the *North American*. He even wrote a story based on Elmira and Edgar called 'The Pirate', in which Edgar becomes 'Edgar-Leonard' and Elmira becomes 'Rose'.[4]

Henry Poe also wrote poetry, and some of it was published in various magazines, including the *Saturday Evening Post* and the *Baltimore Minerva and Emerald*. For a brief period he resumed employment with Henry Didier. At this time he was considered to be the brilliant one in the family, but he suddenly and dramatically went downhill, finding solace in the bottom of a bottle. When Edgar arrived at the house he was entirely 'given up to drink' and penniless. Yet there is no doubt that Edgar loved his brother, and he eagerly listened to stories of far-off voyages to the West Indies, Europe and the Near East, stories that he would remember, sometimes pass off as his own or use in his own tales. They had a similar taste in poetry, and some of their efforts would be remarkably alike, so much so that a collaboration must be suspected.

In the end Allan did write – and, as always, his mind was on West Point. A delay until June 1830 would not have pleased him, but at the back of his mind was the constant fear that Poe might not enlist at all – and that he would spend his life in idleness and, worse still, scrounging from him. Apart from transparent attempts to smooth things over, all Allan could see was that his ward still had his mind full of poetry and the like.

In the latest round of correspondence Poe struck the right note, talking to Allan about his finances. He had realized that he had offended Allan by pursuing a literary career, so none of that was mentioned. He summed up his situation succinctly: if he were lucky enough to get the September appointment, all would be well and good; he had worked out that his living expenses until that time would amount to around $30. If he were unlucky and obliged to wait, he would take on a long-term lease which would cost less per month; he ventured a suggestion of his own but added that he would be happy to leave the exact amount up to Allan. He dutifully passed on news of his relatives as well. This was by far the best way to handle his foster-father.

Aug. 10th 1829.

Dear Pa,

I received yours this morning which relieved me from more trouble than you can well imagine. I was afraid that you were offended & although I knew that I had done nothing to deserve your anger, I was in a most uncomfortable situation – without one cent of money, in a strange place & so quickly engaged in difficulties after the serious misfortunes which I have just escaped. My grandmother is extremely poor & ill (paralytic) My aunt Maria if possible still worse & Henry entirely given up to drink & unable to help himself, much less me.

I am unwilling to appear obstinate as regards the substitute so will say nothing more concerning it – only remarking that they will no longer enlist men for the residue of another's enlistment as formerly, consequently my substitute was enlisted for 5 years not 3.

I stated in my last letter (to which I refer you) that Mr Eaton gave me strong hopes for Sepr at any rate that the appt could be obtained for June next – I can obtain decent board lodging & washing with other expenses of mending &c for 5 & perhaps even for 4½ $ per week.

If I obtain the appt by the last of Sepr the amt of expense would be at most $30. If I should be unfortunate & not obtain it until June I will not desire you to allow as much as that per week because by engaging for a longer period at a cheap boarding house I can do with much less – say even 10 even 8 $ pr month, any thing with which you think it possible to exist. I am not so anxious of obtaining money from your good nature as of preserving your good will.

I am extremely anxious that you should believe that I have not attempted to impose upon you. I will in the meantime (if you wish it) write you often, but pledge myself to apply for no other assistance than what you shall think proper to allow.

Poe still nursed the ambition to become a poet and still had high hopes for 'Al Aaraaf'. He approached his uncle, George Poe, who suggested that he send proofs to the critic John Neal, someone he was acquainted with and who could be of great assistance to him – he was also the critic Poe had written about so disparagingly to Isaac Lea. Neal was the first American correspondent to write for foreign magazines, such as *Blackwood's* – a magazine that Poe would always see as setting the standard in magazine literature. So he sent 'Al Aaraaf' and some of his other material to Neal, beginning his submission with: 'I am young – not yet twenty – am a poet, if deep worship of all beauty can make me one – and wish to be so in the common meaning of the word.'

Neal was a member of the celebrated Delphian Club, which had been inaugurated by the lawyer and editor William Gwynn. It was noted for its wits, and one frequent visitor later played an important role in Poe's life – John Pendleton Kennedy. As Gwynn was an important local figure as well as editor of the *Federal Gazette and Baltimore Daily Advertiser*, it seemed obvious to Poe that he should also approach him. As his cousin Neilson Poe worked for him in the editorial office, it is possible that the suggestion may have come from him. Gwynn, however, was unimpressed, stating that 'Al Aaraaf' was 'indicative of a tendency of anything but the business of matter-of-fact life'.

If Poe was disappointed by Gwynn, Neal gave him unexpected encouragement in a notice published in the September edition of the *Yankee and Boston Literary Gazette*. Although he refers to Poe's poems as 'nonsense', he tempers that by calling them 'exquisite nonsense' and suggests that he may produce 'a beautiful and perhaps a magnificent poem'. Kind, if indulgent, words.

Allan still wanted to be convinced that Poe was doing all he could to secure his West Point place at the earliest opportunity. The theme seems to have recurred throughout Allan's letters of this time. The next intake of cadets for the Military Academy was just over a month away, and he was getting extremely concerned. In fact his concern was well founded. Poe was not among the intake of September 1829 and had to make do with the possibility of a 1830 entrance.

To Poe's great surprise, Allan made a request to see some of his poems. This change of heart was no doubt stimulated by the moderately warm review of Neal and perhaps also the opinion of George Poe, who obviously had more faith in the young man than his guardian did. What if the boy was right? What if his talents were good enough to warrant success? Yet Allan was no fool; he knew perfectly well how difficult it was to make a career out of literature and especially poetry. He himself had been ambitious to write and had written of his desire to Ellis. He now wanted to review Poe's work himself, so that he could judge its merits, so far as his own appreciation allowed. Unfortunately the only spare manuscript was still at Lea & Carey's, but Poe promised to send it when it was available.

Poe was aware of the frustration and simmering unquiet in Allan's letters, and he admitted as much: 'I am sorry that your letters to me have still with them a tone of anger as if my former errors were not forgiven – if I knew how to regain your affection God knows I would do any thing I could.'

During his time in Baltimore he contacted other members of the family, including his cousin Elizabeth Herring, named after her mother and Poe's aunt. He seems to have been fond of her and sent her some verses, one which was a sonnet using her name as an acrostic. As there are sixteen letters in her name, the poem became a sixteen-line sonnet. There is no reason to believe that there was any attraction between them other than friendship – although just as Poe's enemies seek to find evidence of alcohol touching his lips, so they try to infer the worst meaning from the most innocent of relationships.

He was finding it tough to make ends meet. Although he was boarding in an inexpensive house, the landlady was pressing him for his rent. Once again he found himself in financial difficulties, and once again he had no other recourse but to beg from his guardian. 'I would not trouble you so often if I was not extremely pinched – I am almost without clothes and, as I board by the month, the lady with whom I board is anxious for her money. I have not had any (you know) since the middle of August.' This at least brought some cash, but, as usual, there were conditions attached. It seems that Allan went to pains to explain to his foster-son exactly why the sum that he sent should meet all his costs. He still felt that Poe needed to learn the value of money and wrote an itemized list of how the money should be spent, how much pocket money he should have and more. But Poe knew that this would not be enough to manage financially, as Allan had forgotten simple things such as clothing. Even so, he did not want to cause further animosity, so he simply asked Allan to send material and Maria Clemm would make up the required article. Perhaps he derived some secret (if grim) amusement from pulling up his fastidious foster-guardian.

> Dear Pa,
> I duly received your letter enclosing a check for $80, for which I am truly thankful. This will be quite sufficient for all the expenditures you mention but I am afraid if I purchase a piece of linen of which I am much in want I shall have none left for pocketmoney & if you could get me a piece or a ½ piece at Mr Galts & send it to me by the boat, I could get it made up gratis by my Aunt Maria.
>
> The Poems will be printed by Hatch & Dunning of this city upon terms advantageous to me they printing it & giving me 250 copies of the book: I will send it on by Mr Dunning who is going immediately to Richmond.

Frequent visits to the Clemm household had shown Poe how desperate the family's situation was. Their only asset as far as he could see was their Negro slave, Edwin, so he acted as Maria Clemm's agent and went in search of a buyer. Edwin was in the prime of life at twenty-one years of age, and Poe expected to make a good profit from the sale. The best he could do was to sell the slave to one Henry Ridgway, who was willing to pay $40, so a bill of sale was prepared by a clerk called Gibson, and each party set their seal upon it on 10 December 1829 at three in the afternoon. There was one codicil: that the bond should only be valid until Edwin reached the age of thirty. The document was duly signed in the presence of a witness, Henry W. Gray.

Poe was telling the truth about Hatch & Dunning: they did indeed publish *Al Aaraaf, Tamerlane and Minor Poems* by the end of the year. The minor poems included 'Romance', 'To the River', 'To M—' and 'To Science'. To repay Neal's past kindness, Poe asked him if he might dedicate the volume to him, but Neal did not think that it would be beneficial. Poe ignored this advice, however, and dedicated it to him anyway. Now, at last, his magnum opus 'Al Aaraaf' was in print, and Poe had high hopes for the critical reviews of the poem and for the sales of his new book. He looked for help from his tame critic, John Neal, and bluntly told him that some lines from his 'Preface' 'have never been surpassed'. To justify this boast, he stated: '"It is well to think well of one's self" – so sings somebody. You will do me justice however . . .'

He received several copies of his work from Hatch & Dunning, and, packing these with the rest of his belongings, he travelled back to Richmond. Some of these books he gave to Sanxey's, the local bookshop, to sell; doubtless he gave a copy to John Allan. The old year was drawing to a close, and he must have enjoyed a warm feeling back in the house in which he grew up. He will have keenly felt the absence of 'Ma', but at least there was Aunt Nancy, to whom he had always felt a familial affection.

He seems now to have rested on his laurels and looked up old friends, such as the young author Nathan C. Brooks, before starting the new phase in his career; certainly he would have visited the McKenzies, for whom he always had a special regard.

Although Poe's efforts to get into West Point had not yet been successful, he had at least tried his best and would enlist there in six months' time. Allan had decided not to leave things to chance or indeed to the efforts of his foster-son. Charles Ellis had a brother called Powhatan, and Powhatan Ellis was a strong political figure, being US Senator for Mississippi. Allan contacted him, and Powhatan oiled the wheels by applying directly to Major Eaton himself, thus guaranteeing Poe's entry into West Point in June of that year. Eaton must have been tired of hearing the name Edgar Poe. But having settled everything to his satisfaction, there was no reason why Allan should not get along with Edgar well enough, and these first weeks were possibly the most harmonious between them. Free from the task of finding a place in the Academy, Poe may have found it easier to talk about his literary work, and now that he was a published author and needed no financial backing for that purpose Allan probably discussed the matter with him. Allan would have been a steadying influence upon him and would have found it prudent to give practical advice.

However, there was always tension between the two, always ready to burst into something more destructive. It would seem that Allan could not resist bringing Poe's ancestry into the conversation when things became heated, and this is what happened at the beginning of May that year. The cause of the argument is not known, but it may have had something to do with Allan's engagement to a lady who never warmed to Poe, nor he to her – Louisa Gabriella Patterson of New Jersey. Through her Allan might well be able to conceive legitimate heirs, and that would push Poe even more into the background. It is little wonder he felt a constant antagonism against her – and, of course, the liaison would also have seemed to Poe a betrayal of his beloved foster-mother, who had been laid to rest barely more than a year before.

Besides, Allan was once again involved in *affaires d'amour*. He had continued an affair with one Mrs Willis, whom he had known before Fanny's death, and he had been seeing her when Poe was in Baltimore. Now she was heavily pregnant, and paternity was accepted by Allan – in fact, on 1 July she gave birth to twins, to double Allan's headaches.

Perhaps this news put Allan on edge; but at one point his comments must have been very hurtful, as Poe reached the point where his heart 'was almost breaking'. Perhaps it was the news of the forthcoming marriage. Poe's comments irritated Allan, and an argument ensued, wherein Allan proceeded to get angry and then followed that up with abuse of Poe's parentage. According to Poe, these remarks completely embittered him against Allan, although those words, too, were written later and in rage.

At this point another shadow fell across Poe's life in the form of

Samuel 'Bully' Graves, the man who had agreed to act as substitute when Poe left Old Point Comfort. Poe still owed him money, either the remaining $50 (which Poe had assured Allan had been paid) or possibly another debt of the same amount. Graves was getting agitated – it had now been a whole year, and that was long enough to wait for the money. He was now importunate. There was also the matter of money owed to a Sergeant Griffith.

Angrily, shortly after his argument with Allan, on 3 May 1830 Poe sent Graves the following reply:

> Dear Bully,
> I have just received your letter which is the first I have ever got from you. I suppose the reason of my not getting your other was that you directed it to Washington, but I have not been there for some time. As to what you say about Downey, Mr A [Allan] very evidently misunderstood me, and I wish you to understand that I never sent any money by Downey whatsoever. Mr A is not very often sober, which accounts for it. I mentioned to him that I had seen Downey at Balto., as I did, & that I wished to send it on by him, but he did not intend going to the point.
>
> I have tried to get the money for you from Mr A a dozen times but he always shuffles me off. I have been very sorry that I have never had it in my power as yet to pay either you or Sergeant Griffith but altho' appearances are very much against me, I think you know me sufficiently well to believe that I have no intention of keeping you out of your money – the very first opportunity, you shall have it (both of you) with interest & my best thanks for your kindness. I told Sergeant Benton why I never had it in my power – he will explain it.
>
> I suppose some of the officers told you that I am a cadet. If you are, at any time, going to leave the point, write to W. Point and let me know your station. You need be under no uneasiness about your money.

This, for the time being, successfully fobbed Graves off. But now Poe had decided that he would not wait until the entrance examination to go to West Point. Perhaps it had something to do with the fresh argument, or perhaps it was to revisit his old family friends. For whatever reason, he seems to have gone to Baltimore again; and at the time he and Allan were not on especially bad terms, so perhaps they patched up their differences. He left for West Point late in May, just missing a letter from Allan in which he enclosed $20. Henry sent it on to West Point post office, where it sat for some time before Poe was made aware of it.

The days passed by, and Poe at last faced the entrance examinations. These were basically reading, writing and arithmetic, and he had little difficulty with them. When he finally found the letter and received the $20, he read that Allan had a query about the books he had taken from home, the insinuation being that he had taken things which were not his to take. On 28 June he replied: 'The examination for admission is just over – a great many cadets of good family &c have been rejected as deficient . . . Of 130 Cadets appointed every year only 30 or 35 ever graduate, the rest being dismissed for bad conduct or deficiency. The Regulations are rigid in the extreme . . .' He passed his examinations and was formally enrolled in the Military Academy, being stationed at No. 28, South Barracks. Allan must have breathed a sigh of relief.

West Point was the pearl of military academia and had been so since its establishment in 1802. It was originally an army fort, located on a bank of the Hudson River because of its commanding position. George Washington himself ordered its fortifications, which were designed by another military hero, Thaddeus Kosciuszko.[5] Despite the intrigues of Benedict Arnold, the fortress was never captured by the British, and when the Revolutionary War was over several eminent soldiers suggested the founding of a college there to further the science of warfare. The innovative President Jefferson signed the appropriate legislation, and West Point Military Academy was born.

The so-called Father of the Military Academy was Colonel Sylvanus Thayer, who had been in the post of Superintendent since 1811. Thayer stressed the need for civil engineering and the curriculum was based around that. He also insisted that the discipline be tough and that the cadets' behaviour be beyond reproach. Over 300 regulations had been drawn up, many of them draconian. The Academy was certainly a tough place – classes from dawn till 4 p.m., military drill until sunset, and classes again till 9.30 – lights out at 10. Few cadets completed the requisite four years' instruction.

As the first months passed by, Poe applied himself diligently to his course. Although mocked by his colleagues for looking older than they were (as indeed he was),[6] he seems to have settled in well, and he amused his colleagues with fictional accounts of his travels, as well as satirical verses on the officers. The most quoted of these was his squib on Instructor Joseph L. Locke:

John Locke was a notable name
Joe Locke is a greater: in short,
The former was well known to fame
But the latter's well known to 'report'.

Reminiscences of Poe are in the main untrustworthy and gleaned many years afterwards. There is a hint that he may have been subject to fits of manic depression. Tales of his drinking are more than likely false, but if he did drink socially, or sneaked over to Old Benny Haven's for illicit liquor he was never on report for it, and his academic work did not suffer.

With Thayer's permission, he was allowed to gather subscriptions from his friends for a new book of poems. One colleague, Allan B. Magruder, remembered the subscription to be 75 cents and that a publisher from New York (Elam Bliss) visited Poe to discuss terms.

Then came an event which was probably unwelcome to Poe – Allan's remarriage on 5 October 1830. But, once again, financial problems were at the fore when he next wrote to him on 6 November:

> If you would be so kind as to send me on a Box of Mathematical Instruments, and a copy of the Cambridge Mathematics, you would confer a great favor upon me and render my situation much more comfortable, or forward to Col: Thayer the means of obtaining them; for as I have no deposit, my more necessary expenditures have run me into debt.

Suddenly the uneasy relationship between Allan and Poe was blown apart. Bully Graves was angry at being fobbed off for his debt; perhaps he needed the money, as Christmas was approaching. Again finding no satisfaction, he resorted to sending Poe's letter to Allan. The way Poe blamed Allan for non-payment of the debts, the lie that he was always 'shuffled off' by him, and, worse than all, the insinuation of his near-constant drunkenness must have appalled Allan. More than that, it was positively the final straw. This time Poe had gone too far. How dare he abuse and vilify his name in writing, spread lies and libels against him? And after Allan's generosity in forgiving him, helping him, putting him on the ladder to success, supporting him! How was it that Graves was still asking for his money when Poe had assured him that he had paid him off – had used it as an excuse for having little money? It had all been lies, lies, lies. As far as Allan was concerned, he had spent enough time on this selfish charity child whom he had brought up and educated. He wanted to neither see nor hear from him ever again.

Poe read Allan's letter and sent back a furious, unrestrained response, in which he conveyed all his past frustrations and anger.

> West Point. Jan 3rd 1831.
> Sir, I suppose (altho' you desire no further communication with yourself on my part,) that your restriction does not extend to my answering your final letter.
>
> Did I, when an infant, solicit your charity and protection, or was it of your own free will, that you volunteered your services in my behalf? It is well known to respectable individuals in Baltimore, and elsewhere, that my Grandfather (my natural protector at the time you interposed) was wealthy, and that I was his favourite grand-child. But the promises of adoption, and liberal education which you held forth to him in a letter which is now in possession of my family, induced him to resign all care of me into your hands. Under such circumstances, can it be said that I have no right to expect anything at your hands?

As for Poe's education, was it not Allan who, through his own miserliness, had left him to live on nothing and forced him to desperate measures? Did he not refuse to help clear his debts of honour, leaving him at the mercy of his creditors?

> I could associate with no students, except those who were in a similar situation with myself, altho' from different causes. They from drunkenness, and extravagance – I, because it was my crime to have no one on Earth who cared for me, or loved me. I call God to witness that I have never loved dissipation. Those who know me know that my pursuits and habits are very far from any thing of the kind. But I was drawn into it by my companions – and after nearly 2 years conduct with which no fault could be found – in the army, as a common soldier – I earned, myself, by the most humiliating privations, a Cadets' warrant which you could have obtained at any time for asking. It was then that I thought I might venture to solicit your assistance in giving me an outfit – I came home, you will remember, the night after the burial. If she had not have died while I was away there would have been nothing for me to regret – your love I never valued – but she I believed loved me as her own child. You promised me to forgive all, but you soon forgot your promise. You

sent me to W. Point like a beggar. The same difficulties are threatening me as before at Charlottesville, and I must resign.

As to your injunction not to trouble you with farther communication rest assured, Sir, that I will most religiously observe it.

As regards Sergeant Graves – I did write him that letter. As to the truth of its contents, I leave it to God, and your own conscience. The time in which I wrote it was within a half hour after you had embittered every feeling of my heart against you by your abuse of my family, and myself, under your own roof, and at a time when you knew that my heart was almost breaking.

I have no more to say, except that my future life (which thank God will not endure long) must be passed in indigence and sickness. I have no energy left, nor health. If it was possible, to put up with the fatigues of this place, and the inconveniences which my absolute want of necessaries subject me to, and as I mentioned before it is my intention to resign. For this end it will be necessary that you (as my nominal guardian) enclose me your written permission. It will be useless to refuse me this last request, for I can leave the place without any permission – your refusal would only deprive me of the little pay which is now due as mileage.

From the time of writing this I shall neglect my studies and duties at the institution. If I do not receive your answer in 10 days, I will leave the point without – for otherwise I should subject myself to dismission.

On the letter Allan wrote:

I recd this on the 10th & did not from its conclusion deem it necessary to reply. I made this note on the 13th & can see no good Reason to alter my opinion. I do not think the Boy has one good quality. He may do or act as he pleases, tho' I wd have saved him but on his own terms & conditions since I cannot believe a word he writes. His letter is the most barefaced one sided statement.

Like so many of Poe's actions at times of crisis, the writing of this letter was rash and unpremeditated. It was an insuperable barrier to the possibility of reconciliation between them. Had Poe waited a day or two, collected his thoughts and considered the matter carefully and astutely, he might have found a better solution. If he had explained everything, if he had written a more conciliatory letter, perhaps things would have been different. There can be no doubt that behind all the antagonism there was a deep affection. Only people who have love for one another can injure each other so badly.

Yet it is possible that, for the time being, both men were happy enough with the actual outcome. Poe's mind had always been on poetry and literature, and he was now spared the drudgery of army life, the tough regulations and the military drill. On the other hand, he had lost a father and the chance of a secure career. Allan would have been pleased to cast off his responsibility for the troublesome young man and start to make plans for his own life and his new family. This was his second chance, and he still had his heart set on an heir. Yet it is hard to imagine that he would feel no regret at the direction things took.

Poe did in fact subject himself to dismissal by absenting himself from all studies and religious services. The subsequent court martial arraigned him on two counts: first, gross neglect of duty and, second, disobedience of orders. He was found guilty. The trial ended as follows: 'Cadet E.A. Poe will be dismissed the service of the United States and cease to be considered a member of the Military Academy after the 6th of March 1831.'

So ended the military phase of Poe's life, and so came the break with his guardian. He still yearned for a father-figure, but this was the second time there had been a break between John Allan and himself and, after the first, it had taken his wife on her deathbed to persuade Allan to forgive. Now there was no such influence. Edgar Allan Poe was very much alone.

4

⁖ DESCENT INTO THE MAELSTROM ⁖

Dishonourably discharged from the US Army, Poe did not await the expiry of his term at West Point. Freed from service, he was eager to leave, and on 19 February 1831 he travelled to New York. However, he was completely without funds and found himself wondering where he was to get the next cent from. He had found cheap accommodation, but he had caught a chest cold and a painful ear infection. In his last furious letter he had written to his foster-father: 'As to your injunction not to trouble you with farther communication rest assured, Sir, that I will most religiously observe it.' But without food or drink, let alone money to stay in his lodgings, niceties such as self-respect bow down to sheer need. After two days it was an angry and humiliated but needy Poe who again wrote to John Allan:

> I have not strength nor energy left to write half what I feel. You one day or other will feel how you have treated me. I left West Point two days ago and travelled to New York without a cloak or any other clothing of importance. I have caught a most violent cold and am confined to my bed. I have no money – no friends. I have written to my brother, but he cannot help me. I shall never rise from my bed. Besides a most violent cold on my lungs my ear discharges blood and matter continually and my headache is distracting – I hardly know what I am writing. I will write no more. Please send me a little money – quickly – and forget what I said about you.

He had moved to New York because there was nowhere else for him to go. He had only one lead to follow, and as there was nothing else for him to do he followed it – the projected new book of poems for which he had taken up subscriptions among the West Point cadets.

Little did they know what they would get – they expected a book full of satirical puns and squibs on their colleagues and officers, those verbal jokes that had amused them so much when Poe was with them. But Poe had no intention of becoming a humorist just yet, although he would later work in that realm.

He was not the man to lose a second in the promotion of his literary interests, so he went to see Elam Bliss, the publisher who had visited him at West Point to discuss terms for the book. This was an important meeting for Poe, because it was his only chance to raise some money, and his past failures must have been discouraging to him. Still, his breakthrough had to come at some stage, and this was as good a time as any. In fact, very little distinguished the new volume, *Poems*, from the last one; both contained his only two sizeable verses, 'Al Aaraaf' and 'Tamerlane', and they differed only in the shorter pieces. Some of these were now far superior to the earlier poems, however. 'To Helen' made its first appearance, along with 'Israfel', 'Irene' and 'The Doomed City'. It must have been the know-ledge that these were a step up that kept his hopes high.

'Israfel', or 'Israfil', is the Islamic equivalent of the angel Raphael, who is to blow his horn at the coming of Judgement Day, at which time he will stand upon the Holy Rock in Jerusalem. A beautiful four-winged angel, Israfel uses his musical expertise to sing praise to Allah. In a later version, Poe's poem begins:

> In Heaven a spirit doth dwell
> 'Whose heart-strings are a lute;'
> None sing so wildly well
> As the angel Israfel,
> And the giddy stars (so legends tell)
> Ceasing their hymns, attend the spell
> Of his voice, all mute . . .
>
> If I could dwell
> Where Israfel
> Hath dwelt, and he where I,
> He might not sing so wildly well
> A mortal melody,
> While a bolder note than this might swell
> From my lyre within the sky.

'The Doomed City' was later to become 'The City in the Sea', and Poe would accuse Longfellow of imitation in his 'The Beleaguered City'.

If Poe's hopes were kept high, his finances were not. Allan did not respond to his pitiful cry for help, and he became desperate. The last time he was so desperate he had joined the army, but now that was impossible. At least, it was impossible in the USA – but there were other armies he could join. After the Napoleonic War Poland had been swallowed by Austria and Russia, and rebel nationalists were struggling for independence, leading to an all-out war with Russia. Poe now decided on an attempt to join the Polish army in Paris, but he was unsure how to go about it. Although he was seen as disgraced by the American army, he still hoped for assistance from Colonel Thayer, and on 10 March he wrote to him asking for help.

No reply survives. Sick and penniless, Poe had to finish his business with Bliss and find somewhere else to live. Eventually the anticipated volume arrived. The new book of poems was dedicated to the US Corps of Cadets, and once more he must have had great hopes. Once more they were dashed. The book was not profitable, and when the cadets obtained the slim volume they were not impressed – instead of what they expected, they got ethereal verse printed, as they thought, on the cheap.

Poe had no alternative but to beg a bed from his family; he had no income, no cash and no hopes of getting any straight away. John Allan had proved that he wanted no more to do with him, so Poe looked towards Baltimore, where some of his relations were still living – the Herrings and the Clemms. As he had lived at Maria Clemm's dwelling in Mechanics Row, Wilks Street, while angling for the West Point appointment, he went there first, and although her house was full Maria gave him a bed.

The household was the same as ever, except that Henry Clemm does not appear to have been living there. It is thought that, impressed by William Henry Poe's tales of the navy, he went off to sea. Old General Poe's widow was still there, as incapacitated as ever but at least able to provide a little money to the house by means of her widow's pension. William Henry was also there, but in poor condition – his weaknesses had been compounded by a dose of tuberculosis, and he was failing. The only other member of the household was Maria's little girl, Virginia.

It must have been good for Poe to see his brother again and to discuss old times. They would also have discussed the second breach with John Allan, and perhaps William Henry may have given encouragement to his younger brother about the field of literature, in which he himself had had moderate success. Henry's health must have touched Edgar to the quick, and perhaps he thought of his own mother, whose disease had now visited the only remaining member of his immediate family.

It is not hard to imagine the gratitude Poe felt towards his aunt, a gratitude that would be life-long. Doubtless he explained how he would contribute to the upkeep of the house when he gained employment, which would surely now be soon – he had three published books to his name, so surely he could find something in the literature line – perhaps a job with a newspaper or a magazine.

He made overtures to the editor of the local newspaper. It seemed as good a place as any to start; besides, he realized that his cousin Neilson had just left his position there to go on to better things and so there would be a vacancy. He wrote to William Gwynn, owner of the *Federal Gazette and Baltimore Daily Advertiser*, apologizing for his past 'foolish conduct' and seeking a job. This produced nothing, not even a reply, but then we do not know what his 'foolish conduct' was – probably an ill-considered reaction to Gwynn's dismissal of 'Al Aaraaf'.[1]

He made at least one more attempt to find employment in newspaper offices but without success. So he had to look to his writing. Poetry, he felt (and always would), was the form of literature closest to his heart, and he firmly believed that he had passed a milestone in his latest efforts. But his logical mind must have told him that talent itself was not enough to put bread on the table. He had so far seen no profit at all from his publications; what is more, the critics had been lukewarm at best. It was the need to provide a saleable product that pushed Poe towards writing stories – tales of popular interest that he could publish in magazines or perhaps in book form.

Perhaps it was an advertisement in the 4 June edition of the *Philadelphia Saturday Courier* that made Poe sit up and think. The paper announced a prize of $100 for the best tale submitted to them and gave until the beginning of December as the final date for entries. Such a sum must have seemed like a fortune to the impoverished Poe.

The magazine industry had for some time been an alternative for the struggling would-be writer. It had expanded alongside the growth of the economy, assisted by the development of efficient new printing presses that could deliver thousands of periodicals in the shortest time. A pioneer of magazine literature was Joseph Dennie, who, in 1801, founded the *Port Folio*, a magazine in which were found all the ingredients employed by its successors – literature and political commentary as well as literary criticism and poetry. Many other periodicals followed in its wake, and although the *Port Folio* folded in 1827 the middle half of the nineteenth century was the golden age of the magazine.

Poe thought carefully about what he could do with his writings, for the long as well as the short term. Short tales would sell best in the magazines, and yet if he could link them together there might even be a book to be had from them. So he set to work on an idea – 'Tales of the Folio Club'. The link would be the Folio Club itself, a literary society that met to hear each of the tales and then comment on them, in the form of a satire on the criticism of the day. However, the club was 'a mere Junto of *Dunderheadism*' and the members are 'quite as ill-looking as they are stupid'. Poe described the members as Mr Snap, the President, who was 'a very lank man with a hawk nose, and was formerly in the service of the *Down-East Review*'; Mr Convolvulus Gondola, a young gentleman who had 'travelled a good deal'; De Rerum Natura, Esqr, who 'wore a very singular pair of green spectacles', a 'very little man in a black coat with very black eyes'; Mr Solomon Seadrift, who had 'every appearance of a fish'; and Mr Horribile Dictu, with 'white eyelashes, who had graduated at Gottingen'. Then there was Mr Blackwood Blackwood, 'who had written certain articles for foreign Magazines'; the host, Mr Rouge-et-Noir, who 'admired Lady Morgan'; a 'stout gentleman who admired Sir Walter Scott'; and finally Chronologos Chronology, who 'admired Horace Smith, and had a very big nose which had been in Asia Minor'.

Poe then set about the task of writing the tales, and by the time he had finished he had eleven. Many of these were minor pieces, often with a witty turn or even, like 'A Tale of Jerusalem', a running joke. Yet there is a power and an atmosphere that were scarcely equalled in other tales of his day. Other stories with a comic narrative were 'Lionizing', 'Bon-Bon', 'A Decided Loss' and 'The Duc De L'Omelette', in which the Duke gambles with his soul by gaming with the Devil – perhaps a theme close to Poe's heart. 'Epimanes' was a satirical piece on monarchy, whereas 'The Visionary' and 'Metzengerstein' both have a Gothic feel that sets the scene for many of his best-loved tales of terror. These early efforts owe a lot to the style of German

Romantic writer Ernst Theodor Wilhelm Hoffman. He probably also wrote two atmospheric prose poems for the club, too; 'Silence' and 'Shadow'.[2]

The final tale was in a different league. 'MS. Found in a Bottle' is probably the best of his efforts, and Poe's power of description is at its most vivid, particularly the ship in the storm. Of the crew, only two have survived the battering of a tempest, and the sea is a seething mass of mountainous waves, rising to a titanic height above abysses of water beneath.

> We were at the bottom of one of these abysses, when a quick scream from my companion broke fearfully upon the night. 'See! see!' – cried he, shrieking in my ears, – 'Almighty God! see! see!' As he spoke, I became aware of a dull, sullen glare of red light which streamed down the sides of the vast chasm where we lay, and threw a fitful brilliancy upon our deck. Casting my eyes upwards, I beheld a spectacle which froze the current of my blood. At a terrific height directly above us, and upon the very verge of the precipitous descent, hovered a gigantic ship of nearly four thousand tons. Although upreared upon the summit of a wave of more than a hundred times her own altitude, her apparent size still exceeded that of any ship of the line or East Indiaman in existence.

The gigantic ship falls; and the narrator is transferred to the deck of the strange vessel, which is crewed by decrepit, sightless and ancient sailors, who seem not to see him. At last the ship makes its way to uncharted southern seas, where it finds itself in the grip of an irresistible current, drawing it at breakneck speed towards the South Pole . . .

Tragedy now struck the family in Mechanics Row. The disease that had racked Poe's older brother now broke him, and he died on 1 August. Knowing Poe's sensitive nature, the loss must have affected him badly. There was also the matter of the cost of the funeral, and it appears that he put up a note of credit to pay for it, amounting to $80. Afterwards his spirits must have reached a new low, and still there were no prospects of work. He kept writing but also thought deeply about his own life. His need for a father – for a family – was never greater, so he wrote a letter to Allan trying to find common ground for a reconciliation.

> It is a long time since I have written to you unless with an application for money or assistance. I am sorry that it is so seldom that I hear from you or even of you, for all communication seems to be at an end; and when I think of the long twenty-one years that I have called you father, and you have called me son, I could cry like a child to think that it should all end in this. You know me too well to think me interested – if so: why have I rejected your thousand offers of love and kindness? It is true that when I have been in great extremity, I have always applied to you, for I had no other friend, but it is only at such a time as the present when I can write to you with the consciousness of making no application for assistance, that I dare to open my heart, or speak one word of old affection. When I look back upon the past and think of every thing – of how much you tried to do for me – of your forbearance and your generosity, in spite of the most flagrant ingratitude on my part, I can not help thinking myself the greatest fool in existence. I am ready to curse the day when I was born.
>
> But I am fully, truly conscious that all these better feelings have come *too* late. I am not the damned villain even to ask you to restore me to the twentieth part of those affections which I have so deservedly lost, and I am resigned to whatever fate is allotted me.
>
> I write merely because I am by myself and have been thinking over old times, and my only friends, until my heart is full. At such a time the conversation of new acquaintance is like ice, and I prefer writing to you although I know that you care nothing about me, and perhaps will not even read my letter.
>
> I have nothing more to say – and *this time*, no favour to ask. Although I am wretchedly poor, I have managed to get clear of the difficulty I spoke of in my last, and am *out of debt*, at any rate.
>
> May God bless you – E.A.P.
>
> Will you not write one word to me?

It would have taken a heart of marble not to be affected by this letter. Allan did perhaps write back and may have even sent a little money – so much is hinted at in Poe's next letter. But if Allan was beginning to weaken, it was Poe's fate always to be shoulder to shoulder with adversity. He was called to account for an old debt – at least Poe stated that the debt was incurred two years previously, and was as much a debt for Henry Poe as it was for himself. It has been suggested that this was untrue, that Poe was manufacturing an excuse to justify asking for money once again, but he may have been referring to the note of credit with which he paid for his brother's funeral. Whatever the reason, creditors were hunting him down, and, should he be arrested, he was in danger of imprisonment. He had asked around other members of the family, to no avail, so he sent the following letter to Allan on 18 November:

> My Dear Pa,
> I am in the greatest distress and have no other friend on earth to apply to except yourself – if you refuse to help me I know not what I shall do. I was arrested eleven days ago for a debt which I never expected to have to pay, and which was incurred as much on Henry's account as on my own about two years ago.
>
> I would rather have done any thing on earth than apply to you again after your late kindness, but indeed I have no other resource, and I am in bad health, and unable to undergo as much hardships as formerly or I never would have asked you to give me another cent.
>
> If you will only send me this one time $80, by Wednesday next, I will never forget your kindness & generosity. If you refuse God only knows what I shall do, & all my hopes & prospects are ruined for ever.
>
> I have made every exertion but in vain.

He was not gaoled, but he might have been – the local prison was heaving with debtors. He was now in awful straits and needed work badly, but there was nothing available for him. He gathered together five of his Folio Club tales, 'Metzengerstein', 'The Duc De L'Omelette', 'A Tale of Jerusalem', 'A Decided Loss' and 'The Bargain Lost' (the last was the original title of 'Bon-Bon') and sent them off to the *Courier*.

On 30 November his cousin Neilson Poe married Virginia's half-sister, Josephine Clemm. The wedding must have been a welcome change to Poe from all his worries and financial difficulties. He had now been a member of the Clemm family for seven months and was calling Maria 'Muddy' (an affectionate term for 'mother') and little Virginia 'Sissy'. He, in turn, was known as 'Buddie'. Almost neurotic in his need for a family, he took them as his own. He was never an ungenerous man, and his feelings of love and thankfulness towards his Muddy and her family were never to leave him.

After the wedding his creditors started to press Poe even harder. Once again the only man in the world who could help him was John Allan.

Baltimore. Dec. 15th, 1831.
Dear Pa,
I am sure you could not refuse to assist me if you were well aware of the distress I am in. How often have you relieved the distresses of a perfect stranger in circumstances less urgent than mine, and yet when I beg and intreat you in the name of God to send me succor you will still refuse to aid me. I know that I have offended you past all forgiveness, and I know that I have no longer any hopes of being again received into your favour, but, for the sake of Christ, do not let me perish for a sum of money which you would never miss, and which would relieve me from the greatest earthly misery – especially as I promise by all that is sacred that I will never under any circumstances apply to you again. Oh! if you knew at this moment how wretched I am you would never forgive yourself for having refused me. You are enjoying yourself in all the blessings that wealth & happiness can bestow, and I am suffering every extremity of want and misery without even a chance of escape, or a friend to whom I can look up to for assistance.

Think for one moment, and if your nature and former heart are not altogether changed you will no longer refuse me your assistance if not for my sake for the sake of humanity.

I know you have never turned a beggar from your door, and I apply to you in that light, I beg you for a little aid, and for the sake of all that was formerly dear to you I trust that you will relieve me.

If you wish me to humble myself before you I am humble. Sickness and misfortune have left me not a shadow of pride. I own that I am miserable and unworthy of your notice, but do not leave me to perish without leaving me still one resource. I feel at the very bottom of my heart that if you were in my situation and you in mine, how differently I would act.

As Poe waited for the officers to arrive to escort him to prison, on 31 December he received more crushing news. The judges of the *Philadelphia Saturday Courier* had decided on the best tale for their competition, and they had chosen someone else's work – 'Love's Martyr' by Delia S. Bacon.[3] Poe must have wondered how this sentimental story could have been chosen above his literary, imaginative tales. Even more galling was the fact that the newspaper went on to publish all his stories during the next twelve months, and it is unlikely that he saw a cent for any of them.

In the end he was not sent to gaol. Allan was not unmovable, nor was his heart made of marble, and despite his present wife's dislike of Poe he decided to help him once more. He wrote on Poe's letter of 15 December: 'Wrote on 7th December 1831 to John Walsh to procure his liberation & to give him $20 besides to keep him out of further difficulties and value on me for such amount as might be required – neglected sending it on till the 12 January 1832. Then put in the office myself.' The suggestion is that the aid was begrudgingly given and that Allan was by no means keen on once more interesting himself in his prodigal foster-son. To be informed of yet more debts must have irritated Allan in the extreme, and only the dire punishment Poe was facing – a debtors' prison – may have forced his hand. Perhaps the delay in sending the letter was a way of punishing him, too.

His brush with possible imprisonment must have shocked Poe and probably spurred him on to work harder so that the situation could never be repeated. He wrote more tales for his Folio Club, bringing the final tally to seventeen.

The Clemm household now moved to 3 Amity Street in the west end of town; Maria Clemm, her daughter Virginia, her mother Elizabeth Poe and her nephew Edgar. The accommodation was cheaper and comprised two upstairs bedrooms and a living-room and dining-room/kitchen downstairs. The conditions must have been fairly cramped.

There now comes a period in Poe's life which is a happy hunting-ground for romancers and gossip-mongers alike.[4] A favourite story, with no real basis in fact, suggests an amour between Poe and one Mary Devereux in 1831–2; the evidence is flimsy in the extreme.[5] Only one thing is sure: – this was a time of awful privations. There is no evidence of any real source of income, and it is difficult to understand how the rent was paid, since the only trickle of money came from Mrs Poe's pension. Tales of Poe travelling to foreign climes belong in the realms of imagination.

His whereabouts for most of 1832 are fixed by the testimony of an old friend of his, Lambert A. Wilmer, who was in town between the beginning of the year and October. He met Poe often and walked with him on many occasions. Always fastidious about his appearance, Poe kept his old clothes as tidy as he could and always tried to cut an elegant figure, but this was getting harder and harder as time went by. Interestingly, Wilmer also mentioned Poe's total sobriety, as well as his deep affection for the Clemms. He spoke of Poe's industry, too, writing: 'I called to see him at all hours, and always found him employed.' Wilmer's friendship was obviously important for Poe. Wilmer told of the great variety of conversations they had and commented that 'the female creations of his fancy are all either statues or angels'. He also ridiculed any charge of libertinism.

Wilmer had an interest in the *Baltimore Saturday Visitor*, and he persuaded Poe to send some of his tales there. It is doubtful whether he was paid much for them, but at least a complimentary editorial ensued (probably written by Wilmer himself).

Otherwise there seemed to be no relief for Poe's miseries, and he was caught in a downhill spiral of poverty and despair. Even the necessities of life were hard to come by. By April 1833 he was desperate enough to write to Allan once again.

> It has now been more than two years since you have assisted me, and more than three since you have spoken to me. I feel little hope that you will pay any regard to this letter, but still I cannot refrain from making one more attempt to interest you in my behalf. If you will only consider in what a situation I am placed you will surely pity me – without friends, without any means, consequently of obtaining employment, I am perishing, absolutely perishing for want of aid. And yet I am not idle, nor addicted to any vice – nor have I committed any offence against society which would render me deserving of so hard a fate. For God's sake pity me, and save me from destruction.

However, Allan had had enough, and never again contacted Edgar. On the same day that he received this letter, he looked through others Poe had sent and wrote the following on one posted on 21 February from New York:

> It is now upwards of 2 years since I received the above precious relict of the Blackest Heart & deepest ingratitude alike destitute of honour & principle every day of his life has only served to confirm his debased nature – Suffice it to say my only regret is in Pity for his failings – his Talents are of an order that can never prove a comfort for their possessor.

At this crucial point in Poe's life his one driving need was to get something published and to make some sort of a career. He sent his tale 'Epimanes' to Joseph T. and Edwin Buckingham of the *New England*

Magazine, along with a covering letter in which he tried to interest the publishers in all eleven tales, which he had now named 'Tales of the Arabesque'. His ended with a postscript: 'I am poor.'

They showed no interest, so Poe worked on in what must have been a state close to penury, until he discovered that his foster-father was severely ill. According to one story he made his way to Richmond and was confronted by Allan's wife. Poe pushed his way past her to Allan's bed but was ordered to go. A similar tale has been told about an attempted visit after Mrs Allan had given birth to Allan's first heir, during which, it was said, he was again ejected. These stories were later much embroidered and used to delight his enemies. The visit to Allan's death-bed is more plausible than the other, judging by the true affection Poe had for him, but the testimony is suspect, based as it is on second-hand evidence.[6]

On 14 February Allan died and was buried in Shockoe Hill Cemetery. He provided for his illegitimate children, as seen in an odd addendum to the will proper.

> This memo, in my own handwriting is to be taken as a codicil and can be easily proven by any of my friends.
>
> The twins were born sometime about the 1st of July, 1830. I was married the 5th October in New York, my fault therefore happened before I ever saw my present wife and I did not hide it from her. In case therefore these twins should reach the age of twenty-one years and from reasons they cannot get their share of the fifth reserved for them, they are to have $4000 each out of my whole estate to enable them to prosecute some honest pursuit, profession or calling.
>
> March 15th 1833. I understand one of Mrs Willis' twin sons died some weeks ago, there is therefore one only to provide for.

Poe was left nothing. So ended one of the most important, if unsatisfactory, relationships in his life. Even after this, he would retain some measure of nostalgia for the guardian of his youth and would even show interest in Allan's genealogy.

For almost the whole of 1834 there is no data. Perhaps he wrote anonymous articles for journals, but scholars have failed to discover any. The whole family survived on one small pension, plus whatever the resourceful Maria could cajole, borrow or earn. The long year wore on, and Poe became dishevelled in appearance. His clothes were worn and grubby. It must have been a depressing time indeed. Occasionally there would be competitions, and Poe eagerly awaited them in the hope that he could earn at least enough to keep the creditors at bay. One such competition was advertised by the *Baltimore Saturday Visitor*, offering a prize of $50 for the best tale as well as $25 for the best poem. Poe sent in six of his Folio Club tales and several poems.

The announcement of the winning entries was published in the 12 October edition of the paper, and it was probably a pessimistic Poe who opened its pages to learn the decision. He read: 'It will be seen by the following letter that the Committee have decided on the merits of the various productions sent for the premiums offered by us. The "Manuscript Found in a Bottle" is the production of Edgar A. Poe, of Baltimore.' One can imagine the joy Poe felt. Not only had he earned a little money to help with the bills but he had at last been recognized for his story-writing talents. He had, in fact, also won the poetry prize for 'The Coliseum', but the panel felt that it would be unfair to award prizes to just one author, so that premium was given to Henry Wilton's 'The Song of the Winds'. Henry Wilton was in fact the pseudnym of John Hewitt, editor of the *Visitor*!

The judges had been John H.B. Latrobe, J.H. Miller and John P. Kennedy. Encouragingly, they wrote of all the stories: 'These tales are eminently distinguished by a wild, vigorous and poetical imagination, a rich style, a fertile imagination, and varied and curious learning.' For Poe the most important judge was Kennedy, a prominent lawyer who had recently published his first novel, *Swallow Barn*. Kennedy was a kindly man, generous of heart and compassionate, as well as having a fervent love of American literature. He would have taken his job of judging the entries very seriously indeed.

Poe needed very little prompting by the judges to publish his work. Armed with such warm praise, and at Kennedy's suggestion, he sent the package off to Carey & Lea. However, he had had refusals from that firm before, so he made an attempt to enlist Kennedy in his efforts.

> I am thrown entirely upon my own resources with no profession, and very few friends. Worse than all this, I am at length penniless. Indeed no circumstances less urgent would have induced me to risk your friendship by troubling you with my distresses. But I could not help thinking that if my situation was stated – as you could state it – to Carey & Lea, they might be led to aid me with a small sum in consideration of my MS. now in their hands. This would relieve my immediate wants, and

> I could then look forward more confidently to better days. At all events receive assurance of my gratitude for what you have already done.

Kennedy had been busy, having made a trip to Annapolis, but as soon as he returned he set to work on Poe's behalf, asking Carey to do something for Poe as soon as possible and to give him an advance on the work. It seems that Carey had agreed to publish but suggested that very little of profit would be made from a collection of detached stories. He did suggest that the tales be sold to the magazines and that more would be made from them in that way. Carey had gone on to sell one of them to the *Souvenir* – the same periodical to which the firm had suggested Poe send his poems – on the condition that Poe would retain the right to publish the tale in a collected edition. The end result was that Kennedy had got hold of $15 for Poe, with the possibility of much more to come from further sales.

Poe must have been very encouraged by these prospects, and the cash would have seemed like a small windfall – even if it were swallowed up by debts. He still wanted the security of a steady income, and looking through the papers that day he saw an advertisement for a public school teacher. He thought that, with Kennedy's assistance, he might succeed, so on 15 March he wrote to him again. The letter interested Kennedy, and, considering the complex matter of Poe's literary opportunities, he felt it would be more becoming to meet him face to face and see what could be done for him. The best plan was to invite Poe to dinner, which he did. Poe had to suffer the humiliation of explaining why he could not attend, and, as he was in great need, also to beg for cash.

> Your kind invitation to dinner to day has wounded me to the quick. I cannot come – and for reasons of the most humiliating nature – my personal appearance. You may conceive my deep mortification in making this disclosure to you – but it was necessary. If you will be my friend so far as to loan me $20 I will call on you tomorrow – otherwise it will be impossible, and I must submit to my fate.

This letter jolted Kennedy. Only now did he begin to realize Poe's plight. He lost no time, hurrying to visit Poe in person. The scene that he encountered horrified him. The house was small, cramped and quite bare. The whole family were obviously in great need. Poe himself was in a shabby state and looked uncared for and beaten down.

Although he was obviously a proud man, poverty had taken its toll. 'I found him friendless and almost starving,' Kennedy recalled. It was a sight that filled him with pity, and he determined at once to do something about it.

The first concern was that Poe should recover his health, both physical and mental. He needed food and nutrition, as well as exercise. Kennedy made every effort to help him; he later recalled that he 'gave him free access to my table, and the use of a horse for exercise whenever he chose; in fact, brought him up from the verge of despair'. They became firm friends, and chatted about literature, including the style of writing appropriate to the magazines of the day. Gradually Poe built up his strength and confidence, but it was useless to build a man up just to watch him fall back again. He needed employment.

Kennedy was well aware of Poe's talents and potential and determined to use them to find work. He was a successful man and had many contacts; one who sprang to mind was Thomas Willis White. White was a genial man, well built with a roundish face and dark curly hair. He was a printer by trade and had long cherished the thought of running his own magazine; the previous year, in August, he founded the *Southern Literary Messenger*. He had first employed James E. Heath as editor, then Edward V. Sparhawk, but so far circulation was quite low. Kennedy reasoned that if a man of Poe's talents could contribute to the magazine sales figures would probably rise and Poe himself would find employment. So Kennedy wrote to White, praising Poe's talents and suggesting that he might find such a man very useful.

Poe dutifully sent off a selection of his stories, including 'Berenicë' (the diaeresis indicates that the final letter is pronounced). In this tale Poe's style begins to take shape. The heroine is on the point of death, and the narrator is distressed by her coming dissolution. Poe now employs a device he would use again, for example in 'The Tell-Tale Heart'; that of a monomania or *idée fixe*. In this case the obsession is with Berenicë's teeth. After her death she is interred, and (in a paragraph that is usually deleted on account of its horrific content) the narrator recovers the corpse and sees her lips pulled back to reveal the teeth. In a double-shock effect, we find the body has been prematurely interred. The narrator loses his reason; then awakens to find thirty-two teeth scattered over the floor.

White grumbled about some of the content of the story –

particularly the scene that was cut – but was willing to publish it.[7] He also published 'Morella', a kind of prototype of his later masterpiece 'Ligeia'.[8]

By the end of April 1835 Poe was in regular correspondence with White and suggested that he send a tale every month. He also expressed his opinions about the short story and originality in particular:

> To be sure originality is an essential in these things – great attention must be paid to style, and much labour spent in their composition, or they will degenerate into the turgid or the absurd. If I am not mistaken you will find Mr Kennedy, whose writings you admire, and whose Swallow-Barn is unrivalled for purity of style and thought of my opinion in this matter.

Such reflections, along with Poe's obvious writing expertise, must have favourably impressed White. Certainly he seemed to know an awful lot about magazines and literature. Perhaps there could be a place for him in the journal other than as a contributor.

5

⁘ THE LITERARY LIFE OF THINGUM BOB, ESQ. ⁘

Edgar Allan Poe now climbed his first steps on the journalistic ladder, writing stories for the *Southern Literary Messenger*, undertaking reviews and so forth. To begin with, the May edition contained his piece entitled 'Lionizing', a lightweight satirical tale narrated by one Thomas Smith 'from the city of Fum-Fudge'.[1] At last, a little money was coming into the household.

The long period of want had taken its toll. Poe became sickly and often suffered from illness; he also experienced bouts of depression that left him tired and unable to work. How far from the fit schoolboy who could swim against the local river tide, who boxed and who took part in athletics! That seemed worlds away now. But at least he had reason to be optimistic.

He had persuaded White that his stories would appeal to the mass market and that this would be reflected in magazine sales. Now he had to prove it. With typical bad luck, he was ill at the outset of these efforts, and his pieces were not his best. He was at a crossroads at which he was turning to criticism and journalism, and instead of displaying his talents for the world to see he was running at half-power. Such a poor start, just at the moment when he needed to be on top form, must have mortified him, and he admitted as much to the editor.

John P. Kennedy had completed his new novel, *Horse-Shoe Robinson*, which was to elevate his name among other American authors of his time. Poe's review of the work ends:

> A high tone of morality, healthy and masculine, breathes throughout the book, and a rigid – perhaps a too scrupulously rigid – poetical justice is dealt out to the great and little villains of the story – the Tyrrells, the

> Wat Adairs, the Currys, and the Habershams of the drama. In conclusion, we prophecy that *Horse-Shoe Robinson* will be eagerly read by all classes of people, and cannot fail to place Mr Kennedy in a high rank among the writers of this or of any other country. We regret that the late period of receiving his book will not allow us to take that extended notice of it which we could desire.[2]

This was one of Poe's first efforts as a critic, and he wanted to get it right. It was an opportunity for him to do what he longed to do – to give a forthright opinion on the pros and cons of American writing of the period and to take a swipe at the band of literary cliques that had a stranglehold on the country's literature. Poe would be the surgeon to cut away the stagnant flesh and pave the way for original talent. He took to the task with relish.

The first book to feel the swing of Poe's scythe was *Confessions of a Poet* by Laughton Osborne.[3] He gave it a rough time, so much so that a correspondent, 'I' in the *Compiler,* felt compelled to come to Osborne's defence, saying that Poe had obviously never even read the book. Already Poe was getting noticed, and so was the *Southern Literary Messenger*, which must have pleased White.

White wanted a notice of his journal to appear in the *Republican*, and Poe did as requested, albeit he was allotted only a small space. He now questioned White's preference for this particular magazine and argued that it did not command a great deal of respect among the readers he should be trying to entice. Poe went on to suggest a more suitable periodical. 'I have often wondered at your preferring to insert such notices in the *Republican*. It is a paper by no means in the hands of the first people here. Would not the *American* suit as well? Its columns are equally at your service.' White had wanted to know whether Poe was satisfied with the amount he was being paid, and Poe replied: 'You ask me if I am perfectly satisfied with your course. I reply that I am – entirely. My poor services are not worth what you give me for them.'

Within two weeks he had recovered from sickness and was ready to work. He now contributed his tale 'The Adventure of One Hans Phaal' (later to be spelled 'Pfaal'), a parody on current tales of travel to the moon.[4] It combined Poe's love of science with his ability to write good fiction. White could see the value of the story at once, and it appeared in the June number of his magazine. Some readers thought it was a hoax, but it could easily be seen that it was a burlesque and a good one, too. The tale proved to be a huge success, and White must have been considering what to do with his new protégé. Already, sales of his magazine were rising significantly.

Wisely, White began to give Poe other tasks to do for the magazine, and Poe, although still poor, refused payment for them – probably as a means of ingratiating himself with White. This was a game he had to play very carefully, otherwise he might throw everything away. He must not appear too greedy, and he must be industrious. He realized that he was carving himself an important role in the efficient running of the periodical.

By now the advantages of employing Poe full time were obvious. White was able to ask the young newcomer for advice about all things literary and was requesting reviews. Yet, because Poe was green and untried, he was unwilling to make any snap decisions; instead, he suggested a temporary arrangement, say for the winter period, if White should find a need for his services. This was the break that Poe had been waiting for. White had only one criticism to make of Poe – the slapdash appearance and punctuation of his manuscripts, a problem also encountered in many of his letters.

White had decided that, as the third number of his journal had been so good and, as his circulation was growing (thanks in great measure to Poe), it might be an idea to reissue it and advertise the fact in other periodicals. Poe thought this a bad idea and gave very sound reasons why. The public would be much more interested in the present content, he argued, and, besides, the reissue would look suspicious, as if White were shaking them down for more money.

At last Poe had an outlet for his creativity, but now his family suffered another blow. For some time they had relied on Mrs Poe's pension, and on 7 July 1835 the old lady died. The family was now reduced to Maria, Virginia and Poe. The latter was at last making a few dollars from his writing, but money was still tight, so he determined to work hard and be an indispensable member of the *Messenger* team.

White could not help but notice the local interest Poe was starting to excite, and there had been many friendly notices of his Hans Phaal tale (together with some criticism). In fact, White had been sick and had been relying on Poe to perform several jobs – even procuring ink for the printing. As his fame grew, Poe decided it was time to consider the work he had produced to date. It occurred to him that now would be a good time to publish his long-cherished 'Tales of the Folio Club', and he began to overhaul and revise them. He sought out the letter that the judges had written about the stories that were sent to the *Baltimore Visitor*. What better way to capture the public's attention than by publishing that letter? The masses' appetite thus whetted, his book could not fail to achieve some measure of success. So Poe wrote to White, asking him this favour.

> Herewith I send you a *Baltimore Visitor* of October 12th 1833. It contains a highly complimentary letter from Mr Kennedy, Mr Latrobe, and Dr Miller of Baltimore in relation to myself. The Tales of the Folio Club have only been partially published as yet. *Lionizing* was one of them. If you could in any manner contrive to have this letter copied into any of the Richmond Papers it would greatly advance a particular object which I have in view. If you could find an excuse for printing it in the *Messenger* it would be still better.

It is important now to consider the small family group and Poe's relationship to the two ladies. His relationship with Maria was straightforward enough; she was his mother figure. We also know that Virginia was Poe's constant companion, his 'Sissy'. During the hungry years he had clung to them both, and they had clung to him – Virginia especially, since from an early age she had looked upon Poe with an admiration bordering on adoration. Thrown together and suffering together, they found mutual comfort in each other; but recently Virginia had shown signs that she was leaving girlhood behind and was developing fast. The brotherly love and affection Poe had had for her was changing, and, although not quite thirteen, she began to arouse his adult desires. Pretty, plump and loving, she had expressed her devotion to him, just as a little girl would respect any talented relative. Now Virginia began to realize that Poe's feelings were also deepening. In short, he fell in love with his young cousin, and she reciprocated his feelings. Inside his little shelter, the cave in which he had huddled against the buffeting of the harsh world, he felt a companionship which was stronger than any other emotion he had experienced. Whatever others might say against them, the pair found a strength together which they felt would shield them against the world. As Virginia approached the legal age at which she could marry – thirteen – Poe proposed, and she accepted. But there was one person who may have harboured secret doubts: her mother Maria.

Although Maria was devoted to her nephew, she was the practical one of the family. She would have realized that her daughter had only just reached puberty and wondered whether the crush that her little girl had on Poe would be enough to support a loving marriage. What is more, as usual, she worried about money. Although Poe had been offered a temporary job on a magazine, he was earning very little, and the family had still not escaped poverty. Maria might well have had forebodings when she learned that her child was being wooed by her poor relation. On the other hand, her loyalty to her small family was uppermost, and she would not have wanted to estrange herself from the only two people she loved. It seems she gave a guarded consent.

Happier and more optimistic than he had been for some time, Poe packed his bags just before Virginia's thirteenth birthday and made his way to Richmond, where White had his offices. The old sights may have depressed his spirits – the old house where his guardian John Allan had lived and died; the friends of Mrs Allan who had maligned him when he was first cast adrift, those 'enemies' he had written about to Allan. Perhaps he visited Allan's grave on Shockoe Hill. He would have recalled 'the sad experience' of his school days. Almost certainly he would have visited the McKenzies and seen his sister Rosalie, now twenty-three but with a mind that had not yet conquered adolescence.

First of all, Poe had to find lodgings. After some searching he found a modest little house on Banks Street, run by a Mrs Poore. Living with the landlady in the house were her daughter and son-in-law Thomas Cleland.

Poe settled down with Thomas White to work for his journal, an amazing feat considering his total lack of experience. In the *Messenger* he published many of his Folio tales, as well as some biting criticism. For the first weeks all seemed well, and, as was usual when Poe was immersed in something, he was industrious. He even approached White and asked if he would be willing to print his tales in a single volume, and White seems to have given some sort of consent.

But now Neilson Poe made a very unwelcome appearance in Edgar Allan Poe's life. Neilson was the grandson of General Poe's brother George, and he himself had married his first cousin, Josephine Clemm. Maria had told Neilson of Poe's engagement to Virginia, and he did not approve on the grounds of Virginia's age; she was far too young and had not yet grown up in the world. Perhaps Maria had chimed in her agreement, and maybe she had even wheedled an offer from him. Neilson told Maria that he was willing to take Virginia under his wing – she could come and stay with his family and complete her education there. Moreover, he would provide for her upkeep and her future career at his own cost. Perhaps, when she was older, and if she was still of the same mind, a marriage with her cousin might be deemed suitable . . .

Maria wrote to Poe of Neilson's offer and explained that it would be good for Virginia. After all, she would acquire 'accomplishments' and could enter into society, something she had been unable to do. Such an offer was hard to resist, and in Maria's mind it would ensure Virginia's long-term happiness. After all, if Poe were truly in love, surely Virginia's happiness was of paramount importance? What did Poe advise? His reply was so passionate, desperate and heart-broken that he at last showed the full extent of his need.

> Aug. 19th
> My dearest Aunty,
> I am blinded with tears while writing this letter – I have no wish to live another hour amid sorrow, and the deepest anxiety your letter reached – and you well know how little I am able to bear up under the pressure of grief. My bitterest enemy would pity me could he now read my heart. My last my last my only hold on life is cruelly torn away. I have no desire to live and *will not*. But let my duty be done. I love, you know I love Virginia passionately devotedly. I cannot express in words the fervent devotion I feel towards my dear little cousin, my own darling. But what can I say? Oh think for me for I am incapable of thinking. All of my thoughts are occupied with the supposition that both you & she will prefer to go with Neilson Poe. I do sincerely believe that your *comforts* will for the present be secured – I cannot speak as regards your peace, your happiness. You have both tender hearts, and you will always have the reflection that my agony is more than I can bear – that you have driven me to the grave – for love like mine can never be gotten over. It is useless to disguise the truth that when Virginia goes with N.P. that I shall never behold her again – that is absolutely sure. Pity me, my dear Aunty, pity me. I have no one now to fly to. I am among strangers, and my wretchedness is more than I can bear. It is useless to expect advice from me – what can I say? Can I, in honour & in truth say, 'Virginia! do not go! Do not go where you can be comfortable & perhaps happy' – and on the other hand can I calmly resign my – life itself? If she had truly loved me would she not have rejected the offer with scorn? Oh God have mercy on me! If she goes with Neilson Poe what are you to do, my own Aunty?

> I had procured a sweet little house in a retired situation on Church Hill – newly done up and with a large garden and every convenience – at only $5 month. I have been dreaming every day & night since of the rapture I should feel in having my only friends – all I love on Earth – with me there, and the pride I would take in making you both comfortable & in calling her my wife. But the dream is over. Oh God have mercy on me. What have I to *live for*? Among strangers with *not one soul to love me . . .*
>
> The tone of your letter wounds me to the soul. Oh Aunty, aunty you loved me once – how can you be so cruel now? You speak of Virginia acquiring accomplishments, and entering into society – you speak in so *worldly* a tone. Are you sure she would be more happy. Do you think any one could love her more dearly than I? She will have far, very far better opportunities of entering into society here than with Neilson Poe. Every one here receives me with open arms.
>
> Adieu my dear aunty. I *cannot advise you*. Ask Virginia. Leave it to her. Let me have, under her own hand, a letter, bidding me *good bye* – forever – and I may die – my heart will break – but I will say no more. E. A. P.
>
> Kiss her for me – a million times.
>
> For Virginia, My love, my own sweetest Sissy, my darling little wifey, think well before you break the heart of your Cousin, Eddy.

The letter worked, and after some discussion Maria agreed to decline Neilson's offer and to permit Virginia to marry her nephew. That must have come as a great relief to Poe, and although he must have been overjoyed his mood had already swung downwards. From manic, he had reverted to depressive. There were many reasons. There was the recent death of his grandfather's widow, the last in a line of deaths he had witnessed, including his brother's. The pain of the last years, the ghosts of his past that haunted him – and the new burden that Neilson Poe had tried to wreck his marriage – broke his spirit. During hospitable meetings with acquaintances in Richmond he had been duty-bound to drink, and the drink went straight to his head.

But this time it was different. Instead of drinking out of politeness Poe began to drink for drink's sake. He drank long and he drank hard; unable to take it, he became irresponsible and unable to control his actions. It was the summit of a long tough slope to climb as he battled with an addiction that would visit him in times of deep sadness.

There, in the city in which he had been mocked as a child and from where stormed from his foster-father's house in rage and humiliation, he drank. He did not know how much.

On 9 September 1835 he wrote a dismal missive to John P. Kennedy, who, Poe had discovered, was in town. The letter is peculiar in its odd change of mood:

> Excuse me, my dear Sir, if in this letter you find much incoherency. My feelings at this moment are pitiable indeed. I am suffering under a depression of spirits such as I have never felt before. I have struggled in vain against the influence of this melancholy. You will believe me when I say that I am still miserable in spite of the great improvement in my circumstances. I say you will believe me, and for this simple reason, that a man who is writing for *effect* does not write *thus*. My heart is open before you – if it be worth reading, read it. I am wretched, and know not why. Console me – for you can. But let it be quickly, or it will be too late. Write me immediately. Convince me that it is worth one's while – that it is at all necessary to live, and you will prove yourself indeed my friend. Persuade me to do what is right. I do not mean this – I do not mean that you should consider what I now write you a jest – oh pity me! for I feel that my words are incoherent – but I will recover myself. You will not fail to see that I am suffering under a depression of spirits which will ruin me should it be long continued. Write me then, and quickly. Urge me to do what is right. Your words will have more weight with me than the words of others, for you were my friend when no one else was. Fail not, as you value your peace of mind hereafter.

Critics of Poe should scrutinize this letter before making a final decision on Poe's personality. The symptoms of unbearable sadness, his inability to rise from the gloom, his leanings towards suicide – which we have seen before – all point to a state of clinical depression. Even he was in no doubt that he had a mental condition. Last time he was in the deepest trough of melancholy – when he was starving – it had been Kennedy himself who had held out a hand and rescued him. Hearing that Kennedy was in Richmond revived those old memories and the notion that if anyone could help it would be him.

Poe was still drinking heavily and the outcome was obvious. He let his work slide and as a result frequently struggled to do his job. He wrote a number of letters, including one to his old friend John

Neal, asking him to send periodicals in exchange for the *Messenger*, a matter of common courtesy in those days. But as his work deteriorated White became more alarmed, and even more so when he discovered the cause – Poe was inebriated, even in the mornings. White was stunned and disappointed. He dismissed him from his service.

It took Kennedy a few days to meditate on the peculiar letter he had received from Poe, but he was a kindly man and not inclined to let Poe down if he could help it. The last time he had helped Poe he was in dire straits and needed work. Practical help had been easy to supply. But what on earth could Kennedy do now? He made the best attempt he could to help Poe defeat his melancholy, although his suggestions may not have been very useful. As for the practical part of the letter, well, he felt that White would be as good a publisher as Carey & Lea.

> I am sorry to see you in such plight as your letter shows you in. – It is strange that just at the time when every body is praising you and when Fortune has begun to smile upon your hitherto wretched circumstances you should be invaded by these villainous blue devils. – It belongs, however, to your age and temper to be thus buffeted, – but be assured it only wants a little resolution to master the adversary forever. – Rise early, live generously, and make cheerful acquaintances and I have no doubt you will send these misgivings of the heart all to the Devil. – You will doubtless do well henceforth in literature and add to your comforts as well as to your reputation which, it gives me great pleasure to tell you, is every where rising in popular esteem. Can't you write some farces after the manner of the French Vaudevilles? if you can – (and I think you can –) you may turn them to excellent account by selling them to the managers in New York . . .

The day of Poe's marriage arrived, but he must have been a worried man. He had just written to White, apologizing for his actions and asking for his job back. He made every promise he could that he would never err again. Whether or not he told his future bride and mother-in-law about his problems at work is doubtful; more than likely, he hoped that White would forgive him.

Thomas Cleland, son-in-law of Poe's landlady, acted as surety and gave him the marriage bond. On 22 September 1835 Edgar Allan Poe married his thirteen-year-old cousin Virginia in Old Christ Church,

Virginia, being described by Cleland as 'of the full age of twenty-one years'. Such an announcement meant that, although marrying a thirteen-year-old was not illegal, it may have been frowned upon. Still, the couple were undoubtedly happy. Having given up on the idea of a surrogate father, Poe made do with his surrogate mother, Maria Clemm or 'Muddy', and his child bride, Virginia or 'Sissy'. They honeymooned in Petersburg, Virginia.

Luckily for Poe, White was not an ungenerous man. He was willing to forgive and forget and to have him back – if he swore to give up the drink. So on his return from their honeymoon Poe was overjoyed to read the following:

> You have fine talents, Edgar, – and you ought to have them respected as well as yourself. Learn to respect yourself, and you will very soon find that you are respected. Separate yourself from the bottle, and bottle companions, for ever!
>
> Tell me if you can and will do so – and let me hear that it is your fixed purpose never to yield to temptation.
>
> If you should come to Richmond again, and again should be an assistant in my office, it must be expressly understood by us that all engagements on my part would be dissolved, the moment you get drunk.
>
> No man is safe who drinks before breakfast! No man can do so, and attend to business properly . . .

So everything was smoothed over and Poe went back to work. Settled back in the routine, he reverted to the hard-working, conscientious man he could be whenever he applied himself. He put his mind to his articles and kept away from the bottle.

Poe had promised Maria and Virginia a home, and now they began to look for a suitable place. To start with, they decided to move into a boarding-house, and so early in October the Poe family – Maria, Virginia and Edgar – were living in the establishment of one James Yarrington on Eleventh and Bank Streets.

Poe began to serialize *Politian*, his unfinished drama set in Ancient Rome. He based the play upon an actual occurrence, a real Kentucky tragedy. The bones of the tragedy were: one Solomon Sharp seduced Anne Cooke, who later married Jereboam Beauchamp – on condition that he avenge her. He eventually stabbed Sharp; the couple were accused of murder; Anne committed suicide and Beauchamp was executed.

Poe also continued to write reviews of works whenever they became available and learned how to hone his scalpel until it was sharp and cut very deep. He continued to work for the *Southern Literary Messenger* for over a year and in that time wrote many tales as well as incisive criticism. He became famed for this criticism, cutting, often biting but always with an eye to improving American literature. Northern writers such as those centred around the hub of New York got short shrift, much to the delight of his Southern readers. His controversial remarks increased the magazine's circulation, and if White felt he was losing control of the periodical at least his sales figures went up. An early example of his style can be seen from the review of *Confessions of a Poet*, mentioned earlier. Here is how Poe ended his review:

> The author avers upon his word of honour that in commencing this work he loads a pistol, and places it upon the table. He farther states that, upon coming to a conclusion, it is his intention to blow out what he supposes to be his brains. Now this is excellent. But, even with so rapid a writer as the poet must undoubtedly be, there would be some little difficulty in completing the book under thirty days or thereabouts. The best of powder is apt to sustain injury by lying so long 'in the load.' We sincerely hope the gentleman took the precaution to examine his priming before attempting the rash act. A flash in the pan – and in such a case – were a thing to be lamented. Indeed there would be no answering for the consequences. We might even have a second series of the *Confessions*.[4]

Little wonder that the author was not amused. And small wonder, too, that people have blamed Poe for excessive severity. Although he could be overindulgent to friends (particularly lady friends), he was not such a fool that he did not quickly learn how to sell magazines. His cutting, jocular critiques soon earned him a reputation and had the public paying for the magazine. Few people (except the author and target of the work under review) could fail to smile at Poe's witty and biting sarcasm. Of course, he did work towards improving American literature, and, of course, he did give many well-reasoned and admirable notices, but he was also – and had to be – a showman. Being an entertainer sold copy.

During his early formative years with the *Messenger* Poe proved his ability (and his waywardness), and he had more or less moved into the empty chair once occupied by Heath and Sparhawk, White's former editors. White must still have had moments of uneasiness, wondering whether Poe would again start drinking, but as he watched the sales figures rise month by month he must have been satisfied. Poe took every aspect of his job seriously, contributed tales and articles, delivered criticism and drummed up interest in contributors as well as answering correspondence.

Poe's critical writings are best understood in terms of contemporary history, and to understand American society in 1836 we need some appreciation of the political climate of the USA at the beginning of the century. After the Revolution the country had busied itself with implementing a Constitution and drawing together as a nation.[5] Although the Mason-Dixon Line effectively drew a partition between North and South, the cultural differences were of little moment compared to the great affairs of the day.[6] But afterwards, when the New World settled down to enjoy its autonomy, differences between the two halves of the country soon emerged, a divergence emphasized by the advent of the Industrial Revolution. Although the whole country benefited from economic development, the North developed faster than the South, taking advantage of continuously evolving technology, industry and, particularly, commerce. Big, bustling cities displayed a new prosperity, and people began to be drawn to them from the countryside. The South looked on mistrustfully, preferring the old ways, which changed little apart from an advance in working practices. Lives centred around the plantations and cotton, which was in greater demand with the advance of manufacturing depots. The philosophies of North and South diverged, each assured that their way was best.

The plantations were worked by slaves, who formed an integral part of these agricultural enterprises. The family relied on this workforce to manage their cotton crops. But as time went by, campaigns sprang up to abolish the practice. This fitted with a new ethos of social reform, not only concerning slavery but also the position of women and temperance. In 1831 the Abolitionists produced their own magazine, *The Liberator*, mouthpiece of the Anti-Slavery Society.[7] In 1835 the society promoted a huge campaign, distributing leaflets and propaganda throughout the country. These leaflets brought a violent reaction in the Southern states, and they were not altogether welcomed in the North either; members of the society were seen as dangerous cranks and frequently attacked in the streets. Such was the state of affairs in

1836. It was not for another year, with the murder of the abolitionist Lovejoy, before people in the North took the issue seriously and slavery became a central component in the brewing discord between the two halves of the country.[8] In 1836 the abolitionist movement was still spreading in the North, but whites in the South looked on it with disdain, seeing it as a crass expression of anti-Southern prejudice. Poe viewed himself as a Southern gentleman; he had been brought up in Richmond and sympathized with Southern ways. He had been involved in the sale of Edwin, one of Maria's slaves. He never wrote against abolitionism as such, but he did write in defence of the Southern way of life. For instance, he responded to Longfellow's *Poems on Slavery* as follows:

> No doubt, it is a very commendable and very comfortable thing, in the Professor, to sit at ease in his library chair, and write verses instructing the southerners how to give up their all with a good grace, and abusing them if they will not; but we have a singular curiosity to know how much of his own, under a change of circumstances, the Professor himself would be willing to surrender. Advice of this character looks well only in the mouth of those who have entitled themselves to give it, by setting an example of the self-sacrifice.[9]

Whenever Poe took up arms against the smug coterie of Northern authors, his Southern readers would have raised a cheer. However, to see his writings purely as a campaign against the North would be misleading. He was much braver than that. He was about to take on the most powerful men in contemporary American literature and almost single-handedly fight for his beliefs against overwhelming odds.

At this time there was scarcely any copyright protection, and no international copyright law. American publishers could simply steal writings from Britain without paying a cent, whether they were producing books or magazines. Some periodicals did attempt to copyright their material, but their attempts were hardly effective. As Poe later wrote, 'It has long been the custom among the newspapers – the weeklies especially – to copy magazine articles in full, and circulate them all over the country – sometimes in advance of the magazines themselves.'[10] Sometimes this state of affairs worked to the editor's advantage, especially if he wanted an opinion to be widely heard. But there was no incentive for American publishers to advance the interests of native writers, and even if they did decide to take on an

American writer, more often than not they would demand some sort of safety net. This usually took the form of an agreement to make good any losses, as we have already seen in Poe's case.

The writers were thus in a weak position, but their plight was made even worse by the cliques of publishers and writers that had taken over certain cities. Since the early days of the magazine some publishers had worked to develop a stranglehold over American literature and nowhere more malignantly than New York. This smug coterie was an ever-shifting group, but its core membership included some of the leading editors of the day, such as Theodore Sedgwick Fay, associate editor of the *New York Mirror*, and Colonel William L. Stone of the *New York Commercial Advertiser*; but the Godfather of this New York press Mafia was Lewis Gaylord Clark, editor of the *Knickerbocker* and arguably one of the most powerful and influential men in American literature. His influence also extended to other cities through his contacts, particularly his twin brother Willis, who edited the *Philadelphia Gazette*.

If a writer were received into the embrace of this clique his future was relatively secure, regardless of the quality of his writing. He would give notice to the editors of a planned book. They would write favourable notices in all the periodicals under their control – and there were many – before the volume was released; this activity was known as 'puffing'. With so much fulsome praise, the general public would be duped into buying the book. On the other hand, it was career suicide for a writer to turn against the group. Any attack would be met with by a torrent of critical abuse from newspapers and magazines. The inherent worth of a book was not a factor; books were sold on recommendation. Works of great merit might, if the author was disfavoured, be howled down from the bookseller's shelves.

Any attempt to criticize the cliques was dealt with ruthlessly. The Irish writer and critic James McHugh made a brave attempt to draw the public's attention to what was going on, and he was effectively destroyed by the Godfather's henchmen. As Willis Clark wrote to Colonel Stone: 'If you wish me to give a blow on the head of any one whom you despise or contemn . . . my arm and club are *yours*.'[11]

All of this was wormwood to a man of Poe's kidney, a man whose *raison d'être* was to raise the standard of American literature. He was well aware of what was going on, condemned it and at one point mentioned 'the impudent cliques which beset our literature'. More importantly, he decided to do something about it.

His first shot at this New York literary Mafia was fired at none other than Theodore Fay of the *New York Mirror* (co-edited by Nathaniel Willis). Fay had written a book entitled *Norman Leslie: A Tale of Modern Times*. Poe watched with increasing revulsion as he saw puff after puff appear in the journals affiliated to the New York coterie. At last the volume was published, and Poe eagerly scanned its pages: he found a novel of poor quality. In the December issue of the *Messenger* he indulged in a humorous but savage critique:

'Well! – here we have it!' he begins. 'This is *the* book – the book *par excellence* – the book bepuffed, beplastered, and be-*Mirrored* . . . for the sake of every thing puffed, puffing, and puffable, let us take a peep at its contents!' He gives a short synopsis, interspersed with withering scorn, which concludes: 'Thus ends the Tale of the Present Times, and thus ends the most inestimable piece of balderdash with which the common sense of the good people of America was ever so openly or so villainously insulted.' The plot, 'as will appear from the running out line we have given of it, is a monstrous piece of absurdity and incongruity . . . the hero, Norman Leslie . . . is a great coxcomb and a great fool.' Of the writing, 'as regards Mr Fay's *style*, it is unworthy of a school-boy. The "Editor of the *New York Mirror*" has either never seen an edition of Murray's Grammar, or he has been a-Willising so long as to have forgotten his vernacular language.' He comments sardonically on the number of times Fay uses the epithet 'blistering', applying it to 'details', 'truth', 'story' and 'brand'; and concludes: 'Here we have a blistering detail, a blistering truth, a blistering story, and a blistering brand, to say nothing of innumerable other blisters interspersed throughout the book. But we have done with *Norman Leslie* – if ever we saw as silly a thing, may we be blistered.'[12]

Readers, especially those from the South, loved the review, and the circulation of the journal increased. It is hardly surprising that it was becoming a popular periodical. Not only did readers enjoy Poe's stories and his writing skill, but they marvelled and laughed at his critical dexterity and wit. As they paid their money for the next issue, they must have been wondering what on earth he was going to say next.

However, he was starting to make enemies in the literary world, and his friends feared for him if he continued to alienate his contemporaries. But Poe saw his job as fighting for fairness as well as selling copy, and he disregarded all advice – after all, he did not judge his criticism as overly severe by the standards of the day. Besides, if he did go crazy with the scalpel it was usually because the work warranted it.

He had not finished with Fay yet. In February he reviewed Morris Mattson's *Paul Ulric* with some severity, summing it up as 'despicable in every respect. Such are the works which bring daily discredit upon our national literature. We have no right to complain of being laughed at abroad when so villainous a compound, as the thing we now hold in our hand, of incongruous folly, plagiarism, immorality, inanity, and bombast, can command at any moment both a puff and a publisher.'[13] This was an obvious swipe at Lewis Gaylord Clark and company. Poe also commented: 'When we called *Norman Leslie* the silliest book in the world we had certainly never seen *Paul Ulric*.'

While the baleful eyes of the Godfather and his clan were turning slowly upon Poe, he did have allies, mainly in the South but some even in New York. The *New Yorker* said of Poe: He 'examines with impartiality, judges with fairness, commends with evident pleasure, and condemns with moderation. May he live a thousand years!'

At this time Poe was experiencing domestic difficulties. He was not earning the best wages in the world, and times were still difficult for the small family. His ambition was to get a home of his own. Yarrington's was all very well, but it was not as if it were his home. It must have been galling for Poe to look at house prices and compare them with his income – $7 a week after he had paid their rent. It was hardly enough to live on, let alone think of buying a place of their own. So it seemed an impossible dream, and they had to resign themselves to living in rented accommodation for the time being.

Then Poe hit upon a plan, which he discussed with his family. What if they were to open a boarding-house of their own? Quick to learn by example, he had seen how easy it was to make money by taking in lodgers – why could Maria not do the same? It was a fashionable thing for widows of the time to do – a respectable business that also earned them a good living. After all, Maria was a good cook and was skilled in all the domestic sciences. She was more than happy to act as landlady, but where would they get the capital for such an enterprise? It would have to come from loans. It would be difficult to obtain money to build a home of their own but, surely, if he could prove that this was a profitable venture – if he had a good business plan – it should be relatively easy to drum up short-term loans. First of all he turned to his uncle, George Washington Poe, and wrote of his scheme, stressing the financial difficulties mother and daughter were in (and neglecting to mention his marriage to Virginia). George Poe did send the money, but no boarding-house was opened. Despite all his efforts, Edgar could not raise the finance he needed. So the family stayed where they were.

Around this time Poe began to suspect that White was losing confidence in him. It is hard to gauge the reason, although White may have expressed concern over the savagery of some of his criticism. It is probably too much to suggest that a touch of paranoia was developing, but this was not the first time he suspected that someone did not have his interests at heart; he had once written to Allan suggesting that their differences may have been exacerbated by comments of 'enemies at home'. Whether this is of significance or not, Poe was troubled enough to write to a friend, Judge Nathaniel Beverley Tucker, asking him to sort things out. This must have seemed like an odd request, especially as Poe and White worked together, but Tucker obligingly put the matter to the magazine owner. White was somewhat bemused and responded that there was nothing in such a suggestion; Poe was duly mollified and got on with his editorial duties.

The affable John Kennedy answered another of Poe's letters. Everyone was talking about Poe, and Kennedy was pleased that he had fulfilled his potential. 'I am greatly rejoiced at your success not only in Richmond, but every where.' He was also delighted that Poe had recovered from his bout of depression, and he had further words of advice for him.

> Your letter assures me that you have entirely conquered your late despondency. I am rejoiced at this. You have a pleasant and prosperous career before you, if you subdue this brooding and boding inclination of your mind. Be cheerful, rise early, work methodically – I mean, at appointed hours. Take regular recreation every day. Frequent the best company only. Be rigidly temperate both in body and mind.

Poe's reply ended with chit-chat about the magazine, blaming White for the non-appearance of the November issue, although that would have followed Poe's dismissal and on his return it may have taken time to sort out the running of the journal again. White's satisfaction with the increased circulation was reflected in the rise in Poe's wages of $2 per week.

Poe's 'Autography' series was published in the February 1836 edition of the *Messenger;* and it was so popular that it was revived in August.

The idea was simple enough. Poe collected sample notes and signatures from leading lights of the day, and then he analysed the handwriting to draw conclusions about the writer's character. He was very circumspect in this, making few cutting remarks – although there were exceptions, such his comment on Washington Irving: 'Mr Irving's hand writing is common-place. There is nothing indicative of genius about it.' Of course, he could not resist taking a swipe at Fay: 'The MS. however, has an air of *swagger* about it. There are too many dashes – and the tails of the long letters are too long. Mr Messenger thinks I am right – that Mr F. shouldn't try to cut a dash – and that *all* his tales are too long. The swagger he says is respectable, and indicates a superfluity of thought.'[14]

While working in the office, Poe was still searching for a publisher to print his works, and he approached James Kirke Paulding for help. Paulding was a successful writer whose work included *The Backwoodsman, Memoirs of an American Lady*, a life of George Washington and many satires; he was also working for the publisher Harper's, to whom Poe had sent his manuscript. Paulding's reply was friendly, and although he was pessimistic he did make one good suggestion – to write a novel in two volumes, which was the fashion at that time.

The official reply from Harper's came a little later, and it explained to Poe that his writings had been refused for three reasons: first, they had already appeared in print; second, a novel was preferable to detached tales; and, last, the tales were 'too learned and mystical' and would not be appreciated by any but a small percentage of the reading population. They did go on to say: 'We are pleased with your criticisms generally – although we do not always agree with you in particulars, we like the bold, decided, energetic tone of your animadversions, and shall take pleasure in forwarding to you all the works we publish – or at least such of them as are worthy of your notice.'

Word of Poe's disappointment soon reached the ears of the New York coterie, and the *New York Mirror* mocked his efforts, insinuating that his severe criticism was due to envy of those who could write. It was entitled 'The Successful Novel!!', featured Poe as 'Bulldog', and marked the beginning of the war between them.[15] Willis Clark followed suit with an article in the *Philadelphia Gazette* calling Poe 'quacky' and taunting him: 'Many a work has been slashingly condemned – of which the critic himself could not write a page, were he to die for it.'[16] Stone joined in, stating that Poe's method was to employ 'sneers, sarcasm and downright abuse'.[17] But Poe was too slippery and clever for them. He defended himself from all charges, using his recent critique (a harsh one) of the writers Drake and Halleck to support his claims. In this important review he considered the original idea that American letters were in some way inferior to those of abroad (particularly Britain); but now things had changed, and the American press were abusing their authority to indiscriminately puff their own literature, either good or bad:

> We are becoming boisterous and arrogant in the pride of a too speedily assumed literary freedom. We throw off, with the most presumptuous and unmeaning hauteur, all deference whatever to foreign opinion – we forget, in the puerile inflation of vanity, that the world is the true theatre of the biblical histrio – we get up a hue and cry about the necessity of encouraging native writers of merit – we blindly fancy that we can accomplish this by indiscriminate puffing of good, bad, and indifferent, without taking the trouble to consider that what we choose to denominate encouragement is thus, by its general application, rendered precisely the reverse. In a word, so far from being ashamed of the many disgraceful literary failures to which our own inordinate vanities and misapplied patriotism have lately given birth, and so far from deeply lamenting that these daily puerilities are of home manufacture, we adhere pertinaciously to our original blindly conceived idea, and thus often find ourselves involved in the gross paradox of liking a stupid book the better, because, sure enough, its stupidity is American.[18]

Meanwhile, still looking for help for his household, he had written to another cousin, William. This had resulted in a reply as well as $50 for Maria Clemm. This was a fair sum but not enough for comfort, so now Poe decided to make every last effort to raise capital. The boarding-house idea had been scotched but was not dead; there was still someone he could turn to, and that was his boss, Thomas White. The new idea was simple enough. White was to buy a house for $10,000. It was to be rented to Maria Clemm and the Poes, who would turn it into a boarding-house, and the White family would also lodge there. After due consideration, White seems to have agreed to the project; and so, at last, Poe started to look forward to a house for all the family – and another income. But the new house needed to be furnished and, to this end, Poe bought furniture to the tune of $200.

He did not rest there – he had soon found other ways of raising capital. Doubtless having read of similar claims in the press, Poe turned his mind to litigation. He was assured that William Clemm,

Maria's husband, was entitled to an inheritance from the Clemm family. He was convinced of the truth of this, and in fact there probably was a case, so he turned to his old friend Kennedy for help, who agreed to look into the matter. He also considered the claims of his grandmother, Elizabeth Poe. According to Poe, the US government owed General Poe a good deal of money – some $40,000 – and on the strength of that had given Mrs Poe a pension. It should be easy to prove the assertion, and Poe was convinced that a large sum of money would be the result of the settlement. On Kennedy's advice he eagerly wrote to a legal expert, James H. Causten.

Things seemed to be looking up. However, Kennedy eventually got an opinion from his legal adviser, and the news was not good: 'We had a long talk, the result of which was to show me that, the heirs of William Clemm have no claim to anything. There were debts, advances – and I know not what – that had utterly extinguished the claim of W. Clemm himself.' As for Poe's claim concerning Elizabeth Poe, the result was the same; no debt to General Poe was verified.

There were also developments with regard to the boarding-house project. The house was much smaller than had been anticipated; in fact, it was only large enough to hold a single family. So, again, the plan had to be cancelled. But now there were other problems, for Poe had incurred debt for the furniture and the creditors were looking for their money. He therefore suffered the mortification of having to ask Kennedy for help. Kennedy loaned him $100, but it had to be repaid in three months at over $8 per week – virtually all Poe had after the rent had been paid. His disappointment must have been great, and one can imagine the temptation to reach for solace from the bottle. But White's warning was still in his mind, and he worked diligently, never giving his boss occasion to reprimand him. It is hard to believe that a man who had achieved so much success in such a short time, and who should be congratulating himself on his abilities, should have been so unfortunate and so poor.

His skills were never in doubt, and he showed marvellous tact when dealing with contributors. For example, in January 1836 he had written a review of Lydia Huntley Sigourney's book *Zinzendorff and Other Poems*. She had been nicknamed 'The Sweet Singer of Hartford' and dubbed the American Hemans, in honour of the English poetess Felicia Hemans who had died the year before. However, Poe wrote that Sigourney had deserved the epithet simply because she had copied Hemans's style: 'Mrs S. cannot conceal from her own discernment that she has acquired this title *solely* by imitation.'[19] Imitation and plagiarism were the two worst insults that could be given to a writer of that time, and the lady wrote an angry letter to Poe, condemning him for his critique and wanting no more to do with the *Messenger*. However, Poe successfully calmed her with his charm, and even coaxed articles from her.

He wrote a well-regarded article in the April edition, exposing the workings of Maelzel's automaton chess-player, proving that it was operated by a hidden assistant.[20]

Now, after the customary puffing, a long-awaited volume arrived in Poe's hands: *Ups and Downs in the Life of a Distressed Gentleman* by none other than Colonel Stone. Again to Poe's disgust, the quality was poor, so he set about dismembering it in his notice, which begins 'This book is a public imposition' and ends 'It is written, we believe, by Col. Stone of the *New York Commercial Advertiser*, and should have been printed among the quack advertisements, in a spare corner of his paper.'[21] The rage of the New York set can easily be imagined.

Next Poe had an idea for promoting the *Messenger* even more strongly. Under his auspices the magazine's circulation had grown considerably, but he decided to push for a special edition that would include contributions from the leading authors of the time. It would be a one-off showcase for the best talent the USA had to offer. He wrote to potential contributors in two waves of letters, one lot sent out on 7 July and the rest on the 18th.

The replies soon came back; many were complimentary. James Kirke Paulding wrote of the journal:

> It is gradually growing in the public estimation, and under your conduct, and with your contributions, must soon, if it is not already, be known all over the land. You have given sufficient evidence on various occasions, not only of critical knowledge but of high independence; your praise is therefore of value, and your censure not to be slighted. Allow me to say that I think your article on Drake and Halleck one of the finest pieces of criticism ever published in this country.

Fitz-Greene Halleck, a big name among the literati of the time (and a writer Poe had criticized), wrote: 'There is no place where I shall be more desirous of seeing my humble writings than in the publication you so ably support and conduct.' Poe even managed to wrest a poem from Sigourney, as a 'peace offering'. He gathered together all the contributions he had gleaned and prepared the text for the press. It had been hard work, and the issue was indeed one of the best they had produced, but he was leaving nothing to chance. He approached friend and editor Hiram Haines for a puff in his publication, *The Constellation*.

While awaiting the reception of the August edition he made yet another attempt to get his 'Folio Club' tales published. It would have seemed to Poe that, with his new-found reputation in American letters, he should have no difficulty in getting a book printed. He was wrong. No matter how he tried, no one was interested in his idea for a book, not even on the condition that he receive only a few copies by way of payment.

When the August edition of the *Messenger* appeared, the reviews were almost unanimously positive, which must have been gratifying for Poe, considering the industry he had expended on it. One notice, however, caught his eye especially – it was contained in the *Richmond Courier and Daily Compiler*. It followed various malicious notices posted by the Northern clique. This review was not particularly bad until the final paragraph, in which Poe found the following offensive remark: 'the editors must remember that it is almost as injurious to obtain a character for regular cutting and slashing'. He wrote a furious rejoinder.

Most commentators have looked upon this as Poe being hypocritical, unable to accept criticism of his own work even though he did not stint when it came to censuring others. He has been made to appear irascible, childish and inflexible. But that is to misunderstand the man. In fact he could take criticism and often did. If people condemned his writing, he more often that not agreed with them and sometimes even exaggerated his faults. If someone from the coteries had written in a disparaging way, he would retaliate, but there was no animosity between himself and the *Richmond Courier and Daily Compiler*.

Leaving aside a certain amount of showmanship, Poe took the work of criticism seriously. Although his savage humour attracted readers, he used it in a two-fold way – to amuse his audience and, more importantly, to draw the fullest attention to a work's deficiencies. Although cutting, most of his reviews were balanced, pointing out the good as well as lambasting the bad. Nor were they flighty, off-the-cuff character assassinations; Poe felt a responsibility in his work and wanted to further the cause of American letters. Admittedly, he could be very disparaging about a work he despised, and yet in most of his negative reviews he was so persuasive as to carry his reader along with him. If something was derided by Poe, you could be sure it was risible.

Many in the literary world saw this and appreciated it. They often felt that when criticizing a work he could be too severe, but few of them denied that he was a good critic – even Harper's had written saying so. Another fault was that he was sometimes chivalrously kind to lady writers. But there is no doubt that he himself felt that he was doing a good job and that he was setting standards for writing. So to read a notice which described his work as 'regular cutting and slashing' – by a magazine which he had considered friendly to him – was the grossest of insults. In fact the paper quickly made conciliatory overtures.

Problem after problem was crowding in on Poe. He would have felt a failure, and this dragged him back into depression. The promises of an idyllic life that he made when he persuaded Maria and Virginia to throw in their lot with him must have seemed threadbare now; he could hardly make ends meet, and his attempts to provide a business for them had only resulted in more debt, which even now was pressing hard upon him. He had given his all to ensure a profitable, high-profile magazine, and his fame had done nothing to help him publish his own creative writing or even to live a comfortable life. And he could see nothing to promise future improvement. To top it all, he now read in a Southern newspaper that instead of being the conscientious critic he thought himself to be, he was described as little better than a butcher. He had exhausted himself in gathering materials for a superlative issue of the *Messenger* and may well have burned himself out. It is not hard to imagine how the black clouds began to gather and why he took to drink once again.

White was quick to notice. Perhaps he had been watching out for this to happen. Now he was in a predicament. He had sworn to dismiss Poe as soon as there was any evidence of drinking, and yet the man had provided him with one of the best magazines he had issued and had done much to make his magazine venture a success. He warned Poe again, and Poe got back to work.

But his heart was not in it. Although he attended to various editorial tasks he found it hard to concentrate on the job. Depression had brought on drinking which brought on sickness. Slowly his condition deteriorated, and he did little for the magazine. White was at his wits' end. The weeks went by, and there was no improvement.

The last straw came when the December 1836 issue had to be cancelled. On 27 December White wrote to his friend Lucian Minor:

> Highly as I think of Mr Poe's talents, I shall be forced to give him notice in a week or so at farthest that I can no longer recognize him as editor of my *Messenger*. Three months ago I felt it my duty to give him a similar notice – and was afterwards over-persuaded to restore him to his situation on certain conditions – which conditions he has again forfeited.

Poe's drinking was the main cause of his dismissal, but there were other factors; not least, perhaps, White was feeling that his magazine had been hijacked by his celebrity writer. There has also been a suggestion that Poe flirted with White's daughter, but this is simply malicious gossip. White was to remain on good terms with Poe afterwards.

Meanwhile Poe had not entirely idle. He had been working on a book, following the advice of Paulding and Harper's. He was writing a novel in instalments so that he could contribute a chapter to the magazine monthly as well as being able to publish it as a whole novel. He decided on a sea adventure of the most bloodthirsty kind, to cater for the modern taste for such themes, and had entitled it *The Adventures of Arthur Gordon Pym*.[22] The first part was to appear in the next number of the *Southern Literary Messenger*, and Poe asked White if he could fit in more, to which White replied: 'If it be possible, without breaking in on my previous arrangements, I will get more than the 1st portion of *Pym* in – tho' I much fear that will be impossible.' White had also promised to make a financial gift, presumably for services rendered, and of that he said: 'I also made you a promise on Saturday that I would do something more for you to-day, – and I never make even a promise without intending to perform it, – and though it is entirely out of my power to send you up any thing this morning, yet I will do something more for you before night, or early to-morrow – if I have to borrow it from my friends.'

Two instalments of *Pym* were published – in the January and February editions – but that would not fend off Poe's creditors. He was again looking for work and money. It was an all-too-familiar situation.

6

‘YOU SPEAK OF ENEMIES’

At the beginning of 1837 New York was the largest city in America and the commercial hub of the USA. Manhattan and its grid system had been built upon old marshland. The Erie Canal, opened twelve years earlier, boosted trade, which was already prospering thanks to New York's maritime location, and the new railroads promised more. The boom of the early 1830s had resounded all around the country, but with an especial fervour here, and New York had grown with furious intensity. As a result, immigrants swarmed in to claim their share of the new prosperity.

At the very start of the new year a small family may have been seen trudging through the deep snow of an exceptionally bitter winter. The oldest of the three was a large matronly lady with slightly masculine features, the youngest little more than a child. The man, slightly built, with broad forehead, black wavy hair and clipped moustache, was also seeking his fortune in the cosmopolitan melting-pot.

Edgar Allan Poe had passed his apprenticeship with top marks, and he knew it. There was neither a nut nor a bolt of a printing-press that he did not know, and of paper sizes and quality he was an authority. He knew how to run a journal, from rounding up contributions and advertising to design and lay out. As for writing, his efforts had been met with shining praise and his criticism judged, in the main, to be clear and able (if rather severe). His résumé was short but impressive – he had lifted an infant periodical from the gutter to the topmost heights of success, and his talents spoke for themselves.

All things considered, leaving the *Southern Literary Messenger* had probably been for the best. Had he not struggled to make ends meet, worked non-stop for a pittance? It was time to find a position more worthy of him and, bearing in mind the testimonials he had gathered from the nation's literati, he should have no trouble doing that. The only question had been, where? And the answer was obviously New York.

Poe had also been busy on his latest project, and he wanted the largest possible stage on which to exhibit it. He had completed his first attempt at a novel, *The Adventures of Arthur Gordon Pym*.[1] He had sent it to Harper's, who had made the original suggestion, and the company did not hesitate to publish it. The title page would certainly whet the appetite for a thrilling rollercoaster ride of a novel:

> The Narrative Of Arthur Gordon Pym, Of Nantucket; comprising the details of a mutiny and atrocious atrocity on board the American brig *Grampus*, on her way to the South Seas – with an account of the recapture of the vessel by the survivors; their shipwreck, and subsequent horrible sufferings from famine; their deliverance by means of the British schooner *Jane Gray*; the brief cruise of this latter vessel in the Antarctic Ocean; her capture, and the massacre of the crew among a group of islands in the 84th parallel of Southern latitude; together with the incredible adventures and discoveries still further South, to which that distressing calamity gave rise.

Having written what his public most wanted, Poe must have felt that lasting fame was imminent. *Pym* is fascinating, and there is much more in it than implied by his later comment that it was a very 'silly' book. The descriptive writing is among Poe's best and the surreal surprise ending, as they approach the South Pole, enigmatic in the extreme.

> And now we rushed into the embraces of the cataract, where a chasm threw itself open to receive us. But there arose in our pathway a shrouded human figure, very far larger in its proportions than any dweller among men. And the hue of the skin of the figure was of the perfect whiteness of the snow.

In some measure, Poe's hopes were well founded. The book sold out of two editions. This success should have elevated Poe to a high position among his fellow authors – but, sadly, the main interest was in Britain. Owing to the absence of copyright laws, Poe did not see a penny of the profits. In America sales were more sluggish and did not earn him anything at all. The efforts of his enemies in New York may have had much to do with that; across the Atlantic, where there was no negative press, the reaction was more favourable and was based on the merits of the book itself.

Lewis Clark wasted no time in ridiculing Poe's work. In his review he stated: 'There are a great many tough stories in this book told in a rough and slip-shod style, seldom chequered by the more common graces of composition, beyond a Robinson Crusoe-ish sort of simplicity of narration.'[2]

Where the Poes lived on their arrival in New York is a matter of some debate, but it is probable that they stayed in several locations until they found a place in which to settle. Judging by later reports, they stopped in Sixth Avenue and Waverley Place before they settled in 113½ Carmine Street. Throughout these weeks Poe looked around for the position that would most appeal to him and, although we have no records, he must have approached several magazines and newspaper offices.

He soon found that his assumptions about employment were wrong. Openings were not as common as he had supposed, but the main problem was that his reputation preceded him. Magazine and newspaper proprietors had read his cutting reviews of their protégés and were not pleased. There was the occasional ray of hope, such as when Rector Francis L. Hawks of the *North York Review* wrote, 'I wish you to fall in with your broad-axe amidst this miserable literary trash which surrounds us. I believe you have the will, and I know you have the ability . . .'[3] But even that came to nothing. Virtually the only thing he had published in this period was the review of a book by J.T. Stephens, 'Incidents of Travel in Egypt, Arabia and the Holy Land'.

In the meantime Maria was helping the family finances by taking in lodgers. This is fortunate, because we can catch a glimpse of Poe's family life through the eyes of one of them, William Gowans. Gowans was a bookseller who had lived with them at their former residence and had got along with them so well he followed them to New York. As so few contemporary descriptions remain of Poe's family life, it is fascinating to read what he had to say about it:

> During that time I saw much of him [Poe] and had an opportunity of conversing with him often, and I must say that I never once saw him affected by liqueur, nor ever descend to any known vice, while he was one of the most courteous, gentlemanly and intelligent companions

> I have met with during my journeyings and haltings through divers divisions of the globe. Besides, he had an extra inducement to be a good man as well as a good husband, for he had a wife of matchless beauty and loveliness; her eye could match that of any houri, and her face deny the genius of a Canova to imitate; a temper and disposition of unsurpassing sweetness; besides, she seemed as much devoted to him as a young mother is to her first-born.[4]

Saccharine words; yet all other descriptions seem to tally in the main. Maria herself later said: 'How often has Eddie said, "I see no-one so beautiful as my sweet little wife."' The picture is of a couple dependent on each other, and very devoted. Not even his enemies could gainsay this; and it must be borne in mind when, after his death, people wrote various unsavoury and venomous things about his character.

Things got worse for the household. The cost of living in New York was much more expensive than they had realized; as they were relying on rent money, it was hard to budget. The income they had expected from Poe's writing was not forthcoming, and he had failed to find employment. As if that was not bad enough they now faced the Panic of 1837, which began in May and led to a depression that was to drag on for six years.

President Jackson had refused to renew the charter of the Second National Bank, and its functions were farmed out to other, new banks. This led to a boom, but it was based on the banks issuing paper bills which most had not the hard currency to cover; sensing an imminent disaster, Jackson demanded that all government payments be made in cash. The banks were drained of money, and the economy plunged into a recession in which land prices plummeted to extraordinarily low levels. When Van Buren took over as President in 1837 he refused to intervene; the disaster grew, leading to the Panic in May. Within two months virtually half the country's banks had either failed or were on the point of collapse.[5]

In correspondence with James K. Paulding, Poe sought employment as a mere clerk, but unfortunately Poe's break with White did not go unremarked, and this was one of the reasons Paulding was not receptive to Poe's request. There was already talk about Poe's alcoholism, and Poe went to lengths to explain that he was not addicted. He had taken to drink only when under great strain.

> Intemperance, with me, has never amounted to a habit; and had it been ten times a habit it would have required scarcely an effort on my part to shake it from me at once and forever. I have been fully awakened to the impolicy and degradation of the course hitherto pursued, and have abandoned the vice altogether, and without a struggle.

It was obvious now that New York held nothing to tie Poe, so late in August the family packed up their things, said farewell to Gowans and left for Philadelphia. In that city there was not quite so much animosity towards him (unless in the person of Willis Clark), and it, too, had a welter of magazines in full production – enough industry among the presses to promise a career, at any rate. The town was second in size to New York, and there had been a running rivalry between the two. The family moved to a little residence in Arch Street – but their money was almost gone. They had resorted to borrowing cash to move, and now there was nothing coming in. Again Poe had to borrow cash from anyone who would lend it. Things looked bleak.

He borrowed $10 from Nathan C. Brooks, an old friend and the owner of a new magazine called the *American Museum*. Brooks asked if he would like to produce a notice on Washington Irving, and the thought of Poe's assessment of the great writer must have had him rubbing his hands. Oddly enough, Poe declined the offer, claiming ignorance of Irving's work and saying he was busy with another project; he did, however, send Brooks a new tale for the first number which he came to consider his best work.[6] A development from 'Morella', 'Ligeia' plays with the idea of reincarnation.[7] When his soul mate dies, the narrator decides to marry again and takes the Lady Rowena as his bride; but Ligeia eventually takes over his new wife's body and form. Having paid only $10 for the piece, Brooks made another bargain when he rescued 'Siope' (later known as 'Shadow') from Poe's waste bin; it was later published in the *Baltimore Book* for 1839.

Poe had discussed his financial embarrassment with a neighbour, John Cox, who had magnanimously offered him $50. Embarrassed, Poe only accepted $30, but soon afterwards debt forced him to ask for the other $20. Pride was a luxury he could not afford.

It may seem surprising that Poe turned down the offer of a review from Brooks when he needed money so badly. He had mentioned 'engagements' with which he was involved, and one of these was the oddest thing he ever did. It had started with a communication from Professor Thomas Wyatt, who wanted to discuss an urgent matter with him. Intrigued, Poe went to meet the professor, who began by asking him if he wanted to be the author of a book on sea shells. Poe's eyebrows must have risen considerably when he heard the idea, but he wanted to know more.

This was the story. Wyatt had previously published a textbook on conchology with Harper's, but they demurred at publishing a cheaper version because of cost considerations. Now the professor wanted another edition to accompany his lecture notes, but his name was of insufficient weight to persuade the publishers to go ahead. If, however, he could use Poe's name the project would have a much better chance of success. For this service he would be given a fee. It is interesting that Poe's name was of sufficient value to make the sea-shell book viable but not to sell his own work.

Parts of the work were copied from an earlier book, *The Conchologist's Text-Book* by Captain Thomas Brown, which had been published in Glasgow in 1833 – particularly the pictures of shells and the 'Explanation of the Parts of Shells'. Virtually all the rest of the text was taken from Wyatt's own *Conchology*, although Poe made some contributions, such as translations of descriptions 'from Cuvier'.[8] The result was published by Haswell, Barrington & Haswell as *The Conchologist's First Book, or, A System of Testaceous Malacology*.[9]

Later, Poe would defend himself from claims of plagiarism by insisting that all such books are written in the same way; but the most ironic thing about the whole affair was that the book was a success, selling out its first edition. The question of whether Poe's new book was an act of gross plagiarism was contentious at the time because authors were not yet protected by international laws on copyright. The possibility of such a law was on every author's lips, as the year before Britain had passed the first legislation to protect writers and their material. But at the time Poe was writing he was unlikely to be taken to task for plagiarism – legally, at any rate.

The conchology book at least brought in some cash, and any drop of water in the desert would have been welcome. The family moved again, this time to 2502 Coates Street. Although he was not a rich man, Poe was still well enough known to be a minor celebrity, and he began to attend meetings at the Falstaff Hotel with various authors and artists. Here he met Thomas Sully, the uncle of his old school friend Robert Sully. John Sartain, the illustrator and artist, was also a member, and he went on to engrave Poe's portrait.[10] A friendship developed between the two that would continue until the end of Poe's life.

A breakthrough came at last in the spring of 1839 in the form of William Evans Burton, an English comedian and playwright. 'Billy' Burton had fled from England in 1834 to escape the scandal of having bigamously married a sixteen-year-old orphan even though he was already married and had a son. Then a widely acclaimed actor, he continued his success in the USA. He occupied a prominent place, as both actor and manager, in New York City, Philadelphia and Baltimore, the theatre that he leased in New York later being renamed Burton's Theater. He had an enormous library which was to grow to half a million books, and, as part of his interest in literature, in 1835 he decided to start a magazine of his own, the *Gentleman's Magazine*.

He was a large, broad individual with a carrying voice that was a legacy from his life as an actor. A bluff, ebullient, plain-speaking man, he had no time for shilly-shallying or wasting words. In fact his plain speaking could occasionally be construed as rudeness when it was usually only a mannerism of which he was probably hardly aware. He was a determined man, though, who knew exactly what he wanted and who was willing to work industriously to achieve his ends.

Poe now approached him in the hope of finding a job, and he was just the kind of man Burton was looking for, someone who had achieved wonders with his last magazine and who could be expected to do the same for himself. Burton replied to Poe:

> My Dear Sir ,
> I have given your proposals a fair consideration. I wish to form some such engagement as that which you have proposed, and know of no one more likely to suit my views than yourself. The expenses of the Magazine are already woefully heavy; more so than my circulation warrants. I am certain that my expenditure exceeds that of any publication now extant, including the monthlies which are double in price. Competition is high, – new claimants are daily rising. I am therefore compelled to give expensive plates, thicker paper, and better printing than my antagonists, or allow them to win the goal. My contributors cost me something handsome, and the losses upon credit, exchange, etc. are becoming frequent and serious. I mentioned this list of difficulties as some slight reason why I do not close with your offer, which is indubitably liberal, without any delay.

> Shall we say ten dollars per week for the remaining portion of this year? – Should we remain together, which I see no reason to negative, your proposition shall be in force for 1840. A month's notice to be given on either side previous to a separation.
>
> Two hours a day, except occasionally, will, I believe, be sufficient for all required, except in the production of any article of your own. At all events, you could easily find time for any other light avocation – supposing that you did not exercise your talents in behalf of any publication interfering with the prospects of the G.M.
>
> I shall dine at home to-day at 3. If you will cut your mutton with me, good. If not, write or see me at your leisure.

But Poe almost, on his own initiative, wrecked his chance. Hitting another bout of depression, he wrote Burton a melancholy letter that worried the editor. It also seems Poe was doubtful about the quality of the magazine. Burton was not the sort of man to put up with moanings and whimperings – he felt Poe should get a grip on himself and get on with his life. In answer to Poe's letter Burton also voiced his apprehensions concerning Poe's severe criticisms.

They settled their differences, and Poe began working for Burton's magazine. He worked hard and was soon producing some of the best work he had written to date, such as his masterpiece 'The Fall of the House of Usher', and he also reprinted 'William Wilson' and 'Morella'.[11] Late in the year he published 'The Conversation of Eiros and Charmion'.[12] 'William Wilson' is interesting from the biographical standpoint, as the narrator is haunted by a *doppelgänger* which represents his conscience. Through the tale we have descriptions of his school in Stoke Newington as well as student card games.

At the offices of the *Gentleman's Magazine* Poe met a regular contributor, Thomas Dunn English. English was at the time a medical student who was just about to qualify, but he had a penchant for literature and also wrote for Burton. He became a family friend, and would later be an extremely important figure in Poe's life. Through English, Poe was introduced to Henry B. Hirst, the author and poet, with whom he also came to be on friendly terms.

At about this time, with farcical timing, a letter arrived from the *Literary Examiner*. E. Burke Fisher had started this magazine in May, together with W. Whitney, and he was soliciting contributions at a fair price. Of course Poe capitulated but only gave him a single article in the end, as he was dissatisfied with Fisher's treatment of it. The piece was a review of Willis's 'Tortesa', and Fisher had, according to Poe, altered it significantly and added opinions of his own.[13]

Almost immediately Burton demonstrated that he intended to retain control of his periodical and was barking detailed instructions to its new editor. The tone of one note comes across as bluff and a little intimidating. It begins:

> Will you please see Parmelee, and get him to do the enclosed directly, for this next number. I hope you have another chapter of the Miami Valley in, for August. Desire Morrell to obtain Mr R.P. Smith's life from Mr Goodman, if he has not got it yet, but it must be done directly, because we want the matter to begin the September number, and consequently to end the next sheet. If the 'life' will not be ready, we must put in something else, with another plate, for I want the next number out immediately.

In his past journalistic work as a critic Poe had estranged the New York clique and made many enemies. At least one correspondent, J. Beauchamp Jones, was worried for him and warned him in a friendly letter. Poe replied, asking for more information: 'It is always desirable to know who are our enemies, and what are the nature of their attacks . . .' Then, in a later passage: 'You speak of "enemies" – could you give me their names? All the literary people in Baltimore, as far as I know them, have at least professed a friendship.'

It would be wrong to imagine that Poe was gathering only foes; he was also making friends and some (not all) of these would remain friends for his lifetime. One was the physician Joseph Evans Snodgrass whom he had known for some time as editor of the *American Museum of Science, Literature and the Arts*; he had published Poe in the past. Poe still wrote occasional pieces for the *Museum*, including 'Literary Small Talk' and a piece suggesting that Longfellow plagiarized his own 'The Haunted Palace' in 'The Beleaguered City'.

Now Poe was asking for a slightly dubious favour. He wanted Snodgrass to write a review of the latest edition of his magazine and in the puff to incorporate a flattering notice concerning himself taken from the *St Louis Bulletin*. This review was then to be passed to Neilson Poe for insertion into his newspaper. (In the end, Neilson refused.) There is an air of flamboyant optimism in his letter to Snodgrass – he even imagines a profitable connection with Christopher

North and his beloved *Blackwood's Magazine*, who had promised a 'very commendatory review' of his stories.[14] But Snodgrass was to keep quiet about it, at least for the present. As for Neilson Poe's refusal to help his relative out, Poe made his feelings known to Snodgrass thus:

> I felt that N. Poe would not insert the article editorially. In your private ear, I believe him to be the bitterest enemy I have in the world. He is the more despicable in this, since he makes loud professions of friendship . . . I cannot account for his hostility except in being vain enough to imagine him jealous of the little literary reputation I have, of late years, obtained. But enough of the little dog.

It is obvious that Neilson's intrusion into his engagement with Virginia still rankled, and this would not have helped to ease matters. It is a moot point whether Poe should spend so much time complaining about puffing and fighting against it as detrimental to the nation's literary health while asking for a puff himself; but Poe would have drawn the line between a short one-off notice and a deliberate conspiracy to distort American literary standards. Besides, he really had little choice. While the dubious system survived, he had to use it for his own self-protection, otherwise the bad notices of his enemies would drag his work down in the public eye before it had a chance to prosper. Positive press was the only way he could counteract it.

He had approached another publisher, Lea & Blanchard, in an attempt to publish his 'Tales'. Meanwhile he was wondering whether to send his 'Fall of the House of Usher' to the *Southern Literary Messenger*, but he was worried in case White bore him a grudge. However, the former editor, James E. Heath, assured him that this was not the case. Poe was anxious to have his work before the public because he was certain that his tales would soon be published – in the autumn.

By now he had come into contact, through his work, with Philip P. Cooke, an author who was quickly to become a good friend and who, according to Poe, wrote 'some of the finest poetry of which America can boast'. Excited about his forthcoming book, Poe had asked Cooke for an opinion of his tales, especially 'Ligeia'. Cooke wrote flatteringly but questioned the sudden appearance of Ligeia in bodily form instead of a gradual change coming over the Lady

Rowena. Once again, Poe proved that he could accept criticism, even of his best tale, when it was offered by a friendly pen.

> Touching 'Ligeia' you are right – all right – throughout. The gradual perception of the fact that Ligeia lives again in the person of Rowena is a far loftier and more thrilling idea than the one I have embodied. It offers in my opinion, the widest possible scope to the imagination – it might be rendered even sublime.

Carey & Lea, now Lea & Blanchard, at last contacted Poe with an offer to publish his tales. The terms were very meagre, as Poe might have expected. 'As your wish in having your Tales printed is not immediately pecuniary, we will at our own risque & expense print a Small Edition say of 750 copies. This run if sold will pay but a small profit, which if realized is to be ours. The copy right will remain with you, and when ready a few copies for distribution among your friends, will be at your service . . .' Possessed of the information that his tales were about to be published, albeit without profit to himself, Poe was forced to face the prospect of looking for someone to puff his work. As usual, he aimed high and approached none other than Washington Irving, hoping he would say something flattering about his book. Poe was anxious to get good comments from eminent authors to push his tales, so he asked Irving for an opinion on 'William Wilson' (as he had already done for 'Ligeia'). A little later Irving sent the following:

> I have read your little tale of 'William Wilson' with much pleasure. It is managed in a highly picturesque style, and the singular and mysterious interest is well sustained throughout. I repeat what I have said in regard to a previous production, which you did me the favour to send me, that I cannot but think a series of articles of like style and merit would be extremely well received by the public. I could add for your private ear, that I think the last tale much the best, in regard to style. It is simpler. In your first you have been too anxious to present your picture vividly to the eye, or too distrustful of your effect, and have laid on too much colouring. It is erring on the best side – the side of luxuriance. That tale might be improved by relieving the style from some of the epithets. There is no danger of destroying its graphic effect, which is powerful.

Poe had by now received glowing praise from Snodgrass concerning his tales and was evidently pleased; he wrote back to him about Irving's comments and his hopes for the new book. He plainly explained his need for such stuff as Irving's approbation – it would help combat the inevitable hounding he expected from the New York clique.

> I am sure you will be pleased to hear that Washington Irving has addressed me 2 letters abounding in high passages of compliment in regard to my Tales – passages which he desires me to make public – if I think benefit may be derived. It is needless to say that I shall do so – it is a duty I owe myself – and which it would be wilful folly to neglect, through a false sense of modesty.

Now once again Poe contacted his publishers, this time with the idea of selling his copyright. This produced an acidic response. Feeling that he was treading on thinning ice, Poe left the publishers to complete their task and in a short while was rewarded with seeing his new volume, *Tales of the Grotesque and Arabesque*, on sale.[15] His dedication was a nod back to his army days – to Colonel William Drayton.[16] He received his twenty free copies and began distributing them – the first to Snodgrass. A week later he was full of optimism and expectation – he even imagined that the run had been sold out, which was far from the truth. He was pleased with all the notices so far, and the Philadelphia press had given him 'the very highest possible praise', but he was nervously awaiting the others. Benjamin Park had promised a review in his *New World* – and the book had just reached New York . . .

Poe had good reason to expect a curt response from New York, as he had once again upset the cliques with a severe critique of Longfellow's latest offering, *Hyperion*.[17] Oddly enough, although he defended Longfellow's work, Lewis Clark studiously ignored Poe's book. Not long after, Longfellow published a book of verse, well puffed beforehand, called *Voices of the Night*, which (unlike *Hyperion*) won a great deal of critical acclaim. Poe recognized Longfellow's genius and was particularly taken with 'Hymn of the Night': 'Had he written always thus, we should have been tempted to speak of him not only as *our* finest poet, but as one of the noblest poets of all time.' But what Poe could not stomach was his 'imitation', an accusation at least partly convincing; and his concern was with one particular piece concerning the Old Year:

> . . . then nearly all that is valuable in the piece of Tennyson is the first conception of personifying the Old Year as a dying old man, with the singularly wild and fantastic *manner* in which that conception is carried out. Of this conception and of this manner he is robbed. Could he peruse today the 'Midnight Mass' of Professor Longfellow, would he peruse it with more of indignation or of grief?[18]

This attack was quickly answered by Willis Clark:

> A neighbouring periodical, we hear, has been attempting to prove that Professor Longfellow's sublime and beautiful 'Midnight Mass for the Dying Year' has been imitated from a poem by Tennyson. Preposterous! There is nothing more alike in the two pieces than black and white, with the exception of the personification – and *that* was Longfellow's long before the Scotch writer thought of 'doing' his poem.[19]

Perhaps one of the strangest gifts Poe ever received was now offered by his friend and editor of the *Star*, Hiram Haines – a fawn for Virginia. Somewhat bemused, Poe could not think of a way to transport the animal to his home. 'What can be done? Perhaps some opportunity may offer itself hereafter – some friend from Petersburg may be about to pay us a visit. In the meantime accept our best acknowledgments, precisely as if the little fellow were already nibbling the grass before our windows in Philadelphia.'

Back at the *Gentleman's Magazine*, things were not all going well. Burton obviously meant what he said about literary criticism, so Poe was working in uncongenial conditions, subject to the orders of a man whose ideas he did not share. In fact, Burton had refused to publish some of Poe's reviews and articles. Burton's latest diktat – that payments for contributions were to cease – also angered Poe. Burton was trying to cut costs because he was involved in a theatre project that was costing him a lot of cash – the National Theater on Chestnut Street, which was to open in August. Instead of paying fees to contributors, he had hit upon the idea of awarding prizes, and these attempts at penny-pinching gnawed at Poe. He himself needed money from whatever source he could earn it. It was bad enough that an American writer found it hard to get into print, without taking away his fee for the work. In fact, Poe doubted whether any cash would be paid at all, and in the end the scheme folded.

Relations between Burton and Poe were souring; it had been

obvious from their first meeting that a clash was inevitable. For one thing, Poe was hardly well paid and still short of money for everyday expenses. The extent of his problems may be seen by the fact that his neighbour John Cox had still not received payment of the money he loaned him over a year ago, and Poe suffered the humiliation of explaining his financial position to him. He did, however, send him a copy of his book.

Burton would not have been pleased to hear of the rumours circulating abroad that Poe was about to launch his own magazine. The rumours were true. Had he not warned Poe, in his very first letter, that 'you could easily find time for any other light avocation – supposing that you did not exercise your talents on behalf of any publication interfering with the prospects of the G.M.'? And what was he now planning to do but set up a journal whose purpose was to do just that?

On the other side, Poe had discovered that Burton was planning to sell his magazine to George R. Graham, editor of *The Casket*. Of course, Burton felt that such a business transaction had nothing to do with his employee. Poe would hardly have agreed with such a contention and felt slighted.

Burton was not a man to keep his feelings to himself and made his opinions clear in a letter which he sent to Poe on Saturday, 30 May. Poe was furious with the contents and allowed himself time to recover from his rage before replying on the Monday. If the first paragraph is anything to go by, it is as well he waited – it is hard to imagine what he might have written in the heat of the moment:

> In the first place – your attempts to bully me excite in my mind scarcely any other sentiment than mirth. When you address me again preserve if you can, the dignity of a gentleman. If by accident you have taken it into your head that I am to be insulted with impunity I can only assume that you are an ass.

Poe now suggested that, because Burton had once published a severe review of *Arthur Gordon Pym*, he assumed that Poe had resented, and still resented, it. Furthermore, Burton had stated that Poe owed him $100, and with his usual clinical detail Poe denied it. As for Poe losing interest in the magazine – that was because Burton had continuously rejected his work. So much for Burton's grievances. As for his own:

> You first 'enforced', as you say, a deduction of salary: giving me to understand thereby that you thought of parting company – You next spoke disrespectfully of me behind my back – this as an habitual thing – to those whom you supposed your friends, and who punctually retailed me, as a matter of course, every ill-natured word which you uttered. Lastly you advertised your magazine for sale without saying a word to me about it.

The relationship between the two men was untenable, and Poe left. Later, when the fires died down, neither nurtured a lasting resentment, and they both eventually spoke well of the other.

Poe had not written many original articles for the magazine in 1840, just 'The Philosophy of Furniture' and 'The Journal of Julius Rodman'.[20] For *Alexander's Weekly Messenger* he had contributed the more interesting 'cryptography' pieces. But now he had no permanent position. Once again he had to shift for himself.

7

⁖ IN SEARCH OF ELDORADO ⁖

TO THE PUBLIC. SINCE resigning the conduct of the *Southern Literary Messenger*, at the commencement of its third year, I have constantly held in view the establishment of a Magazine which should retain some of the chief features of that Journal, abandoning the rest. Delay, however, has been occasioned by a variety of causes, and not until now have I felt fully prepared to execute the intention.

To the mechanical execution of the work the greatest attention will be given which such a matter can require. In this respect, it is proposed to surpass, by very much, the ordinary Magazine style. The form will nearly resemble that of the *Knickerbocker.* The paper will be equal to that of the *North American Review*. The pictorial embellishments will be numerous, and by the leading artists of the country, but will be only introduced in the necessary illustration of the text. The *Penn Magazine* will be published in Philadelphia, on the first of each month, and will form, half yearly, a volume of about 500 pages. The price will be $5 per annum, payable in advance, or upon the receipt of the first number, which will be issued on the first of January, 1841.[1]

These are extracts from 'Prospectus of the Penn Magazine, a monthly literary journal, to be edited and published in the City of Philadelphia, by Edgar A. Poe'. It may seem very strange that a man who has just found himself unemployed and penniless should be embarking on such a high-cost project as starting up his own magazine. Over-optimistic as he was, Poe could in no way be called foolish. He had not worked for two major magazines without learning enough to understand how to make a journal successful.

Starting such a periodical required a large amount of cash, but Poe argued that it need not come from his own coffers (which were empty anyhow) but from subscriptions. Should he obtain enough of these – say 500 – the necessary money would be available.

It did not take long for news of the prospectus to reach the eyes of the New York clan, and the threat that the Penn would rival both the *Knickerbocker* and the *North American Review* was not missed. Although Lewis Clark despised Poe, there can be little doubt that the 'new kid on the block' could be a troublesome addition to the magazine family. He made mention of the prospect in the July edition of the *Knickerbocker*, altering the facts to Poe's detriment. The *Gentleman's Magazine* had folded, and who was to blame but Poe, described as 'the principal editor'? What is more, the new magazine is not said to be intending to take 'the form' of the *Knickerbocker* but to be presented 'in the style of' it, implying that Poe meant to imitate it not only in appearance but in content:

> The *Gentleman's Magazine* . . . is offered for sale; 'the proprietor being about to engage in a more profitable business'. Mr E.A. Poe, a spirited writer, and hitherto the principal editor of the miscellany in question, announces his retirement from its supervision. He has issued proposals for a new monthly magazine, 'to be executed in the neatest style, after the manner of the *Knickerbocker*', to which he promises to bring great additions to the literary aid he has hitherto diverted into a different channel.[2]

Poe immediately set about touting for business, mailing the prospectus to anyone who could be of any help. On 3 June he turned to his first critic and friend, John Neal:

> My Dear Sir
> As you gave me the first jog in my literary career, you are in a measure bound to protect me & keep me rolling. I therefore now ask you to aid me with your influence, in whatever manner your experience shall suggest. It strikes me that I never write you except to ask a favour, but my friend Thomas will assure you that I bear you always in mind – holding you in the highest respect and esteem.

But Neal was unable to assist – apart from giving Poe a lesson in elementary grammar:

> You say 'I will be pardoned,' for 'I shall be pardoned', 'For assurance that I will fulfil' &c., for shall &c. Are you Irish – or have you associated much with the Irish – the well-educated Irish I mean? They always make this mistake, and the Scotch too sometimes; and you, I am persuaded, are either connected by blood or habits with the Irish of the South. Forgive me this liberty I pray you, and take it for granted that I should not complain of these two little errors, if I could find anything else to complain of.

Before Poe left Burton's magazine Snodgrass had sent in an essay, which he wanted back. Poe was certain that it still lay with Burton, and explained this, as well as expressing his feelings about Burton, which obviously still rankled:

> Were I in your place I would take some summary method of dealing with the scoundrel, whose infamous line of conduct in regard to this whole premium scheme merits, and shall receive exposure. I am firmly convinced that it was never his intention to pay one dollar of the money offered; and indeed his plain intimations to that effect, made to me personally and directly, were the immediate reasons of my cutting the connexion as abruptly as I did. If you could, in any way, spare the time to come on to Philadelphia, I think I could put you in the way of detecting this villain in his rascality. I would go down with you to the office, open the drawer in his presence, and take the MS. from beneath his very nose. I think this would be a good deed done, and would act as a caution to such literary swindlers in future. What think you of this plan? Will you come on? Write immediately in reply.

In the meantime, what news of Poe's *Tales*? It seemed that Poe was the last to know:

> Touching my Tales, you will scarcely believe me when I tell you that I am ignorant of their fate, and have never spoken to the publishers concerning them since the day of their issue. I have cause to think, however, that the edition was exhausted almost immediately. It was only six weeks since that I had the opportunity I wished of sending a copy to Professor Wilson, so as to be sure of its reaching him directly. Of course I must wait some time yet for a notice, – if any there is to be . . .

It was now dangerous for anyone to pen a letter to Poe about anything – they would inevitably be roped into his magazine scheme. For example, the Philomathean Society had been founded eight years earlier, originally as a student body based at New York University. It had accumulated its own library and augmented knowledge by means of debates and lectures; and Poe was a regular guest there. Now it could be a useful connection. He wrote to A.S. Cummings: 'Your personal influence with the institution in behalf of the "Penn Magazine" (of which I forward a Prospectus) I would esteem a very great favor – as the patronage of such bodies is always of the highest importance in all enterprises of the kind.'

He wrote to his two cousins, William and Washington. To William (and brother Robert) in Augusta he wrote: 'I take pride in earnestly soliciting your support, and that of your brothers and friends,' and 'Will you oblige me by acting as my agent for the Penn Magazine in your city, this letter being your authority?' A day later he was writing to Washington, stating that the two brothers had promised every aid and asking him to find subscriptions for him in Macon.

> My chances of establishing the Magazine depend upon my getting a certain number of subscribers previously to the first of December. This is rendered necessary by my having no other capital to begin with than whatever reputation I may have acquired as a literary man. Had I money, I might issue the first numbers without this list; but as it is, at least 500 names will be required to enable me to commence. I have no doubt in the world that this number can be obtained among those friends who aided me in the *Messenger*; but still it behooves me to use every exertion to ensure success. I think it very probable that your influence in Macon will procure for me several subscribers, and, if so, you will render me a service for which I shall always be grateful.

On 7 August he received a letter from a correspondent who was to become one of his best friends – at least, while he was alive. This was the Georgia poet Thomas Holley Chivers, who had graduated as a physician but hardly ever practised medicine, especially when an inheritance made him independently wealthy. He turned his mind to literature, and by the time he met Poe he had written a book of autobiographical poems as well as the play *Conrad and Eudora*.

Chivers's literary style was, to say the least, unusual, festooned as it was with flowery epithets and weighed down with archaic follies, often done for humorous effect. His writing was not without merit, but it takes some getting used to. Poe must have wondered who on earth this was as he read in the first paragraph: 'My absence from the City, among the emerald highlands of the beautiful Hudson, prevented my answering it sooner than to-day.' He is happy to support Poe's venture, for 'In the Paradise of Literature, I do not know one better calculated than yourself to prune the young scions of their exuberant thoughts.' However, he offers words of warning about the severity of Poe's critiques: 'In some instances, let me remark, you seemed to me to lay aside the pruning-knife for the tomahawk, and not only to lop off the redundant limbs, but absolutely to eradicate the entire tree.' We lose track of Chivers for almost two years, but then he will return to play a leading part in Poe's tale.

The mail-shots produced some results, and within a month John Tomlin, Postmaster of Jackson, Tennessee, and a regular contributor to the *Gentleman's Magazine* (as well as an admirer of Poe), had sent him nine subscribers. Poe was quick to express his gratitude. 'I hope you will think me sincere when I say that I am truly grateful for the interest you have taken in my welfare. A few more such friends as yourself and I shall have no reason to doubt of success.' To this Tomlin replied enthusiastically: 'The abiding interest which I feel for your welfare, gives at all times the most cheering hopes of your success. It cannot be that you will not succeed! For the warmhearted Southerners, by whom you are known, will not let the Work die for the want of patronage. They are your friends for they know you well, and will sustain you.' He also promised more subscribers after a visit to Nashville.

Poe also received a reply from Pliny Earle, a famous psychiatrist and poet, who at least contributed a poem. Poe replied with thanks but enclosed a prospectus in the hope that he might yet drum up interest:

> I hasten to thank you for the interest you have taken in my contemplated Magazine, and for the beautiful lines 'By an Octogenarian'. They shall certainly appear in the first number. You must allow me to consider such offerings, however, as any thing but 'unsubstantial encouragement.' Believe me that good poetry is far rarer, and therefore far more acceptable to the publisher of a journal, than even that rara avis money itself. Should you be able to aid my cause in Frankford by a good word with your neighbours, I hope that you will be

> inclined to do so. Much depends upon the list I may have before the first of December. I send you a Prospectus – believing that the objects set forth in it are, upon the whole, such as your candor will approve . . .

There followed the first in a string of correspondence to a friend of Poe's, Frederick W. Thomas. He was a minor author, having published a novel called *Clinton Bradshaw*, as well as being a lawyer and politically active. As their relationship, and political issues, were to become an important aspect of Poe's story, it would be helpful to give a brief historical sketch of American politics at this time.

After the Revolutionary War two parties emerged: the Federalists and the Republicans. When George Washington left office the two parties fought it out in the first presidential campaign. John Adams of the Federal Party was victorious, but Thomas Jefferson, the Republican candidate, became Vice-President. This was not a good arrangement, so Adams introduced the 12th Amendment in 1802, ensuring that in future both President and Vice-President must be of the same party. Monroe was, however, the last Federal candidate to be put forward for President.

By 1830 the changing face of America, brought about by the Industrial Revolution, split the existing Republicans into two distinct parties: the Democratic Republican Party (later the Democratic Party), led by Andrew Jackson, and the National Republican Party, led by John Quincy Adams. Like the former Federalists, the National Republican Party was in favour of economic nationalism, to which Jackson was strongly opposed. But after the furore over the Second National Bank war the National Republican Party foundered, paving the way for the new Whig Party, headed by Henry Clay and Daniel Webster. The Whigs pressed for expanding the national government and more commercial development, while the Democrats still favoured the agrarian ideals championed by Jefferson, so popular with the farmers of the Southern states.

Van Buren had exacerbated the panic of 1837, as we have already seen, and even so intended to run for President for a second term.[3] However, there was much animosity against him, and the Whigs mounted a strong challenge, putting up General William Henry Harrison along with his second-in-command, John Tyler. Harrison, famed for his part in the battle against native Americans known as the Battle of Tippecanoe, was nicknamed Old Tip, and the Whigs' election slogan was 'Old Tip and Tyler too!'

Frederick W. Thomas was a staunch Whig supporter and strenuously canvassed for Harrison; it was at this time he met Poe. Harrison won the election but fell ill after making his inaugural speech and died after a term of one month. Tyler took over the presidency, and after angering some of his party members, such as Henry Clay, he was expelled from the party in his second year of office. But none of this had yet happened; Thomas was still campaigning for Harrison.

The first known letter between Thomas and Poe is one from Thomas dated 6 November (no longer in existence). They soon became firm friends, Thomas visiting the family at home. Thomas had just published *Howard Pinckney* in the wake of his other novels, *Clinton Bradshaw* and *East and West*, and they came before Poe's critical eye. Not even for a friend would Poe abandon his critical principles:

> I like H.P. very well – better than E. & W. & not nearly so well as C.B. You give yourself up to your own nature (which is a noble one, upon my soul) in *Clinton Bradshaw*; but in *Howard Pinkney* you abandon the broad rough road for the dainty by-paths of authorism. In the former you are interested in what you write & write to please, pleasantly; in the latter, having gained a name, you write to maintain it, and the effort becomes apparent.

Of course, Poe enlists Thomas's help in pursuing the dream of the *Penn*:

> Perhaps you may be able to have the accompanying Prospectus (which you will see differs from the first) inserted once or twice in some of the city papers – if you can accomplish this without trouble I shall be greatly obliged to you. Have you heard that that illustrious graduate of St John's College, Cambridge, (Billy Barlow,) has sold his Magazine to Graham, of the 'Casket'?

By 'Billy Barlow' Poe means Billy Burton, who had indeed sold his magazine to George Rex Graham, who promptly incorporated it into his own magazine, *The Casket*. Thomas's reply came soon after: he had found a magazine agent, 'who to all appearances is honest; he is a one-legged man on a crutch and I would fain therefore believe so'.

Poe was now having trouble meeting deadlines; to make matters worse, he was ill. The first edition was therefore postponed. It must have been galling to Poe to have to write announcing this to all his well-wishers and contributors, but there was nothing else to do. On 30 December he wrote to L.J. Cist, who was a friend of one of his subscribers, Joseph Boyd, and possibly a contributor with the pseudonym 'Gnoman':

> Your letter of the 7th found me labouring under a severe illness, which has confined me to bed for the last month, and from which I am now only slowly recovering. The worst result of this illness is that I am forced to postpone the issue of the first number of the Mag. until the first of March next when it will certainly appear, and I trust under the best auspices . . .

There was more to the delay than Poe's sickness – in fact, the illness was probably brought on by depression. Although he had done his best, finances were still wanting for the project to go ahead. Even though the magazine was in serious difficulties, Poe still laboured with the idea of bringing out the *Penn* and wrote to his old friend Kennedy for help.

> I am about to commence, in this city, a Monthly Magazine somewhat on the plan of the '*Southern Messenger*', and of which you may have seen a Prospectus in some of the Baltimore papers. The leading feature proposed is that of an absolutely independent criticism. Since you gave me my first start in the literary world, and since indeed I seriously say that without the timely kindness you once evinced towards me, I should not at this moment be among the living – you will not feel surprise that I look anxiously to you for encouragement in this new enterprise – the first of any importance which I have undertaken on my own account. What I most seriously need, in the commencement, is caste for the journal – I need the countenance of those who stand well in the social not less than in the literary world. I know that you have never yet written for Magazines – and this is a main reason for my now begging you to give me something for my own. I care not what the article be, nor of what length – what I wish is the weight of your name. Any unused scrap lying by you will fully answer my purpose.

Untiringly Poe continued to contact anyone who might help him produce an issue of which he could be proud, and uphold the promises he had made in his prospectus. He wrote to Snodgrass, who was still asking about the missing manuscript. He begins with his *idée fixe*, the *Penn*:

> You wish to know my prospects with the 'Penn'. They are glorious – notwithstanding the world of difficulties under which I labored and labor. My illness (from which I have now entirely recovered) has been, for various reasons, a benefit to my scheme, rather than a disadvantage; and, upon the whole, if I do not eminently succeed in this enterprise the fault will be altogether mine own. Still, I am using every exertion to ensure success, and, among other manœuvres, I have cut down the bridges behind me. I must now do or die – I mean in a literary sense . . .

He goes on to discuss other journals and the fate of William Burton who, it seems, has been going downhill:

> Burton that illustrious 'graduate of St John's College, Cambridge' is going to the devil with the worst grace in the world, but with a velocity truly astounding. The press here, in a body, have given him the cut direct. So be it – *suum cuique*. We have said quite enough about this genius.
>
> Mr Graham is a very gentlemanly personage. I will see him tomorrow, and speak to him in regard to your essay: although, to prevent detection, Burton may have destroyed it.

He continued to send out soliciting letters, working towards the launch of the magazine, until he received a letter from Judge Joseph Hopkinson. The letter includes the following warning:

> Allow me to remind you that the ruin of our periodicals has been distant subscribers, who never send their money, and the collection of which costs more than is received – A late very popular work, that set out with great strictness in exacting punctual payment from its subscribers, had, nevertheless, thirty thousand dollars due to it in five or six years, and was compelled to stop, with an immense list of subscribers.

The good judge was no fool, and Poe soon discovered the wisdom of his words. Desperate for cash, he offered a partnership to a man named Pollock, but this could not save him. Suddenly, his bank suspended all loans, which made the project completely unthinkable. Nothing could now save the *Penn*. When he realized it was impossible to produce an edition in March, Poe had to admit defeat and postpone the idea. The announcement was made in the *Saturday Evening Post* on 20 February. The project was put to bed – 'scotched, but not killed'.[4]

8

‘YOU MUST GET AFLOAT BY YOURSELF, POE’

The failure to launch the *Penn* must have knocked the wind out of Poe’s sails. He had made the best effort he could and had received so many complimentary messages and helpful contributions that he must have wondered what went wrong. Of course, it was the age-old problem of finance. There is no doubt that if he had managed to overcome the initial problems and, given enough backing to put the machinery into operation, he would have made a resounding success of it and would probably have been fighting Lewis Clark for the title of Magazine King. But the backing was not there. Even if he had found enough money to produce the first issue, he would have needed capital to keep the magazine going until it proved profitable. He needed a backer.

He was not the only person to be disappointed at the collapse of the *Penn* project. Many readers, such as John Tomlin, were looking forward to a magazine run by the fearless and talented editor. Snodgrass also conveyed his sympathy, as did others. But the important thing for Poe now was to find employment, and where else should he look but to George Rex Graham, ex-cabinet-maker and lawyer, who had taken over the *Gentleman’s Magazine*, combined it with *The Casket* and was now producing a new periodical called *Graham’s Magazine*; he was also a proprietor of the *Saturday Evening Post*. So Poe introduced himself to Graham and explained his recent problems with the *Penn*. As the periodical was no longer an option, would Graham consider employing him?

For Poe this would be a much-needed money-earner, but it was also a blessing for Graham. He needed someone to take over the editorial rudder, and who better than the man who had done such a good job on the *Southern Literary Messenger*. Graham was happy to take him on, and Poe took up the post immediately. He wrote some good work for Graham, including 'A Descent into the Maelstrom', 'The Colloquy of Monos and Una' and an 'Autography' series.[1]

He had hardly settled into his editorial chair when disturbing news came from Snodgrass, who had by now heard some of the things Burton had been saying about Poe – none too complimentary things at that. It was the first time the rumour had been spread about him that he was a drunkard. White knew about his drinking habits when he was fired from the *Messenger*, but if gossip was being spread about him none of it had reached Poe's ears. Snodgrass, fearful for Poe's reputation, felt it his duty to warn him about it. Poe angrily retorted:

> You are a physician, and I presume no physician can have difficulty in detecting the *drunkard* at a glance. You are, moreover, a literary man, well read in morals. You will never be brought to believe that I could write what I daily write, as I write it, were I as this villain would induce those who know me not, to believe. In fine, I pledge you, before God, the solemn word of a gentleman, that I am temperate even to rigor. From the hour in which I first saw this basest of calumniators to the hour in which I retired from his office in uncontrollable disgust at his chicanery, arrogance, ignorance and brutality, *nothing stronger than water ever passed my lips*.
>
> It is, however, due to candor that I inform you upon what foundation he has erected his slanders. At no period of my life was I ever what men call intemperate. I never was in the habit of intoxication. I never drunk drams, &c. But, for a brief period, while I resided in Richmond, and edited the *Messenger*, I certainly did give way, at long intervals, to the temptation held out on all sides by the spirit of Southern conviviality. My sensitive temperament could not stand an excitement which was an everyday matter to my companions. In short, it sometimes happened that I was completely intoxicated. For some days after each excess I was invariably confined to bed. But it is now quite four years since I have abandoned every kind of alcoholic drink – four years, with the exception of a single deviation, which occurred shortly after my leaving Burton, and when I was induced to resort to the occasional use of cider, with the hope of relieving a nervous attack.

For the April issue of *Graham's Magazine* Poe had written one of his most famous tales, 'The Murders in the Rue Morgue'.[2] Here he introduced the Chevalier C. Auguste Dupin, prototype of Sherlock

Holmes, who had all of the latter's analytical powers. Poe plays the part of Watson. Possessed of incredible powers of deduction (once following the train of Poe's thoughts just as Holmes would later do with Watson), Dupin was often enlisted by the Prefect of Police (Poe's Lastrade equivalent) to solve knotty problems. In this story two grotesque murders have been committed in a room to which there is seemingly no ingress; we follow Dupin's reasoning as he eventually solves the puzzle. The perpetrator turns out to have been an escaped orang-utan. The tale was a great success. Later, Conan Doyle said: 'Edgar Allan Poe was father of the detective tale, and covered its limits so completely I fail to see how his followers can find ground to call their own.'[3]

John McKenzie travelled to see Poe around this time, and Poe had the chance to see his sister Rosalie ('Rose'), who spent a week with the family while McKenzie travelled to Boston on business. It must have cheered Poe to see his sister again, and he wrote about it to his old friend Thomas Wyatt.

In the April issue, Poe proved that he was still a showman and an audience-grabber. He issued a challenge: he would solve any cryptogram, and the key phrase 'may be either in French, Italian, Spanish, German, Latin or Greek'. This was an incredible boast, and the New Yorkers must have been waiting for him to slip on his own banana skin. But he proved that he was possessed of an extraordinary ability to solve such riddles, and his skill amazed everyone who tried to outwit him. Perhaps readers had simply assumed him to be a poet and writer of romance – he now proved he had a precise mathematical mind.

This was not the only sensational idea he had for selling magazines. Charles Dickens had begun to serialize his book *Barnaby Rudge* and had so far published three chapters.[4] Somewhat egotistically, Poe boasted that he could deduce the full plot of the novel simply from the work he had before him. This he did in the same issue, and although his speculation was not perfect it was close enough to Dickens's design that it had the author wondering if Poe was the Devil.

Poe set about his usual task of drumming up support for *Graham's*, and as he looked through the list of possibles he must have shuddered when he saw the name Henry Wadsworth Longfellow. He had already taken Longfellow to task in his reviews and in terms unlikely to be soon forgiven. Still, he took a deep breath and wrote, mentioning that he had 'no reason to think myself favourably known to you'. Professor

Longfellow replied to Poe's request in the most generous terms: 'You are mistaken in supposing that you are not "favorably known to me." On the contrary, all that I have read, from your pen, has inspired me with a high idea of your power; and I think you are destined to stand among the first romance-writers of the country, if such be your aim.'

Next Poe met someone who would play an important part in his life and a more important role after his death, the Reverend Rufus Wilmot Griswold. Griswold was a journalist and anthologist, and they met through their journalistic careers. He was compiling *The Poets and Poetry of America*,[5] and Poe had little reason to admire him, being, as he was, a close friend of the New York clique. However, Poe had left two letters of introduction; so Griswold visited him and they talked literature. In his first letter to Griswold, Poe writes: 'Dr Griswold, Will you be kind enough to lend me the No. of the Family Magazine of which we spoke – if you have received it? I would be much obliged, also, if not, at any new book of interest. Truly yours, Poe.' Now Griswold contacted Poe asking for contributions for his forthcoming anthology, for he was an astute critic and appreciated Poe's talent. Poe was proud to send him some examples, from which Griswold could choose whichever took his fancy.

Poe's friend Frederick Thomas proved a continual and wordy letter-writer. Through Thomas Poe had met Jesse Dow, a convivial, amiable type who took Poe's fancy; as Poe's friendship with Thomas increased, so did his friendship with Dow. After Harrison's success and Tyler's inauguration, both Thomas and Dow had been given government posts, Thomas in the Treasury Department. Thomas wrote regularly throughout May 1841, mostly small talk and of happenings in the government offices. Dow's success had been short lived, as he had been dismissed. It seems that, as a writer, he could not resist discussing politics out of court and so made himself unpopular among those in power. It was a sad time for Dow, as he had a wife and three children to support.

Being in the government buildings, Thomas saw a great deal of what went on in the corridors of power and felt that the characters he constantly met there provided wonderful material for an author. Thomas was always a great source of interesting news. For example, the controversy over the Second National Bank was still raging. Moreover, Henry Clay, who supported the bank, was now trying to pass legislation to safeguard copyright. That, thought Thomas, was surely worth a Poe editorial.

Among other such snippets of information, Thomas suddenly ended a letter with a proposition which came at Poe out of the blue and left him in deep thought.

> How would you like to be an office holder here at $1500 per year payable monthly by Uncle Sam who, however slack he may be to his general creditors, pays his officials with due punctuality. How would you like it? You stroll to your office a little after nine in the morning leisurely, and you stroll from it a little after two in the afternoon homeward to dinner, and return no more that day. If during office hours you have anything to do it is an agreeable relaxation from the monstrous laziness of the day. You have on your desk everything in the writing line in apple-pie order, and if you choose to lucubrate in a literary way, why you can lucubrate. Come on and apply for a clerkship, you can follow literature here as well as where you are, and think of the money to be made by it. 'Think of that, Master Brooke,' as Sir John sayeth – write to me if you love me on the reception of this.

This was no pipe-dream. A clerkship could indeed be had – and it would put an end to Poe's financial worries as well as allowing him time to continue with his literary work. Not only that, but Poe had friends on the inside, as it were, who were willing to advance his application – and if he became successful as an editor or writer, why, he could resign. Such a safety-net was just what Poe needed, and he wanted to know more about it from his wordy friend.

Thomas had been unwell, as he often was, but soon resumed his correspondence. Aside from the government sinecure, Thomas wanted to see Poe at the head of a leading journal. The only way for him to move ahead would be to carve out a reputation for himself:

> You must get afloat by yourself, Poe – or some friend with you – who would contribute not by intellectuality, but by popularity to your joint publication as much as in him is, to your work. I believe such a publication with your acknowledged talent in it, would contribute greatly not only to your popularity but to that of the literature of the west . . .

'You must get afloat by yourself, Poe – or some friend with you.' For a dizzy moment it seemed that Poe's dream might come true, because it looked as though Graham had given provisional agreement to publish the precious *Penn* with Poe. Poe had discussed every aspect with him – and even though the journal promised to be expensive and difficult to launch, Graham could see that if anyone could pull it off, that man was Poe. No sooner had Poe convinced Graham of the potential of the plan than a mail-shot was sent to everyone Poe could think of, including Washington Irving, Henry Longfellow, John P. Kennedy, Fitz-Greene Halleck and James F. Cooper.

Although he spoke of Graham with a friendly tone, some world-weariness was creeping into Poe's letters. He was once again tired of eking out a living for others and longed for his independence. It was the same as it was on the *Southern Literary Messenger*, and, like White, Graham was at least civil and kind. The more despondent Poe got, the more he thought of what Thomas had written concerning the government job. It could solve so many problems for him. As if to accentuate such a possibility, Thomas had just stepped into a job for $1,000 per annum. His position was only temporary, but he was sure that Poe could indeed get something. There was one man who could undoubtedly assist him – John P. Kennedy, who was, after all, a Congressman . . .

Kennedy! Of course! Did Kennedy not first help him out of the gutter and into a job at White's? Unfortunately, Poe was too poor to make the journey to Washington, but he asked Thomas to approach Kennedy and seek his assistance, as well as that of the Secretary of War. After a short delay, it seemed that Poe was in luck. Although Thomas hadn't seen Kennedy yet, he was due to see the President's son. With Thomas working on Poe's behalf, the chances of his getting the position were very good indeed. Soon Poe received more positive news from his friend; he was full of optimism – but there would be delays. Kennedy had promised to do all he could, and the President's son was behind him. Besides, his 'cryptography' column was causing quite a stir in the corridors of government.

So Poe had to wait. Meanwhile he picked up his correspondence with Snodgrass and discussed his recent work. Willis Gaylord Clark, editor of the *Philadelphia Gazette* (and twin brother of Lewis), criticized Poe for speaking favourably of the poet McJilton even though he had described the man's work thus: 'There are always fine imaginative passages: – but their merit is scarcely discernible through the clouds of verbiage, false imagery, bad grammar, and worse versification in which they are enveloped.' Snodgrass had also praised Poe for his tale 'Descent into the Maelstrom'. Poe disagreed, feeling that 'it was finished in a hurry, and therefore its conclusion is imperfect'. The self-criticism is fair, but the build-up of excitement in the first part of the story is marvellous, as the fishermen have lost sense of time and find themselves facing the terrible whirlpool. The ending is just too technical and mathematical – dispassionate, compared to the atmosphere carefully constructed in the foregoing work.

For that month's issue of *Graham's* Poe wrote a review of Wilmer's *Quacks of Helicon*, in which several leading poets are criticized. Poe did not like having to pan his old friend's work, especially as the theme (an attack on the literary cliques) was so congenial to him; but his duty was sacrosanct. So he pulled Wilmer up for 'imitation, for vulgarity, for the gross obscenity, the filth' and for 'indiscriminate censure . . . It will not do in a civilized land to run a-muck like a Malay. Mr Morris *has* written good songs. Mr Bryant is not *all* a fool. Mr Willis is not *quite* an ass. Mr Longfellow *will* steal, but perhaps he cannot help it, (for we have heard of such things).' A run-of-the-mill critique, as far as it went. But the subject matter was much more appealing to Poe, and he used it to fire damaging broadsides against the power of the clique. And he did so with a sure aim and a steady hand:

> We repeat it: – *it is* the truth which he has spoken, and who shall contradict us? He has said unscrupulously what every reasonable man among us has long known to be 'as true as the Pentateuch' – that, as a literary people, we are one vast perambulating humbug. He has asserted that we are *clique*-ridden, and who does not smile at the obvious truism of that assertion? He maintains that chicanery is, with us, a far surer road than talent to distinction in letters. Who gainsays this? The corrupt nature of our ordinary criticism has become notorious. Its powers have been prostrated by its own arm. The intercourse between critic and publisher, as it now almost universally stands, is comprised either in the paying and pocketing of black mail, as the price of a simple forbearance, or in a direct system of petty and contemptible bribery, properly so called – a system even more injurious than the former to the true interests of the public, and more degrading to the buyers and sellers of good opinion, on account of the more positive character of the service here rendered for the consideration received. We laugh at the idea of any denial of our assertions upon this topic; they are infamously true. In the charge of general corruption there are undoubtedly many noble exceptions to be made. There are, indeed, some very few editors, who, maintaining an entire independence, will receive no books from publishers at all, or who receive them

> with a perfect understanding, on the part of these latter, that an unbiassed *critique* will be given. But these cases are insufficient to have much effect on the popular mistrust: a mistrust heightened by late exposure of the machinations of *coteries* in New York – *coteries* which, at the bidding of leading booksellers, manufacture, as required from time to time, a pseudo-public opinion by wholesale, for the benefit of any little hanger on of the party, or pettifogging protector of the firm.[6]

It was time for Poe to consider his options. For the present he was working for *Graham's*, and that could not immediately be changed. Second, he had at least a good chance of getting a government clerkship, which would at once relieve him of financial problems. Third, he could continue to work towards becoming a celebrated author. To do the last, he had to get his work before the public; and as he had written eight more tales since his last published volume he considered that now might be the time to try again. So he wrote to his publishers; but Lea & Blanchard's reply was less than encouraging, and Poe discovered that the last edition of his tales had not yet been sold. 'In answer we very much regret to say that the state of affairs is such as to give little encouragement to new undertakings. As yet we have not got through the edition of the other work & up to this time it has not returned to us the expense of its publication.' This was another great disappointment to Poe, and he had to settle down and earn while he awaited news of the government job. He racked his brain to think of ideas for *Graham's*; he resurrected the old 'Autography' series with new characters, gathering more signatures as he awaited news from Thomas.[7]

Griswold intended to include Frederick Thomas in his *Poets and Poetry of America* and approached Poe to write his biography, to which he readily agreed and immediately wrote to Thomas for some details. Thomas replied with a very long history of himself and his family. Poe had meanwhile used his expertise to crack a code sent by him, which greatly impressed him: 'I do not wonder that you have been annoyed by cryptographic connoisseurs. Your astonishing power of deciphering secret writing is to me a puzzle which I can't solve. That's a curious head-piece of yours, and I should like to know what phrenologists say about it. Did you ever have your head examined?'

Thomas was also asking a favour: he wanted to get a song published. Poe found a publisher by the name of 'Willig', who 'says he cannot afford to give anything for it beyond a few copies – but will promise to get it up handsomely'. He adds: 'I received your last some days ago, and have delayed answering it, in hope that I might say your song was out, and that I might give you my opinion and Virginia's about its merits.' Too many people consider Virginia a mere child, almost a dumb witness to all that went on. Admittedly she was a quiet girl, but she could sing well and play the piano, as well as having an appreciation of music, and Poe genuinely valued her opinion. By this time she had passed her nineteenth birthday and was a cultured young lady.

Over the months Poe had increased the sales of *Graham's* from 5,000 to 25,000, and he was frustrated that he could not do the same for a magazine of his own. Between November 1841 and January 1842 he published his second series of articles on 'Autography'. It followed a similar format as before, but now he took a stab at some of the New York coterie, including his old opponents Theodore Fay and Colonel Stone. Of Fay he wrote:

> The author of 'Norman Leslie' and 'The Countess Ida' has been more successful as an essayist about small matters, than as a novelist. 'Norman Leslie' is more familiarly remembered as 'The Great Used Up,' while 'The Countess' made no definite impression whatever. Of course we are not to expect remarkable features in Mr Fay's MS. It has a wavering, finicky, and over-delicate air, without pretension to either grace or force; and the description of the chirography would answer, without alteration, for that of the literary character. Mr F. frequently employs an amanuensis, who writes a very beautiful French hand. The one must not be confounded with the other.[8]

These columns were making Poe more famous by the day. As Thomas next wrote: 'You, my dear Poe, have a very high reputation here among the literati and more than once in "dining out" I have discussed you and made conversational capital out of you – If I were permanently fixed in office, I could get leave of absence, without stoppage of pay, and then I could slip on to the city of brotherly love and shake you by the hand. God bless you.'

The Poes were a sociable family and often asked friends and family over for evening get-togethers. These included literary friends Poe had made, including Frederick Thomas and Thomas Dunn English, as well as other authors. Henry B. Hirst was a regular visitor who liked to arrive on Sunday mornings, when the two men would go walking.

Poe did not reply to Thomas's letter straight away because at one of their soirées Virginia had been singing and playing for their visitors; Poe loved to see his wife entertain, as she was a good singer and everyone seemed to love her. On this night, just as they were all enjoying a song, Virginia stopped and coughed violently. Blood streamed into her mouth, and Poe ran to her rescue. According to him, she had 'burst a blood vessel in her throat'. After this episode she was very ill, and Poe was devastated. He told Thomas about it a fortnight afterwards. Virginia was never to completely recover her health.

The day after Virginia became ill Poe went to Graham and asked for an advance of salary, but he was refused. To take his mind off things, he turned to work. Perhaps he was not in the best humour when he picked up *Wakondah* by Cornelius Mathews, but he gave it a ferocious drubbing. 'We should be delighted to proceed – but how? to applaud – but what? Surely not this trumpery declamation, this maudlin sentiment, this metaphor run-mad, this twaddling verbiage, this halting and doggerel rhythm, this unintelligible rant and cant!'[9] It is greatly to Mathews's credit that he bore no animosity towards Poe for such a damning critique.

Poe was determined to publish his own magazine at any cost and even contemplated approaching President Tyler's son, Robert, who was known to Thomas, to see if he would have any interest in some kind of partnership. Poe wrote to Thomas, in a strange mood half of depression and half of business, and suggested Tyler's involvement. It came to nothing. It may seem strange, perhaps even cold, that Poe should give the business of the magazine and borrowing money top priority when his wife was lying sick. But it was for that very reason that he needed money. He was not a rich man – constantly in debt – and had to raise money for medicine and for food, so that he could look after Virginia properly. As it transpired, he was again doomed to disappointment – Tyler was willing to help with articles but no more. Poe's only hope of salvation was the chance of that government post.

Charles Dickens visited America, arriving early in January 1842 and toured around; Poe asked to meet him. Dickens replied:

> March 6, 1842.
> My Dear Sir,
> I shall be very glad to see you whenever you will do me the favor to call. I think I am more likely to be in the way between half-past eleven and twelve, than at any other time. I have glanced over the books you

have been so kind as to send me, and more particularly at the papers to which you called my attention. I have the greater pleasure in expressing my desire to see you on this account.

Faithfully yours always,
Charles Dickens

They did meet, and seem to have got along very well, although there is no record of their meeting; they subsequently maintained a mutual respect. Dickens took away a copy of *Tales of the Grotesque and Arabesque* and tried to find a publisher for it in England. As with most of Poe's hopes, this was destined to be dashed, however.

Poe was next attempting to get his new story, 'The Pit and the Pendulum', published. Although this was another of his masterpieces, set in Castile in the time of the Spanish Inquisition, he was finding it hard to drum up any interest at all.[10]

In fact, this minor problem was a minor irritant on top of a larger sore. He had reached the end of his tether. All his past misgivings now came back to him, and he felt he could go no further. He had tired of the magazine and its poor quality (even though his own contributions had been of a constantly high standard), and he was tired of doing a tough job of work for a pittance. Graham's refusal to give him an advance still rankled, though in no other way had he shown any animosity towards Poe. Besides, it is highly likely that Poe wanted to spend more time with his sick wife. So he decided to quit his job. Perhaps he thought that his success in building up the circulation of the magazine would open doors to other employment. It didn't. Poe and Graham parted on good terms. Later, Graham described him as 'a quiet, unobtrusive, thoughtful scholar', 'a devoted husband' and 'the soul of honour'. There was no question of Poe drinking or behaving in any way other than as a professional gentleman.

His successor at *Graham's Magazine* was Rufus Wilmot Griswold. Negotiations had begun in April, and Griswold was offered $1,000, $200 more than Poe. Enmity began to develop between the two men.

9

THE VALLEY OF UNREST

Frederick Thomas did not have the money to help Poe launch the *Penn*, but he did have news about the prospect of a government job. He had been speaking to the President's son Robert, and now wrote to his friend:

> Last night I was speaking of you, and took occasion to suggest that a situation in the Custom House, Philadelphia, might be acceptable to you, as Lamb (Charles) had held a somewhat similar appointment, etc., and as it would leave you leisure to pursue your literary pursuits. Robert replied that he felt confident that such a situation could be obtained for you in the course of two or three months at farthest, as certain vacancies would then occur.

For a while things began to look a little brighter. Virginia seemed to be better, and now there was a good job on the horizon. But future prospects do not pay bills, and the family had to face the fact that money was scarce. They moved from Coates Street to North 7 Street, Spring Garden – not as pleasant, maybe, but at least a home. Eventually Maria took in lodgers.

Poe wrote back to Thomas as quickly as he could. The lengths that his friend was going to to help him touched him to the heart. As for the Custom House job – of course he would be interested in it.

> What you say respecting a situation in the Custom House here, gives me new life. Nothing could more precisely meet my views. Could I obtain such an appointment, I would be enabled thoroughly to carry out all my ambitious projects. It would relieve me of all care as regards a mere subsistence, and thus allow me time for thought,

which, in fact, is action. I repeat that I would ask for nothing farther or better than a situation such as you mention. If the salary will barely enable me to live I shall be content. Will you say as much for me to Mr Tyler, and express to him my sincere gratitude for the interest he takes in my welfare?

I am rejoiced to say that my dear little wife is much better, and I have strong hope of her ultimate recovery. She desires her kindest regards – as also Mrs Clemm.

In another letter to a friend, James Herron, a civil engineer in Washington, Poe gave an insight into his feelings at the time. Virginia's illness tormented him, and he had abandoned all work. At times he took to drink. Now Virginia had had a fresh bleed from the lungs. This was no simple ruptured blood vessel. Perhaps deep down Poe dreaded what it might be; and memories may have stirred of a young boy sitting by his mother's death bed. Perhaps his wife had contracted tuberculosis. That his love for the lady Virginia was real and deep can be seen in Graham's reminiscence: 'His love for his wife was a sort of rapturous worship of the spirit of beauty that he felt was fading before his eyes.'[1] He could not bear to see Virginia so ill. There was only one hope – the Custom House job. With that he could again take care of his family.

You have learned, perhaps, that I have retired from '*Graham's Magazine*'. The state of my mind has, in fact, forced me to abandon, for the present, all mental exertion. The renewed and hopeless illness of my wife, ill health on my own part, and pecuniary embarrassments, have nearly driven me to distraction. My only hope of relief is the 'Bankrupt Act', of which I shall avail myself as soon as possible. Had I resolved upon this at an earlier day, I might now have been doing well – but the struggle to keep up has, at length, entirely ruined me. I have left myself without even the means of availing myself of the act . . .

You will be pleased to hear that I have the promise of a situation in our Custom-House. The offer was entirely unexpected & gratuitous. I am to receive the appointment upon removal of several incumbents – the removal to be certainly made in a month. I am indebted to the personal friendship of Robert Tyler. If I really receive the appointment all may yet go well. The labors of the office are by no means onerous and I shall have time enough to spare for other pursuits. Please mention nothing of this – for, after all, I may be disappointed.

> Mrs Poe is again dangerously ill with hemorrhage from the lungs. It is folly to hope.

Sick or not, Poe had to rouse himself from his torpor and earn some money. Given the success of the detective story 'The Murders in the Rue Morgue', Poe decided to resurrect sleuth C. Auguste Dupin and employed the interesting idea of using his powers to solve a contemporary murder, that of cigar-girl Mary Rogers. Poe offered the tale, 'The Mystery of Marie Rogêt', to George Roberts, editor of the *Boston Mammoth Notion*, for half price. It was refused. Poe then turned to his old friend Snodgrass, to whom he offered the tale for a mere $40.[2]

Meanwhile the enmity between himself and Griswold had grown. Daniel Bryan had sent Poe some verses, addressing them to *Graham's*, but Poe had never received them. As the package had been sent to *Graham's*, he concluded that Griswold had been opening his mail. This was just another example, in Poe's eyes, of Griswold's untrustworthiness. By now he had come to consider Griswold's anthology as biased, produced in concert with the New York clan. Such a collaboration would never be seen in his own *Penn*, when it appeared.

> I am anxious, above all things, to render the journal one in which the true, in contradistinction from the merely factitious, genius of the country shall be represented. I shall yield nothing to great names – nor to the circumstances of position. I shall make war to the knife against the New-England assumption of 'all the decency and all the talent' which has been so disgustingly manifested in the Rev. Rufus W. Griswold's 'Poets & Poetry of America'.

Even now he was still confident of pulling off the *Penn* project. The lack of money did not deter him; should he get together a large enough list of subscribers, he could interest a backer in investing. Poe had contacted Graham, who had by now turned down the idea of the *Penn*, the reason (according to Poe) being that Poe had made a great success of his own magazine, and his own success had worked against him.

Poe had more on his mind than literary matters, magazines and his growing dislike of Rufus Griswold. He was still desperately worried about his wife, he had virtually no money and had health problems of his own. He resorted to writing to friends asking for cash. These pleading letters are often seen as low and ignoble, but the reason he wrote them was sheer need. He had no choice. There were times when he could only survive by begging – yet, apart from episodes of drinking, he applied himself well, wrote constantly, and throughout his life he tried to map out a career for his own sake and his family's.

One thing, apart from the chimerical *Penn*, kept his optimism going, and that was the Washington job. To enlist more help he wrote again to James Herron, to ask if he could oil some cogs; also, could he also lend some money to see him through these hard times? Herron was ready to help as best he could and did whatever was in his power; he went to see Robert Tyler, the President's son, and seemed to get certain assurances. He also sent Poe $20. As always when helped, Poe seems both grateful and slightly embarrassed.

> I am more deeply indebted to you than I can express, and in this I really mean what I say. Without your prompt and unexpected interposition with Mr Tyler, it is by no means improbable that I should have failed in obtaining the appointment which has now become so vitally necessary to me; but now I feel assured of success. The $20, also, will enable me to overcome other difficulties – and, I repeat, that I thank you from the bottom of my heart. You have shown yourself a true friend.

Poe had annoyed Thomas Holley Chivers with one of his 'Autography' articles, in which he summarized the poet's handwriting to ascertain his merits and character:

> His productions affect one as a wild dream – strange, incongruous, full of images of more than arabesque monstrosity, and snatches of sweet unsustained song. Even his worst nonsense (and some of it is horrible) has an indefinite charm of sentiment and melody. We can never be sure that there is any meaning in his words – neither is there any meaning in many of our finest musical airs – but the effect is very similar in both. His figures of speech are metaphor run mad, and his grammar is often none at all. Yet there are as fine individual passages to be found in the poems of Dr Chivers, as in those of any poet whatsoever.[3]

Chivers does not seem to have been mortally offended – he had submitted an article thinking Poe was still editing *Graham's* – but guessing that he was annoyed (and wanting his help), Poe writes to him by way of apology.

The paper had scarcely gone to press before I saw and acknowledged to myself the injustice I had done you – an injustice which it is my full purpose to repair at the first opportunity. What I said of your grammatical errors arose from some imperfect recollections of one or two poems sent to the first volume of the *S.L. Messenger*. But in more important respects I now deeply feel that I have wronged you by a hasty opinion . . .

As I have no money myself, it will be absolutely necessary that I procure a partner who has some pecuniary means. I mention this to you – for it is not impossible that you yourself may have both the will & the ability to join me. The first number will not appear until January, so that I shall have time to look about me.

Chivers was not unmoved by Poe's letter, and accepted his offer of friendship. He had indeed been somewhat irritated by the autography article, which led to his comment:

I receive, with grateful pleasure, your polite remarks in regard to the autograph article. I had always spoken so highly of your talents as a poet, and the best critic in this Country, that, when my friends saw it, believing you were what I represented you to be, they came almost to the conclusion that they were not only mistaken, but that I was a bad writer, and a fit subject for the Insane Hospital.

I shall ever take great pride in acknowledging you the noblest of all my friends. May all your days be forever brightened by the sunshine of prosperity; and if there should ever come over you a cloud, may it overshadow you like the wing of an Angel, which, when it has departed, lets down from heaven a tenfold radiance to light you round about.

Poe's finances were by now desperate. He wrote to the editors of the *Democratic Review* admitting as much and enclosed an article, 'Landscape Garden', asking no price and leaving the question of remuneration to them.[4]

Around this time he wrote a short note that has achieved a certain fame. The text simply ran: 'It gives me pleasure to comply with the very flattering request embodied in your letter of June 18th. My absence from this city will, I hope, serve as sufficient apology for the tardiness of this reply.' It was written on 18 July 1842 to Oscar T. Keeler. Keeler was an avid autograph hunter from 1838 until about 1868. This letter, well preserved, became known as the 'Philadelphia Shroud' because it has a faint imprint of Poe on it. But the existence of the ghostly image is easy to explain – it was kept in contact with a portrait of Poe for many years.

Virginia, oscillating between ill health and slight improvement, had now taken a turn for the worse, so Poe made further efforts to advance his career in the two directions open to him – the new magazine and the government job. As to the first, in the *New York Mirror* Poe once again announced that the *Penn* was back in business. Concerning the second, he renewed correspondence with Thomas, from whom he had heard nothing for some time. He told a strange and true anecdote about Griswold. He had considered writing a review of Griswold's anthology for the *Democratic Review* but found that someone else had done it before him. He mentioned this to Griswold, who suggested Poe simply write the review and leave the publication to himself – he would see that Poe got the payment due as well as a charge for his labour. Poe was surprised at this open bribe, but being short of money he agreed, writing the review just as he would have done if Griswold was not paying him and, according to him, with little praise in it. Poe also told Thomas that he himself had annoyed Griswold by not replying promptly enough to his request for information on the poetess Amelia Ball Welby. According to Poe, Graham wanted him back, as he was not pleased with Griswold's work.

The Custom House appointment was approaching fast, and Poe thought again about the *Penn*. Although he would soon have time on his hands, and a salary, he still needed capital. He discussed his situation with his new friend Chivers and calculated that he needed a capital of $1,000 to ensure success. And who better placed to aid him than the now-rich Chivers.

> The only real difficulty lies in the beginning – in the pecuniary means for getting out the two (or three) first numbers; after this all is sure, and a great triumph may, and indeed will be achieved. If you can command about $1000 and say that you will join me, I will write you fully as respects the details of the plan, or we can have an immediate interview . . .
>
> I repeat that it would give me the most sincere pleasure if you would make up your mind to join me. I am sure of our community of thought & feeling, and that we would accomplish *much*.

He now had the *Penn* bit once again between the teeth and was planning a new prospectus. For a short while things suddenly began to look up. Just before the week of the Custom House appointment, he learned that James Russell Lowell was about to publish a new journal, the *Pioneer*.

Lowell had had a chequered career to date. After graduating from Harvard he became a jack of all trades, his career vacillating between the law and business; he also wrote several pieces for magazines and became known as one of the Fireside Poets. In 1840 he had become engaged to Maria White, who was a great beauty and a strong influence on his life. The year before he set up the *Pioneer* he had published a volume entitled *A Year's Life*.

Poe was quick to enquire about the possibility of working for the new magazine to earn money while he awaited the outcome of his various projects:

> Nov 16 1842
> Dear Sir,
> Learning your design of commencing a Magazine, in Boston, upon the first of January next, I take the liberty of asking whether some arrangement might not be made, by which I should become a regular contributor.
>
> I should be glad to furnish a short article each month – of such character as might be suggested by yourself – and upon such terms as you could afford 'in the beginning'.
>
> That your success will be marked and permanent I will not doubt. At all events, I most sincerely wish you well; for no man in America has excited in me so much of admiration – and, therefore, none so much of respect and esteem – as the author of 'Rosaline'.

The time for making government appointments was coming round, and Poe awaited the results anxiously. On 14 November Thomas wrote to him to tell him that the positions were about to be filled. When the newspapers arrived he searched through them, finding that there had been four removals appointments. Among the names he found that a post had been given to a certain 'Pogue'; thinking the likeness to his own name too much of a coincidence, Poe rushed to the Custom House to get clarification.

He met the official in charge of the collectorship, a man by the name of Smith, who was hassled and busy. Poe did discover, however, that there was no one called Pogue, so the name must have been a mistake; obviously someone had misheard his name being pronounced and misspelt it. Smith was not an easy man to deal with, and under the impression that Poe had been appointed he told him that he would call for him when the time came for him to be sworn into office. After two days, still hearing nothing, Poe once again returned to the Custom House and accosted Smith, asking in a friendly fashion whether he had any good news for him.

> He replied – 'No, I am instructed to make no more removals.' At this, being much astonished, I mentioned that I had heard, through a friend, from Mr Rob. Tyler, that he was requested to appoint me. At these words he said roughly, – 'From *whom* did you say?' I replied from Mr Robert Tyler. I wish you could have seen the scoundrel – for scoundrel, my dear Thomas in your private ear, *he is* – 'From Robert Tyler!' says he – 'hem! I have received orders from *President* Tyler to make no more appointments and shall make none.' Immediately afterward, he acknowledged that he had made one appt *since* these instructions.

Disappointment was to follow disappointment. Hardly had he time to consider this blow when another hope was dashed. Charles Dickens had promised to aid Poe however he could and had made extensive efforts to get his book into print. But even his illustrious name had not forced the issue through, and Dickens had to admit failure:

> I have mentioned it to publishers with whom I have influence, but they have, one and all, declined the venture. And the only consolation I can give you is that I do not believe any collection of detached pieces by an unknown writer, even though he were an Englishman, would be at all likely to find a publisher in this metropolis just now.
>
> Do not for a moment suppose that I have ever thought of you but with a pleasant recollection; and that I am not at all times prepared to forward your views in this country, if I can.

It is hard not to sympathize with Poe; and under these hard blows of fate he would resort to drink. It was a time in his life when he needed hope and something to lighten his spirits; some good news about the *Penn*, perhaps – he had been expecting a letter from Chivers any day. But when it did come it was hardly the cheering words he had expected, the flowing humour of Chivers's usual banter. It was written in Chivers's style, but the subject was sombre. His little three-year-old daughter had died, and Chivers poured out his agony:

> Now my hope is dead – the beautiful saintly winged dove which soared so high from the earth – luring my impatient soul to wander, delighted, from prospect to prospect – has been wounded in her midway flight to heaven by the keen icy arrows of Death! My anticipations are sorrowful – every thing in the round world is dark to me! The little tender innocent blue-eyed daughter of my heart – the soul of my own soul – the life of my own life – 'my joy, my food, my all – the world' – is dead!

Poe had written 'The Tell-Tale Heart', one of his best tales about a monomaniac who murders an old man because of a hatred for his 'filmed' eye; buries him under the boards; but when the police arrive he hears the beating of the corpse's heart and confesses his crime to them. It has a strong psychological feel to it and sits well even with modern horror stories. Poe submitted the tale to the *Boston Miscellany*, not realizing that H.T. Tuckerman was the present editor; he had panned Tuckerman in his 'Autography' series by stating: 'He is a correct writer so far as mere English is concerned, but an insufferably tedious and dull one.' The tedious and dull writer accordingly rejected the tale.

At the nadir of Poe's misfortunes, hope began to peer through the mist. One glimmer of sunlight for Poe was brought by Lowell, who had agreed to print Poe's work. The rate of pay was not great; he would receive only $10 for 'The Tell-Tale Heart',[5] but it was a much-needed $10. Poe went on to send more contributions, and for a while the journal seemed to flourish. He also sent contributions to other magazines, such as 'The Pit and the Pendulum', which he finally sold to the *Gift*.

Even a small income was welcome, as Virginia was still ill. She was popular with all who met her, and many people sent worried notes asking after her. For example, to a Jane Clark, Poe wrote this reply: 'I am happy to say that our dear Virginia's cough is much better and we have great hopes of her speedy recovery.' It was still an anxious time for him, but at least there seemed to be some kind of stability, and although there were times of wild desperation he usually came to terms with his wife's sickness. He was in especially good spirits whenever she felt better.

Now came a piece of news which elated him. Indeed it was a turning-point for him. He had been in discussion with Thomas Cottrell Clarke, erstwhile editor of the *Saturday Evening Post* who now published the *Saturday Museum* of Philadelphia, and the main topic had been the establishment of a new magazine, the *Stylus* (*Penn* was thought too provincial, too local a name). Poe of course had all the facts and figures in his head, and he once more argued for a journal of which the American public could be proud; not cheap but of the highest quality. Hadn't he been solely responsible for the huge increase in circulation not only of the *Southern Literary Messenger* but also of the *Gentleman's Magazine*? The testimonials he had from a multitude of sources would have proved his reputation as well as his drawing power. The success of such a magazine would be assured; and, as Clarke was a publisher already, some costs could be effectively cut at the start.

Thomas Clarke was a man of business and was persuaded by Poe's strong business plan. He was very impressed by Poe's track record, so much so that he was willing to make an offer. Clarke would be willing to join Poe in this literary venture, and the prospectus could therefore be prepared. Illustrator Felix Darley was to do the artwork.[6] But there was a proviso – that Poe allow his name to appear as a member of the *Saturday Museum* staff. This was an interesting development, in that it proves just how much Poe's name was worth, in spite of the broadsides fired at him by the powerful New York clique. Poe had taken them on fearlessly and recklessly and had emerged victorious. It had been some achievement. Papers were signed on 31 January 1843 by Poe, Clarke and Darley, and witnessed by Poe's friend Henry B. Hirst and W.D. Riebsam.

As part of his inauguration as a nominal member of staff, it was required that the journal should furnish a biography of Poe, so he was asked to have one prepared. Poe approached Thomas, who was flattered by the request but had to turn it down, pleading pressure of work. So Poe turned to his friend Hirst, who still visited the family and went for his walks with Poe. Hirst agreed and began work on the text straight away. A portrait was also made for the occasion; Poe was far from impressed by it, but it was too late to change it. He thought it was more like a caricature: 'I am ugly enough God knows, but not quite so bad as that.'

He was just as excited about the *Stylus* as he was about the *Penn* – more so, as he now had sound financial backing. The prospectus appeared in the *Saturday Museum* on 4 March 1843:

PROSPECTUS OF THE STYLUS:
A Monthly Journal of General Literature

TO BE EDITED BY EDGAR A. POE.
And Published, in the City of Philadelphia, by
CLARKE & POE.

Poe began by explaining the change of name. 'The *Penn Magazine*,' it had been thought, was a name somewhat too local in its suggestions, and 'the *Stylus*' had been finally adopted.

> It will include about one hundred royal octavo pages, in single column, per month; forming two thick volumes per year. In its mechanical appearance – in its typography, paper and binding – it will far surpass all American journals of its kind. Engravings, when used, will be in the highest style of Art, but are promised only in obvious illustration of the text, and in strict keeping with the Magazine character . . . the price will be Five Dollars per annum, or Three Dollars per single volume, in advance.

He had hit upon the idea of introducing biographical and critical sketches of authors, and the New York clan must have shuddered when they contemplated what Poe was up to.

> An important feature of the work, and one which will be introduced in the opening number, will be a series of Critical and Biographical Sketches of American Writers. These Sketches will be accompanied with full length and characteristic portraits; will include every person of literary note in America; and will investigate carefully, and with rigorous impartiality, the individual claims of each.

The concluding paragraph was another veiled snipe at the cliques:

> It shall, in fact, be the chief purpose of 'The *Stylus*,' to become known as a journal wherein may be found, at all times, upon all subjects within its legitimate reach, a sincere and a fearless opinion. It shall be a leading object to assert in precept, and to maintain in practice, the rights, while, in effect, it demonstrates the advantages, of an absolutely independent criticism; – a criticism self-sustained; guiding itself only by the purest rules of Art; analyzing and urging these rules as it applies them; holding itself aloof from all personal bias; and acknowledging no fear save that of outraging the Right.[7]

Things now happened with amazing speed. Through Thomas's intercession Poe was again given a chance of a government job. Once more Thomas had had a long chat with Robert Tyler, and explained how Poe was not given the Custom House job in spite of Tyler's recommendation. Thomas stressed Poe's reliability and good standing in society – he showed him Poe's biography as written in the *Museum* and mentioned his station in American life – that he was about to edit the most influential magazine in the country's history. Having heard all of this and after reading the prospectus, Robert Tyler was impressed and agreed that Poe was just the kind of man the government needed. He would back Poe all the way.

The first thing was to avoid unfortunate incidents such as the one with Smith. Poe had to have a recommendation from the highest quarter, and as President Tyler made the appointments the best idea was for Poe to have an interview with him. It was all arranged; and as an extra bonus Poe could lecture in Washington and drum up subscriptions for the magazine. It was all perfect, although a minor problem was Poe's lack of money, and the fact that this whirlwind negotiation meant that he would have to leave for Washington within a few days. He admitted his difficulties to Carter, the *Pioneer* co-editor, and asked for $30 that was owing to him. Whether he received it or not, he was still in need when he arrived in Washington. He stayed at 'The Widow Barrett's'.

He wrote straight away to Clarke, asking for some cash.

> My expenses were more than I thought they would be, although I have economised in every respect, and this relay (Thomas' being sick) puts me out sadly. However all is going right. I have got the subscriptions of all the Departments – President, &c. I believe that I am making a sensation which will tend to the benefit of the Magazine.
>
> Day after to-morrow I am to lecture.
>
> Send me $10 by mail, as soon as you get this. I am grieved to ask you for money in this way – but you find your account in it – twice over.

He now had the chance he wanted – to meet the President, after which the offer of a government post would be a formality. The need to borrow money must have seemed ironic to him, now that he was scaling the heights of success. He had a partnership in a high-quality magazine, which under his influence was bound to succeed. He had the gift of a job in the government to supplement his earnings. And as a safety net he had the *Pioneer* to write articles for. No one could say he did not deserve it.

He was to meet Thomas in Washington, but Thomas was sick and could not come. At least Poe had one friend there – Jesse Dow, who was only too happy to meet him and act as host. What happened next is described in a letter Dow wrote to Thomas C. Clarke:

> Washington. March 12, 1843.
> Dear Sir –
> I deem it to be my bounden duty to write you this hurried letter in relation to our mutual friend, E.A.P.
>
> He arrived here a few days since. On the first evening he seemed somewhat excited, having been over-persuaded to take some Port wine.
>
> He exposes himself here to those who may injure him very much with the President, and thus prevents us from doing for him what we wish to do and what we can do if he is himself again in Philadelphia. He does not understand the ways of politicians, nor the manner of dealing with them to advantage. How should he?
>
> Mr Thomas is not well and cannot go home with Mr P. My business and the health of my family will prevent me from so doing.
>
> Under all the circumstances of the case, I think it advisable for you to come on and see him safely back to his home. Mrs Poe is in a bad state of health, and I charge you, as you have a soul to be saved, to say not one word about him to her until he arrives with you. I shall expect you or an answer to this letter by return of mail.
>
> Should you not come, we will see him on board the cars bound for Philadelphia, but we fear he may be detained in Baltimore and not be out of harm's way.
>
> I do this under a solemn responsibility. Mr Poe has the highest order of intellect, and I cannot bear that he should be the sport of senseless creatures who, like oysters, keep sober, and gape and swallow everything.
>
> I think your good judgment will tell you what course you ought to pursue in this matter, and I cannot think it will be necessary to let him know that I have written you this letter; but I cannot suffer himself to injure himself here without giving you this warning.
>
> Yours respectfully,
> J.E. Dow

A party had been given on Poe's arrival in Washington, and it was the sociable thing to drink a bumper with the guests. He did not want to, knowing how alcohol affected him, but he did as he was asked – and very soon after became drunk and then totally incapable. After the first taste he reached for the bottle over and again, getting drunk and making a fool of himself. To Dow's mortification, some of the guests found Poe's antics hugely entertaining, and he became the butt of their laughter. He found a Spaniard's moustache hilarious and made offensive remarks about it and at one point wore his cloak the wrong way round.

Dow had helped the reeling Poe to visit Robert Tyler, but he was in such a state that it was not advisable for him to see the President. Having squandered the opportunity provided by his visit, he was too drunk to deliver his lectures, so they had to be cancelled. In all respects the visit was a catastrophe. He made his way back alone to Philadelphia, and when he sobered up he realized he had ruined any chance he had of the government job.

He also realized that he had let down two of his best friends, and although he tried to hide behind jest it was a mortified Poe who wrote to Dow and Thomas.

> . . . this is for Dow. My dear fellow – Thank you a thousand times for your kindness & great forbearance, and don't say a word about the cloak turned inside out, or other peccadilloes of that nature. Also, express to your wife my deep regret for the vexation I must have occasioned her. Send me, also, if you can the letter to Blythe. Call also, at the barber's shop just above Fuller's and pay for me a levy which I believe I owe. And now God bless you – for a nobler fellow never lived.
>
> And this is for Thomas. My dear friend. Forgive me my petulance & don't believe I think all I said. Believe me I am very grateful to you for your many attentions & forbearances and the time will never come when I shall forget either them or you. Remember me most kindly to Dr Lacey – also to the Don, whose mustachios I do admire after all, and who has about the finest figure I ever beheld – also to Dr Frailey. Please express my regret to Mr Fuller for making such a fool of myself in his house, and say to him (if you think it necessary) that I should not have got half so drunk on his excellent Port wine but for the rummy coffee with which I was forced to wash it down . . .

Now that the government position was no longer a possibility, Poe did at least have two things to fall back on – the *Pioneer* and the *Stylus*. It came as a great shock to him to receive a communication from James Lowell telling him that his magazine had folded. The story was a simple one. When Lowell started up the journal he relied on payments from his publishers to keep his creditors happy, at least until the magazine was firmly established. Sadly, the very first payment received from his publishers was 'protested for non-payment', and as an inevitable result the magazine foundered. Lowell could not finance himself, as he was already $1,800 in debt and was in the process of borrowing enough money to cover his debt. He acknowledged owing Poe for work and promised to remit it as soon as he could.[8]

Although the folding of the *Pioneer* and the loss of revenue must have been another blow to him, Poe chivalrously waived the money owed to him, something he could ill afford to do. He enclosed a copy of his prospectus for the *Stylus* and asked if he could use Lowell himself as the first of the literati promised to the public. If he was agreeable, Poe wondered if he could forward a likeness.

Thomas was still optimistic that Poe could pull off the job in government. He had smoothed things over with the President's son and still thought something could be done. Certainly, Poe could not complain about the efforts his friend had made for him. The President himself had been asking questions about Poe and seemed very interested in him:

> I rejoice to know that your wife is better. I cannot leave the office at present to see Robert Tyler, as you suggest, to get a line from him. But this I can tell you that the President, yesterday, asked me many questions about you, and spoke of you kindly. John Tyler, who was by, told the President that he wished he would give you an office in Philadelphia, and before he could reply a servant entered and called him out. John had heard of your frolic from a man who saw you in it, but I made light of the matter when he mentioned it to me; and he seemed to think nothing of it himself. He seems to feel a deep interest in you.

Poe had asked Robert Tyler if he would be willing to repeat his earlier recommendation; if so, Poe believed that Judge Blythe would still give him a post in the Custom House. Tyler was positive, but nothing was to come of it all; and Poe never again applied for a clerk's post in government.[9]

He now put his energies into the *Stylus*. Postmaster John Tomlin had written to tell Poe that his old boss, Thomas W. White, had died the previous January, and there might be the opportunity to take up the old magazine. As it now seemed to be floating on the market, Poe thought it could possibly be bought and absorbed by his own journal. With this in mind, he wrote to White's son-in-law; however, the latter was not interested, and the *Messenger* carried on for a further twenty-one years.[10] Having obtained no reply, Poe wrote to a member of the McKenzie family (who had fostered his sister Rosalie) in Richmond to see if they could discover anything about it; he would soon learn that White's son-in-law was determined to go his own way. Once again Poe swung into depression, writing a melancholy letter to his cousin William.

There was some small success. He had sold a story, 'The Gold Bug', to George R. Graham for the fair price of $52. Then he noticed that the *Dollar Newspaper* was offering a prize of $100 for the best tale, so he asked Graham if he could have the piece back so that he could enter the competition. Good-natured Graham agreed, and accordingly Poe entered it. The judges were R.T. Conrad, H.S. Patterson and W.L. Lane, and they awarded the prize to Poe.[11] It must have been a great relief. 'The Gold Bug' was a fine tale of hidden treasure, involving the cracking of a code and the final discovery of Captain Kidd's hoard. Poe used reminiscences from his own past for the background, setting it in Sullivan's Island, where he had passed some of his time as a soldier.

There was to be one more blow. Thomas C. Clarke had finally decided to back out of the *Stylus* project. The reasons are not known, but he was possibly discouraged by Poe's behaviour in Washington; and maybe he had heard the tales that Griswold was telling about Poe's drinking and unreliability. More than probably, Poe's enemies among the clans of New York and Philadelphia wanted to do him harm and succeeded. For whatever reason, Clarke had no more to do with the *Stylus*, and that was, no doubt, the cause of Poe's recent gloom. Since April he had stopped writing. Was he drinking? Almost certainly.

10

ONCE UPON A MIDNIGHT DREARY

Poe had to force himself to recover from his latest setbacks and sort out the loose ends, particularly the fate of the *Stylus*. His disappointment was shared by his admirers, and there were many. John Tomlin wrote blaming the Philadelphia clique for the failure of the *Stylus*: 'the belief that the devilish machinations of a certain clique in Philadelphia, had completely baulked your laudable designs . . . your final triumph over this clique, will give me more pleasure than anything I wot of now'. But that was not to be, not just yet.

There was something else on Poe's mind. Burton's and Griswold's constant gossip-mongering over Poe's drinking had started to pay dividends in that rumours of Poe's alcoholism were becoming common knowledge. Poe's old friend Lambert Wilmer had even written to Tomlin about it. All of this infuriated Poe, and he asked Tomlin, as he valued his friendship, to let him look at the words Wilmer had written. Tomlin obediently sent on the letter, with some reservations. The offending passage ran thus:

> Edgar A. Poe (you know him by character, no doubt, if not personally), has become one of the strangest of our literati. He and I are old friends – have known each other since boyhood, and it gives me inexpressible pain to notice the vagaries to which he has lately become subject. Poor fellow! He is not a teetotaller by any means, and I fear he is going headlong to destruction, moral, physical, and intellectual.

The description was perhaps not unjust. Poe was in dire straits and even had to ask Lowell for the contribution fees he had so generously waived.

At this point Poe received a letter from an admirer, a man in his late teens by the name of Abijah Metcalf Idle. He wrote timidly enough and called Poe 'the Peter McPrawler of *Graham's Magazine*'. Poe was generous with his time and sought always to nurture new talent. It is gratifying to read how he encouraged and befriended Idle, giving him advice and strengthening his resolve. The pair continued their correspondence for some time, Poe constantly reviewing Idle's work and offering literary advice; but Idle never achieved literary eminence.[1]

Debts and bills were still coming in, but no earnings. Even Graham was asking for cash, and Poe had to send an itemized account of their business to date to prove exactly what was owing.[2] It came to Poe's notice that Maria Clemm, as the widow of William Clemm, had right of dower to a plot of ground in Baltimore. Would the owner, John B. Morris, like to buy this right? 'Mrs Clemm is in excellent health, and may live forty years. At the same time she is in indigent circumstances, and would regard your purchase of the Right as a favor for which she would be grateful. May I ask you, on her behalf, what would be the value of the Right to yourself?'

There was another way of earning money, which could be profitable if organized properly. He had intended to do this in Washington, but his drunkenness had stopped him. He could lecture. In his preparation for the *Stylus* he had already done a lot of research into the American literati – besides, after reviewing and reading so much literature there were few people more knowledgeable than he on the poetry of the country. He made inquiries and was satisfied that he would be quite a popular speaker, so began to organize a lecture tour. The dates of his lectures would be: on 21 November 1843 at the William Wirt Literary Institute in Philadelphia; on 28 November at the Temperance Hall for the Franklin Lyceum in Wilmington, Delaware; and on 23 December at the Newark Academy in Newark. The talk would be entitled 'American Poetry'. In it, he thoroughly carpeted Griswold for his anthology:

> There is no one who, reading the 'Poets and Poetry of America,' will not, in a hundred instances, be tempted to throw it aside, because its prejudices and partialities are, in these hundred instances, altogether at war with his own. Had the work, nevertheless, been that of the finest critic in existence – and this, we are sorry to say, Mr Griswold is *not* – there would still have been these inevitable discrepancies of opinion, to startle and to vex us, as now.[3]

As New Year 1844 dawned, Poe realized that lecturing had become his main source of income and was keen to do as much of it as possible. He repeated his poetry lecture at the Philadelphia Museum on 10 January. He succeeded in booking the Egyptian Saloon of the Oddfellows Hall in Gay Street, then on the day of the event he wrote to the *Patriot* to get some advertising. He also accepted an offer of a lecture at the Academy Hall for the Mechanics Institute, Reading, responding to a request from Samuel Williams and William Graef. He delivered the talk on 10 March. He then asked Lowell about the possibility of a tour in Boston, and Lowell suggested that it was too late that year but that he would help to get things moving next year. Lowell himself was full of excitement – his new book, *Poems*, had just been published.

During the next month Poe read and wrote a critique of the work which appeared in the March edition of *Graham's Magazine*. His praise was complimentary indeed, beginning:

> This new volume of poems by Mr Lowell will place him, in the estimation of all whose opinion he will be likely to value, *at the very head* of the poets of America . . . These are *crowded* with excellences of the loftiest order . . . we repeat, that he has given evidence of at least as high poetical genius as any man in America – if not a loftier genius than any.[4]

But even Lowell does not escape a barb from Poe's critical pen. 'The defects observable in the "Legend of Brittany" are, chiefly, consequent upon the error of didacticism.' The book did well and ran into a third edition.

George Lippard, Pennsylvanian author and advocate of a socialist political philosophy, now wrote to Poe asking for his opinion on a manuscript, 'The Ladye Annabel', as well as advice on how to handle personal enemies. Poe's advice about enemies is excellent and unfortunate in that Poe never seemed to be able to follow it himself:

> And as for these personal enemies, I cannot see that you need put yourself to any especial trouble about THEM. Let a fool alone – especially if he be both a scoundrel and a fool – and he will kill himself far sooner than you can kill him by any active exertion . . .

Lowell's next letter was friendly, but it may have been the last straw as far as Poe was concerned:

> When will Graham give us your portrait? I hope you will have it done well when it is done, & quickly too. Writing to him a short time ago I congratulated him upon having engaged you as editor again. I recognized your hand in some of the editorial matter (critical) & missed it in the rest. But I thought it would do no harm to assume the fact, as it would at least give him a hint. He tells me I am mistaken & I am sorry for it. Why could not you write an article now and then for the *North American Review*? I know the editor a little, & should like to get you introduced there. I think he would be glad to get an article. On the modern French School of novels for example. How should you like it? The Review does not pay a great deal ($2 a page, I believe) but the pages do not eat up copy very fast.

These words may have given Poe a jolt. After all, what had he done since he left *Graham's*? Performed a few lectures, written a few articles – no more. Now he was idling and stagnating while his career was slipping back into obscurity. Yet here was a good working example of how to deal with adversity, in the form of Lowell. He had just faced a catastrophe – his magazine had folded, and he was left in debt – and now he was the author of a book of poetry that was in its third edition. Poe had left Graham with the intention of opening doors and making an impression on the literature of America – but he was reduced to writing small pieces for a pittance. It had all gone wrong. Even young Idle was still writing, asking for advice on how to get on in the world. Poe must have felt the irony. Even that young man had somehow come upon money, and yet his literary mentor was still penniless.

It seems that Graham had talked to Poe about writing Lowell's biography, so Poe asked him for some details. And once again he took the opportunity to promote his dream of the ideal American magazine:

> How dreadful is the present condition of our Literature! To what are things tending? We want two things, certainly: – an International Copy-Right Law, and a well-founded Monthly Journal, of sufficient ability, circulation, and character, to control and so give tone to, our Letters. It should be, externally, a specimen of high, but not too refined Taste: – I mean, it should be boldly printed, on excellent paper, in single column, and be illustrated, not merely embellished, by spirited wood designs in the style of Grandville. Its chief aims should be Independence, Truth, Originality . . .

Things were now so bad that he had no option other than to move his family away from Philadelphia and make a new start elsewhere. To move to a provincial town would be suicide for all his aspirations, so there was only one other place to go – back to New York. So he and Virginia packed their bags and set off, leaving Maria to sort out any loose ends. The following letter makes a pleasant change. This is Poe the family man:

> New-York, Sunday Morning April 7, just after breakfast.
> My dear Muddy,
> We have just this minute done breakfast, and I now sit down to write you about everything. I can't pay for the letter, because the P.O. won't be open to-day. In the first place, we arrived safe at Walnut St wharf. The driver wanted to make me pay a dollar, but I wouldn't. Then I had to pay a boy a levy to put the trunks in the baggage car. In the meantime I took Sis in the Depot Hotel. It was only a quarter past 6, and we had to wait till 7. We saw the Ledger & Times – nothing in either – a few words of no account in the Chronicle. We started in good spirits, but did not get here until nearly 3 o'clock. We went in the cars to Amboy about 40 miles from N. York, and then took the steamboat the rest of the way. Sissy coughed none at all. When we got to the wharf it was raining hard. I left her on board the boat, after putting the trunks in the Ladies' Cabin, and set off to buy an umbrella and look for a boarding-house. I met a man selling umbrellas and bought one for 62 cents. Then I went up Greenwich St and soon found a boarding-house. It is just before you get to Cedar St on the West side going up – the left hand side. It has brown stone steps, with a porch with brown pillars. 'Morrison' is the name on the door. I made a bargain in a few minutes and then got a hack and went for Sis. I was not gone more than ? an hour, and she was quite astonished to see me back so soon. She didn't expect me for an hour. There were 2 other ladies waiting on board, so she wasn't very lonely. When we got to the house we had to wait about ½ an hour before the room was ready. The house is old & looks buggy . . . The landlady . . . gave us the back room . . . for 7 $ – the cheapest board I ever knew, taking into consideration the central situation and the living. I wish Kate could see it – she would faint. Last night, for supper, we had the nicest tea you ever drank, strong & hot – wheat bread & rye bread – cheese – tea-cakes (elegant), a great dish (2 dishes) of elegant ham, and 2 of cold veal piled up like a mountain and large slices – 3

dishes of the cakes and, and every thing in the greatest profusion. No fear of starving here. The landlady seemed as if she couldn't press us enough, and we were at home directly. Her husband is living with her – a fat good-natured old soul. There are 8 or 10 boarders – 2 or 3 of them ladies – 2 servants. For breakfast we had excellent-flavored coffee, hot & strong – not very clear & no great deal of cream – veal cutlets, elegant ham & eggs & nice bread and butter. I never sat down to a more plentiful or a nicer breakfast. I wish you could have seen the eggs – and the great dishes of meat. I ate the first hearty breakfast I have eaten since I left our little home. Sis is delighted, and we are both in excellent spirits. She has coughed hardly any and had no night sweat. She is now busy mending my pants which I tore against a nail. I went out last night and bought a skein of silk, a skein of thread, & 2 buttons, a pair of slippers & a tin pan for the stove. The fire kept in all night. We have now got 4 $ and a half left. Tomorrow I am going to try & borrow 3 $ so that I may have a fortnight to go upon. I feel in excellent spirits & haven't drank a drop – so that I hope so to get out of trouble. The very instant I scrape together enough money I will send it on. You can't imagine how much we both to miss you. Sissy had a hearty cry last night, because you and Catterina weren't here. We are resolved to get 2 rooms the first moment we can. In the meantime it is impossible we could be more comfortable or more at home than we are. It looks as if it was going to clear up now. Be sure and go to the Post Office. & have my letters forwarded. As soon as I write Lowell's article, I will send it to you, & get you to get the money from Graham. Give our best loves to Catterina.[5]

The family settled into 130 Greenwich Street, cat and all, and soon got into a domestic routine. Galvanized by his new surroundings, Poe made an effort to break into the publishing world. At first it seemed that fortune may have turned her wheel for Poe. He sold an article to the *Sun* newspaper – a balloon hoax story, with the headline:

ASTOUNDING NEWS!
BY EXPRESS VIA NORFOLK:
THE ATLANTIC CROSSED IN THREE DAYS!
SIGNAL TRIUMPH OF MR MONCK
MASON'S FLYING MACHINE!!!

Arrival at Sullivan's Island, near Charlestown, S.C., of Mr Mason,
Mr Robert Holland, Mr Henson, Mr Harrison Ainsworth,
and four others, in the
STEERING BALLOON 'VICTORIA,'
AFTER A PASSAGE OF SEVENTY-FIVE HOURS
FROM LAND TO LAND.
FULL PARTICULARS OF THE VOYAGE!!!

The public were completely taken in, and there was a giant wave of excitement, people fighting to get a copy of the extra edition. Monck Mason was a real balloon pilot who had flown from England to Germany – and now, according to Poe, he had made the first transatlantic crossing. Poe was extremely proud of his hoax, even though the public should have guessed it simply by looking at the list of passengers – Harrison Ainsworth, for example, was a well-known writer of romances such as *The Lancashire Witches* and *The Tower of London*. Of the item's reception, Poe wrote:

> As soon as the few first copies made their way into the streets, they were bought up, at almost any price, from the news-boys, who made a profitable speculation beyond doubt. I saw a half-dollar given, in one instance, for a single paper, and a shilling was a frequent price. I tried, in vain, during the whole day, to get possession of a copy.[6]

He found more work, writing several articles about New York in a column entitled 'Doings of Gotham' for the *Columbia Spy*. This journal was edited by two young men, Eli Bowen and Jacob L. Gossler, both still in their teens and doubtless overjoyed to get Poe as a contributor.

The fact that Poe was short of money seems to have been spread around town, with the result that he was never given plum payment for any effort he made. Sometimes he found it hard to find a publisher at all. 'The Oblong Box' was refused by the *New York Mirror*, so he sent it to the *Opal*. Sarah Josepha Hale was in charge of selection (as well as editing *Godey's Lady's Book*).[7] Poe had known her son at West Point and had given him fictional accounts of his adventures and foreign travel. His forceful pushing of 'The Oblong Box' and his admission of financial embarrassment suggest desperation:

> I have thought it best to write you this letter, and to ask you if you could accept an article from me – or whether you would wish to see the one

> in question – or whether you could be so kind as to take it, unseen, upon Mr Willis's testimony in its favor. It cannot be improper to state, that I make the latter request to save time, because I am as usual, exceedingly in need of a little money.

Doubtless sensing this desperation, Sarah Hale made Poe a pitiable offer – fifty cents per page – but finding nowhere else to go, Poe was forced to accept it: 'The price you mention – 50 cts per page – will be amply sufficient; and I am exceedingly anxious to be ranked in your list of contributors . . .'

Poe had also sold a story to the *Gift* – a new Dupin tale called 'The Purloined Letter'.[8] It was a popular story, clever in its simplicity, if a little overwritten. It is perhaps a pity that Poe, unlike Conan Doyle, did not fully grasp the potential of his creation. With Poe's analytical mind it would have been a relatively easy task to create a regular series of Dupin adventures, and his detective might, like Holmes, have become a household name. Perhaps also, like Conan Doyle, he might have become so associated with the character that he would have been unable to escape from him; but to Poe in 1844 that may have not seemed too great a danger. However, Dupin's hunt for the stolen letter would be his last assignment.

Lowell had agreed to write a biography of Poe, to appear in *Graham's Magazine* as one of 'Our Contributors', and he wanted some details from his subject. Nothing could be easier – Poe simply sent him Hirst's original effort (as well as the hated portrait). There was one piece of excellent news, though: 'The Gold Bug' had been extremely popular and had sold a staggering number of copies.

> Touching the Biography – I would be very proud, indeed, if you would write it – and did, certainly, say to myself, and I believe to Graham – that such was my wish; but as I fancied the job might be disagreeable, I did not venture to suggest it to yourself. Your offer relieves me from great embarrassment, and I thank you sincerely. You will do me justice; and that I could not expect at all hands.
>
> . . . Of the 'Gold-Bug' (my most successful tale) more than 300,000 copies have been circulated.

One of the tales Poe mentioned to Lowell, 'The Black Cat', deserves especial mention, if only for its popularity.[9] Once again the narrator is a madman. In a freak act of sadism, and in a state of drunkenness, he maims his favourite cat, a black pet named Pluto. Eventually he murders his wife and bricks her up in the cellar. When the police arrive he taps the brickwork with his cane, which produces a howl from behind. The walls are beaten down.

> The corpse, already greatly decayed and clotted with gore, stood erect before the eyes of the spectators. Upon its head, with red extended mouth and solitary eye of fire, sat the hideous beast whose craft had seduced me into murder, and whose informing voice had consigned me to the hangman. I had walled the monster up within the tomb!

Apart from earning some cash from lecturing, Poe had also sold articles on 'The Omnibus' to Philadelphia's *Public Ledger* and the celebrated 'The Premature Burial' to the *Dollar Newspaper*.[10] 'The Premature Burial' is one of the most morbid of Poe's tales and concerns itself with a subject that haunts Poe – being buried alive.

There now began a long correspondence between Poe and his two friends Chivers (who was expecting to inherit some of his father's estate the following month) and Lowell. Lowell was preparing to write Poe's life story, and he asked for a 'spiritual autobiography' from Poe.

The latter was moved by Lowell's suggestion and wrote on the subject of spirituality. He considered 'particled' matter as making up the visible world and humans; but matter can become so very rarefied as to become unparticled and so permeate all things. This Poe saw as God. This idea was expanded much later in 'Eureka', but in its nascent stage it became the subject of an article to be published in the *Columbian Magazine* with the title 'Mesmeric Revelation'.[11] In his enthusiasm he related the theme to Lowell. This letter is interesting because it touches upon several important aspects of Poe's character:

> You speak of 'an estimate of my life' . . . My life has been whim – impulse – passion – a longing for solitude – a scorn of all things present, in an earnest desire for the future. I am profoundly excited by music, and by some poems – those of Tennyson especially – whom, with Keats, Shelley, Coleridge (occasionally) and a few others of like thought and expression, I regard as the sole poets. Music is the perfection of the soul, or idea, of Poetry. The vagueness of exultation aroused by a sweet air

> (which should be strictly indefinite & never too strongly suggestive) is precisely what we should aim at in poetry. Affectation, within bounds, is thus no blemish.

Lowell set to work on the biography, and when it was at last ready he sent the manuscript to Poe. Lowell himself was not pleased with it: 'It is not half so good as it ought to be, but it was written under many disadvantages, not the least of which was depression of spirits which unfits a man for anything.' He praised Poe overall, but did mention his acidic critiques: 'He seems sometimes to mistake his phial of prussic-acid for his inkstand.' He described Poe's 'facility of vigorous, yet minute analysis, and a wonderful fecundity of imagination'.[12]

To Chivers Poe had naturally broached the idea of his own magazine, and Chivers seemingly agreed to consider going in on the project, but he wanted to know more.

> I expect to receive my part of my father's estate in July next, and should like to unite with you, provided it would be to my interest to do so. I should like for you to make a perfect exposition of the manner in which you wish me to join you. Would not the publication of such a Magazine as *Graham's* be more profitable to us? I should like very much to know your opinion about the matter. I shall return to New York as soon as I receive my part of the estate.

One thing Chivers disagreed with Poe about was the value of Transcendentalism. This was extremely fashionable at the time; it was based on Immanuel Kant's teachings, as opposed to the sensualism of John Locke. Kant had called 'all knowledge transcendental which is concerned not with objects but with our mode of knowing objects'. In simple terms, it meant grounding one's ideas on spiritual rather than earthly feelings and principles. This lofty ideal was also represented in socialistic ideas, which were also current at the time; various writers such as Carlyle and Coleridge expressed this philosophy in their work. A great influence at this time was Emanuel Swedenborg. It is easy to see how a rift would develop between Chivers and Poe; Poe believed in materialism, seeing God as almost an afterthought; whereas Chivers was deeply religious and saw everything in terms of the Holy Spirit. Chivers commented: 'I cannot say that I like very much your dislike to Transcendentalism. All true Poetry is certainly transcendental – although it is the beautiful expression of that which is most true.'

With his Baptist background and his love of Transcendentalism and Swedenborgism, Chivers was not going to be content with Poe's undervaluation of the human as matter and soul. 'Unparticled matter' could not convey to Chivers the spirit, soul or intention of God. Its 'agitation' was too simple a concept to convey thought and volition. As Poe's ideas could not, to Chivers's mind, allow for the volition of God, they must be wrong. Poe described the Will of God as an 'agitation' of the unparticled matter – God – which is inextricably mixed with the baser 'particled' matter of man. Chivers would have none of that and added:

> From the inaudible thoughts of God were the stars born. Thunder is the voice of Nature hushing her own self to repose. It is that voice by which she wishes to sing herself into silence of the Deity. Silence is bliss. Thought is silence. Therefore, thought is bliss. It is the sapphire silence of the soul. Paracelsus says that silence is the language of spirits. – This is my answer to your 'agitation.'

Poe was interested in furthering his own cause. If Griswold could make a profit from anthologizing the poets of America, then why could not Poe make just such a profit from anthologizing a critical review of American literature? After all, most of his correspondents were impressed with his past efforts, for whatever reason; and if he had successfully wielded his tomahawk for public magazines, why not in a serious work in book form? What's more, Poe was developing his materialistic theory of the universe, and his interest in cosmology would later grow into something bigger. His 'Mesmeric Revelation' had appeared in the *Columbian Magazine*; Poe sent a copy to Lowell, and asked about the progress of the biography.

An old friend reappeared at this point – Frederick Thomas, who was still working for the Government in a patents department. He had tracked Poe down – at least to Philadelphia – and had had his verse 'The Beechen Tree' published, but it had received a bad review by Thomas Dunn English in his magazine *Aurora*; he stated that it 'gave him "nausea" and that it was all twattle'. Poe wrote back to Thomas, promising to right the critical wrong done to his poem. He went on to describe English as 'a bullet-headed and malicious villain'. Poe and English were destined to fall out in graver terms later on, but it seems that relations between the two men had already deteriorated, perhaps because English had vilified Robert Tyler, whom Poe remembered kindly as someone who made a lot of effort to secure him a government job.

Thomas also relayed news about Jesse Dow. The last Poe had heard of Dow was that he had lost his position – but the irrepressible epicurean bounced back. Thomas had half expected Dow to end up in poverty, but in the event he found himself another government job and a good one – door keeper to the House of Representatives, which brought with it a good salary. As an agent for various claimants he had accrued a fair amount of money – so much so that he had bought a house and was living in comparable luxury.

In contrast, Poe's lack of funds was still a pressing concern, and he needed a fixed income. Just then his luck changed for the better –this time engineered by his mother-in-law and aunt Maria Clemm. She had for some time acted in the role of secretary to her nephew, and it was a common sight to see her walking around the streets of New York carrying messages and manuscripts. One day she visited the offices of the *New York Mirror* and called to see the editor, Nathaniel P. Willis. She asked if there was no opportunity of work for Poe there. Willis was a kind-natured man and no fool – he knew well enough what a draw it would be to have such a contentious figure working for him. Poe has created sparks enough along the corridors of Gotham, and hiring him could do no worse than increase his sales. So straight away Willis offered Poe a position. Taking his past career into account, he offered him a post as sub-editor as well as critic. The wages may not have been a fortune but, still, this was regular work, and Poe was grateful to Willis for it. This was the beginning of a lasting friendship. Poe worked hard and with his usual flair, and Willis found nothing for which to criticize his new editor. In fact, Willis would later describe him as a 'quiet, patient, industrious, and most gentlemanly person, commanding the utmost respect and good feeling by his unvarying deportment and ability'.[13]

However, two incidents now occurred that proved that Poe was in a potentially irritable mood. A correspondent, Samuel D. Craig, angered by something Poe had written, had sent an angry letter filled with lies about Poe himself, probably cobbled together from the old rumours. Craig also enclosed a letter on the subject which he ordered Poe to hand over to Willis. Poe summarily dealt with the nuisance with a strongly worded letter containing veiled threats:

The tissue of written lies which you have addressed to myself individually, I deem it as well to retain. It is a specimen of attorney grammar too rich to be lost. As for the letter designed for Mr Willis (who, beyond doubt, will feel honoured by your correspondence), I take the liberty of re-inclosing it. The fact is, I am neither your footman nor the penny-post.

The second incident involved William Duane, a friend of Poe's, who had lent him via Henry Hirst a bound edition of the *Southern Literary Messenger* which Maria Clemm had subsequently sold to Leary's (a Philadelphia bookseller). Now Duane was asking for his book back, and Poe explained that Maria had returned it to Hirst a number of months before. To do Poe justice, it could be that Maria had sold it on her own initiative and told Poe that it had been returned. After a while Duane wrote again to Poe about the missing volume; he had approached Hirst, who declared that the idea that he was given the book back was 'a damned lie'. Poe responded that he had been trying to get together copies of the missing articles, but Duane had rediscovered the book (with his signature in it) and bought it. Poe still insisted it had been returned to Hirst. And there the matter ended, although the friendship was at an end.

Poe's final tale of detection, 'Thou Art the Man', was published in the November edition of *Godey's Lady's Book*, and 'Marginalia' was published in the next two numbers of the *Democratic Review*.[14] He was not unproductive during this time. He also wrote a satirical piece entitled 'The Literary Life of Thingum Bob, Esq.' which was published in the *Southern Literary Messenger*.[15] He now called his collection of tales 'Phantasy Pieces'.

'The Literary Life of Thingum Bob, Esq.' was an obvious satirical attack on the clique editors, who in the story reject Dante and enthuse over a line of rubbish submitted by Thingum. Thingum is told that payment was not to be expected; but the *Lollipop* journal takes him under his wing. The *Lollipop* is an obvious snipe at the *Knickerbocker*.

Poe must have had quite a surprise to receive a note through the post from his old enemy Rufus Wilmot Griswold. In it he told Poe that, although the pair were not friends, he wished to publish some of his work in his forthcoming *The Prose Authors of America and Their Works*.

Jany 14 1845
Although I have some cause of personal quarrel with you, which you will easily enough remember, I do not under any circumstances

permit, as you have repeatedly charged, my private griefs to influence my judgment as a critic, or its expression. I retain, therefore, the early formed and well founded favourable opinions of your works, which in other days I have expressed to you, and in a new volume which I have in preparation, I shall endeavor to do you very perfect justice. Hence this note. Carey & Hart are publishing for me 'The Prose Authors of America, and their Works,' and I wish, of course, to include you in the list, – not a very large one – from whom I make selections. And I shall feel myself your debtor if there being any writings of yours with which I may be unacquainted, you will advise of their titles, and where they may be purchased; and if, in the brief biography of you in my Poets &c. of America, there are any inaccuracies, you will point them out to me. If the trouble were not too great, indeed, I should like to receive a list of all your works, with the dates of their production.

Yours &c. R. W. Griswold.

Poe could be chivalrous, and a kind word could often buy his forgiveness. In fact, there was no proffered hand of friendship in Griswold's note – he simply wished to include some of Poe's work in his anthology – but Poe immediately held out an olive branch, blaming a mischief-maker and slanderer for coming between them:

{Confidential} New-York: Jan. 16. 45.
Dear Griswold – if you will permit me to call you so – your letter occasioned me first pain and then pleasure: – pain because it gave me to see that I had lost, through my own folly, an honorable friend: – pleasure, because I saw in it a hope of reconciliation. I have been aware, for several weeks, that my reasons for speaking of your book as I did (of yourself I have always spoken kindly) were based in the malignant slanders of a mischief-maker by profession. Still, as I supposed you irreparably offended, I could make no advances when we met at the Tribune Office, although I longed to do so. I know of nothing which would give me more sincere pleasure than your accepting these apologies, and meeting me as a friend. If you can do this and forget the past, let me know where I shall call on you – or come and see me at the Mirror Office, any morning about 10. We can then talk over the other matters, which, to me at least, are far less important than your good will.

Very truly yours
Edgar A. Poe.

Unfortunately, Poe was not fully aware of the extent of Griswold's vindictiveness and malice – nor would he come to know of it. But posterity certainly would.

He now met someone else who would play an important role in his life: Evert Augustus Duyckinck, who was first a lawyer, then a man of letters, being editor (with Cornelius Mathews) of the *Arcturus* in 1841–2. He was still contributing articles to magazines, as well as editing Wiley & Putnam's *Library of American Books*. Duyckinck wrote to Poe because the latter had mistakenly attributed an article in the *Broadway Journal* to him; Poe had also made a mistake concerning Duyckinck and the *Tribune* and the *Morning News*. Inauspicious as it was, this meeting became the starting point for a long and friendly relationship in which Duyckinck would more or less play the part of Poe's agent.

Then came an important piece of news from Lowell. He had sent a letter of introduction for Poe to Charles F. Briggs, author of *The Adventures of Henry Franco*; Briggs was about to start the *Broadway Journal*, to be published by John Bisco, once editor of the *Knickerbocker*.

> My object in writing this is to introduce you to my friend, Charles F. Briggs, who is about to start a literary weekly paper in New York & desires your aid. He was here a month or two since, & I took the liberty of reading to him what I had written about you & today I received a letter from him announcing his plan & asking your address. Not knowing it, & not having time to write him I thought that the shortest way would be to introduce you to him. He will pay & I thought from something you said in your last letter that pay would be useful to you. I also took the liberty of praising you to a Mr Colton, who has written 'Tecumseh' . . . & whom I suspect, from some wry faces he made on first hearing your name, you have cut up. He is publishing a magazine & I think I convinced him that it would be for his interest to engage you permanently. But I know nothing whatever of his ability to pay.

Now, at last, the tide seemed to be turning for Edgar Allan Poe. Briggs took him on as sub-editor and critic for the *Broadway Journal*. The editorial duties were shared between Poe, Briggs and someone called Henry C. Watson, whose speciality was music. All now seemed well in the world. If the *Broadway Journal* was no *Stylus*, at least it offered a steady wage, and Poe was given virtual *carte blanche* to write whatever took his fancy.

He had hardly had time to accustom himself to his editorial seat when, on 29 January 1845, he published in the *Evening Mirror* a poem that changed his fortunes and raised him to the dizzy heights of fame. It caused such a sensation that imitations were rife, and everyone suddenly wanted to know all about the author. Originally, Poe had published it under the *nom de plume* 'Quarles', but now he admitted authorship. The poem was called 'The Raven'. It has been described with some justice as the best poem ever to come from American hands. The picture of the grieving man – who has just lost his love, Lenore – giving vent his anguish to a dumb bird who has learned only one word ('nevermore') is powerful indeed, especially when the poem reaches its climax and the narrator begins to believe in the raven's intelligence:

> Then, methought, the air grew denser,
> perfumed from an unseen censer
> Swung by Seraphim whose foot-falls tinkled
> on the tufted floor.
> 'Wretch,' I cried, 'thy God hath lent thee –
> by these angels he has sent thee
> Respite – respite and nepenthe from thy
> memories of Lenore!
> Quaff, oh quaff this kind nepenthe, and for-
> get this lost Lenore!'
> Quoth the raven, 'Nevermore.'
>
> 'Prophet!' said I, 'thing of evil! – prophet
> still, if bird or devil! –
> Whether tempter sent, or whether tempest
> tossed thee here ashore,
> Desolate yet all undaunted, on this desert
> land enchanted –
> On this home by horror haunted – tell me
> truly, I implore –
> Is there – *is* there balm in Gilead? – tell me –
> tell me, I implore!'
> Quoth the raven, 'Nevermore.'
>
> 'Prophet!' said I, 'thing of evil! – prophet
> still, if bird or devil!
> By that Heaven that bends above us – by that
> God we both adore –

Tell this soul with sorrow laden if, within the
distant Aidenn,
It shall clasp a sainted maiden whom the
angels named Lenore –
Clasp a rare and radiant maiden, whom the
angels named Lenore?'
Quoth the raven, 'Nevermore.'

Overnight Edgar Allan Poe became a celebrity. He was nicknamed 'The Raven'. He was invited to soirées and functions – a celebrity whose presence graced the tables of the most illustrious literati in the land. Publishers became interested in his tales and his poems. In a moment, everything he ever dreamed of appeared at his fingertips.

11

⁘ 'AT LEAST THE PROSPECTS ARE GOOD' ⁘

Few people would have denied Poe his success, after all his years of hard effort and swathes of misfortune. This was a well-earned reward. And if 'The Raven' stood apart as a piece of work above the common run of literature it was a poem of such a standard that probably only appears once in a lifetime to a gifted writer. Even so, marvellous as the poem was, Poe the perfectionist could not resist making small improvements here and there. But, whatever he did to the poem, people were vociferous in their praise.

Even Lewis G. Clark had to give it praise to begin with, however reluctantly.[1] The poet Mary E. Hewitt stated: 'After the "Raven," my verse seemed to me but a broken chime', and Elizabeth Barrett Browning thought 'there is a fine lyrical melody in it'. Robert Browning 'was struck much by the rhythm of that poem'.[2] The tributes poured in.

Poe knuckled down and did his best for his new employer. Charles F. Briggs was around forty, of slight build and with a moustache. He had been a sailor, voyaging around Europe and South America before becoming a merchant in New York; some time later he took to writing and achieved some success with *The Adventures of Henry Franco*. After that, Henry Franco became his *nom de plume*, and in 1843 he published 'The Haunted Merchant'. Magazine editing was a new venture for him, and he had taken John Bisco into partnership with him. He welcomed Poe as someone who could make up for his lack of experience.

Poe wrote for the *Broadway Journal* with industry, and first of all revised 'The Raven' for the next issue.[3] He remained proud of his greatest creation. According to one story, a great actor named Murdock paid a visit to the offices of the *Broadway Journal*, and Poe asked him if he would care to do a favour, to which the actor agreed. Poe gathered together all members of the office, and the actor recited 'The Raven' to the assembly, much to their delight.

He wrote many pieces for the *Journal*, such as 'Some Words with a Mummy', 'Three Sundays in a Week', 'Magazine Writing – Peter Snook', 'Lenore', 'The Tell-Tale Heart', 'The Island of the Fay' and 'The Spectacles'.[4] 'Peter Snook' had the New York coterie irritated, containing, as it did, criticisms of the whole magazine business; it rubbed salt in the wound that had been caused by 'Thingum Bob'.

Briggs was pleased with Poe's progress, and wrote to Lowell: 'I like Poe exceedingly well; Mr Griswold has told me shocking bad stories about him, which his whole demeanour contradicts.'[5] He must have been patting himself on the back for having caught such an influential fish as Poe. The only slightly worrying problem was Poe's determination to attack Longfellow at every opportunity.

Now there would be changes. Poe was at the height of his fame and yet even so he was earning very little. This could not last, and he was making noises of discontent. It soon became apparent to Briggs and Bisco that they could not keep Poe for long under the present arrangement; 'The Raven' was now a household name and his fame was spreading far and wide, yet even so he was surviving on the pittance he was paid as employee of their magazine. It was small wonder, then, that he was looking to make mileage out of his newfound star status. Already the articles written by him were selling copy, and their sales were increasing. It must have been worrying to think that their best draw was tempted to resign and go on to better things, and it was clear that his name would attract many of their rivals. Then there was still the threat that Poe would at last succeed in his ultimate ambition to develop a magazine of his own, which would be a serious rival to their own. His track record with the *Southern Literary Messenger* and the *Gentleman's Magazine* was well established, and the former was already making overtures to get him back on board. They needed to offer Poe an incentive great enough both to keep him and to ensure that he remained with them.

Poe wanted nothing short of a partnership, and to this the two gave their deepest consideration. A partnership would necessarily mean a diminution in their own shares; but such a loss would be offset by the increased circulation of the *Broadway Journal*, if their figures were right. If Poe proved as successful as he had been in his past endeavours, the *Journal* would go from strength to strength. Currently, in the golden age of the magazine, new publications rose and fell with clockwork regularity. Rivals were appearing everywhere and it was harder to keep afloat on such a sea of literature. To succeed, it was imperative to have a guaranteed quantity and quality of writing as well as the flair to attract the attention of the reading public. The best of all magazinists was Poe – he had proven himself time and time again and there was no gainsaying his value as a contributor. Of course, there were dangers – everyone had heard the tales told by such as Griswold about Poe's unreliability and his drinking. There was also the worry that Poe was a controversial writer – his monomania about Longfellow's plagiarism was one such danger. But on the other hand, Poe had the natural gift of showmanship which had made his name so familiar even before 'The Raven' made its appearance and shot him to stardom.

Briggs and Bisco made up their mind to take Poe on as a partner, entitled to a third of all the profits. A contract was accordingly drawn up and was signed on 21 February 1845. This was a landmark for Poe; greatly encouraged, he took up his pen and wrote with renewed industry for what was fast becoming his own magazine in every sense of the word.

One of Briggs's main concerns – the Longfellow war – continued unabated. Longfellow was the darling of the New York coterie, and the especial property of the Clark brothers. Lewis Gaylord Clark had been responsible for an inordinate amount of 'puffing' for Longfellow's work *Outre-Mer*, and for five years Longfellow submitted pieces for the *Knickerbocker* without payment. Thus – quite aside from his undeniable genius – was his success assured. It was not so much the quality of Longfellow's work that irritated Poe so much as the methods employed by the cliques to assuring his success even before his work was in print. Poe had already attacked the coterie's favourite several times, and now battle recommenced. A broadside came on 13 and 14 January in the form of a review of Longfellow's anthology of lesser poets, known as *The Waif*, in which Longfellow himself wrote the 'Proem'. Poe ended his critique with:

> We conclude our notes on the 'Waif,' with the observation that, although full of beauties, it is infected with a *moral taint* – or is this a mere freak of our own fancy? We shall be pleased if it be so; – but there *does* appear, in this exquisite little volume, a very careful avoidance of all American poets who may be supposed especially to interfere with

> the claims of Mr Longfellow. These men Mr Longfellow can continuously *imitate* (*is* that the word?) and yet never even incidentally commend.[6]

Within a week there came a reply from a friend of Longfellow – 'H'. 'H' was in fact George S. Hillard, of the Cambridge 'Five of Clubs' group, one of whose members was Longfellow. Hillard took exception to the charge of 'imitation', a dirty word at the time, and the allegation that Longfellow had omitted several leading American poets.[7]

Unfortunately for Longfellow, a strong proof of his plagiarism came not from Poe but from an unexpected source, the Buffalo *Western Literary Messenger*, which showed that his translation of 'The Good George Campbell' was stolen wholesale from the British ballad 'Bonnie George Campbell'.[8] But Poe's words had created such a storm that more of Longfellow's friends came to his defence, including Charles Sumner and, more importantly, a correspondent who signed himself 'Outis' ('No one', taken from Odysseus' speech to the Cyclops). He defends Longfellow by launching a scathing attack on 'The Raven', accusing Poe of imitating 'The Rime of the Ancient Mariner' and claiming to find fifteen 'imitations' in it; this is probably why Poe took so much exception to the article.[9]

That the letter from Outis rattled Poe can be seen by the fact that in each weekly edition of the *Broadway Journal* until 29 March he continued to blast away at Outis and at Longfellow. He successfully answered each charge of the Coleridge 'imitations', conceding only two – they both contain a bird and that 'there is an allusion to the departed'. He ends the whole sequence as follows:

> Had I accused him, in loud terms, of manifest and continuous plagiarism, I should but have echoed the sentiment of every man of letters in the land beyond the immediate influence of the Longfellow *coterie*. And since I, 'knowing what I know and seeing what I have seen' – submitting in my own person to accusations of plagiarism for the very sins of this gentleman against myself – since I contented myself, nevertheless, with simply setting forth the *merits* of the poet in the strongest light, whenever an opportunity was afforded me, can it be considered either decorous or equitable on the part of Professor Longfellow to beset me, upon my first adventuring an infinitesimal sentence of dispraise, with ridiculous anonymous letters from his friends, and moreover, with malice prepense, to instigate against me the pretty little witch entitled

> Miss Walter; advising her and instructing her to pierce me to death with the needles of innumerable epigrams, rendered unnecessarily and therefore cruelly painful to my feelings by being first carefully deprived of the point?[10]

The 'pretty witch', editor of the *Boston Tribune* (and therefore a member of the powerful Boston coterie), had annoyed Poe with a few disparaging remarks, ending in his mock epitaph:

> There lies, by Death's relentless blow,
> A would-be critic here below;
> His name was Poe
> His life was woe,
> You ask, 'What of this Master Poe?'
> Why nothing of him that I know;
> But Echo, answering, saith: 'Poh!'[11]

Outis had so incensed Poe that he even stooped to writing (or at the very least co-writing) an anonymous piece in Thomas D. English's *Aristidean*, claiming that Longfellow had stolen a great deal from himself: 'Footsteps of Angels' from 'The Sleeper', 'The Beleaguered City' from 'The Haunted Palace' and 'The Spanish Student' partly from his 'Politian'. The article was his most savage yet, and part of it ran:

> It is, indeed, for that whereas, Mr LONGFELLOW has stolen so much from Mr POE, that we have alluded so much to the *exposé* of the latter; for it appeared to us, our course was but just. The latter, driven to it by a silly letter of Mr LONGFELLOW'S friends, has exposed the knavery of the Professor, and any one who reads the '*Broadway Journal*,' will acknowledge he has done it well.
>
> There are other plagiarisms of Mr LONGFELLOW which we might easily expose; but we have said enough. There can be no reasonable doubt in the mind of any, out of the little clique, to which we at first alluded, that the author of 'Outre Mer,' is not only a servile imitator, but a most insolent literary thief.[12]

The idea that Longfellow had stolen lines of *his own* for 'The Spanish Student' was extra fuel to the fire, and Poe wrote a strong critique of it, expecting Graham to publish it in his magazine. But it was too hot for Graham to handle. Poe himself had the courage of a lion, but few others were so brave. Graham was well aware that the wasps were buzzing around Poe's head, and did not wish to become embroiled in a war of the presses. Poe took *Graham's* refusal in good part.

The bottle of vitriol was put away for the next edition of the *Broadway Journal*, dated 5 April 1845. Possibly still irritated by the half-humorous claims of plagiarism levelled at himself (and possibly also realizing the many other claims which could be made against him for his earlier efforts), Poe had been thinking hard about the subject of plagiarism. It suddenly dawned on him that writers of genius had limited sources of inspiration and could all be stimulated by the same early spark. As in the idea of a collective unconscious, we all dip from the same well of the appreciation of beauty. That a long-forgotten work can later inspire the same feelings in later years can in part explain the similarity of its expression. As Poe put it:

> It appears to me that what seems to be the gross *inconsistency* of plagiarism as perpetrated by a poet, is very easily thus resolved: – the poetic sentiment (even without reference to the poetic power) implies a peculiarly, perhaps an abnormally keen appreciation of the beautiful, with a longing for its assimilation, or absorption, into the poetic identity. What the poet intensely admires, becomes thus, in very fact, although only partially, a portion of his own intellect. It has a secondary origination within his own soul – an origination altogether apart, although springing, from its primary origination from without. The poet is thus possessed by another's thought, and cannot be said to take of it, possession. But, in either view, he thoroughly feels it as *his own* – and this feeling is counteracted only by the sensible presence of its true, palpable origin in the volume from which he has derived it – an origin which, in the long lapse of years it is almost impossible *not* to forget – for in the mean time the thought itself is forgotten. But the frailest association will regenerate it – it springs up with all the vigor of a new birth – its absolute originality is not even a matter of suspicion – and when the poet has written it and printed it, and on its account is charged with plagiarism, there will be no one in the world more entirely astounded than himself. Now from what I have said it will be evident that the liability to accidents of this character is in the direct ratio of the poetic sentiment – of the susceptibility to the poetic impression; and in fact all literary history demonstrates that, for the most frequent and palpable plagiarisms, we must search the works of the most eminent poets.[13]

This was a brave and contrite statement. And just before this he had even asked pardon from those he might have insulted in the earlier sequence of letters in the Longfellow war – even Longfellow himself.

So the battle abruptly came to a confused end. Although Longfellow himself was well aware of the attacks made on him, he kept a restrained silence throughout. A gentleman in every way, it was beneath him to retaliate, and he stood aside and let the war continue, obviously hoping that it would run its own course and end in its own good time. His own reputation was hardly in doubt, although it may have been slightly tarnished by the 'Bonnie George Campbell' incident. Longfellow wanted only a quiet life, even if it meant working for his support for no fee. He did write a comment in his diary, however, stating that if Lowell were to continue to write such good work Poe would 'pound him'.

The cliques were not so forgiving. Having already marked Poe as a possible troublemaker, they now looked on him with a malignant eye. Not only was he a nuisance, he was a potential danger. Lewis Gaylord Clark in particular added the latest string of insults to his personal grudge bank, and hatred for this upstart poet and critic was smouldering.

While this somewhat unsavoury battle was in progress Poe did not neglect his editorial duties. Nor could he have been unaware that, although the potential for earning money was at his fingertips, precious little of it had as yet come his way. He had to find other ways of making ends meet, so he took once again to lecturing. There was no difficulty in attracting an audience, as his name now drew audiences far and wide. On the evening of 28 February 1845 he delivered his lecture on '*The Poets and Poetry of America*' at the Historical Society Library of New York. As befitted his new friendship (as he thought it) with Griswold, he omitted all negative references to him. At the lecture was the author William Mitchell Gillespie, who had just published *Rome as Seen by a New Yorker* through Wiley & Putnam. Poe had complimented the poetess Frances Sargent Osgood, but she was unable to attend because a friend let her down and left her waiting at her hotel.

At this time Poe's war with Longfellow was still raging, the cliques were defending their idol and attacking Poe. After his lecture an article appeared in the *National Archives*; the final paragraph alluded an attack made by the *New York Tribune*, scoffing at the audience of 300 and stating that 'any dancing dog or sommersetting monkey would have drawn a larger house'.[14] Ms Walter, the 'pretty witch', had added in her 'Transcript' that she would have preferred the animals to the man who had made such remarks about Longfellow. 'If he was to come before a Boston audience with such stuff, they would *poh* at him at once.'[15]

The *Southern Literary Messenger* had not given up hope of retrieving the services of its erstwhile editor, and Briggs and Bisco must have been astonished when they read the *Messenger*'s April edition, in which an announcement appeared: 'It needs an Argus to guard and watch the Press and, to enable the *Messenger* to discharge its part, we have engaged the services of Mr Edgar A. Poe, who will contribute a monthly critique . . .'[16] Although Poe wrote some pieces for the journal he was not employed in a full-time capacity, and he made that clear to his two partners. He still desperately needed the cash.

Around this time Poe wrote to his old friend in politics, Frederick W. Thomas. He had not heard from him since the 'Raven' catapulted him to fame. Poe was well aware that he still owed Jesse Dow money after borrowing from him during his ill-fated visit to Washington, so he suggested that he write articles for him until his debt was paid:

> And yet, Thomas, I have made no money. I am as poor now as ever I was in my life – except in hope, which is by no means bankable. I have taken a 3d pecuniary interest in the '*Broadway Journal*', and for every thing I have written for it have been, of course, so much out of pocket. In the end, however, it will pay me well – at least the prospects are good. Say to Dow for me that there never has been a chance for my repaying him, without putting myself to greater inconvenience than he himself would have wished to subject me to, had he known the state of the case. Nor am I able to pay him now. The Devil himself was never so poor. Say to Dow, also, that I am sorry he has taken to dunning in his old age.

In fact, Poe would have been able to discuss his suggestion for paying off his debt with Dow personally, as the latter was on his way to New York in any case.

At this time Poe met two of his correspondents. First, he met Chivers, but the first impression made by Poe was not auspicious, as Chivers recorded in a later Poe biography. He stated that when he saw him in Nassau Street he was 'drunk as an Indian', and they walked down the street together. Here is the incident in Chivers's own words:

By this time we had gotten opposite the Trait House, where we met Lewis Gaylord Clark, the Editor of the *Knickerbocker* Magazine. The moment Poe saw him – maddened by the remembrance of something that he had said in a recent Number of the Magazine touching one of his own articles which had appeared in the *Broadway Journal* – he swore, while attempting to rush away from my hold, that he would attack him.

'No!' said I, 'Poe! You must not do so while walking with me!'

'I will, by God!' continued he, pulling me along. Clark was then talking with another man, but as soon as this man saw the determined attitude of Poe, he immediately left him and went on his way – when Poe approached him, giving him his hand. As Clark responded to the offer of his hand, he exclaimed:

'Why, Poe! Is this you?'

'Yes, by God! This is Poe!' answered he, 'Here is my friend Dr Chivers from the South.'

'What!' exclaimed Clark, giving me his hand, 'Dr Chivers, the author of so many beautiful Poems?'

'Yes, by God!' said Poe, 'Not only the author of the beautifullest Poems ever written anywhere, but my friend too, by God!'

'I was very much pleased', said I, 'with Willis Gaylord Clark's Poems.'

'Yes, he was a noble fellow', said Clark, 'and I am his twin brother!'

'Good Lord!' said I internally – while Poe looked Good Lord all over – exclaiming in a rather belligerent tone:

'What business had you to abuse me in the last Number of your Magazine?'

'Why, by God! Poe!', exclaimed Clark, siding off towards the curbstone of the pavement – 'How did I know the Article referred to was yours? You had always attached your name to all your articles before, and how in Hell, did I know it was yours?'

By this time Clark had completely bowed himself away from the middle of Nassau Street, on his way to his office.

Poe, then, turning suddenly round to me, and locking his arm in mine, and pulling me impetuously along with him, in a selfconsciousness of his triumph, exclaimed in an indignant chuckle:

'A damned coward! By God!' and went on his way rejoicing.[17]

The second meeting was with James Russell Lowell. Lowell was visiting New York, and the two arranged to meet. They had never seen each other before, and their friendship had blossomed simply through their correspondence and their old working relationship. However, both had the greatest respect for each other, Poe having given glowing praise to Lowell's poetry and Lowell admiring Poe's fiction and poems. There must have been much anticipation in Lowell's mind when he knocked at Poe's door.

Sadly, things did not go well. Although at the zenith of his fame Poe was still in financial straits, and worry about Virginia's health did not help matters; a Dr Mitchell had diagnosed bronchitis. So Poe began to do what he always did in times of great stress or depression – he drank. When Lowell called he had already had a drink (one glass of wine would have an adverse effect on him), so when he was announced Poe quickly tried to sober up before he went to meet him. In this he was only partially successful. Later, Lowell wrote to George E. Woodberry, one of Poe's biographers: 'He was small; his com plexion of what I would call a clammy-white; fine, dark eyes, and fine head, very broad at the temples, but receding sharply from the brow backwards. His manner was rather formal, even pompous, but I have the impression he was a little soggy with drink – not tipsy – but as if he had been holding his head under a pump to cool it.' Much later Maria wrote to Lowell excusing her son-in-law:

> How much I wish I could see you, how quickly I could remove your wrong impression of my darling Eddie. The day you saw him in New York *he was not himself.* Do you not remember that I never left the room. Oh if you only knew his bitter sorrow when I told him how unlike himself he was while you were there you would have pitied him, he always felt particularly anxious to possess your approbation. If he spoke unkindly of you (as you say he did) rely on it, it was when he did not know of what he was talking.[18]

Poe himself, perhaps by way of saving face, reported to Thomas Chivers that 'I was very much disappointed in his appearance as an intellectual man. He was not half the noble-looking person that I expected to see.'

Chivers had visited the Poe household not long after this meeting. The Poes, and Maria, had moved to 195 East Broadway. When Chivers came Poe was unwell and spent a good deal of time in bed. But Chivers was far from convinced by Poe's illness – he had qualified as a doctor and, even though he did not practise medicine, he knew enough to suspect that Poe was malingering, and it seemed even more suspicious that Poe was due to deliver a poem at New York University. He was more than likely right; Poe always felt a great strain at appearing in public, and his latest depression would have made the ordeal even harder. Even Maria agreed that he was putting on an act.

Chivers, as we have seen, was an ebullient, poetical, flowery and religious individual; his relationship with Poe was a strange one, yet there is no doubt that they had great affection for each other – at least, while Poe was alive. Chivers was not a reliable witness to Poe's life, however, and he coloured facts to the point of distortion. But he did leave a detailed portrait of Poe's appearance. He described Poe's temperament as 'bilious, nervous, sanguinous – but, upon first view, appeared to be bilious, sanguinous, nervous'.[19] His forehead was broad. His hair was 'dark as a raven's wing' and his eyes were 'of a neutral violet tint, rather inclining to hazel' and shone 'with a mildly subdued serenity of intellectual splendour'. His eyelashes were 'long dark and sillian', hanging over his eyes 'like willow weeping by the Moon'. His mouth, 'like Apollo's bow unbent', contained a set of teeth 'as evenly set as the *Opal* walls of Eden', and could look beautiful when in a cheerful temper. His smile cheered but seemed to Chivers to be 'not a smile of joy, more one of Genius, a "smiling review" of all he had said just before'. His face was rather oval, 'tapering in the contour rather suddenly to the chin, which was very classical – and, especially when he smiled, really handsome'. His neck was long and slender, and when sitting gave the impression that he was taller than he really was. A peculiarity that struck Chivers was the way in which Poe's torso seemed to taper towards the shoulders. His arms and hands were also slender, but Chivers seems to have been mostly taken with his hands. 'In fact, his hands were truly remarkable for their roseate softness and lily-like, feminine delicacy. You could have judged of his nobility by his hands.' As for his clothes, 'his dress was always remarkably neat for one in his circumstances'. Imitating Chivers's example, Poe bought a cane, which he loved to carry while walking, and he flourished it 'with considerable grace'.[20] Such was the man who had, to the outward eye, achieved greatness, yet on closer inspection had achieved little besides. If wealth could be measured in terms of metre and literature, Poe was indeed a rich man, but in terms of hard currency he was still poor and looking for further ways of generating income.

Fear about Virginia's health, and his need for money, continued to haunt him. It seemed to him as if, no matter how much he worked and toiled – fifteen hours a day at times – he was no nearer to his goal.

Was he an alcoholic? The word 'alcoholic' was not invented until 1849. Its definition remains open to dispute, but it is defined by the *Journal of the American Medical Association* as 'a primary, chronic disease characterized by impaired control over drinking, preoccupation with the drug alcohol, use of alcohol despite adverse consequences, and distortions in thinking'.[21] There are known to be several risk factors predisposing to alcoholism. The obvious one is drinking constantly over a prolonged period. The age at which one starts to drink may be important. Males are more likely to succumb than females. Emotional states, such as depression and anxiety, can foster alcohol dependence. A genetic link has been proved, and family history can also play a vital role, especially if a parent has been victim to the problem.

Although there is no positive proof, it has been said that Poe drank at university when in his teens, although at that time it had no adverse effect, and at West Point. There also seems to be strong evidence of a genetic trait – his father, we know, took to drink towards the end of his career as an actor, and his brother William Henry developed a serious drink problem. A single glass of wine would be sufficient to send Rosalie off to a deep sleep. Moreover, Poe was prone to fits of depression and anxiety, as is evident from his letters. Certainly he would seem to be a strong candidate for alcoholism. On the other hand, he was a very intelligent man and was painfully aware of his problem, hating the hold alcohol had over him in times of stress. The dangers of drinking were not new to America – the depression after the War of Indepedence had resulted in crime and an increase in the levels of alcohol consumed; and as a backlash the first temperance society was formed in Connecticut in 1789. Others followed, often led by the Church, and by 1826 the American Temperance Society had been formed. So by the time Poe found himself fighting his own personal demon the problem was well known, established in print and preached from the sidewalks. Poe was always ashamed of his lapses and would often admit his weakness to friends and acquaintances in letters.

As for drug abuse, the only time that he took opium was much later, and there is no proof that he took the drug at any other time; Thomas D. English stated that on his visits he found no evidence of such a habit.

By this time there is little doubt that Poe had a serious drink problem, and he had probably had it since his first dismissal from the *Southern Literary Messenger*. It seemed to flare up especially in times of great stress or depression, as was the case now. His drinking affected his work to such an extent that Briggs became aware of it. Unable to countenance this behaviour, even at the risk of losing their prize contributor, Briggs removed Poe's name from the paper.

But Poe was not finished with the *Broadway Journal*. In a flurry of activity he entered into secret talks with Bisco while Briggs was in negotiations to take on a new publisher (a Mr Homans) and buy Bisco's share. To Briggs's surprise, Bisco held out against him, and a short battle took place between them, with the result that Bisco won full possession of the journal. What Briggs had not known was that Bisco was planning to oust him in any case. Poe was retained as sole editor (Watson continuing with the musical side of things) and was to receive 50 per cent of the profits. Briggs was embittered by all this and in his anger reversed his original good opinion of Poe.[22]

Poe now found himself again at the head of the journal, and with a greater financial incentive to work for its success. He published several revised versions of his pieces and some new work, including 'How to Write a Blackwood Article'. This article ridiculed the style of current magazines, picking on the famous *Blackwood's Magazine* as its victim. The narrator is one 'Suky Snobbs', who goes by the *nom de plume* 'the Signora Psyche Zenobia'.

> Of course I don't speak of the political articles. Everybody knows how they are managed, since Dr Moneypenny explained it. Mr Blackwood has a pair of tailor's-shears, and three apprentices who stand by him for orders. One hands him the *Times*, another the *Examiner* and a third a *Culley's New Compendium of Slang-Whang*. Mr B. merely cuts out and intersperses.

The article was accompanied by a piece entitled 'The Predicament', in which Poe took great satisfaction from having Suky stuck in a Gothic cathedral beneath the pendulum of an immense clock, which proceeds to decapitate her.

Following the success of 'The Raven' Wiley & Putnam published a book of his *Tales*. He must have been delighted by the terms: instead of a few copies for his friends, he now commanded whopping royalties of 8 cents per 50-cent book. Of course, he sent copies out to his friends in any case; and Thomas was warm in his praise: 'I have obtained your book published by Wiley & Putnam and have been delighted with it – I have just loaned it to a lady friend of mine who is an admirer of yours.'

It is time now to turn to a matter of the utmost importance when considering the rest of Poe's life – his relationship with women. Poe was endlessly susceptible to women and would on occasion have great cause to regret it. But it is completely wrong to think of Poe as a Don Juan or a Casanova. That he could have been is certain, but the idea of physical relationships with the women of his acquaintance was as foreign to him as it was hoped for by some who were not quite so fastidious.

Since the death of his own mother, his foster-mother and Mrs Stanard, Poe's ideals had reached the realms of Arcadia. His excessive need for love had never left him, and as a poet he longed for it. But this passion was evermore associated with the tragedy of loss, which he embodied in all his poetry and tales – the ethereal heroine teetering on the brink of destruction. This feeling of love was nothing short of adulation, and the power of his emotions raised these figures to the realms of the sublime. In so many ways his feelings towards the opposite sex had barely left adolescence, and he loved with all the passion of a never-ending puberty.

As for physical relationships, he had all he wanted with Virginia. His child-bride had grown to be his constant companion and helpmate, and he was totally devoted to her and to her mother. Despite assertions to the contrary, he lived with and for his family. After the deaths of all who were near to and beloved by him, he clung to Virginia like a lifeline. Nor was Virginia the dull child that some would make her out to be – she was his confidante, she had poetic leanings and was a skilled singer and musician. Just as Poe held fast to her, so did she devote herself to him. She had seen bad times and had nursed him through his illnesses and drunken binges – but her love for him never wavered, and they were inseparable. Poe could write about his goddesses, but their feet were clay – Virginia was his only real love and object of desire.

Poe's fame continued to make him a desirable ornament for soirées. The host was often James Lawson, the author; or Dr Orville Dewey, the preacher, in Mercer Street; or at Waverley Place, the poetess Anne C. Lynch. At these gatherings he was able to read his poetry and hear that of others, meet ladies of letters and flirt with them – these included Mary Gove (later Mrs Nichols), Elizabeth Oakes-Smith, Mary E. Hewitt and Mrs Elizabeth Frieze Ellett. Sometimes Virginia attended these get-togethers with her husband, and sometimes he would go alone.

At some stage, Poe and his family moved home, to 85 Amity Street, not far from the home of Anne C. Lynch. He was now in a position to attend her meetings regularly.

Women were fascinated by his slight build, his apparent vulnerability, his esoteric poems and his rakish reputation. Like Byron, they saw him as 'mad, bad and dangerous to know'. The element of danger and the thrill of getting to know this elusive poet with his dubious past interested them even further. Rumours of his drinking and his unreliability were common gossip; and since 'The Raven' his poems became better known, too. For a while, he was the man to be seen with.

In turn, Poe got to meet the leading lady poets of the time. Of all the literary ladies he met and admired, his attention at the time was centred upon Frances Sargent Osgood, whom he first met in Astor House in March. Later she would say: 'From that moment until his death we were friends.' Fanny, a Massachusetts girl, married an artist – Samuel Stillman Osgood – and they visited England for about five years, where she published a book of poems entitled *A Wreath of Flowers from New England*. On their return they settled in New York and Fanny became an important figure among the literati. Poe described her as 'about medium height and slender; complexion usually pale; hair black and glossy; eyes a clear, luminous grey, large and with great capacity for expression'.[23] There was more to her than that. She was petite, attractive and not a little coquettish; she loved flirting and loved attention. She, like the others, was intrigued by Poe and wanted to get to know him more. Earlier Poe had praised her poetry, and he wrote of her work:

> In fancy, as contradistinguished from imagination proper, in delicacy of taste, in refinement generally, in *naïveté*, in point, and, above all, in that inexpressible charm of charms which, for want of a better term or a more sufficient analysis than at present exists, we are accustomed to designate as *grace*, she is absolutely without a rival, we think, either in our own country or in England.[24]

Fanny Osgood was the type of female upon whom the troubadour Poe could unleash his passionate verses. As he always did when writing of his female creations, he waxed lyrical with emotional power as he worshipped at the altar of beauty. Fanny was an outlet for the pent-up forces within his soul, though he loved her not as a wooer, more as an acolyte. It was with a poet's eye he saw the inner goddess, an imago that in fact had little to do with the rather flighty person of Fanny; he was worshipping the beauty in femininity. This, as he said to Chivers, was the 'damnest amour' he felt. Of course, few women could resist such accolades, and Fanny returned his passion as was 'right fit'; she wrote to him, the Raven, as a poetical symbol. Fanny's husband realized this, and did nothing to dissuade them. In fact, he saw things as clearly as anyone. Just as this literary exchange posed no risk to Virginia, it presented none to Samuel Osgood. Like Poe, he was secure in his marriage and knew that there was no need for jealousy or discomfort. In fact, he painted Poe's portrait. In the same vein, Virginia welcomed Fanny's friendship, and she also became good friends with her husband's correspondent.

Poe and Fanny began their corrspondence in April, when Fanny, under the pseudonym Violet Vane, wrote him a piece entitled 'So Let It Be'. In it, Osgood gives guarded consent to the 'friendship' that had grown between them. Poe quickly followed up with his response, a poem entitled 'To F—'. Thus encouraged, Fanny wrote him a rejoinder, which began:

> I know a noble heart that beats
> For one it loves how 'wildly well!'
> *I* only know for *whom* it beats;
> But I must never tell!
> *Never* tell!
> Hush! Hark! How echo soft repeats, –
> Ah! Never tell![25]

The 'wildly well' was a quote from Poe's own 'Israfel'. Poe responded with a verse addressed directly to her, and the exchange became more frequent. One of Poe's most famous pieces, 'To F— O—', published in the *Broadway Journal*, runs in part:

> Thou wouldst be loved? – then let thy heart
> From its present pathway part not!
> Being everything which now thou art,
> Be nothing which thou art not.
> So with the world thy gentle ways,
> Thy grace, thy more than beauty,
> Shall be an endless theme of praise,
> And love – a simple duty.[26]

Although they flirted in a literary style, they remained simply good friends. She would visit him and Virginia, and she wrote that he was

Top left: Elizabeth 'Eliza' Poe (1796–1811), Poe's mother, from an original miniature given to Marie Louise Shew by Virginia Poe just before her death
Top right: John Allan (1779–1834), Poe's foster-father, with whom he had a tempestuous relationship
Above: Frances Keeling Allan (1785–1829), Poe's beloved foster-mother, also known as 'Ma'

Virginia Eliza Clemm (1822–47), also known as 'Sissy'; Maria's daughter and Poe's wife. This drawing was after an anonymous painting made soon after her death.

Edgar Allan Poe in the last year of his life; painting after the 1849 daguerreotype

Maria Clemm (1790–1871), also known as 'Muddy', Poe's aunt and future mother-in-law, who became his surrogate mother

George Rex Graham (1831–94), editor of *Graham's Magazine* and Poe's employer from 1841 to 1842

Rufus Wilmot Griswold (1815–57), author, anthologist and Poe's literary executor

Lewis Gaylord Clark (1808–73), editor of the *Knickerbocker*, leader of the New York literary coterie and Poe's enemy

Thomas Holley Chivers (1807–58), doctor, poet and Poe's close friend

Thomas Dunn English (1819–1902), doctor, writer, politician and bitter enemy of Poe, although late in life he defended him against the charge of drug abuse

James Lowell Russell (1819–91), Romantic poet, magazine editor and Poe's one-time friend; Poe worked for him when he ran the *Pioneer* journal

Elizabeth Fries Ellett (1812–77), historian and poet, whose friendship with Poe turned to enmity

Frances Sargent Osgood (1811–50), poet and playwright, whose flirtation with Poe led to a scandal, although she was to remain a lifelong friend

Anne Charlotte Lynch (1815–91), poet and socialite; Poe was a regular attendee of her Saturday literary soirées

Sarah Helen Whitman (1803–78), Poe's fiancée towards the end of his life and author of *Edgar Poe and His Critics*

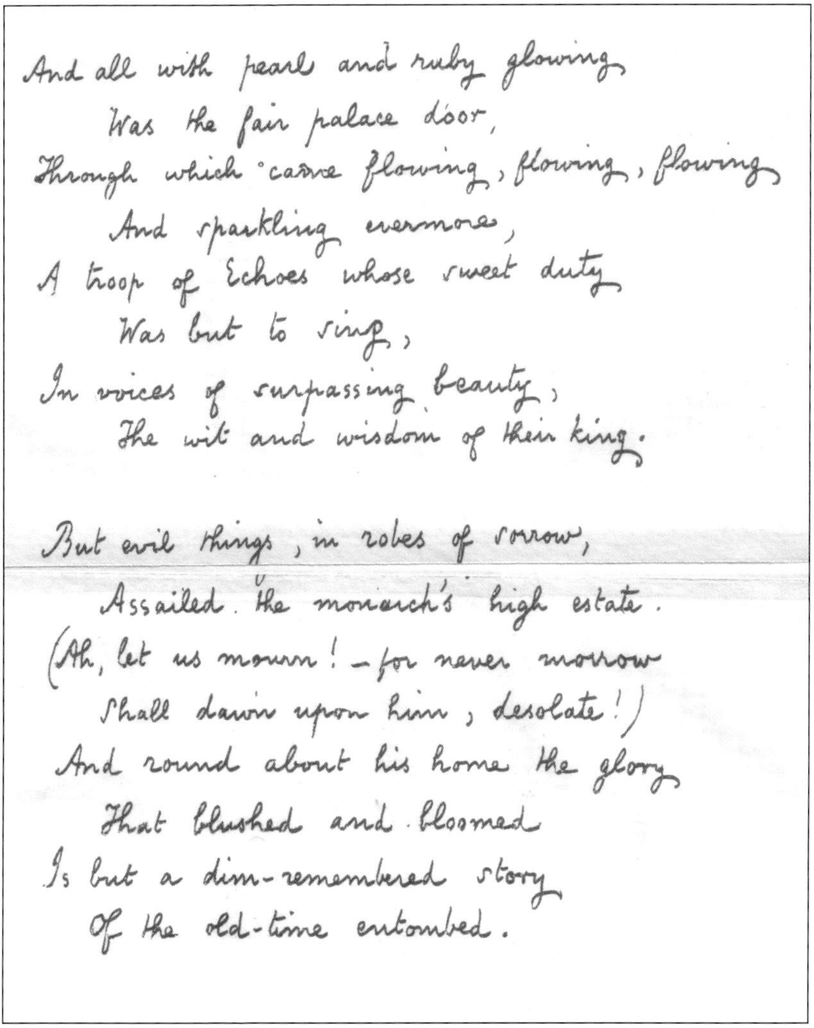
And all with pearl and ruby glowing
Was the fair palace door,
Through which came flowing, flowing, flowing
And sparkling evermore,
A troop of Echoes whose sweet duty
Was but to sing,
In voices of surpassing beauty,
The wit and wisdom of their king.

But evil things, in robes of sorrow,
Assailed the monarch's high estate.
(Ah, let us mourn! – for never morrow
Shall dawn upon him, desolate!)
And round about his home the glory
That blushed and bloomed
Is but a dim-remembered story
Of the old-time entombed.

Extract from 'The Haunted Palace' by Poe, in his own hand, first published in 1839 (a full transcript of this page can be found in Appendix 1)

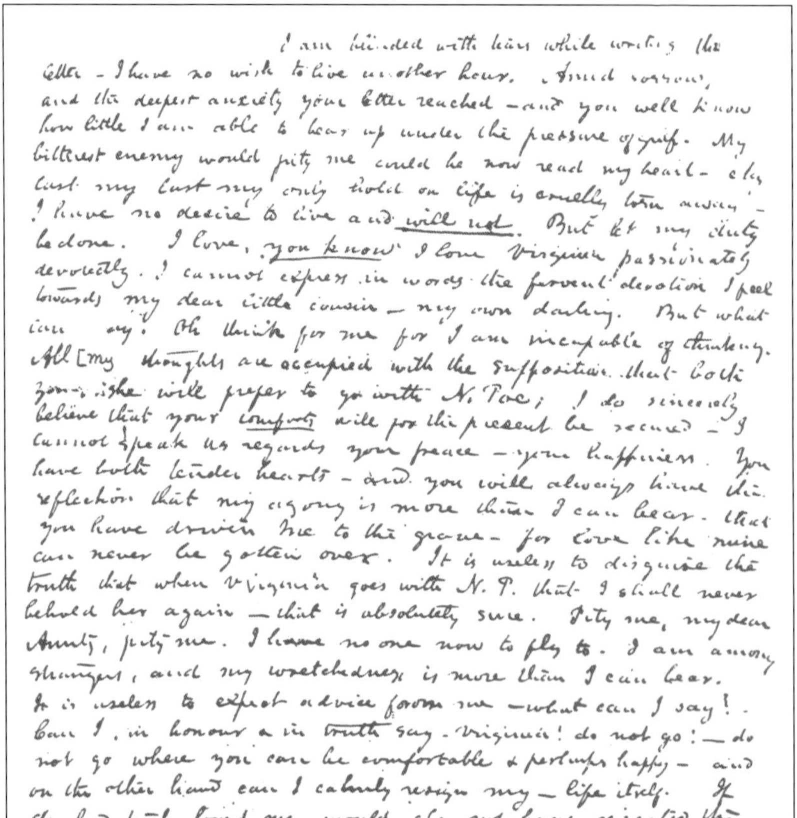

I am blinded with tears while writing this letter — I have no wish to live another hour. Amid sorrow, and the deepest anxiety your letter reached — and you well know how little I am able to bear up under the pressure of grief. My bitterest enemy would pity me could he now read my heart — My last my last my only hold on life is cruelly torn away — I have no desire to live and will not. But let my duty be done. I love, you know I love Virginia passionately devotedly. I cannot express in words the fervent devotion I feel towards my dear little cousin — my own darling. But what can I say? Oh think for me for I am incapable of thinking. All [my] thoughts are occupied with the supposition that both you & she will prefer to go with N. Poe; I do sincerely believe that your comforts will for the present be secured — I cannot speak as regards your peace — your happiness. You have both tender hearts — and you will always have the reflection that my agony is more than I can bear — that you have driven me to the grave — for love like mine can never be gotten over. It is useless to disguise the truth that when Virginia goes with N. P. that I shall never behold her again — that is absolutely sure. Pity me, my dear Aunty, pity me. I have no one now to fly to. I am among strangers, and my wretchedness is more than I can bear. It is useless to expect advice from me — what can I say? Can I, in honour & in truth say — Virginia! do not go! — do not go where you can be comfortable & perhaps happy — and on the other hand can I calmly resign my — life itself. If she had truly loved me would she not have rejected the offer with scorn? Oh God have mercy on me!

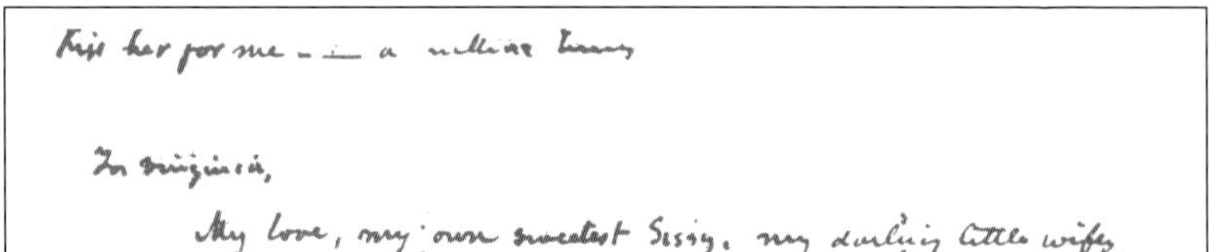

Kiss her for me — a million times

For Virginia,

My love, my own sweetest Sissy, my darling little wifey, think well before you break the heart of your cousin. Eddy.

Top: A desperate letter of 29 August 1839 from Poe to Maria Clemm, begging for an early marriage
Above: An agonized postscript to Virginia from the same letter
(see Appendix 1)

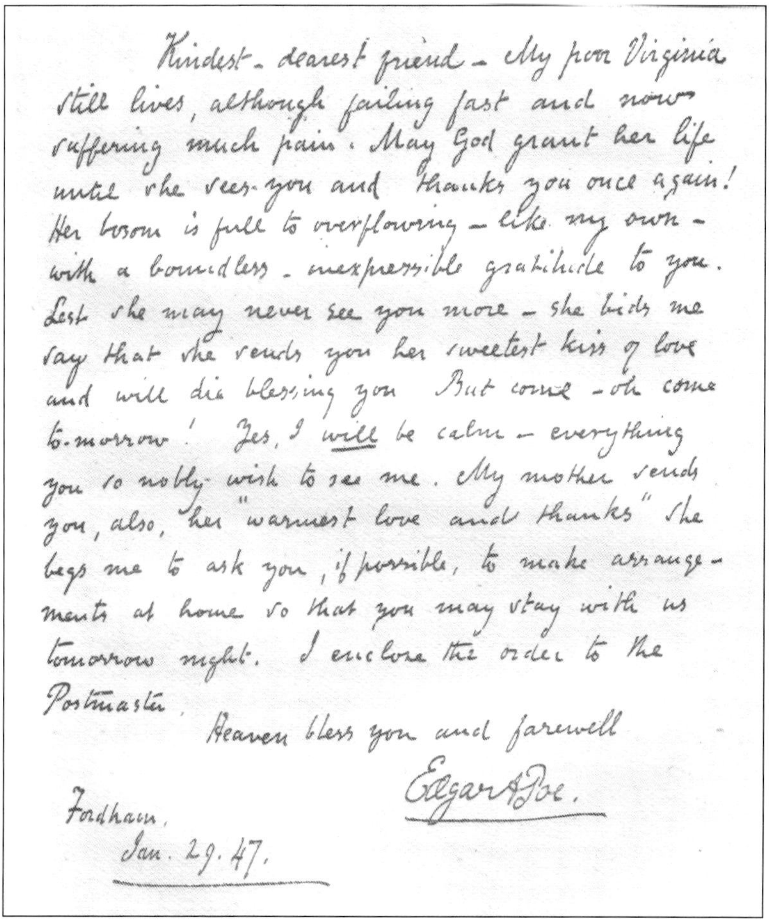

Kindest – dearest friend – My poor Virginia still lives, although failing fast and now suffering much pain. May God grant her life until she sees you and thanks you once again! Her bosom is full to overflowing – like my own – with a boundless – inexpressible gratitude to you. Lest she may never see you more – she bids me say that she sends you her sweetest kiss of love and will die blessing you But come – oh come to-morrow! Yes, I <u>will</u> be calm – everything you so nobly wish to see me. My mother sends you, also, her "warmest love and thanks" She begs me to ask you, if possible, to make arrange-ments at home so that you may stay with us tomorrow night. I enclose the order to the Postmaster.

Heaven bless you and farewell

Edgar A Poe.

Fordham,
Jan. 29. 47.

A letter from Poe to Marie Louise Shew, begging for help as Virginia lay dying (see Appendix 1)

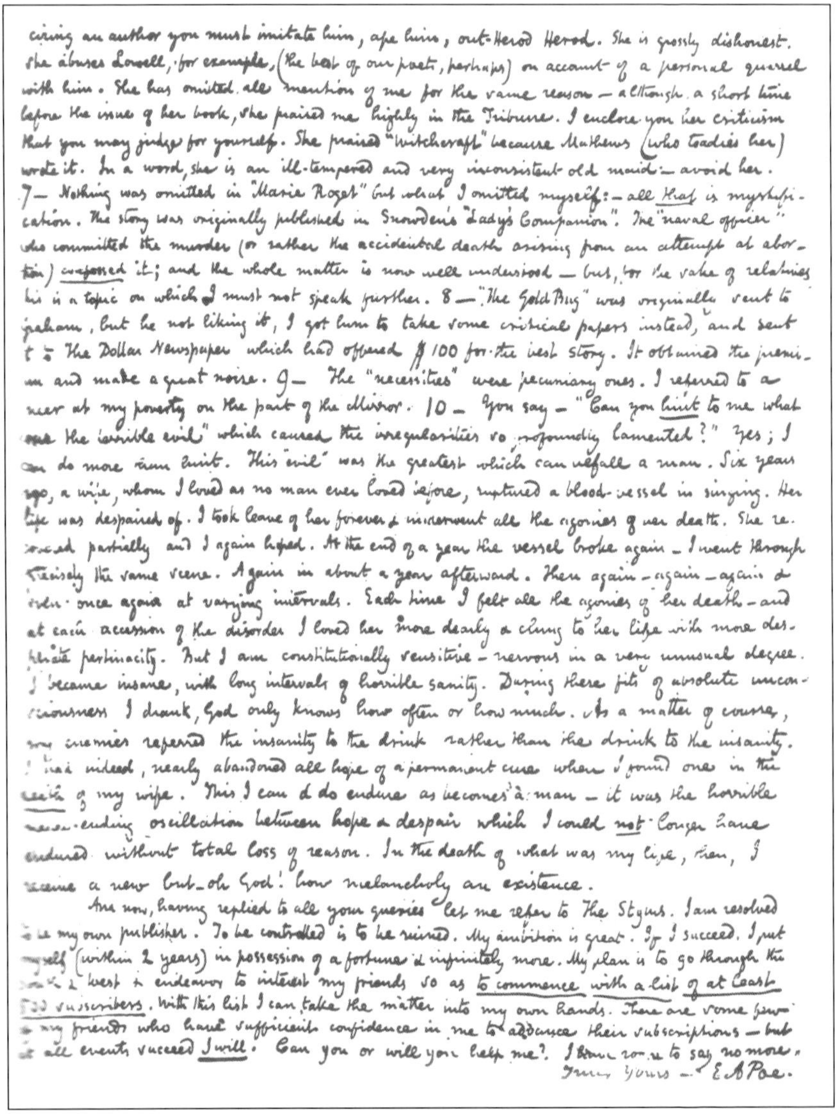

viewing an author you must imitate him, ape him, out-Herod Herod. She is grossly dishonest. She abuses Lowell, for example, (the best of our poets, perhaps) on account of a personal quarrel with him. She has omitted all mention of me for the same reason — although, a short time before the issue of her book, she praised me highly in the Tribune. I enclose you her criticism that you may judge for yourself. She praised "Witchcraft" because Mathews (who toadies her) wrote it. In a word, she is an ill-tempered and very inconsistent old maid — avoid her. 7 — Nothing was omitted in "Marie Roget" but what I omitted myself: — all that is mystification. The story was originally published in Snowden's "Lady's Companion". The "naval officer" who committed the murder (or rather the accidental death arising from an attempt at abortion) confessed it; and the whole matter is now well understood — but, for the sake of relatives, this is a topic on which I must not speak further. 8 — "The Gold Bug" was originally sent to Graham, but he not liking it, I got him to take some critical papers instead, and sent it to The Dollar Newspaper which had offered $100 for the best story. It obtained the premium and made a great noise. 9 — The "necessities" were pecuniary ones. I referred to a sneer at my poverty on the part of the Mirror. 10 — You say — "Can you hint to me what was the 'terrible evil' which caused the irregularities so profoundly lamented?" Yes; I can do more than hint. This "evil" was the greatest which can befall a man. Six years ago, a wife, whom I loved as no man ever loved before, ruptured a blood-vessel in singing. Her life was despaired of. I took leave of her forever & underwent all the agonies of her death. She recovered partially and I again hoped. At the end of a year the vessel broke again — I went through precisely the same scene. Again in about a year afterward. Then again — again — again & even once again at varying intervals. Each time I felt all the agonies of her death — and at each accession of the disorder I loved her more dearly & clung to her life with more desperate pertinacity. But I am constitutionally sensitive — nervous in a very unusual degree. I became insane, with long intervals of horrible sanity. During these fits of absolute unconsciousness I drank, God only knows how often or how much. As a matter of course, my enemies referred the insanity to the drink rather than the drink to the insanity. I had, indeed, nearly abandoned all hope of a permanent cure when I found one in the death of my wife. This I can & do endure as becomes a man — it was the horrible never-ending oscillation between hope & despair which I could not longer have endured without total loss of reason. In the death of what was my life, then, I receive a new but — oh God! how melancholy an existence.

And now, having replied to all your queries let me refer to The Stylus. I am resolved to be my own publisher. To be controlled is to be ruined. My ambition is great. If I succeed, I put myself (within 2 years) in possession of a fortune & infinitely more. My plan is to go through the South & West & endeavor to interest my friends so as to commence with a list of at least 500 subscribers. With this list I can take the matter into my own hands. There are some few of my friends who have sufficient confidence in me to advance their subscriptions — but at all events succeed I will. Can you or will you help me? I have room to say no more.

Truly Yours — E A Poe.

A letter of 4 January 1848 to George Eveleth in which Poe discusses his drink problem, exacerbated by the death of his wife Virginia (see Appendix 1) 'playful, affectionate, witty . . . for his young, gentle, and for his idolised wife – he had . . . a kind word, a pleasant smile, a graceful and courteous attention'. Poe told her that when he wrote about the literati of New York the length of the notice was in proportion to the estimation he held of their worth; with Virginia's help he measured them all, and whose was the longest? 'Just as if her little vain heart didn't tell her it's herself!'[27]

Behind the scenes all was not well with the *Broadway Journal*. In fact they were finding it tough to keep their heads above water. Having taken over, Bisco found that he had inherited financial problems. This could, apparently, be rectified with a loan of $50, so Poe looked to his old, and rich, friend Chivers:

> Mr Bisco says to me that, with the loan of $50, for a couple of months, he would be put out of all difficulty in respect to the publication of the '*Broadway Journal*'. Its success is decided, and will eventually make us a fortune. It would be, therefore, a great pity that anything of a trifling nature (such as a want of $50) should interfere with our prospects. You know that I have no money at command myself, and therefore I venture to ask you for the loan required. If you can aid us, I know you will. In 2 months certainly the money will be repaid.

Chivers wrote Poe a typically long and rambling reply. Poe can have the money when his friend returns a loan, but . . .

> You are always talking to me about the 'paper.' 'Cuss' the paper! what do I care for the 'paper'? The 'paper' will do me no more good than it will any body else. I have no interest in it – it is in your individual welfare and happiness that I have an interest – an abiding, disinterested, heartborn interest – although I should like to see the paper flourish, as it would be an interest to you. For Heaven's sake! do not connect my respect for you with any worldly matter – as it does not belong to the world at all. I see plainly that you do not know me. I would not let you have a cent for any other consideration than the heartborn respect which I feel for you, as your friend – one who desires, from the bottom of his heart, your welfare and happiness, in every respect whatever. My dear Poe! you must not practice lip service with me – you must talk from the bottom of your heart when you talk to me. I am your friend, and, therefore, whenever I talk to you, it is out of the substance of my heart. It is an absolute waste of time, as well as a sin against God, to talk any other way.

As for Poe's assertion that he has stopped drinking: 'You say you have not touched a drop of the ashes of Hell since I left New York. That's a man. For God's sake, but *more* for your own, never touch *another drop*.'

Apart from worries about the *Broadway Journal*, Poe was still trying to raise more cash on his own, and to that purpose he began making moves to have a collection of his poems published, hoping that sales would be buoyed up by the inclusion of 'The Raven'; the volume was to be called *The Raven and Other Poems*.[28]

Now he was invited to the Boston Lyceum for a poetry reading, and he willingly accepted in spite of the warnings of 'the pretty witch' and the fact that he had attacked their beloved Longfellow. The reading was not a success; he followed a three-hour lecture by the politician Caleb Cushing, who had already bored the crowd to tears, and they were in no mood to listen to much more. Cushing's speech was calculated to appeal to the audience, and in it he extolled the virtue of the American state while criticizing her natural enemy, Britain. His intentions were good, but his monologue was overlong. When he finally sat down it was Poe's turn to take the podium. He had little to give them in the vein of 'The Raven', so he turned to his old favourite, 'Al Aaraaf', which he had always felt was misjudged and had not reached its audience. Perhaps now, with his enhanced reputation, it would come into its own. It did not. After a short talk on didacticism he recited the poem, but some members of the audience began to leave before it ended. Then a request was made that he read out 'The Raven', and although more of the audience were leaving, thinking that the night was over, Poe acquiesced. After the reading he compounded matters by taking a drink with eminent Bostonians, including Cushing, and under the influence he told them that he had tricked the audience by reading a poem he had written when he was twelve. To say the least, they were little impressed.

Cornelia Walter must have rubbed her hands when she heard that Poe was going to make a personal appearance in Boston. Her review of the reading was not complimentary, but also not excessively harsh, although she did state that she had trouble hearing the poem because of the noise of members of the audience departing before it had finished. Most Bostonians would have applauded her; but her criticisms were not accepted wholesale. In the *Sunday Times and Messenger* a Major M. M. Noah was plainly embarrassed by the treatment at the hands of both press and audience of a poet of such eminence as Poe.[29]

When the Boston press heard of Poe's comments to Cushing and the others, they were incensed and began to roundly pan him for his efforts. Cornelia Walter wrote: 'Should Mr Poe be desirous of knowing further what is thought of the matter in these parts, we refer him to the pleasant adventure of the immortal Barabello, the "Broadway Poet of Rome", who was crowned with cabbage in the Capitol.'[30] As the days went by the Boston clique hounded him, anonymously and otherwise; and it soon became obvious that he would have to face the brewing storm. Some of his allies had rallied around, but it was time for Poe to address the matter. He gave a statement in the *Broadway Journal* on 1 November and defended himself well. Unfortunately, however, he ended with a stringent attack on Boston, with such insults that it made him strong enemies among the Bostonian clique – or the 'Frogpondians', as he dubbed them.

> We like Boston. We were born there – and perhaps it is just as well not to mention that we are heartily ashamed of the fact. The Bostonians are very well in their way. Their hotels are bad. Their pumpkin pies are delicious. Their poetry is not so good. Their Common is no common thing – and the duck-pond might answer – if its answer could be heard for the frogs.
>
> But for all these good qualities the Bostonians have no soul. They have always evinced towards us individually the basest ingratitude for the services we rendered them in enlightening them about the originality of Mr Longfellow. When we accepted, therefore, an invitation to 'deliver' a poem in Boston – we accepted it simply and solely, because we had a curiosity to know how it felt to be publicly hissed – and we wished to see what effect we could produce by a neat little *impromptu* speech in reply. Perhaps, however, we overrated our own importance, or the Bostonian want of common civility – which is not quite so manifest as one or two of their editors would wish the public to believe. We assure Major Noah that he is wrong. The Bostonians are well-bred – as *very* dull persons very generally are.[31]

This made things much worse, and there was a cry of outrage from all quarters of Boston. Cornelia Walter had already scoffed that Poe's talents had deteriorated since he was ten years old, 'his best poems having been written before that period'.[32] It was some time before the storm abated.

The affairs of the *Journal* were getting worse, and in desperation an offer came from Bisco to Poe. Bisco was willing to sell the *Journal* to him for a mere $50 – plus the debts incurred. Poe was eager to accept and signed a promissory note endorsed by Horace Greeley, an erstwhile contributor to the *Journal*. Now at last Poe was at the helm of his very own journal – albeit one that was beset with financial difficulties. He had already shown that he was more than capable of editing a successful magazine, but even the best editor in the country (and some would claim that *was* Poe) could not produce copy from fresh air. Not only did Poe need to borrow the money to pay Bisco for control of the periodical, he also needed capital to run the business until it proved profitable. It was a hopeless task, but he was not to be easily beaten down. He approached Rufus Griswold and John Kennedy, among others. Some did indeed comply with his wishes and sent money to him.

Wiley & Putnam announced the publication of *The Raven and Other Poems* on 8 November. Poe's preface contains the famous lines:

> Events not to be controlled have prevented me from making at any time any serious effort in what, under happier circumstances, would have been the field of my choice. With me poetry has been not a purpose, but a passion; and the passions should be held in reverence; they must not – they cannot at will be excited, with an eye to the paltry compensations, or the more paltry recommendations, of mankind.[33]

On the whole, the critical notices were not good. It was to be expected that Lewis G. Clark would not be complimentary. He even felt ready to take a swipe at 'The Raven', saying that it 'would not bear scrutiny'. He scoffed at Poe's metre and his claims to precocity and claimed that Poe was an 'imitator'. He also took the opportunity to reject Poe's criticisms, dismissing them as 'coarse personal abuse'; 'in ladies' magazines he is an Aristarchus, but among men of letters his sword is a broken lath'.[34]

The pressure again drove Poe towards depression. He needed money to keep the *Broadway Journal* afloat, and this seemed a never-ending problem. He wrote to Duyckinck in the hope he could wheedle owed money out of his publisher. He also wrote to the poet Halleck, blaming his current difficulties on the efforts of certain persons to sabo-tage the *Journal*. This is not as paranoid as it may seem, as there were many people among the cliques of Boston and New York who had reason to dislike Poe personally and possibly to fear him professionally. He requested

$100, and it is to his credit that Halleck actually complied with his request. Poe also turned to Thomas D. English for advice, and English suggested that he contact Thomas H. Lane at the Custom House. Although some negotiations ensued, nothing came of them.

While battling against fortune and time Poe wrote another successful hoax. This time it was 'The Facts in the Case of M. Valdemar'.[35] He purports to be a doctor with an interest in hypnotism. He hypnotizes a willing volunteer to the point of death and holds him in an animated state until the patient begs to be freed; as the doctor makes certain passes over the subject with his arms, the volunteer's body melts before the terrified eyes of witnesses. The ending is suitably horrific:

> As I rapidly made the mesmeric passes, amid ejaculations of 'dead! dead!' absolutely *bursting* from the tongue and not from the lips of the sufferer, his whole frame at once – within the space of a single minute, or even less, shrunk – crumbled – absolutely *rotted* away beneath my hands. Upon the bed, before that whole company, there lay a nearly liquid mass of loathsome – of detestable putrescence.

This was published in the December edition of *American Review: A Whig Journal* and subsequently in the *Broadway Journal*. An English hypnotist, Robert H. Collyer, was totally taken in:

> Dear Sir, – your account of M. Valdemar's case has been universally copied in this city, and has created a very great sensation. It requires from me no apology, in stating, that I have not the least doubt of the possibility of such a phenomenon; for I did actually restore to active animation a person who died from excessive drinking of ardent spirits. He was placed in his coffin ready for interment. You are aware that death very often follows excessive excitement of the nervous system; this arising from the extreme prostration which follows; so that the vital powers have not sufficient energy to react. I will give you the detailed account on your reply to this, which I require for publication, in order to put at rest the growing impression that your account is merely a splendid creation of your own brain, not having any truth in fact.

Collyer was not the only one to be taken in. The tale was believed by some English papers, including the *Popular Record of Modern Science* and the *Morning Post*.

In the mail Poe also received a fan-letter from a 'rustic youngster from the backwoods of Maine'. The author was a medical student who became a constant correspondent, George W. Eveleth. He wrote of his admiration: 'To be short and direct, Mr Poe is the one I have selected from all the writers of whom I know any thing, for my especial favourite. I am passionately fond of reading his productions of all kinds' and concluded: 'Will Mr Poe not address me?'

Poe would. In his next letter Eveleth even sent $3 towards the *Journal*. However, by Christmas it was obvious to Poe that he could not go on with the magazine, and it folded. The tasks involved in its dissolution were carried out by Thomas H. Lane and, apparently, Thomas Dunn English. A valedictory then appeared, dated 16 December: 'Unexpected engagements demanding my whole attention, and the objects being fulfilled so far as regards myself personally, for which "The *Broadway Journal*" was established, I now, as its editor, bid farewell – as cordially to foes as to friends. EDGAR A. POE.'[36] The loss of the *Journal* was of course a crushing blow, but as ever he was reluctant to let go of his hopes. He had soon resuscitated his plan for the *Stylus* and was doing the groundwork. It was a project he clung to with the desperation of a drowning man. In a postscript to a letter to the editor Sarah Hale, dated 16 January 1846, he wrote:

> The *B. Journal* had fulfilled its destiny – which was a matter of no great moment. I have never regarded it as more than a temporary adjunct to other designs. I am now busy making arrangements for the establishment of a Magazine which offers a wide field for literary ambition. Professor Chas. Anthon has agreed to take charge for me of a Department of Criticism on Scholastic Letters. His name will be announced. I shall have, also, a Berlin and a Parisian correspondent – both of eminence. The first No. may not appear until Jan. 1847.

He decided to write sketches of New York's men and women of letters and to append a description not only of the work but also of their physical appearance. It seems a good journalistic plan and would attract readers. He began his research by asking Duyckinck to ascertain the personal details of a number of these leading figures.

Returning to Poe's social life, an event was fast approaching that would have serious repercussions for his future. He was still involved in literary flirtations with a number of the lady authors of the city, in particular Fanny Osgood and Elizabeth Ellett. Elizabeth was married to chemistry professor William Henry Ellett and had been born and bred in New York. She turned to letters with some success; her first published volume, in 1835, had been *Poems, Translated and Original*. No doubt drawn to Poe by his chivalrous and elegant manner, she became enamoured of him and, like Fanny Osgood, began to send him poems. On 17 December 1845 she sent a note to him concerning her husband's removal from his college; but the real reason lies in the following German postscript.

> Iche habe einen Brief fur Sie – wollen Sie gerfalligst heute Abend nach Uhr den sebbe bein mir entnehmen oder abholen lassen.
>
> O welchen Riss erregst du mir im Herzen
> Die Sinne sind in deinen Banden noch
> Hat gleich die Seele blutend sich befreit!

which may be translated:

> I have a letter for you. Will you not most kindly pick it up or have it sent for after seven o'clock this evening.
>
> O, what a rent you have made in my heart
> The senses are still in your bonds
> Though the bleeding soul has freed itself.

Like other friends, the two women, Elizabeth and Fanny, were frequent visitors to the Poe household and knew Virginia well. Fanny herself was genuinely fond of Poe's wife and could see the bond that linked the couple together, but Elizabeth was in the toils of love and wanted Poe for herself – at least, she wanted to be the only object of his desires. Fanny was simply a literary friend of Poe, and although she was a minor irritant she was no real rival. At least, so Elizabeth thought until she unexpectedly paid a visit. Whether she went searching among Poe's private papers (something she would be caught doing in the future) or whether, less likely, she just happened upon it, she found and read one of Fanny's letters. There she found the romantic style she had thought reserved for herself alone. From that second she became Poe's bitter enemy. Not only did she show Virginia 'that fearful letter', she went on to hound her with anonymous letters for the rest of her life.

Jealousy gnawed at her and fuelled her rage. She lost no time but started spreading rumours of Poe's infidelity with Fanny Osgood, which soon had spread far and wide and became common gossip. These tales would not have pleased Rufus Griswold, who himself had harboured desires for the lady. Elizabeth's notes reached Virginia, and she even had the temerity to approach Samuel Osgood himself. But here she overreached herself. Osgood was no fool, and, knowing about the friendship between his wife and Poe, he was outraged at the slurs made on the reputation of his wife. Immediately he threatened Elizabeth with a lawsuit for libel, which temporarily put her off her stride. But only temporarily – her fury was too all-consuming for her to baulk at that. She went on to suggest that the letter might not have been written by Fanny at all, but had been a forgery written by Poe himself.

Virginia had seen her husband in adversity before and had supported him through all eventualities. So did she now, but this time she, too, was enmeshed in Elizabeth Ellett's toils. The continuous gossip, and the notes from Ellett, depressed her immeasurably, as can be seen in the Valentine she wrote to Poe. It is an acrostic, each first letter spelling out Poe's name; and in it she betrays her wish to leave the world and its gossip behind, to live only with him:

> Ever with thee I wish to roam –
> Dearest my life is thine.
> Give me a cottage for my home
> And a rich old cypress vine,
> Removed from the world with its sin and care
> And the tattling of many tongues,
> Love alone shall guide us when we are there –
> Love shall heal my weakened lungs,
> And oh the tranquil hours we'll spend
> Never wishing that others may see!
> Perfect ease we'll enjoy, without thinking to lead
> Ourselves to the world and its glee –
> Ever peaceful and blissful we'll be.

However, things were not allowed to rest, and Mrs Ellett's poison began to do its work. The friends that Fanny had made at the literary soirées began to fear for her reputation, and they spoke to her about it. She conceded that she had written Poe some letters and verses but categorically denied any romantic liaison. But could she not see, they argued, the danger she was in? At the moment Poe was the object of everyone's talk, but should it prove that he was in possession of damaging evidence against her how would things look then? Her letters could be misinterpreted, after all, much to Fanny's disadvantage – and coupled with the verses they knew she had written they might be enough to spark further rumours. There was only one possible course of action. She must retrieve her letters; Poe must be forced to give them up.

Poor Fanny was in a dilemma of her own making. To refuse to reclaim the letters would be tantamount to a confession. Yet Poe was dear to her, and she did not wish to hurt him or to aggravate the wrongs he felt. She could call on him herself, but that would be too risky in the light of all the rumours. Now her reputation had been called into question, and she had no choice but to comply. She agreed to allow two representatives to call on Poe and ask for the letters back – the social hostess Anne C. Lynch and the feminist Margaret Fuller.

When Fuller and Lynch knocked on Poe's door that day he must have wondered what was going on. He was less than pleased when they explained their errand and was indignant that such a matter should be pursued to his home. However, if Fanny had asked for the return of her letters, he was too much of a gentleman to deny her. Bristling with chagrin, he went to collect them and angrily handed them over. But he knew very well who was at the bottom of all this, and in a rash instant, as the women left, he told them to tell Mrs Ellett that she should look to her own letters. After that, the women took the correspondence back to Fanny – and reported Poe's parting remark.

When Elizabeth heard of Poe's remark she was livid and determined to use this as extra fuel to attack him. Although Poe did return her correspondence she refused to let matters drop and consulted her brother, a Colonel Lummis. The good colonel was convinced that Poe's actions had touched his sister's honour and demanded satisfaction. To a soldier and a man of honour there was only one recourse. He challenged Poe to a duel.

Poe was no coward, and these new events galled him even further. Losing no time, he saw Thomas Dunn English and asked him to lend him a pistol. But English had heard the stories and was not at all convinced that Poe was innocent; besides, he had no intention of lending him a pistol to exacerbate an already dangerous situation. Poe became irate with him, and English got angry in his turn. An exchange of words followed in which English called Poe a liar. So animated did the argument become that it ended in a fist fight, after which Poe claimed he had to be dragged off English's 'rascally carcass', and English claimed he had taught Poe a lesson he would never forget.

Although the duel never took place, Poe himself was in a dilemma of Elizabeth Ellett's making. He had two impossible choices – either to continue to tell the truth, that Elizabeth's letters really had existed, or to pretend that they had not. He now had no proof to back up the first assertion; and even if he had it would mean compromising a lady, something that would be repugnant to Poe even in the case of Elizabeth. On the other hand, if he denied the letters he would brand himself a liar and lend fuel to the damaging rumours that were already afloat.

Colonel Lummis let the matter rest, presumably after finding that Mrs Ellett had received the letters. But the damage done to Poe's reputation was incalculable, and English, who had once been on good terms with Poe, became his fiercest enemy. The talk continued about Poe, his drunkenness, his debauchery and his reputation with women. But to all of these was added another, darker whisper, which gained in currency and was soon common gossip. Poe was mad.

12

THE MAN THAT WAS USED UP

Once again, in the tragic carousel ride that was his life, Poe was without work and had to rely upon his magazine contributions for money. Things were once again tough for the Poe family. In the aftermath of the Ellett affair, Poe's mental state deteriorated and he fell ill. It is more than likely that he took to the bottle. Depression dominated him.

Unaware of his condition, not even his pen friends could comfort him. Instead they were more interested in what had happened to the money they had sent him. Abijah M. Idle was wondering what was going on, and their correspondence ended here.[1] Another friend, George Eveleth, was also concerned about the $3 he had sent to Poe, but Poe returned it with a note in which he commented: 'You seem to take matters very easily and I really wonder at your patience under the circumstances.'

By now the Poes had moved to Fordham, West Fields, some thirteen miles from the city; the cottage was on Fordham Hill and surrounded by an acre or so of fenced-in meadow. Poe leased it from its owner, John Valentine, for $100 per annum. His lifestyle can be glimpsed through a note of Maria's: 'He passed the greater part of the morning in his study, and, after he had finished his task for the day, he worked in our beautiful flower garden, or read and recited poetry to us.'[2] He still hoped his influential friends would drum up work for him. He had sent his *Tales* to Dickens, as well as a suggestion that the *Daily News* might publish some of his work, but Dickens was not associated with the editorship: 'In reference to your proposal as regards the *Daily News*, I beg to assure you that I am not in any way connected with the Editorship or current Management of that Paper. I have an interest in it, and write such papers for it as I attach my name to. This is the whole amount of my connection with the Journal.'

Naturally, after the Osgood–Ellett débâcle, Poe did not see fit to resume his attendances at the soirées of which he had been so prominent a member. But he was still talked about and often. Mary Hewitt, the poet, had great admiration for Poe, and had had many a chat with Fanny Osgood. Knowing the true state of affairs, she was eager to assure Poe that he was sorely missed. In a sensitive and honourable way she hinted that Fanny was still Poe's friend. The letter must have been a comfort to Poe.

> We were all exceedingly sorry to hear of your illness in Baltimore, and glad when we heard that you had so far recovered as to be able to return to our latitude, though it were to play hide-and-seek with your friends. Our charming friend Mrs Osgood, and myself, indulge often in talking of you and your dear wife. Next to seeing those we remember, is the luxury of talking of them – and you know the power of the feminine organ at laudation, as well as its opposite.
>
> All Bluedom misses you from its charmed circle, and we often ask when are we to have Mr Poe back again among us.

The poet Philip Cooke was back in touch, and Poe mentioned his work on the literati and hopes of writing a book on the subject, using Lowell's memoir:

> I am now writing for Godey a series of articles called 'The N.Y. City Literati'. They will run through the year & include personal descriptions, as well as frank opinions of literary merit. Pending the issue of this series, I am getting ready similar papers to include American litterateurs generally – and, by the beginning of December, I hope to put to press (here and in England) a volume embracing all the articles under the common head 'The Living Literati of the U.S.' – or something similar.

He was never happier than when he had projects in hand and kept himself busy. The inkstand replaced the bottle. He worked with his customary diligence, and after a time he had completed the drafts for the 'Literati of New York' sketches, which were to appear between May and October in *Godey's Lady's Book*. Signatures from the individual authors were included in a reissue of the May number. Poe wrote to Godey enclosing all the autographs he had gathered and awaiting their publication.

At this time the poet Elizabeth Barrett wrote to thank Poe for his *Tales.*

> Your 'Raven' has produced a sensation, a 'fit horror,' here in England. Some of my friends are taken by the fear of it and some by the music. I hear of persons haunted by the 'Nevermore,' and one acquaintance of mine who has the misfortune of possessing a 'bust of Pallas' never can bear to look at it in the twilight. I think you will like to be told our great poet, Mr Browning, the author of 'Paracelsus,' and the 'Bells and Pomegranates,' was struck much by the rhythm of that poem.
>
> Then there is a tale of yours ('The Case of M. Valdemar') which I do not find in this volume, but which is going the round of the newspapers, about mesmerism, throwing us all into 'most admired disorder,' and dreadful doubts as to whether 'it can be true,' as the children say of ghost stories. The certain thing in the tale in question is the power of the writer, and the faculty he has of making horrible improbabilities seem near and familiar.

The 'Literati' sketches appeared in *Godey's Lady's Book* throughout the period May to September. But soon after publication of the first instalment things began to look ominous. The New York clique viewed the series with a mixture of contempt and apprehension, although by Poe's standards the articles were mild indeed. In his piece on Charles F. Briggs, however, he criticized his work as an imitation of Smollett and then infuriated his erstwhile co-editor with the following portrait:

> Mr Briggs's personal appearance is not prepossessing. He is about five feet six inches in height, somewhat slightly framed, with a sharp, thin face, narrow and low forehead, pert-looking nose, mouth rather pleasant in expression, eyes not so good, gray and small, although occasionally brilliant . . . He walks with a quick, nervous step. His address is quite good, frank and insinuating . . . He has, apparently, traveled; pretends to a knowledge of French (of which he is profoundly ignorant); has been engaged in an infinite variety of employments, and now, I believe, occupies a lawyer's office in Nassau street. He is married, goes little into society, and seems about forty years of age.[3]

Lewis Clark was not pleased with the article, but was even less pleased when he was informed that he himself was to make an appearance at some stage. Louis Godey himself had told him so, thinking he would be pleased to be included in such august company. At least, that is what Godey said; secretly he wanted to assess Clark's reaction. He was not disappointed; instead of pleasure, the prospect 'put him in a perfect agony of terror'.[4] The delighted Godey quoted this in the *New York Evening Mirror*.

To combat this threat, Clark issued a veiled threat of his own, using the latest rumours about Poe against him. To the piece on Briggs he replied in the *Knickerbocker*:

> There is a wandering specimen of 'The Literary Snob' continually obtruding himself upon public notice; today in the gutter, tomorrow in some milliner's magazine: but in all places, and at all times, magnificently snobbish and dirty, who seems to invite the 'Punchy' writers among us to take up their pens and impale him for public amusement. Mrs Louisa Godey has lately taken this snob into her service in a neighbouring city, where he is doing his best to prove his title to the distinction of being one of the lowest in his class at present, infesting the literary world. The *Evening Gazette and Times* speaks of our literary 'snob' as one 'whose idiosyncrasies have attracted some attention and compassion of late' and adds: 'We have heard that he is at present in a state of health which renders him not completely accountable for all his peculiarities'!
>
> But after all, why should one speak of all this? Poh! Poe! Leave the 'idiosyncratic' man 'alone in his glory'.[5]

The sketches were, however, so popular that Godey had to rerun May's issue. Public excitement was intense. After the June issue had been published, again containing mild reviews, an article suddenly appeared in the *Evening Mirror* by its editor, Hiram Fuller. Whether instigated by Clark or not, it was a coarse affair, stooping so low as to attack Poe from every angle. He began with a scoffing account of the effects produced by Poe's articles – that two apprentices never slept all night and that some students were induced to make a pilgrimage to the asylum in which Poe was confined. He goes on:

> Mr Poe is the last man in the country who should undertake the task of writing 'honest opinions' of the literati. His infirmities of mind and body, his petty jealousies, his necessities even, which allow him neither time nor serenity for such work, his limited information on local subjects, his unfortunate habits, his quarrels and jealousies, all

unfit him for the performance of such a duty, as the specimens already published abundantly prove.[6]

To cap this, Fuller added an objectionably insulting personal portrait of Poe, describing him as 'in height about five feet one or two inches', his weight 'about 115 pounds', his forehead flat (suggesting a 'lack of moral sentiments'), his tongue too large for his mouth and which 'shows itself unpleasantly when he speaks earnestly' and that his walk was 'quick, jerking, sometimes waving'.

Poe was not the man to allow this to pass unanswered, and he turned to Joseph Field, editor and founder of the *Reveille*, for help. He began by stirring the murky waters of Fuller's past and quoted Elizabeth Barrett's letter (although he made slight alterations).

He was a schoolmaster, about 3 years ago, in Providence, and was forced to leave that city on account of several swindling transactions in which he was found out. As soon as Willis & Morris discovered the facts, they abandoned the *Mirror*, preferring to leave it in his hands rather than keep up so disreputable a connexion.

All that I venture to ask of you in the case of this attack, however, is to say a few words in condemnation of it, and to do away with the false impression of my personal appearance it may convey, in those parts of the country where I am not individually known. You have seen me and can describe me as I am. Will you do me this act of justice, and influence one or two of your editorial friends to do the same? I know you will.

Poe's sketches continued. In the third instalment, still smarting from the Ellett incident, he took a swing at Thomas Dunn English, ending:

No spectacle can be more pitiable than that of a man without the commonest school education busying himself in attempts to instruct mankind on topics of polite literature . . .

. . . he was not, I say, laughed at so much for his excusable deficiencies in English grammar (although an editor should certainly be able to write *his own name*) as that, in the hope of disguising such deficiency, he was perpetually lamenting the 'typographical blunders' that 'in the most unaccountable manner' *would* creep into his work. Nobody was so stupid as to suppose for a moment that there existed in New York

> a single proof-reader – or even a single printer's devil – who would have permitted *such* errors to escape. By the excuses offered, therefore, the errors were only the more obviously nailed to the counter as Mr English's own.
>
> I make these remarks in no spirit of unkindness. Mr E. is yet young – certainly not more than thirty-five – and might, with his talents, readily improve himself at points where he is most defective. No one of any generosity would think the worse of him for getting private instruction.
>
> I do not personally know Mr English . . .[7]

The war of the literati continued and indeed reached new heights of unsavouriness. A response from English arrived, in Fuller's newspaper. The article, fascinating in its brutality, began by accusing Poe of owing him money, of forgery (as accused by a merchant in the city) and of drunkenness and included a distorted account of his part in the Ellett affair:

> He told me that he had vilified a certain well-known and esteemed authoress, of the South, then on a visit to New York; that he had accused her of having written letters to him which compromised her reputation; and that her brother . . . had threatened his life unless he produced the letters he named. In a day or so, afterwards, being confined to his bed from the effect of fright and the blows he had received from me, he sent a letter to her brother of the lady he had so vilely slandered, denying all recollection of having made any charges of the kind alleged, and stating that, if he had made them, he was labouring under a fit of insanity to which he was periodically subject.
>
> He is not alone thoroughly unprincipled, base, and depraved, but silly, vain, and ignorant – not alone an assassin in morals, but a quack in literature. His frequent quotations from languages of which he is entirely ignorant, and his consequent blunders, expose him to ridicule; while his cool plagiarisms, from known or forgotten writers, excite the public amazement.[8]

This article was studiously ignored even by Poe's enemies, so vicious was its content – Griswold himself shuddered at it. But Poe did not let English's attack pass. He composed a reply and sent it to Godey; the latter, although he was pleased with the huge interest the series had inspired, was feeling nervous about the furore they were causing, and wanting nothing to do with the private row he sent Poe's piece to the *Spirit of the Times*, where they charged $10 for publication: then Godey sent the bill to Poe.[9] Poe was not pleased about this, as he explained to Godey directly.

In his reply to English he refuted the charges made about Elizabeth Ellett and threatened a lawsuit concerning the charge of forgery. In his 'Reply to Mr Poe's Rejoinder' English then repeated his charges, 'which prove him to be profligate in habits and depraved in mind'. As for the threat of a lawsuit, 'Let him institute a suit, if he dare . . .'[10]

Poe indeed dared, having obtained proof from the merchant in question that the forgery story was a tissue of lies. Knowing that he had gone too far, English fled to Washington but refused the let matters rest even there. In his serialized novel *1844* he included the character of Marmaduke Hammerhead, a drunkard, wife-beater and critic who had written 'The Black Crow' and 'The Humbug and Other Tales'; he also has a relationship with a poetess named 'Miss Flighty'.[11] Later, even after Poe's suit had come to court, he constantly abused Poe in print until eventually he was threatened with so many libel suits from others that he ceased publication.[12]

English's assaults must have wounded Poe, and times were getting tougher and tougher. His depression returned, and again he fell ill. He had received payment for the 'Literati' sketches some months ago, and since then no money had come into the house. He turned to his old friend Chivers. He had not heard from him for some time, when all of a sudden six letters arrived on his doorstep, all having been sent to his old address. Poe was obviously pleased to hear from him:

> We are in a snug little cottage, keeping house, and would be very comfortable, but that I have been for a long time dreadfully ill. I am getting better, however, although slowly, and shall get well. In the meantime the flocks of little birds of prey that always take the opportunity of illness to peck at a sick fowl of larger dimensions, have been endeavoring with all their power to effect my ruin. My dreadful poverty, also, has given them every advantage. In fact, my dear friend, I have been driven to the very gates of death and a despair more dreadful than death, and I had not even one friend, out of my family, with whom to advise. What would I not have given for the kind pressure of your hand!

Although in despair, he has battled against alcohol and still retains optimism for the future:

There is one thing you will be glad to learn: – It has been a long while since any artificial stimulus has passed my lips. When I see you – should that day ever come – this is a topic on which I desire to have a long talk with you. I am done forever with drink – depend upon that – but there is much more in this matter than meets the eye. Do not let anything in this letter impress you with the belief that I despair even of worldly prosperity. On the contrary although I feel ill, and am ground into the very dust with poverty, there is a sweet hope in the bottom of my soul.

As Poe once again spiralled into the clutches of poverty he must have felt uplifted when he received a letter from his old friend and correspondent Frederick Thomas – but any pleasure must have faded when he read the contents. There was terrible news. His sister and her two children had drowned at sea.

While the battle with English was raging another combatant entered the fray – the great Godfather of the Press himself, Lewis Gaylord Clark. Clark had been awaiting his caricature with some nervousness and was already armed for the attack when it was eventually published. In fact, the review was relatively mild.

Mr Clark is known principally as the twin brother of the late *Willis* Gaylord Clark, the poet, of Philadelphia, with whom he has often been confounded from similarity both of person and of name. He is known, also, within a more limited circle, as one of the editors of the *Knickerbocker* magazine, and it is in this latter capacity that I must be considered as placing him among literary people. He writes little himself, the editorial scraps which usually appear in fine type at the end of the *Knickerbocker* being the joint composition of a great variety of gentlemen (most of them possessing shrewdness and talent) connected with diverse journals about the city of New York . . .

It is not, of course, to be understood from anything I have here said, that Mr Clark does not occasionally contribute editorial matter to the magazine. His compositions, however, are far from numerous, and are always to be distinguished by their style, which is more 'easily to be imagined than described.' It has its merit, beyond doubt, but I shall not undertake to say that either 'vigor,' 'force' or 'impressiveness' is the precise term by which that merit should be designated. Mr Clark once did me the honor to review my poems, and – *I forgive him*.

[As for the *Knickerbocker*] . . . as the editor has no precise character, the magazine, as a matter of course, can have none. When I say 'no precise character,' I mean that Mr C., as a literary man, has about him no determinateness, no distinctiveness, no saliency of point; – an apple, in fact, or a pumpkin, has more angles. He is as smooth as oil or a sermon from Doctor Hawks; he is noticeable for nothing in the world except for the markedness by which he is noticeable for nothing.

What is the precise circulation of the *Knickerbocker* at present I am unable to say; it has been variously stated at from eight to eighteen hundred subscribers. The former estimate is no doubt too low, and the latter, I presume, is far too high. There are, perhaps, some fifteen hundred copies printed.

At the period of his brother's decease, Mr Lewis G. Clark bore to him a striking resemblance, but within the last year or two there has been much alteration in the person of the editor of the *Knickerbocker*. He is now, perhaps, forty-two or three, but still good-looking. His forehead is, phrenologically, bad – round and what is termed 'bullety.' The mouth, however, is much better, although the smile is too constant and lacks expression; the teeth are white and regular . . .[13]

This was fairly mild stuff, but Clark was incensed at the small innuendos, at the belittling of what he considered the finest magazine in America, the snide barbs at his talent as an editor and the snipes at his personal appearance. He pulled himself up to his full height and let his weight fall squarely on Poe. It is difficult to imagine that a man of Clark's reputation could have stooped so low as to have written the following in his journal:

The jaded hack who runs a broken pace for common hire . . . might revel in his congenial abuse of this Magazine and its Editor from now till next October without disturbing our complacency for a single moment. He is too mean for hate, and hardly worthy scorn. In fact there are but two classes of persons who regard him in any light – those who despise and those who pity him; the first for his utter lack of principle, the latter for the infirmities which have overcome and ruined him. Here is a faithful picture, for which he but recently sat. We take it from one of our most respectable daily journals.

It is melancholy enough to see a man maimed in his limbs, or deprived by nature of his due proportions: the blind, the deaf, the mute, the lame, the impotent, are all objects that touch our hearts, at least all whose hearts have not been indurated to the fiery furnace of sin;

> but sad, sadder, and saddest of all is the poor wretch whose want of moral rectitude has reduced his mind and person to a condition where indignation for his vices and revenge for his insults are changed into a compassion for the poor victim himself. When a man has sunk so low that he has lost the power to evoke vengeance, he is the most pitiful of all pitiable objects. A poor creature of this description called at our office the other day. In a condition of sad imbecility, bearing in his feeble body the evidences of evil living, and betraying by his talk such radical obliquity of sense, that every spark of harsh feeling toward him was extinguished, and we could not even entertain a feeling of contempt for one who was evidently committing a suicide upon his body, as he had already done upon his character. Unhappy man! He was accompanied by an aged female relative who was going a weary round in the hot streets, following his steps to prevent his indulging in a love of drink, but he had eluded her watchful eye by some means, and was already far gone in a state of inebriation. After listening awhile with painful feelings in his profane ribaldry, he left the office, accompanied by his good genius, to whom he owed the duties which she was discharging for him.

Clark closes with other comments, including the day he encountered Poe with Chivers:

> He is equally unknown to those he abuses. The Editor hereof has no reminiscence of ever having seen him save on two occasions. In the one case, we met him in the street with a gentleman, who apologised the next day. In a note now before us, for having been seen while in his company 'while he was labouring under such an excitement'. In the other, we caught a view of his retiring skirts as he wended his 'winding way', like a furtive puppy with a considerable kettle to his tail, from the publication office, whence – having left no other record of his tempestuous visit upon the publisher's mind than the recollection of a coagulum of maudlin and abusive jargon – he had just emerged, bearing with him one of his little rolls of manuscript, which had been previously submitted for insertion in our 'excellent Magazine', but which, unhappily for his peace [*sic*], had shared the fate of its equally attractive predecessors.[14]

This last paragraph (apart from the meeting of Poe and Chivers) rings false, especially the submission of a number of articles to the *Knickerbocker*, where he would have expected a frosty reception. And the statement that he had met Poe only twice before was a plain falsehood.

Clark had an arsenal of the press at his beck, but Poe was running out of options. He did have time, however, to make an amendment to one of the articles in the final instalment of the 'Literati', concerning Charles F. Hoffman. In it he wrote:

> Mr Hoffman was the original editor of the *Knickerbocker* Magazine, and gave it while under his control a tone and character, the weight of which may be best estimated by the consideration that the work thence received an impetus which has sufficed to bear it on alive, although tottering, month after month, through even that dense region of unmitigated and unmitigable fog – that dreary realm of outer darkness, of utter and inconceivable dunderheadism, over which has so long ruled King Log the Second, in the august person of one Lewis Gaylord Clark.[15]

If things were looking poor before Poe wrote the 'Literati' sketches, now they were truly dismal. Virginia was getting worse. In the past Poe had been through some bad times, but now he hit rock bottom. The eruption after the 'Literati' sketches had an adverse effect on him, and the public attacks hit their mark. People talked about his drunkenness, his affairs and his mental instability. Publishers began to think of him as a liability. Almost certainly, the huge weight of problems began to crush him. And ever-waiting in the wings was the terrible urge to drink, an urge which became ever more tempting. The family began to sell their belongings, and soon there would be very little left. Throughout the next two months he wrote to no one, although he did receive a letter from George Eveleth.

Poe was now bankrupt. Maria Clemm foresaw the poorhouse. Having no one to turn to, the family kept to themselves. Nobody visited, so nobody was aware of the levels to which the three had fallen. Virginia was sinking day by day, and now even Poe could no longer doubt that she was entering the last stages of tuberculosis. Yet there was nothing he could do to help her, not even supply the money to buy her the right foods. It was a worse horror than anything he had written about in his tales. He could not lose her. If he did, he would lose his final hold on sanity. Not even Maria could find a way to help.

At last a visitor did knock on the door – one of Poe's old friends, Mary Gove Nichols. Reluctantly Poe admitted her, and she got a shock when she saw the bare home; and if that made her appalled, she was horrified when she saw Virginia: 'There was no clothing on the bed, which was only straw, but a snow-white counterpane and sheets. The weather was cold, and the sick lady had the dreadful chills that accompany the hectic fever of consumption. She lay on the straw bed, wrapped in her husband's great coat, with a large tortoise-shell cat in her bosom.' Poe was also unwell. Mrs Nichols did what she could, but she could see the family needed help, both financial and medical. Worried about Poe, and even more so about Virginia, she called on a neighbour, Mrs Marie Louise Shew, a doctor's daughter, who came round to see for herself what was going on. She, too, was horrified, and set about looking after the family. With the medical training she had, she was an invaluable ally and was able to give them solid practical help. So kind was she that Virginia gave her a portrait of Poe and a small jewel-case that had belong to Poe's mother.

Mary Nichols put out a call for subscriptions, which raised $60 in a week – rainfall in the desert. It enabled proper bedding to be provided for Virginia. But it did not fend off destitution.

This unexpected aid temporarily lifted Poe's spirits. Probably because of this, and through Mrs Shew's help, he weaned himself off drink and set about putting his life in order. Although he had considered himself washed up, he looked to literature to save him. After all, there was still the guiding star of the *Stylus* to think of and his book on American writers. In the midst of this, he read a letter that must have cheered him a little. It was from a Scot, Arch Ramsay, who was trying to ascertain whether the M. Valdemar tale was a hoax or not. Poe did not answer him until he felt well enough to do so, and when he did it was with playful humour: 'Some few persons believe it – but I do not – and don't you.'[16]

The family was surviving, but hardly more. Well-meaning friends now banded together in an attempt to help them. Mary Nichols wrote to Fanny Osgood, who had moved to Albany soon after the Poe–Ellett business; alarmed, she notified her sister-in-law, Mrs Locke, who sent a poem and cash. On 15 December the following article was published by the *New York Morning Express*:

> ILLNESS OF EDGAR A. POE. – We regret to learn that this gentleman and his wife are both dangerously ill with the consumption, and that the hand of misfortune lies heavy upon their temporal affairs. We are sorry to mention the fact that they are so far reduced as to

be barely able to obtain the necessaries of life. That is, indeed, a hard lot, and we do hope that the friends and admirers of Mr Poe will come promptly to his assistance in his bitterest hour of need. Mr Poe is the author of several tales and poems, of which Messrs Wiley & Putnam are the publishers, and, as it is believed, the profitable publishers. At least, his friends say that the publishers ought to start a movement in his behalf.[17]

The article uncomfortably mirrors the one written years ago for Elizabeth Poe as she lay on her death-bed. Another notice, in Philadelphia's *Saturday Evening Post*, ended: 'they are without money and without friends . . .' Nathaniel Willis was shocked to read this, and took it upon himself to write an editorial, with the best intentions. It was inserted in the 26 December edition of the *Home Journal,* in which he stated that an anonymous admirer had sent money, and Willis would be happy to forward any other contributions to Poe. Poe was not pleased with the editorial and felt humiliated, although there is nothing that could be said against Willis's motives. In one of his most dignified letters he wrote:

MY DEAR WILLIS: – The paragraph which has been put in circulation respecting my wife's illness, my own, my poverty etc., is now lying before me; together with the beautiful lines by Mrs Locke and those by Mrs —, to which the paragraph has given rise, as well as your kind and manly comments in the *Home Journal.*

The motive of the paragraph I leave to the conscience of him or her who wrote it or suggested it. Since the thing is done, however, and since the concerns of my family are thus pitilessly thrust before the public, I perceive no mode of escape from a public statement of what is true and what erroneous in the report alluded to.

That my wife is ill, then, is true; and you may imagine with what feeling I add that this illness, hopeless from the first, has been heightened and precipitated by her reception, at two different periods, of anonymous letters – one enclosing the paragraph now in question; the other, those published calumnies of Messrs —, for which I yet hope to find redress in a court of justice.

Of the facts, that I myself have been long and dangerously ill, and that my illness has been a well understood thing among my brethren of the press, the best evidence is afforded by the innumerable paragraphs of personal and literary abuse with which I have been latterly assailed.

This matter, however, will remedy itself. At the very first blush of my new prosperity, the gentlemen who toadied me in the old, will recollect themselves and toady me again. You, who know me, will comprehend that I speak of these things only as having served, in a measure, to lighten the gloom of unhappiness, by a gentle and not unpleasant sentiment of mingled pity, merriment and contempt.

That, as the inevitable consequence of so long an illness, I have been in want of money, it would be folly in me to deny – but that I have ever materially suffered from privation, beyond the extent of my capacity for suffering, is not altogether true. That I am 'without friends' is a gross calumny, which I am sure you never could have believed, and which a thousand noble-hearted men would have good right never to forgive me for permitting to pass unnoticed and undenied. Even in the city of New York I could have no difficulty in naming a hundred persons, to each of whom – when the hour for speaking had arrived – I could and would have applied for aid and with unbounded confidence, and with absolutely no sense of humiliation.

I do not think, my dear Willis, that there is any need of my saying more. I am getting better, and may add – if it be any comfort to my enemies – that I have little fear of getting worse. The truth is, I have a great deal to do; and I have made up my mind not to die till it is done.

Sincerely yours,
Edgar A Poe.[18]

He was back in his stride again, and he reconsidered his situation. Virginia was ill, but she had been so ill in the past that he had despaired of her life. Now, under Marie Shew's supervision, she seemed better, and there was no doubt that she would continue to improve. As for himself, it was up to him to get the momentum going again. He began to gather materials for his work and turned to Evert Duyckinck. It was useful having friend who was also a reader for Wiley & Putnam: Poe asked him to obtain Arthur Gilfillan's *Sketches of Modern Literature and Eminent Literary Men* as well as a poem he believed was imitated by Longfellow.

As the New Year of 1847 came and went, Poe had every hope that he could rise again from the literary ashes. He had improved in health, and he was no longer drinking. His projects were under way. He still had enough friends in the publishing business to enable him to work. As he had done so many times before, he clawed himself free from his personal hell.

However, towards the end of January Virginia's health took a bad turn. This time she seemed not to be recovering. The disease was now taking her over, and there seemed to be no stopping it. On the night of 29 January she looked so ill that Poe frantically sent this note to Marie Shew:

> Kindest – dearest friend – My poor Virginia still lives, although failing fast and now suffering much pain. May God grant her life until she sees you and thanks you once again! Her bosom is full to overflowing – like my own – with a boundless – inexpressible gratitude to you. Lest she may never see you more – she bids me say that she sends you her sweetest kiss of love and will die blessing you. But come – oh come to-morrow! Yes, I will be calm – everything you so nobly wish to see me. My mother sends you, also, her 'warmest love and thanks'. She begs me to ask you, if possible, to make arrangements at home so that you may stay with us tomorrow night. I enclose the order to the Post-master. Heaven bless you and farewell, Edgar A Poe.

The next day came, and Virginia was much worse. She herself felt that her time had come. Knowing of her husband's weaknesses and dependency, she waited until Poe was not in earshot, then called her mother to her. 'Darling, darling Muddy, you will console and take care of my poor Eddy – you will *never, never* leave him? Promise me, my dear Muddy, and then I can die in peace.'[19] Maria promised.

Virginia deteriorated. Poe watched by her bedside with Maria. It would be impossible to guess the agony he went through, watching his little wife slowly fading from him. But no amount of love or attention could save her. She was in the last extremities of the disease that had consumed her lungs for so long, and now she could fight no more. Suddenly, she stopped breathing.

Poe did not even have enough money for the funeral, so Mrs Shew provided it, along with the coffin. They had permission from the owner of the Fordham Cottage, the Valentines, to bury her in a vault belonging to them at the Reform Church.

The loss of Virginia was the greatest calamity of Poe's life. His one wish, for a family and for love and affection, was collapsing around his ears, and he was devastated. He no longer felt that he had anything to live for.

Each night he would go and sit by Virginia's grave, weeping.

13

EUREKA

> You say – 'Can you hint to me what was the terrible evil which caused the irregularities so profoundly lamented?' Yes; I can do more than hint. This 'evil' was the greatest which can befall a man. Six years ago, a wife, whom I loved as no man ever loved before, ruptured a blood-vessel in singing. Her life was despaired of. I took leave of her forever & underwent all the agonies of her death. She recovered partially and I again hoped. At the end of a year the vessel broke again – I went through precisely the same scene. Again in about a year afterward. Then again – again – again & even once again at varying intervals. Each time I felt all the agonies of her death – and at each accession of the disorder I loved her more dearly & clung to her life with more desperate pertinacity. But I am constitutionally sensitive – nervous – in a very unusual degree. I became insane, with long intervals of horrible sanity. During these fits of absolute unconsciousness I drank, God only knows how often or how much. As a matter of course, my enemies referred the insanity to the drink rather than the drink to the insanity. I had indeed, nearly abandoned all hope of a permanent cure when I found one in the death of my wife. This I can & do endure as becomes a man – it was the horrible never-ending oscillation between hope & despair which I could not longer have endured without the total loss of reason. In the death of what was my life, then, I receive a new but – oh God! how melancholy an existence.[1]

So wrote Poe later in the year to his pen-friend George Eveleth. Poe was in a poor condition after his wife's death, and Mrs Shew, not willing to let him destroy himself, nursed him back to health. She also approached a friend belonging to the New York Union Club, who had a whip-round, and others contributed, so that there was enough to pay the pressing bills. Poe was not ungrateful for her ministrations, and he acknowledged his gratitude to 'Louise' by writing the poem 'To M— L— S—'.

Interestingly, Mrs Shew made her own diagnosis of Poe and took it to a Dr Mott: 'I decided that in his best health he had a lesion of one side of the brain, and . . . he could not bear stimulants or tonics without producing insanity . . .'[2] It was not the only time a diagnosis had been made concerning Poe's health. On one occasion he slept for twelve hours away from home, and was examined by a Dr Francis, who diagnosed heart disease.

Poe's other faithful friend was his aunt and mother-in-law, Maria. To her he wrote the personal and beautiful poem, 'To My Mother':

> Because I feel that, in the heavens above,
> The angels, whispering to one another,
> Can find, among their burning terms of love,
> None so devotional as that of 'mother' –
> Therefore by that sweet name I long have called you –
> You, who are more than mother unto me,
> And fill my heart of hearts, where Death installed you,
> In setting my Virginia's spirit free.
> My mother – my own mother – who died early –
> Was but the mother of myself; but you
> Are mother to the one I loved so dearly,
> And thus are dearer than the mother I knew;
> By that infinity with which my wife
> Was dearer to my soul than its soul-life.[3]

When he felt better, Poe liked to wander around the countryside near the cottage – down to the High Bridge (a high aqueduct) and around the rocky terrain. He never lost his love for nature, which stretched back to the days as a student in Charlottesville, when he used to wander in the Ragged Mountains. Later, Helen Whitman described the area where he walked:

> During Mr Poe's residence at Fordham a walk to High Bridge was one of his favourite and habitual recreations. The water of the aqueduct is conveyed across the river on a range of lofty granite arches, which rise to the height of a hundred and forty-five feet above high-water level. On the top a turfed and grassy road, used only by foot passengers,

and flanked on either side by a low parapet of granite, makes one of the finest promenades imaginable.

The winding river and the high rocky shores at the western extremity of the bridge are seen to great advantage from this lofty avenue. In the last melancholy years of his life – 'the lonesome latter years' – Poe was accustomed to walk there at all hours of the day and night; often pacing the then solitary pathway for hours without meeting a human being. A little to the east of the cottage rises a ledge of rocky ground, partly covered with pines and cedars, commanding a fine view of the surrounding country and of the picturesque college of St John's, which had in that time an avenue of venerable old trees. This rocky ledge was also one of the poet's favourite resorts. Here through long summer days and through solitary, star-lit nights he loved to sit, dreaming his gorgeous waking dreams . . .[4]

Poe was victorious in his court case against English: he was awarded $225 plus expenses, which was manna to him.[5] He boasted unconvincingly to Eveleth that it was quite a victory, considering English had done him 'no real damage'. Yet English's attack was still news, enough so at any rate to be the subject of an editorial in the *New York Tribune*, and Poe wrote to its editor, Horace Greeley, for satisfaction.

Unfortunately, Chivers had not heard Poe's bad news when he wrote his next letter, asking after Virginia. It is obvious from his tone that, at this point at any rate, Chivers was a real friend to Poe and was worried about his constitution, as well as the attacks that had been made upon him. He urged Poe to leave New York and live in the South with him:

If you will come to the South to live, I will take care of you as long as you live – although, if ever there was a perfect mystery on earth, you are one – and one of the most mysterious. However, come to the South and live with me, and we will talk all these matters over at our leisure . . .

I do not intend this for a letter, but write to let you know that New York is not the place to live in happiness. I have lived there, and know all about it. Come to the South. The stage is coming.

To claw himself free from ruin Poe had needed friends, one of the most compassionate being Mrs Shew. But she had not been alone in her solicitations. One of the most helpful of his admirers was Mrs

Ermina Starkweather Locke, 'Jane', a poet from Lowell, Massachusetts. It was her letter which Willis had included in his when he had written the well-meaning editorial on Poe's poverty. In his letter of thanks Poe's words are so mutilated and it is so altered as to be almost unreadable. Part of it runs:

> Your beautiful lines appeared at a time when I was indeed very ill, and I might never have seen them but for the kindness of Mr Willis who enclosed them to me – and who knew me too well to suppose as some of my friends did that I would be pained by so sweet an evidence of interest on the part of one of whose writings, with whose fervid and generous spirit which they evince, he had so often heard me express sympathy.

Mrs Shew had allowed Poe to plan the furnishing of her new house (music room and library), presumably following the tenets he put forward in his 'The Philosophy of Furniture'. On one such visit he was complaining that he could not concentrate because of the noise of church bells. According to her, she wrote down 'The Bells, by Edgar A. Poe', and gave the first line of the first and last verses of the famous poem.[6] He responded:

> I have been engaged all day on some promised work – otherwise I should have replied immediately as my heart inclined. I sincerely hope you may not drift out of my sight before I can thank you. How kind of you to let me do even this small service for you, in return for the great debt I owe you. Louise – my brightest – most unselfish of all who ever loved me . . .

He made a brief trip to Philadelphia around this time and visited the office of *Graham's*. His want of money had not diminished. He sent two articles to Judge Conrad, editor of the *North American* and at this time assistant to Graham, in an attempt to raise money from them.

It had now been ten months since the death of Virginia, and Poe was in mental turmoil. As can be seen by some of the letters, he had not recovered from Virginia's death; and the house seemed empty without her. Maria was always around to care for him, but for friendship he had become attached to Louisa Shew. He was still depressed and still dangerously short of money, although he continued to formulate his plans and write. What was now occupying his mind was death itself, and the meaning of existence. One night he went to a midnight service with Mrs Shew, low in spirits. As he sat mulling over his hardships, he heard the priest say: 'He was a man of sorrows.' He burst into tears and ran outside.

Now he had no one to whom he could attach his enormous emotional need. Mrs Shew he loved as a dear friend and a medical assistant. But his tormented passion needed an outlet, and the necessity grew stronger as time went by. His scorched fingers had now healed, and he looked for another idol to worship. At first he was mildly obsessed with the poet Stella Lewis and with his old salon friend Mrs Locke; women seemed to find his melancholy passion irresistible. He sent Stella Lewis a letter enclosing a sonnet in which was hidden her name:

> A thousand thanks for your repeated kindness, and, above all, for the comforting and cheering words of your note. Your advice I feel as a command which neither my heart nor my reason would venture to disobey. May Heaven forever bless you and yours!
>
> A day or two ago I sent to one of the Magazines the sonnet enclosed. Its tone is somewhat too light; but it embodies a riddle which I wish to put you to the trouble of expounding.

The sonnet was a modified acrostic. One needs to take the first letter of the first line, the second letter of the second line, and so on, to spell 'Sarah Anna Lewis':

> 'Seldom we find,' says Solomon Don Dunce,
> 'Half an idea in the profoundest sonnet.
> Through all the flimsy things we see at once
> As easily as through a Naples bonnet –
> Trash of all trash! – how can a lady don it?
> Yet heavier far than your Petrarchan stuff –
> Owl-downy nonsense that the faintest puff
> Twirls into trunk-paper the while you con it.'
> And, veritably, Sol is right enough.
> The general Petrarchanities are arrant
> Bubbles – ephemeral and so transparent –
> But this is, now, – you may depend upon it –
> Stable, opaque, immortal – all by dint
> Of the dear names that lie concealed within 't.

His poem 'Ulalume' was finally printed in Colton's *American Review* anonymously; he sent a copy to his friend Willis, also asking for anonymity.[7] The reason was simple – he wished to create the same sort of uproar as happened with 'The Raven'. Sadly, that was not to be, yet it was certainly one of the finest pieces of writing he had done since those dizzy times. Suggested by the death of Virginia, it tells of the narrator leading Psyche into a dim vale against her will, as she senses something terrible there. This vale is in a place by a lake called Auber, in the woods of Weir. The poem ends:

> Thus I pacified Psyche and kissed her,
> And tempted her out of her gloom –
> And conquered her scruples and gloom:
> And we passed to the end of the vista,
> And were stopped by the door of a tomb;
> By the door of a legended tomb: –
> And I said – 'What is written, sweet sister,
> On the door of this legended tomb?'
> She replied – 'Ulalume – Ulalume –
> 'Tis the vault of thy lost Ulalume!'
>
> Then my heart it grew ashen and sober
> As the leaves that were crispéd and sere –
> As the leaves that were withering and sere,
> And I cried – 'It was surely October
> On *this* very night of last year
> That I journeyed – I journeyed down here –
> That I brought a dread burden down here –
> On this night of all nights in the year,
> Oh, what demon has tempted me here?
> Well I know, now, this dim lake of Auber –
> This misty mid region of Weir –
> Well I know, now, this dank tarn of Auber,
> In the ghoul-haunted woodland of Weir.'

Poe was writing some Marginalia for *Graham's*, which appeared in the first three editions of 1848. He also was working on the project of the expanded 'Literati', a book now to be entitled 'Literary America' (it never came to fruition). But his main occupation was with a consideration of the origins of the universe, which would soon burst upon the world. He had been pondering the meaning of existence for some time. Cosmology was popular, and Laplace's nebular theory was in vogue.[8] Poe combined his theory with those of Kepler and the idea of gravitation, and formulated his own theory of the origins of the universe.[9] At first there was nothing, then matter was created from nothing; so each particle tends to be drawn back to the other (gravitation). If they ever succeeded, and matter combined, there would be nothingness again. The drawing apart of particles is caused by the will of God. The universe of stars is finite, so there may be other universes, and, by association, other gods. The end of the present universe may not be the end of the matter.

> Guiding our imaginations by that omniprevalent law of laws, the law of periodicity, are we indeed more than justified in entertaining a belief – let us say, rather, in indulging a hope – that the processes we have here ventured to contemplate will be renewed forever, and forever, and forever, a novel Universe welling into existence, and then subsiding into nothingness, at every throb of the Heat Divine. And now – this Heart Divine – what is it? *It is our own.*[10]

Scientific speculation written in the first half of the nineteenth century will necessarily look dated now. Yet there is much about his work that feels modern, and it demonstrates Poe's power of logic to a extraordinary degree. He argues that the universe is finite; otherwise there would be stars in every direction we look and therefore a background luminosity.[11] His argument that all began as a single particle, and that the universe is expanding, foreshadows the Big Bang theory. The possibility that all may recommence is a nod to the 'oscillating universe' theory. His theory of electricity and infinity chimes with many theories of modern physics. And he had a wonderful grasp of astronomical distances and structures. Although some ideas were wrong (the self-luminosity of the moon, for example), his monograph is a model of precise thought and repays reading today.

He called his work 'Eureka'. Lectures succeeding from the theory, and profits from the book expounding his ideas, could furnish the means for Poe to launch his beloved *Stylus*. However, he could not even afford the money to hire the lecture hall of the Society Library, New York, so he approached H.D. Chapin to see if anything could be done. Chapin had given him a letter of introduction to Colonel James W. Webb, editor of the *Morning Courier.*

I have been thinking that a better course would be to make interest among my friends here – in N.Y. city – and deliver a Lecture, in the first instance, at the Society Library. With this object in view, may I beg of you so far to assist me as to procure for me the use of the Lecture Room? The difficulty with me is that payment for the Room is demanded in advance and I have no money. I believe the price is $15. I think that, without being too sanguine, I may count upon an audience of some 3 or 4 hundreds – and if even 300 are present, I shall be enabled to proceed with my plans. Should you be so kind as to grant me the aid I request, I should like to engage the Room for the first Thursday in February.

It is impossible not to admire Poe's tenacity. Once again he is promoting his own journal and looking for 500 subscribers. To this end, he plans a trip to Richmond and a lecture. He also enlists the help of Willis.

Jan 22
I am about to make an effort at re-establishing myself in the literary world, and feel that I may depend upon your aid. My general aim is to start a Magazine, to be called the *Stylus*; but it would be useless to me, even when established, if not entirely out of the control of a publisher. I mean, therefore, to get up a *Journal* which shall be my own, at all points. With this end in view, I must get a list of, at least, five hundred subscribers to begin with: – nearly two hundred I have already. I propose, however, to go South and West, among my personal and literary friends – old college and West Point acquaintances – and see what I can do. In order to get the means of taking the first step, I propose to lecture at the Society Library, on Thursday, the 3d of February – and, that there may be no cause of squabbling, my subject shall not be literary at all. I have chosen a broad text – 'The Universe.' Having thus given you the facts of the case, I leave all the rest to the suggestions of your own tact and generosity.

He delivered his lecture on 3 February at the Society Library but was disappointed with the turnout – a mere sixty persons. Perhaps that was due to the inclement weather. It was not enough to provide the profits he had anticipated, and meanwhile Willis had placed an advertisement for his new magazine in his journal. However, the press were in the main appreciative of his efforts, and the *Courier and Enquirer* was very complimentary.[12]

Poe walked into Putnam's offices and saw George Putnam himself. He declared that he had made a discovery that even belittled those of Newton. He suggested that the first edition of his book should comprise a minimum of 50,000 copies; but Putnam printed only 500, giving Poe an advance of $14, on condition he sign a document promising to repay the money if the profits from sales had not covered that sum by the end of the year.

Poe prefaced the volume with the following:

> To the few who love me and whom I love – to those who feel rather than to those who think – to the dreamers and those who put faith in dreams as in the only realities – I offer this book of Truths, not in its character of Truth-Teller, but for the Beauty that abounds in its Truth, constituting it true. To these I present the composition as an Art-Product alone, – let us say as a Romance; or, if I be not urging too lofty a claim, as a Poem.
>
> *What I here propound is true*: – therefore it cannot die; or if by any means it be now trodden down so that it die, it will 'rise again to the Life Everlasting.'
>
> Nevertheless, it is as a Poem only that I wish this work to be judged after I am dead.[13]

He wrote to Eveleth answering some minor points and describing his drinking habit, which any critic of Poe should read carefully.

> The fact is thus: – My habits are rigorously abstemious and I omit nothing of the natural regimen requisite for health: – i.e. – I rise early, eat moderately, drink nothing but water, and take abundant and regular exercise in the open air. But this is my private life – my studious and literary life – and of course escapes the eye of the world. The desire for society comes upon me only when I have become excited by drink. Then only I go – that is, at these times only I have been in the practice of going among my friends: who seldom, or in fact never, having seen me unless excited, take it for granted that I am always so. Those who really know me, know better. In the meantime I shall turn the general error to account.

Theological student John Hopkins had noticed the pantheistic references in 'Eureka' and was concerned about them. As such references would be construed as heresy, the success of Poe's venture in publishing the lecture as a book could be seriously affected.

> My dear Sir,
> On glancing over your MS. the other day at Mr Putnam's, I perceived that you had added a new development of your ideas. After the closing the magnificent and sublime idea of a new universe springing into existence at every throb of the Divine heart, (a passage at which my humble judgment, the work should end,) you go to explain the Divine heart as being our own, and then lay down a system of complete and pure pantheism.

Mrs Locke had by now become quite besotted with Poe, but he did not realize it. He judged the feelings of others by his own, and up to this point he had hardly written anything which could possibly be misconstrued. But his own need to express love and affection was undeniable, and in return he expected the same sort of response he had received from Fanny Osgood. He was more than capable of entering a literary flirtation again, and who knows? Perhaps eventually things could have blossomed further. In the meanwhile, Mrs Locke had helped Poe by organizing a lecture in Lowell; Poe wrote to her (although they had not met) in a mysterious romantic style, wondering if she were free. Mrs Locke took Poe's sentiments very seriously indeed – and when Poe discovered that she was married he never again addressed such words to her.

> You will not suspect me of affectation, dear friend, or of any unworthy passion for being mysterious, merely because I find it impossible to tell you now – in a letter – what that one question was which I 'dare not even ask' of you . . . Tell me only of the ties – if any exist – that bind you to the world: – and yet I perceive that I may have done very wrong in asking you this: – now that I have asked it, it seems to me the maddest of questions, involving, possibly, the most visionary of hopes. I have seen much that you have written, but 'now that I know you' I have a deep curiosity to see all.

He needed money to get to Richmond and turned to Charles Bristed, who had sent him $10 after the public appeal.

> I fear that, on reading this note, you will think me (what God knows I am not) most ungrateful for your former kindness – and that I presume upon it more than I should, in asking you to aid me again. My only excuse is, that I am desperately circumstanced – in very bitter distress

> of mind and body – and that I looked around me in vain to find any friend who both can and will aid me, unless it be yourself. My last hope of extricating myself from the difficulties which are pressing me to death, is in going personally to a distant connexion near Richmond, Va, and endeavoring to interest him in my behalf. With a very little help all would go well with me – but even that little I cannot obtain; the effort to overcome one trouble only serving to plunge me in another. Will you forgive me, then, if I ask you to loan me the means of getting to Richmond.

Poe now considered a letter that had arrived from Anna Blackwell, an English writer, who had lodged with Poe's family for a short while in the autumn of 1847. She now wrote asking advice about the publishing of her poems, *Legend of the Waterfall*. Poe remembered Sarah Helen Whitman, whom he had once met at a literary soirée; as she lived in the same area (Rhode Island), could Anna tell him more about her?

> Do you know Mrs Whitman? I feel deep interest in her poetry and character. I have never seen her – but once. Anne Lynch, however, told me many things about the romance of her character which singularly interested me and excited my curiosity. Her poetry is, beyond question, poetry – instinct with genius. Can you not tell me something about her – any thing – every thing you know – and keep my secret – that is to say let no one know that I have asked you to do so? May I trust you? I can – and will.

He gave Stella Lewis a glowing report on her work *Child of the Sea*. At this time she and Mrs Locke seemed to be vying for his affections. But of all Poe's friends and acquaintances, the one nearest to Poe's heart, and the one towards whom he felt enormous gratitude, was of course Louisa Shew. Unfortunately she had been told of the pantheism in 'Eureka', and as a staunch Christian she could not condone a heretic. She therefore reluctantly felt it her religious duty to sever all ties with him. This rejection pained him, and, as usual when in a state of anguish, he spilled his pain on to the page, groans intermingled with literary beauty.

> Can it be true Louise that you have the idea in your mind to desert your unhappy and unfortunate friend and patient. You did not say so, I know,

> but for months I have known you was deserting me, not willingly but none the less surely – my destiny –
>
> Disaster following fast, following faster &c . . .
>
> . . . Is it possible your influence is lost to me? Such tender and true natures are ever loyal until death, but you are not dead, you are full of life and beauty!
>
> . . . I shall hardly last a year longer, alone! a few short months, will tell, how far my strength – (physical, and moral) will carry me in life here. How can I believe in Providence when you look coldly upon me, was it not you who renewed my hopes and faith in God? . . . & in humanity? Louise I heard your voice as you passed out of my sight leaving me with the Parson, 'The man of God, The servant of the most High.' He stood smiling and bowing at the madman Poe! But, that I had invited him to my house, I would have rushed out into God's light and freedom!

But no amount of pleading could convince Louise. Their friendship was at an end.

At the invitation of his admirer, Mrs Locke, Poe gave a lecture on 'The Poets and Poetry of America' at Wentworth Hall on 10 June. While in Lowell, he saw Mrs Locke, and also by chance he met Locke's neighbour, Mrs Annie Richmond. It seems that by this time Poe's pent-up emotions were slowly breaking loose, and he began to form attractions to several ladies at once. It was apparent from the start that he felt an attraction for Annie, which would hardly have pleased Jane Locke. But jealous as she was, she would hardly expect anything to grow from such a small seed – after all, like herself, Annie was married. So nothing was said, and after the lecture Poe made his way home again. His question, at least, had been answered – Jane was married, too.

On his return Poe was anxious to see Chivers, and sent him a note. '. . . I am very anxious to see you – as I propose going on to Richmond on Monday. Can you not come out to Fordham & spend tomorrow & Sunday with me? We can talk over matters, then, at leisure . . .' On it, Chivers scribbled: 'The following is the last letter that I ever received from him.'

On 17 July Poe travelled again to Richmond, but the visit was not a success. According to the editor at the time of the *Southern Literary Messenger*, John Thompson, he was constantly inebriated, and was so when he sold him 'The Rationale of Verse' and a review of Mrs Lewis's *The Child of the Sea and Other Poems*. He described him as 'horribly drunk, and discoursing "Eureka" every night to the audiences of the Bar Rooms', although the two versions he wrote of that were contradictory, and no one else seems to corroborate it. Poe found time to visit the McKenzies (John and Louisa) and his sister Rosalie. He also met John M. Daniel, editor, and argued about the causes of duels – debt and a lady – then challenged him to a duel himself.

The only letter from this period was to Maria Clemm:

> Richmond – August 5.
> My own dearest Muddy – What can be the reason that you have not written to me? Here I have been a whole fortnight & not one line from you yet. I did not think you would treat your poor Eddy in such a way as that. Be sure & write the moment you get this and, if possible, send the 'article'. Mr Thompson has accepted it. I gave him, also, the article about Mrs Lewis & he will publish it. Of course, I could not ask him anything for it – as it was a great favor to get him to insert it at any rate. I am still out at John's – although I have been to Mrs M's & am going back in a day or two to stay some time. Mrs M. was very cordial – but Louisa still more so. I think she is the sweetest creature in the world and makes John the best of wives. She is hardly changed in the least. You know how often I have spoken to you of her heavenly smile . . .

Soon he returned to New York. But if his magic had not worked on Thompson, it certainly had on Mrs Locke. Possibly she had decided to wager all on a romantic appeal to Poe – but she was to be disappointed.

> I hope you will acknowledge the receipt of this immediately, tho' more than this I shall not entreat of you, leaving all to your own discretion and feelings, mine are written out, and you cannot mistake them; therefore you can judge of the safety of any thing you may say to me, or of the manner in which it will be received. But the courtesy due, if you do not believe my heart – I beg you will not deny me, that I may know you have received this. – Have these given you even greater sympathy than I now feel.

She included a long poem entitled 'Ermina's Tale' which included the verse:

Henceforth the 'RAVEN'S' beak my heart shall bear;
And the strange flapping of his ebon wings,
Fan my sad spirit to a deep despair
Wild as the '*nevermore*' it ceaseless sings!

Sadly for Mrs Locke, at that moment Poe was obsessed with another woman – Helen Whitman. And now his emotions were to enter another state, and he found himself embroiled in a frenzied tug-of-love.

14

'WHOSE HEART-STRINGS ARE A LUTE'

The story goes that Poe first saw Helen Whitman after his ill-fated lecture at the Boston Lyceum; that he wandered (around midnight) to the area she resided in, and saw her in her garden. He had praised her poems, and in February 1848 she had addressed verses to him:

> Then, oh! Grim and Ghastly Raven!
> Wilt thou to my heart and ear
> Be a Raven true as ever
> Flapped his wings and cried 'Despair'?
> Not a bird that roams the forest
> Shall our lofty eyrie share.[1]

This effusion at least demonstrates how much more innocent such rhymes were in those days and may serve as a warning to those who too quickly accept the sentiments contained therein, although it seems likely she was attracted to Poe even then.

Poe had not forgotten about her. He sent 'To Helen' to Bayard Taylor on 15 June. It begins:

> I saw thee once – once only – years ago:
> I must not say how many – but not many.
> It was a July midnight; and from out
> A full-orbed moon, that, like thine own soul, soaring,
> Sought a precipitate pathway up through heaven,
> There fell a silvery-silken veil of light,
> With quietude, and sultriness, and slumber,
> Upon the upturned faces of a thousand
> Roses that grew in an enchanted garden,

> Where no wind dared to stir, unless on tiptoe –
> Fell on the upturn'd faces of these roses
> That gave out, in return for the love-light,
> Their odorous souls in an ecstatic death –
> Fell on the upturn'd faces of these roses
> That smiled and died in this parterre, enchanted
> By thee, and by the poetry of thy presence.[2]

Now he turned his attention to seeking her out. Fanny Osgood was aware of his mission and wrote to Helen describing Poe as 'a glorious devil, with large heart and brain'.[3] To find out whether or not she was in Providence, he wrote to her under the pseudonym Edward S.T. Grey. His need for affection and adoration – and his need to love and worship – had led to trifling with Mrs Locke and Mrs Lewis. Now the need grew stronger and his passions more serious. Helen Whitman had not replied to his last note, so Poe took a letter of introduction from one Mrs McIntosh and travelled to Rhode Island to see her in person. There he presented himself to her and wooed her passionately, at least once in a cemetery. There, he whispered to her: 'Helen, I love now – now – for the first and only time.' He also proposed. Helen sent him home and promised to write to him. She was reticent, yet obviously conquered by his impetuosity and passion. She also worried about her looks and her age. 'I can only say to you that had I youth and health and beauty, I would live for you and die with you. Now, were I to allow myself to love you, I could only enjoy a bright, brief hour of rapture and die . . .'

Poe was ecstatic at the progress he had made. He gushed out his feelings with literary skill and fire, praised her poem 'April Nights', persuaded her of his undying love and begged a reply. This very private and passionate letter could hardly fail to melt her heart:

> . . . but grant that what you urge were even true. Do you not feel in your inmost heart of hearts that the 'soul-love' of which the world speaks so often and so idly is, in this instance at least, but the veriest, the most absolute of realities? Do you not – I ask it of your reason, darling, not less than of your heart – do you not perceive that it is my diviner nature – my spiritual being – which burns and pants to commingle with your own? Has the soul age, Helen? Can Immortality regard Time?
>
> And how am I to answer what you say of your personal appearance? Have I not seen you, Helen, have I not heard the more than melody of your voice? Has not my heart ceased to throb beneath the magic

> of your smile? Have I not held your hand in mine and looked steadily into your soul through the crystal Heaven of your eyes? Have I not done all these things? – or do I dream? – or am I mad? Were you indeed all that your fancy, enfeebled and perverted by illness, tempts you to suppose that you are, still, life of my life! I would but love you – but worship you the more: – it would be so glorious a happiness to be able to prove to you what I feel! But as it is, what can I – what am I to say? Who ever spoke of you without emotion – without praise? Who ever saw you and did not love?

Of course, Helen had strong feelings for Poe, as her verses to him had proved. She was also moved by his wooing, by his passionate pleas and by the fact that he had knelt before her and asked for her hand in marriage. She discussed it with her friends, but many of these were of the literary group which had been all too familiar with the latest gossip about Poe and about his drunkenness and his apparently dishonourable part in the Ellett affair. She had been told of the stories about him and the enemies he had made in public life; she knew of the calumnies spread in the press and the furious accusations of English and Clark. It is reasonable enough that she should become wary of this smooth-tongued suitor, and she was in an agony of indecision.

While awaiting her reply, Poe wrote a letter to introduce Jane Locke to Stella Lewis. It is possible that Mrs Locke was fuming over her lack of success with Poe and was already angry with him; and it is also possible that Poe was unaware of her feelings or ability to cause trouble. For Poe to recommend an attractive poetess to her would not have appeased her.

He next wrote a note of introduction to Annie Richmond, whose family he had met in Lowell, on behalf of Mrs Lewis. On occasion he would stay with the Richmonds when he visited Lowell, and he became a friend of the family. Apart from Annie and her husband, he got along very well with Annie's sister, Sarah Heywood, and a small child called Caddy or Carrie. At this juncture his feelings towards Annie were those of a dear friend.

At this time he received an invitation to lecture in Providence, from T.L. Dunnell, which he promptly accepted.

Encouraged by so many signs, he became intoxicated by the neurotic flood of passion that had taken over him. Helen had become the embodiment of his literary ideal, and the closer he got to his goal the more intense he became. But in the attaining of his goal there were obstacles to be overcome, as he sensed after reading her reticent reply. In his next letter, still overcharged with emotion, he battled to defend himself and to convince Helen of his honest intentions. First he mentioned Helen's initial reaction when she read his letter, reminding her that she felt 'the love that glowed within its pages'. But, convinced that Helen had been dissuaded by her friends, he feared she was turning away from him. He argued that, should this be so, she could not really love him, and that would be a torment to him; the only solution for him would be death: 'my heart is broken – that I have no farther object in life – that I have absolutely no wish but to die'. He went on to express the terrible emotion he felt when he read what people had told her of him. He defended his own honour, and in a dark moment lied about his marriage to Virginia:

> If I have erred at all . . . it has been on the side of what the world would call a Quixotic sense of the honorable – of the chivalrous. The indulgence of this sense has been the true voluptuousness of my life. It was for this species of luxury that, in early youth, I deliberately threw away from me a large fortune, rather than endure a trivial wrong. It was for this that, at a later period, I did violence to my own heart, and married, for another's happiness, where I knew that no possibility of my own existed.

Helen was never taken in by Poe's protestation that he had married against his will. She knew of the terrible deprivations he endured but acknowledged the strength of the bond of devotion between husband and wife. This conviction later became one of the foundations of her strong defence of his character.[4]

He went on to describe the malice of Elizabeth Ellett, 'the most malignant and pertinacious of all fiends – a woman whose loathsome love I could do nothing but repel with scorn – to slander me, in private society, without my knowledge and thus with impunity', protesting how honourably he acted to save the lady's honour and how he acquitted himself in the face of the subsequent attacks of Fuller and English. Next, he truthfully asserted the real reason he has so many enemies – that he had stood up fearlessly against the cliques and fiercely maintained his own independence from them. However, he wrote, these accusations could not have hurt him if he had been assured of all he wanted in the world – Helen's love.

> But the cruel sentence in your letter would not – could not so deeply have wounded me, had my soul been first strengthened by those assurances of your love which I so wildly – so vainly – and, I now feel, so presumptuously entreated . . . towards you there is no room in my soul for any other sentiment than devotion: – it is Fate only which I accuse: – it is my own unhappy nature which wins me the true love of no woman whom by any possibility I could love.

He insisted that his one goal was the magazine, a goal he pursued for her sake. '"I will erect", I said, "a prouder throne than any on which mere monarch ever sat; and on this throne she – she shall be my queen".'

There was another problem. He had heard that Helen might possess some property, which would make his advances improper, for how could he hope to woo a lady of means when he himself was so poor?

One can easily imagine the mixed emotions with which Helen read this epistle. Her heart was greatly moved, and Poe had cleverly defended himself against the charges levelled against him, while evoking much sympathy for his past. But there was a disquieting intensity to his words, suggesting that he was not himself. The events of the last few years played heavily on his mind, and he was close to a breakdown. The passionate furies had taken hold of his mind, and only mental disturbance could explain his shameful reference to his dead wife. This mental aberration was to become clearer as the days went by. But there was also much logic in his words, and they were written in a style which, although furiously passionate, seemed to indicate the strength of his feelings of love. Poor Helen was in a perfect agony of indecision.

The pitch of intensity that Poe's passions had reached is apparent in his behaviour over the next few days. Not wanting to precipitate a quick and possibly unwelcome decision, he asked Helen to defer her decision for a week; she promised to write to him at Lowell, where he was stopping *en route* to New York. Her note was indecisive; he rushed back to Providence but was not able to see her. The fears and doubts that filled his mind became dark and unwholesome. His thoughts became even blacker. He travelled to Boston. There, his mind unhinged and in a bout of depression, he went through with the veiled threat he had already made and tried to commit suicide by taking an opium overdose. Luckily he vomited up the poison.

Becoming more and more unstable, he returned to Providence with the intention of clearing the air and visited Helen at her home. He was insistent, but Helen was upstairs and quite at a loss to know what to do. She did not want a scene then and there, and besides, she did not know what to do or say. She sent a message downstairs to say that she would see him at noon the next day, but in his state that was not good enough. He sent back a message that he must see her now, as he had an engagement; she replied, still suggesting noon. Poe demanded some paper and wrote her a note:

> Dearest Helen – I have no engagements, but am very ill – so much so that I must go home, if possible – but if you say 'stay', I will try & do so. If you cannot see me – write me one word to say that you do love me and that, under all circumstances, you will be mine . . .

He continued in the same vein for two days, and eventually, at the Athaeneum, she did meet him. His efforts at persuasion were brought to a halt; she showed him letters she had received warning her against the union. Feeling that all was in vain, he walked away. That seemed to put an end to his chances, and he pondered hard over his failure. This last meeting had an even more detrimental effect on his mind and drove him to despair. He decided that he would not give her up and that he must see her again.

The following morning he called again, now in a delirium and on the point of breakdown. In Helen's words, 'he was in a state of wild and delirious excitement calling upon me to save him from some terrible impending doom. The tones of his voice were appalling and rang through the house. Never have I heard anything so awful, awful even to sublimity.'[5] Alarmed, Helen called for her doctor, a Dr Okie, who examined Poe and diagnosed 'congestion of the brain', a loose description for any form of mental aberration that could be put down to a diseased brain. He was put up at the house of a neighbour, William J. Pabodie, whose family looked after him.

The thought that she had driven Poe to such extremity weighed heavy on Helen and finally convinced her that he was genuinely besotted with her. At last she succumbed – but she set down conditions. The main one, and one on which she was adamant, was that he drank no more. Poe was transported, made the promise and set off back to New York. On the steamboat back, the *Long Island Sound Boat*, he wrote to her expressing his joy, although he felt 'a strange shadow of coming evil'. He was indeed still mentally deranged. His heart beat powerfully within him, and Helen, although the object of his desires, was simply the embodiment of the idol, the unattainable female, which had always beguiled him.

The next letter, sent two days later, comes as something of a surprise. It is a love letter, as passionate as those written to Helen – but addressed to his friend Annie Richmond. Annie had advised Poe to marry Helen but, still in the throes of his passion, Poe transfers his adoration to her. It would be comic if not so tragic. Surely Poe was now a man with serious psychological problems.

It has been suggested that there was a difference between the two love affairs – that his affair with Helen had an ethereal, intellectual side, whereas the affair with Annie was based on mutual physical attraction. This does not accord with the tone of his letters. Certainly he writes with the same elevated passion to both women.

He had known Annie throughout his mad wooing of Helen. He had seen her at Richmond and had expressed his devotion to her also. After winning Helen's consent, on his return to Fordham he took pen and paper and wrote to Annie:

> Nov. 16th 1848 –
> Ah, Annie Annie! my Annie! what cruel thoughts about your Eddy must have been torturing your heart during the last terrible fortnight, in which you have heard nothing from me – not even one little word to say that I still lived & loved you . . . Why am I not with you now darling that I might sit by your side, press your dear hand in mine, & look deep down into the clear Heaven of your eyes – so that the words which I now can only write, might sink into your heart, and make you comprehend what it is that I would say – And yet Annie, all that I wish to say – all that my soul pines to express at this instant, is included in the one word, love.

The words are painfully familiar. The woman-imago to which he was so violently drawn was projected on to both Helen and Annie. The language he uses is dramatic and powerful. He loses himself in the abject, altruistic desire to reach out for a safe harbour, and his need to be adored and to adore batters down his reason. He is suffering all the torments of the mentally ill. In the throes of his passion he would willingly sacrifice anything, even the happiness he plans with Helen.

> To be with you now – so that I might whisper in your ear the divine emotions, which agitate me – I would willingly – oh joyfully abandon this world with all my hopes of another: – but you believe this, Annie – you do believe it, & will always believe it – So long as I think that you know I love you, as no man ever loved woman – so long as I think you comprehend in some measure, the fervor with which I adore you, so long, no worldly trouble can ever render me absolutely wretched. But oh, my darling, my Annie, my own sweet sister Annie, my pure beautiful angel – wife of my soul – to be mine hereafter & forever in the Heavens – how shall I explain to you the bitter, bitter anguish which has tortured me since I left you? You saw, you felt the agony of grief with which I bade you farewell – You remember my expressions of gloom – of a dreadful horrible foreboding of ill – Indeed – indeed it seemed to me that death approached me even then, & that I was involved in the shadow which went before him – As I clasped you to my heart, I said to myself – 'it is for the last time, until we meet in Heaven . . .'

Annie had talked with Poe about Helen. She herself was happily married and saw Helen as the best alternative for Poe. Seeing that he was distracted, she urged him in his wooing of Helen: 'Here I saw her, & spoke, for your sake, the words which you urged me to speak . . .'

Poe went on, as he had with Helen, to describe his idyll, his little cottage – he, Annie and Muddy, together in a state of bliss. It is no accident that he wrote of similar hopes. In his mind that was his ultimate hope – it was the state of bliss in which he had lived with Virginia, and in his heart he wanted to bring back that security with a faceless lady, the epitome of what was impossible, his perfect soulmate, the goddess he had tried so hard to describe in his poetry and which was no more than a figment of his imagination. The wedding Poe had proposed would be another bar between them:

> Think – oh think for me – before the words – the vows are spoken, which put yet another terrible bar between us – before the time goes by, beyond which there must be no thinking – I call upon you in the name of God – in the name of the holy love I bear you, to be sincere with me – Can you, my Annie, bear to think I am another's?

In his delirium he had bared his tortured heart to the only one he could freely talk to – his 'Muddy'. Frightened by Poe's derangement, and probably pressed by him, Maria had written to Annie asking her to visit Poe in Fordham:

> . . . she tells me that she has written you, begging you to come on to Fordham – ah beloved Annie, IS IT NOT POSSIBLE? I am so *ill* – so terribly, hopelessly ILL in body and mind, that I feel I CANNOT live, unless I can feel your sweet, gentle, loving hand pressed upon my forehead – *oh my pure, virtuous, generous, beautiful, beautiful sister Annie!* – is it not POSSIBLE for you to come – if only for one little week? – until I subdue this fearful agitation, which if continued, will either destroy my life or, drive me hopelessly mad – Farewell – here & hereafter – forever your own Eddy.

Poe's depression was now hounding him. To succeed in life – and at that pressing moment, with Helen – he needed to advance himself in the public eye once again, and the only vehicle he knew was his beloved *Stylus*. Although the project now looked impossible, he would not give up. He was still writing to friends and relatives to help him.

He wrote to thank Helen. Now that she had been won, it is noticeable that Poe no longer indulged in the highly charged love-letters that he had previously sent. Olympus had been climbed, the impossible had become the possible. But still there lurked that shadow: 'Still the Shadow of Evil haunts me, and, although tranquil, I am unhappy. I dread the Future. – and you alone can reassure me. I have so much to say to you, but must wait until I hear from you.'

A week had passed since Poe wrote his appeal to Annie, and she had not answered, so he wrote to her sister, Sarah Heywood, expressing his love. On the very same day he was writing to Helen, swearing that his latest trials had only served to strengthen him:

> In a little more than a fortnight, dearest Helen, I shall, once again, clasp you to my heart: – until then I forbear to agitate you by speaking of my wishes – of my hopes, and especially of my fears. You say that all depends on my own firmness. If this be so, all is safe – for the terrible agony which I have so lately endured – an agony known only to my God and to myself – seems to have passed my soul through fire and purified it from all that is weak.

He then warned her against the machinations of Mrs Ellett, and her propensity to write anonymous letters, as she had done to his wife. 'My poor Virginia was continually tortured (although not deceived) by her anonymous letters, and on her death-bed declared that Mrs E. had been her murderer. Have I not a right to hate this fiend & to caution you against her?'

It seems that Poe was battling not only his enemies but also Helen's family, who regarded him as a gold-digger. Both Helen's mother and sister had made it plain what they thought of him:

> Be careful of your health, dearest Helen, and perhaps all will yet go well. Forgive me that I let these wrongs prey upon me – I did not so bitterly feel them until they threatened to deprive me of you. I confess, too, that the intolerable insults of your mother & sister still rankle at my heart – but for your dear sake I will endeavor to be calm.

Two days later, in another letter, he discusses their literary ambition and sees them both at the head of the *Stylus*: 'Would it not be "glorious", darling, to establish, in America, the sole unquestionable aristocracy – that of intellect – to secure its supremacy – to lead & to control it? All this I can do, Helen, & will – if you bid me – and aid me.'

All seemed to be going well with the courtship, although Helen's mother was still against the match. She insisted an agreement be drawn up transferring all of Helen's property to herself; this was done and signed on 15 December. Poe returned to Providence, and on that day he met an old friend, the poet Mary Hewitt. When she asked if he was going to be married, he answered coldly: 'No, Madam, I am not going to Providence to be married, I am going to deliver a lecture on poetry. That marriage may never take place.' Obviously, he was still worried about the interference of Helen's family and especially her mother, who now insisted that he sign a document assenting to the transfer of property.[6] This he did on 22 December.

He delivered his lecture on 'The Poetic Principle' for the Franklin Lyceum at Howard's Hall, Providence, on 20 December – he had obviously been persuaded to change the date by Dunnell. It was shrewd advice: the reading attracted no less than 1,800 people. Poe was staying at the Earl House, and as a celebrity he was invited to join in the carousing; sadly, he succumbed. He also visited Helen but, fortunately, was not in a state of intoxication.

The wedding date was approaching, and on 23 December he wrote a draft of a request for the priest, the Reverend Crocker, to publish the wedding banns (this was not sent but handed to Pabodie to deal with the matter): 'Will Dr Crocker have the kindness to publish the banns of matrimony between Mrs Sarah Helen Whitman and myself, on Sunday and on Monday. When we have decided on the day of the marriage we will inform you, and will thank you to perform the ceremony.' Then he wrote to Maria of his intention to marry: 'My own dear Mother – We shall be married on Monday, and will be at Fordham on Tuesday, on the first train.'

So the second wedding of Edgar Allan Poe was approaching; but it was not to be. It was called off. While out riding, Helen had visited a circulating library, where a note was handed to her telling her of 'recent events' in Poe's life, and that he had been drinking that very morning. Suspicion falls heavily on Mrs Locke, whose enmity had been aroused by jealousy. Whoever wrote the note, it tipped the scales against Poe, and Helen decided against the wedding.

Helen herself gave an account of Poe returning to her house and their last meeting. She sniffed her ether-soaked handkerchief in an effort to lose consciousness, while Poe entreated her to say one word to him.

'Say that you love me, Helen.'

'I love you,' she replied, and no more was spoken between them.

This pretty interlude is contradicted by a later letter from Poe in which he asserts that Helen's ruse was successful and that when he reached her she was totally unconscious, so that no word passed between them.

Helen wrote to Mary Hewitt of how she felt for Poe: not exactly 'love' but 'something at once more intimate & more remote – a strange inexplicable enchantment that I can neither analyse nor comprehend'. This was perspicacious of her and reflects Poe's feelings as well as anything.

There was little to suggest that Poe was in deep mourning; perhaps, like Icarus, he felt that he had flown too close to the sun. Despite his clouded mind, he had always intended to do the honourable thing. He had arranged the banns and had planned to be Helen's husband. It was Helen herself who called off the wedding, and in that Poe was blameless. But he was not in control of his senses. Having been jilted at the last moment, he later wrote to Annie saying that, after they had separated, he had decided to call off the engagement! One idol had fallen as soon as she had become attainable, but there still remained Annie, the unattainable, who now filled his imagination.

News of the broken engagement travelled fast, and Annie heard some slanderous things about it and about why Helen went to the priest to stop the banns being read for the second time. Poe wrote to Annie putting his side of the story. He began by saying that he forgave Helen for anything she may have said. He realized that Helen's friends – and his enemies – would speak vilely of him. He also suspected that Annie's husband harboured ill feeling towards him. (In fact this was not true.) Poe then avowed that if Annie truly loved him he would be armed against all eventualities.

> But as long as you and yours love me, my true and beautiful Annie, what need I care for this cruel, unjust, calculating world? Oh, Annie, there are no human words that can express my devotion to you and yours. My love for you has given me renewed life. In all my present anxieties and embarrassments, I still feel in my inmost soul a divine joy – a happiness inexpressible – that nothing seems to disturb. For hours at a time I sit and think of you – of your lovely character – your true faith and unworldliness. I do not believe that any one in this whole world fully understands me except your own dear self.

Annie had asked Poe to recommend some literature, and he did so; but the actions of Mrs Ellett and Mrs Locke had shaken his faith in literary ladies. Only Fanny Osgood still stood high in his esteem. He ended with this worrisome line: 'I have had a most distressing headache for the last two weeks.'

He also wrote to Helen to straighten things out. He was in a quandary, because he could not exculpate himself without seeming to speak badly of her, and he was not prepared to do that. He laid the blame for the rupture firmly at the door of Helen's mother and also mentioned Helen's dependence on ether (she always had a handkerchief with her soaked in the substance). He suggested they agree to tell the same story, that the marriage was called off because of Helen's ill health. She complied with this suggestion, but that did not put a stop to the rumours. His name was once again tarnished as a result.

Helen had not replied to Poe's letter (she never did); and he wrote again to Annie, now seeing the world through rosy spectacles. Annie was now his only real confidante and as such was a great inspiration to him. She alone was now the object of his fascination, and he became much more settled in himself. It was better thus; Annie was inaccessible and thus a safe outlet for his effusions of affection. As a wooer he had been a disaster, but now he could worship his idol out of harm's reach. Annie had also become close to Maria. Poe told of his hopes of leaving Fordham next year and mentioned that he had written a new tale, 'Hop-Frog':

> The prose pages I finished yesterday are called – what do you think? – I am sure you will never guess – 'Hop-Frog!' Only think of your Eddy writing a story with such a name as 'Hop-Frog'! You would never guess the subject (which is a terrible one) from the title, I am sure.[7]

'Hop-Frog' was a fascinating tale, as it seemed in many ways to reflect Poe's life at that point. The world of his enemies takes the form of a King and his entourage; the hero is Hop-Frog, a distorted dwarf who is the King's jester and who hails from 'some barbaric region'. The King, for amusement, forces Hop-Frog to drink a glass of wine: 'He knew that Hop-Frog was not fond of wine, for it excited the poor cripple almost to madness; and madness is no comfortable feeling.' Hop-Frog's hatred of the King becomes unbearable when the King throws wine in the face of his beloved friend, another dwarf, Trippetta. At a masquerade Hop-Frog persuades the King and his governors to dress as orang-utans, then he manages to haul them up on a string hanging from the ceiling and burns them alive. Thus was Hop-Frog revenged on his tormentors.

This was not the first time that Poe had written about revenge. In November 1846 Godey had published his famous story, 'The Cask of Amontillado', in which the narrator Montresor wreaks a terrible vengeance upon his antagonist, Fortunato.[8] In the classic climax, so often quoted and copied in books and on film, Montresor entices Fortunato into his catacombs on the pretext of examining a cask of wine; he then chains him in a recess which he subsequently bricks up.

Poe's old friend Frederick Thomas had written to him in November, but the letter took some time to arrive. Poe welcomed the communication as it reconnected him with his old world of literary contacts, and in reply he comments on his love of literature:

> Right glad am I to find you once more in a true position – in the field of Letters. Depend upon it, after all, Thomas, Literature is the most noble of professions. In fact, it is about the only one fit for a man. For my own part, there is no seducing me from the path. I shall be a

> litterateur, at least, all my life; nor would I abandon the hopes which still lead me on for all the gold in California.

Thomas had published the prospectus for his new *Chronicle*, and Poe was complimentary. It stirred up his contempt for the cliques and especially the Bostonians, or 'Frogpondians' as he called them. He also mentioned a new work by Lowell, *A Fable for Critics*.[9]

> I suppose you have seen that affair – the 'Fable for Critics' I mean. Miss Fuller, that detestable old maid – told him, once, that he was 'so wretched a poet as to be disgusting even to his best friends'. This set him off at a tangent and he has never been quite right since: – so he took to writing satire against mankind in general, with Margaret Fuller and her protégé, Cornelius Mathews, in particular.

Poe was smarting over the famous verse of Lowell's concerning him:

> Here comes Poe with his Raven,
>   like Barnaby Rudge
> Three-fifths of him genius,
>   and two-fifths sheer fudge.

He went on to foresee a great future for the *Chronicle* which, he assumed, would not be browbeaten by the cliques into a weak and impotent journal. Rallying his old convictions, he was ready to face the literary world again. Fearless as ever, he imagined himself taking on the cliques again and settling old scores.

> By and bye I mean to come out of the bush, and then I have some old scores to settle. I fancy I see some of my friends already stepping up to the Captain's office. The fact is, Thomas, living buried in the country makes a man savage – wolfish. I am just in the humor for a fight.

Just as he seemed to be recovering, along came more trouble to blight his happiness. He had first seen Annie when he paid a visit to Richmond, and since that time Mrs Locke had resented the friendship that grew between them. Now that the relationship had blossomed, she was consumed with jealousy and planned to wreck it. She became Mrs Ellett to Annie's Fanny Osgood. She set about spreading scandal about Poe far and wide, even going so far as to inform Annie's husband of a fictional affair. She had a good model to follow, having witnessed the development of the Ellett–Poe affair. She had also seen its consequences and, with great malice, decided to replicate them herself. Poe was looking forward to a visit to the Richmonds when he became aware of what was happening, and he hurriedly wrote to Annie about it.

He described his history with Mr and Mrs Locke. It was she who had helped him so much when he was in dire straits before and after Virginia's death; and a debt of gratitude allowed their friendship to continue. But on the strength of an exchange of letters Mrs Locke had become convinced that there was more to be had from their relationship and from the start took a dislike to Annie, mainly out of jealousy, although as it happened she was a relative of Annie's. Poe had not become aware of Mrs Locke's feelings towards him until he paid the couple a visit and quite innocently brought up the subject of Annie; Mrs Locke became annoyed, apparently because she felt snubbed and declared that Annie had only been admitted into society through their connection. At this, Poe had grown angry and left the house, thereby ending the cordial relationship between them. But Mrs Locke would not easily suffer such an affront, and envy led her to hate Poe.

Poe suspected that Annie's husband had taken sides against him because he has misinterpreted their friendship. He was wrong about this. Just as Annie was of the ilk of Fanny Osgood, so her husband was made in the mould of Samuel Osgood. When the Lockes visited and made their accusations against Poe, Mr Richmond was outraged and showed them the door – but Poe did not know that. He saw only one honourable course; to protect Annie from further calumny. He therefore determined to sever contact with her, although to do so would wound him immeasurably. But Annie was not willing to drop their friendship.

Poe himself was still angry about the remarks made by Mrs Locke and was desperate to find proof that all he had said was true. He asked Maria to look through his correspondence to see if any of Mrs Ellett's letters remained, but none came to light. At that point Mrs Locke incriminated herself through her own vindictiveness. She wrote to Poe, and in her letter she let slip that she had spoken against Annie, something she had strenuously denied to the Richmonds.

> Well! what do you think? Mrs L has again written my mother, and I enclose her letter. Read it! You will find it thoroughly corroborative of

all I said. The verses to me which she alludes to I have not seen. You will see that she admits having cautioned me against you, as I said, and in fact admits all that I accused her of.

Meanwhile he was revising his lecture, 'The Poetic Principle'. He had no choice but to devote himself to his work, as financial difficulties were haunting him. He turned to his friend Willis, asking him to publish his poem 'For Annie'.[10] Some people were beginning to assume that Willis himself wrote 'Ulalume', so Poe asked him to correct this misapprehension, which Willis did.

Depression gripped him again, as he told Annie. The reasons were many, financial worries among them. His hopes of publishing in various magazines had been dashed, and he worried whether he could make any money at all. On top of this, Mrs Locke had written again. She was proving hard to shake off. Again imitating what had gone before, she was considering copying Thomas Dunn English's ruse of publishing a novel caricaturing Poe. The strain proved too much, and he fell sick once more.

Annie, – You will see by this note that I am nearly, if not quite, well – so be no longer uneasy on my account. I was not so ill as my mother supposed, and she is so anxious about me that she takes alarm often without cause. It is not so much ill that I have been as depressed in spirits – I cannot express to you how terribly I have been suffering from gloom . . . I begin to have a secret terror lest I may never behold you again . . . Abandon all hope of seeing me soon . . .

What do you think? I have received a letter from Mrs L, and such a letter! She says she is about to publish a detailed account of all that occurred between us, under guise of romance, with fictitious names, &c., – that she will make me appear noble, generous, &c. &c. – nothing bad – that she will 'do justice to my motives,' &c. &c. She writes to know if 'I have any suggestions to make.' If I do not answer it in a fortnight, the book will go to press as it is – and, more than all this – she is coming on immediately to see me at Fordham. I have not replied – shall I? and what?

Maria wrote a footnote: 'Do not believe Eddy; he has been very ill, but is now better – I thought he would die several times. God knows I wish we were both in our graves – it would, I am sure, be far better.'

15

A DREAM WITHIN A DREAM

When Poe tore open a letter from Mr Edward Howard Norton Patterson, he must have thought he was dreaming. Patterson, only twenty-one, had been given a local newspaper by his father, but he wanted to publish a magazine, and, being an admirer of Poe, he wished it to be solely under his control. Only Poe, he reasoned, had the determination and mettle to ensure the success of a new journal.

This was a dream come true for Poe, and ironically it had come, not as a result of any effort on his part but out of the blue. He answered positively, although he could not quite believe his luck.

> Experience, not less than the most mature reflection on the topic, assures me that no cheap Magazine can ever again prosper in America, We must aim high – address the intellect – the higher classes – of the country (with reference, also, to a certain amount of foreign circulation) and put the work at $5: – giving about 112 pp. (or perhaps 128) with occasional wood-engravings in the first style of art, but only in obvious illustration of the text. Such a Mag. would begin to pay after 1000 subscribers . . . I need not add that such a Mag. would exercise a literary and other influence never yet exercised in America. –
>
> My plan, in getting up such a work as I propose, would be to take a tour through the principal States – especially West & South – visiting the small towns more particularly than the large ones – lecturing as I went, to pay expenses – and staying sufficiently long in each place to interest my personal friends (old College & West Point acquaintances scattered all over the land) in the success of the enterprise. By these means, I would guarantee, in 3 months (or 4) to get 1000 subs. in advance, with their signatures.

Patterson could not be more obliging, agreeing with Poe on virtually every point and leaving him to choose the title for the journal. He thought he could drum up 500 subscribers – interestingly, by using the power of Poe's name. He further suggested that the magazine begin with ninety-six pages, which could be increased later.

After some reflection, Poe accepted Patterson's offer. He suggested they get over the difficulty of publishing in the provincial backwater of Oquawka, a small town in Illinois, by stating in the journal that it was published in New York and St Louis. He planned to leave for Lowell and Boston and then travel on to Richmond; he requested that Patterson forward half of his expenses – $50 – to be collected in Richmond.

He must by now have been in a buoyant mood. Not only were his financial problems set to be overcome, he was standing on the brink of his greatest magazine venture. The cliques of New York may have battered him to his knees, but they had not defeated him. He was still alive and full of fight. It was now imperative that he re-establish himself in the literary world, and to that end he sent two contributions to Griswold's anthology, 'For Annie' and 'Annabel Lee'.[1]

'For Annie' was of course his tribute to Annie Richmond. It is a love poem, ending:

> But my heart it is brighter
> Than all of the many
> Stars of the Heaven –
> Sparkles with Annie –
> It glows with the thought
> Of the love of my Annie –
> With the thought of the light
> Of the eyes of my Annie.

He delayed his departure for Richmond. There may have been several reasons for this – the want of money probably a major factor. It seems also that Thompson (of the *Southern Literary Messenger*) had a letter for him from Patterson, and he wanted to see it.

He now turned his attention back to his beloved Annie. He sent her various poems and warned her against Dr Locke, assuring her that if Mrs Locke were to call he would not admit her.

June 16 Fordham –
My own *darling* Annie –
You must have been thinking all kinds of hard thoughts of your Eddie for the last week – for you asked me to write before I started for Richmond and I was to have started last Monday (the 11th) – so perhaps you thought me gone, and without having written to say 'good bye' – but indeed, my Annie, I could not have done so. The truth is, I have been on the point of starting every day since I wrote – and so put off writing until the last moment – but I have been disappointed – and can no longer refrain from sending you at least a few lines to let you see why I have been so long silent. When I can go now, is uncertain – but perhaps I may be off to-morrow, or next day: – all depends upon circumstances beyond my control. Most probably, I will not go until I hear from Thompson (of the S.L. *Messenger*) to whom I wrote 5 days ago – telling him to forward the letter from Oquawka, instead of retaining it until he sees me.

At last, Poe was ready for his lecturing trip to Richmond, but he once again fell prey to melancholy. On the day before he left New York he and Mrs Clemm spent the night with the Lewises. He seemed 'very sad' and asked Stella to write his life story if he never returned, a task which Stella felt to be beyond her powers. On his way to the steamboat he turned to Maria and said: 'God bless you, my own darling Mother! Do not fear for Eddy! See how good I will be while I am away from you, and will come back to love and comfort you!'[2]

He got as far as Philadelphia when a strange incident happened. He visited the editor John Sartain and looked pale and distressed, so Sartain took him in and sat him down. Poe was very excitable, constantly in fear of something. Sartain calmed him to some extent and asked him what on earth was wrong. Poe begged him to help him and wanted his protection. On being asked why, Poe explained that he had settled on the train when his attention was drawn to two men talking together. He strained his ears to catch their conversation. To his horror they were talking about him, and the point of their discussion was that Poe had involved himself in 'women trouble' and now they wanted revenge. There was only one course open to them: now that they had found Poe they would have to kill him; they could dispose of his body by throwing it from the train at some convenient point. Only then would their revenge be complete.[3]

In a panic, Poe decided he had to give his would-be assassins the slip, so he made his move when the train pulled in at Bordentown. He rushed off the train, successfully eluding his murderers, and made his way back to Philadelphia; but certainly the two men were following him. He had to find refuge, so he called on Sartain. Now, if he travelled further, the two men would find him again and carry out their threat. Sartain must help him or he was doomed. He needed to go unnoticed, and then he hit upon the idea of disguise. It would help if he could change his appearance.

Afraid of Poe's mental state, Sartain felt he had no alternative but to humour his mad friend. He took a pair of scissors and helped to clip off Poe's moustache. (Whether he did that or not, Poe still had a moustache when he finally arrived in Richmond.) Poe now wanted to go outside, so Sartain accompanied him. They took a bus to Callowhill Street, where they alighted and continued on foot to the Schuylkill Reservoir; they climbed down some steps and sat on a landing that was equipped with seats.

Poe continued his strange story. He had been in Moyamensing Prison, he said, for forging a cheque for $50, and the warders were also planning to kill him. They put him in a cell, leaving him to ponder his fate. As in 'The Pit and the Pendulum', Poe waited to see what they would do next. The door opened, and to his amazement they pushed in Maria Clemm. Poe had to sit in torment while they threatened to maim his mother-in-law; they planned to chop her into bits before his eyes. The whole scene terrified him. Later, he sat at his prison window and looked out. He could make out a tall stone tower, and on top of that he saw a radiant female standing alone. Transfixed, he stared at her, and she began to speak to him, even though she was far off. In a later version (to John R. Thompson) he said he went flying with his vision, which was transformed into a black bird that said it was cholera.

Sartain put all of this down to drink and later gave a different account of Poe's activities. He had had one too many, along with other people, and had been taken before the authorities. When Mayor Gilpin saw him, he remarked: 'Why, this is Poe, the poet', and let him go without a fine.[4]

As Poe sat in his house making such odd utterances, Sartain became afraid for his sanity, so he contacted Lippard (the novelist) and Burr (editor of *Nineteenth Century*); all Friday night they sat with him and helped him as best they could until he was fit to move on. Unfortunately, another disaster had occurred: Poe's valise, containing his lecture notes, had gone missing. Although he did eventually retrieve the case, his notes were gone, so he had to rewrite the whole speech.

Poe's psychotic attack did not end there. He wrote a frenzied letter to Maria:

> July 7. New York,
> My dear, dear Mother, – I have been so ill – have had the cholera, or spasms quite as bad, and can now hardly hold the pen. The very instant you get this, *come* to me. The joy of seeing you will almost compensate for our sorrows. We can but die together. It is no use to reason with me now; I must die. I have no desire to live since I have done 'Eureka.' I could accomplish nothing more. For your sake it would be sweet to live, but we must die together. You have been all in all to me, darling, ever beloved mother, and dearest, truest friend. I was never *really* insane, except on occasions where my heart was touched. I have been taken to prison once since I came here for getting drunk; but *then* I was not. It was about Virginia.

The letter was sent via Stella, but his note to her reveals his paranoia at that time. 'Dearest Anna, Give the enclosed speedily to my darling mother. It might get into wrong hands.'

The note cannot have been much comfort to Maria Clemm. She had expected to hear from him well before this and became worried over his safety. She had expressed her concern to Annie:

> Eddy has been gone for ten days, and I have not heard one word from him. Do you wonder that I am distracted? I fear everything.
>
> Do you wonder that he had so little confidence in any one? Have we not suffered from the blackest treachery? Eddy was obliged to go through Philadelphia, and how much I fear he has got into some trouble there; he promised me so sincerely to write thence. I ought to have heard last Monday, and now it is Monday again and not one word.
>
> Oh if any evil has befallen him what can comfort me? . . . If Eddy goes to Richmond safely and can succeed in what he intends doing, we will be relieved of part of our difficulties, but if he comes home in trouble and sick, I know not what is to become of us.[5]

On the 13th he made his way towards Richmond. *En route*, he wrote a morose letter to Maria, in which his dependence on his 'mother' can be plainly seen; he was homesick and ill. He continued with another on his arrival.

July 14. Near Richmond
The weather is awfully hot, and, besides all this, I am so homesick I don't know what to do. I never wanted to see any one half so bad as I want to see my own darling mother. It seems to me that I would make any sacrifice to hold you by the hand once more, and get you to cheer me up, for I am terribly depressed. I do not think that any circumstances will ever tempt me to leave you again. When I am with you I can bear anything, but when I am away from you I am too miserable to live.

Later that day, he continued:

Richmond, Saturday night.
Oh, my darling Mother, it is now more than three weeks since I saw you, and in all that time your poor Eddy has scarcely drawn a breath except of intense agony. Perhaps you are sick or gone from Fordham in despair, or dead. If you are but alive, and if I but see you again, all the rest is nothing. I love you better than ten thousand lives – so much so that it is cruel in you to let me leave you; nothing but sorrow ever comes of it.

Oh, Mother, I am so ill while I write – but I resolved that come what would, I would not sleep again without easing your dear heart as far as I could.

My valise was lost for ten days. At last I found it at the depot in Philadelphia, but (you will scarcely credit it) they had opened it and stolen both lectures. Oh, Mother, think of the blow to me this evening, when on examining the valise, these lectures were gone. All my object here is over unless I can recover them or re-write one of them.

I am indebted for more than life itself to B—. Never forget him, Mother, while you live. When all failed me, he stood my friend, got me money, and saw me off in the cars for Richmond.

I got here with two dollars over – of which I inclose you one. Oh God, my Mother, shall we ever again meet? If possible, oh come! My clothes are so *horrible,* and I am so ill. Oh, if you *could* come to me, *my mother*. Write instantly – oh *do* not fail. God forever bless you.

Eddy.

Five days later the psychotic attack, which Poe clearly saw as 'hallucination', was over, and he wrote much more happily to Maria. On his arrival in Richmond he stayed at the Swan Tavern.

July 19. Richmond
My Own Beloved Mother –
You will see at once, by the handwriting of this letter, that I am better – much better in health and spirits. Oh, if you only knew how your dear letter comforted me! It acted like magic. Most of my suffering arose from that terrible idea which I could not get rid of – the idea that you were dead. For more than ten days I was totally deranged, although I was not drinking one drop; and during this interval I imagined the most horrible calamities . . .

All was hallucination, arising from an attack which I had never before experienced – an attack of mania-a-potu. May Heaven grant that it prove a warning to me for the rest of my days. If so, I shall not regret even the horrible unspeakable torments I have endured.

All is not lost yet, and 'the darkest hour is just before daylight.' Keep up heart, my own beloved mother – all may yet go well. I will put forth all my energies. When I get my mind a little more composed, I will try to write something. Oh, give my dearest, fondest love to Mrs Lewis. Tell her that never, while I live, will I forget her kindness to my darling mother.

The Swan Tavern was a little faded, but it was still regarded as a respectable place to stay.[6] It was a modest-sized building on Broad Street, with a long veranda and high chimneys, run by a Mr Blakey. Dr George W. Rawlings lived in a small frame house next door and was later to state that, in a delirium, Poe grabbed a pistol and tried to shoot him. If true, this underlines Poe's mental imbalance at the time.

Poe found Patterson's package containing the promised $50 waiting for him. Poe wrote to acknowledge it and explained that he had been suffering from cholera, something he may well have come to believe.

July 19th Richmond
My Dear Sir,
I left NewYork six weeks ago on my way to this place, but was arrested in Philadelphia by the Cholera, from which I barely escaped with life. I have just arrived in Richmond and your letter is only this moment received – or rather your two letters with the enclosures ($50. etc.) I have not yet read them and write now merely to let you know that they are safe. In a few days – as soon as I gather a little strength – you shall hear from me in full.
Truly Yours ever,
Edgar A. Poe.

Patterson was eager to ensure the success of the new magazine, so he worked to put Poe's name before the public. He made an announcement in the *Oquawka Spectator* on 5 September 1849: 'Edgar A. Poe, the celebrated poet, is now lecturing in Richmond, Virginia. His great erudition, added to his gigantic intellect and most felicitous command of language, cannot fail to render his lectures very popular.'

But even Patterson had some reservations. Either on his own initiative or after taking advice, he had decided that, after all, he would prefer to publish a $3 magazine, and he told Poe this. Patterson would have conversed with all those he knew in the magazine trade, and they probably advised him that Poe's plan had too many risks – better to aim for a lower-priced magazine to assure success. Poe was not enthusiastic and stated that it would fail; besides, personally he could not give such an enterprise his full heart.

> 'To fail' would be ruinous – at least to me; and a $3 Magazine (however well it might succeed (temporarily) under the guidance of another) would inevitably fail under mine. I could not undertake it *con amore*. My heart would not be in the work. So far as regards all my friends and supporters – so far as concerns all that class to whom I should look for sympathy and nearly all of whom I proposed to see personally – the mere idea of a '$3 Magazine' would suggest namby-pambyism & frivolity. Moreover, even with a far more diminished circulation than you suggest, the profits of a $5 work would exceed those of a $3 one.

The risk of losing Poe was too much for Patterson. He quickly replied:

> In publishing a $5 magazine, of 96 pp., monthly, page same size as *Graham's* – in bourgeois or brevier (instead of long primer and brevier, as first proposed), it would be necessary for me to make an outlay of at least $1,100 (this amount including a supply of paper for three months for 2,000 copies). Now, if you are sure that, as you before thought, 1,000 subscribers can be obtained who will pay upon receipt of the first number, then you may consider me pledged to be with you in the undertaking.

He further suggested Poe makes his way to St Louis, taking his time, to arrive by the middle of October.

Poe looked out over Richmond and felt a pang of nostalgia. The town was changing, and it had caught up with the industrial boom of the time. New furnaces and rolling mills had been set up, and here stood the third-largest iron foundry in the United States – the Tredegar Iron Works, which had combined the Virginia Foundry with the newer works. The railroad system had arrived. In 1831 the Chesterfield Railroad Company opened its horse-drawn rail line between Manchester and the Chesterfield coal mines. The first steam locomotive service to the city began with the Richmond, Fredericksburg and Potomac Railroad in 1836. A new company, the Richmond and Danville Railroad, had also been founded in 1838, with the idea of extending the service to Danville. The old world was slowly giving way to the new.

Much of the old town was still standing as it was when Poe was a child, but he now saw it through more mature eyes. He would now have had more appreciation for the Capitol building, built in a classical style, surrounded by stone columns. He would also have seen the old Allan house and perhaps felt a little bitter when he saw the two new wings which had been added to accommodate Allan's two sons. There was the old Ewing School where he had been taught as a child and where he first became aware of the social differences between him and the other childen. There was no such stigma now: he had come home as a hero, a poet of great standing, and the town welcomed him as their own.

He never visited his beloved aunt, Fanny Allan's sister Nancy, because she was away at the time, at Columbia. One report suggests that he went to Shockoe Hill graveyard and put flowers on the grave of his beloved Fanny Allan. It is unlikely that he saw the grave of John Allan without mixed feelings. He would also have seen the resting-place of one of his first loves – his first 'Helen', Mrs Stanard. It is said that he visited the cemetery of St John's to see the obscure burial-place of his own mother, Elizabeth Poe. Such visits would have filled his heart with sorrow.

Of the various people he met, he spent some time with the Sullys (he had been to school with Robert Sully) as well as Robert Stanard and even little Catherine Poitiaux, who had written a line to him when he was a boy in England. He spent most of his time at Duncan Lodge with the McKenzies and had a chance to meet and chat with his sister Rosalie, who idolized him. He was even invited to the house of a cousin of Mr Allan's second wife, Julia Mayo Cabell, where she entertained him and invited her friends along to meet him. Poe had known the Mayo family when he was a child and had on occasion visited their house.

Rosalie was a sweet lady, but she worshipped him and followed him around like a lap-dog, which greatly embarrassed him at times. She took him to visit the Talley family at their house, Talavera, where he made the acquaintance of the poet Susan Talley (later Mrs Weiss), who would afterwards paint his portrait. She was to write of Poe's 'indescribable charm, I might almost say magnetism, which his eyes possessed',[7] as well as 'in knowledge of human nature, he was, for a man of his genius, strangely deficient'. He became very friendly with the family and visited them on several occasions.

He also remembered little Elmira Royston, now Mrs Shelton, was still living in Richmond. His new acquaintances may have known of Poe's early romance with her and told him that she had often asked about him; he also heard something else – that she had been a widow for five years. Knowing that she was again unattached, already a hope was kindled in him. He recalled the first of his loves, their teenage engagement and the verses he had written to her. He was determined to see her again, so he made his way to her house on Grace Street; a three-storey building with a small porch sitting on the tree-lined street. Poe knocked on the door, and was greeted by a servant; Poe told her that he had come to see Mrs Elmira Shelton. The servant told Elmira that a gentleman was waiting to see her, and she came to the door, astonished to see her old wooer standing before her. He took one look and said: 'Oh! Elmira, is this you?'[8]

She recognized him immediately but could spare no time for him as she was about to go to church. Poe returned another day, and they talked about old times. He would now have discovered that all his old letters had been kept from her by her father until her marriage. The need for love and affection flared up in him again, and it seemed fitting that his first love should become his last. With all of his old powers of persuasion, he began to court her. At first she laughed at his protestations, but soon saw that he was in earnest. 'He looked very serious, and he said he was in earnest and had been thinking about it for a long time. Then I found out that he was very serious and I became serious. I told him if he would not take a positive denial he must give me time to consider of it.'[9]

On 17 August he gave a successful lecture on 'The Poetic Principle' in the Exchange Concert Rooms, for which admission was priced at 25 cents. The talk began with a discussion on the appropriate length of a poem. He cited several poems in support of his theories, including Longfellow, Bryant, Pinckney, Moore, Hood, Byron and Tennyson. He offered this definition: 'I would define, in brief, the Poetry of words as *The Rhythmical Creation of Beauty*. Its sole arbiter is Taste. With the Intellect or with the Conscience it has only collateral relations. Unless incidentally, it has no concern whatever either with Duty or with Truth.'[10]

The event attracted a very good review in the *Richmond Whig*, as well as some mixed comments from John M. Daniel of the *Examiner*. His article concluded: 'His voice is soft and distinct, but neither clear nor sonorous. He does not make rhyme effective; he reads all verse like blank verse; and yet he gives it a sing-song of his own more monotonous than any versification.'[11] Despite this Poe allowed him to publish 'The Raven' and entered into a contract with him to write for his newspaper.

Poe drank in Richmond, and it is likely that at least one bout began during the celebrations after his lecture. Perhaps his old memories, coupled with native conviviality, persuaded him. Yet he was still fighting the dependence. On the second occasion of his inebriation he was taken to the McKenzie house, and there he was examined by Dr Gibbon Carter, who had a long conversation with him about the evils of drink. Poe explained his past problems and his unavailing efforts to break the habit; but he also swore that he would do all in his power to end his addiction for good. Dr Carter welcomed this but stressed the seriousness of his situation – he warned him that further relapses could well be deleterious, even fatal, to him.

Poe was as good as his word. He even joined the local Temperance Society, as confirmed by William J. Glenn, the presiding officer for the Shockoe Hill division of the Sons of Temperance. The company met in a room above a carpenter's shop on Broad Street, a frame building opposite Brook Avenue. According to Glenn, 'There has been no intimation that Mr Poe had violated his pledge before leaving Richmond . . . and the consensus of opinion of the Sons of Temperance was that he had kept his pledge inviolate.'[12] It is obvious that Poe hated the habit and tried hard to recover from it at several points in his life.

He delighted in the company of so many friends. Whenever he went to see Elmira he would call in on Dr Carter, whose house was between his hotel and Elmira's house. But this delight was often mixed with a feeling of sadness. One afternoon he went for a walk with Susan

Talley, and they went towards the old Mayo house, which he remembered having visited when a boy. Susan later described the visit:

> I observed that he was unusually silent and preoccupied, and, attributing it to the influence of memories associated with the place, forbore to interrupt him. He passed slowly by the mossy bench called the 'lover's seat', beneath two aged trees, and remarked, as we turned towards the garden, 'There used to be white violets here'. Searching amid the tangled wilderness of shrubs, we found a few late blossoms, some of which he placed carefully between the leaves of a note-book. Entering the deserted house, he passed from room to room with a grave, abstracted look, and removed his hat, as if involuntarily, on entering the salon, where in old times many a brilliant company had assembled. Seated in one of the deep windows, over which now grew masses of ivy, his memory must have borne him back to former scenes, for he repeated the familiar lines of Moore . . .
>
> I feel like one:
> Who treads alone
> Some banquet hall deserted.
>
> and passed with the first expression of real sadness I had ever seen on his face. The light of the setting sun shone through the drooping ivy-boughs into the ghostly rooms, and the tattered and mildewed paper-hangings, with their faded tracery of rose garlands, waved fitfully in the autumn breeze. *An inexpressibly eerie feeling came over me.*[13]

His visit to Catherine Poitiaux ended in a similar way. When he was about to leave, a strange expression came over him, reminding her of the look she had seen 'on the countenance of the dying'. When asked when she would see him again, he answered 'nevermore'. Both of these reminiscences may have been coloured in the later descriptions, but it does seem as if Poe was in a sad mood for at least some of the time.

He renewed his wooing of Elmira. The force of his words and his protestations eventually broke down Elmira's defences. Like Helen, Elmira had been warned about Poe's past, and she was nervous about his reputation for drinking. But Poe was able to reassure her, just as he had done with Helen, and could even prove that he had joined the Sons of Temperance on Broad Street. His whirlwind romance, played with his usual insane fervour, reached its climax when he asked her to marry him. Although later she denied the engagement, her denial does not bear scrutiny. She finally submitted and agreed to be his wife. All of Poe's old acquaintances offered their congratulations.

He wrote triumphantly to Muddy about the success of his lecture. On top of this, a Mr Loud had offered him $100 to edit the poems of his wife (Mrs St Leon Loud), and his old flame Elmira had agreed to marry him. However, the ending of the letter suggests that the clouds had not yet departed his mind: 'Do not tell me anything about Annie – I cannot bear to hear it now – unless you can tell me that Mr R. is dead. – I have got the wedding ring – and shall have no difficulty, I think, in getting a dress-coat.'

Elmira was out of town when Poe next travelled on his lecture tour to Norfolk, Virginia. On 9 September he spent a pleasant evening at the Hygeia Hotel at Old Point Comfort with friends, one of whom was the young Susan Ingram. They recited a number of his poems, including 'Ulalume'. Susan told him how much she admired it, and the next day he gave her a letter with a transcription of the poem.

Poe visited the Ingrams again. While he and Susan were talking, Poe noticed the smell of orris root on her clothes. She later recalled:

> 'I like it too', he said. 'Do you know what it makes me think of? My adopted mother. Whenever the bureau drawers in her room were opened there came from them a whiff of orris root, and ever since when I smell it I go back to the time when I was a little boy and it brings back thoughts of my mother.[14]

On 14 September he delivered his 'Poetic Principle' lecture in the Norfolk Academy. Again he had great success, and the *Norfolk American Beacon* repeatedly praised his efforts, stating that they had been received with 'rounds of applause from the intelligent audience'.[15] There was some profit, too; he had made enough to pay his bills at the Madison House, where he stayed, with $2 left over.

He and Elmira had made plans about where to live after the wedding:

> Mrs J.S. French . . . proposes for me to go, immediately after the marriage, to one of her houses – the one she is in now – and send for you to join us at once – there we will remain, only for the present, until we can

make what other arrangements we please. So hold yourself in readiness as well as you can, my own darling mother – but do not sell off or anything of that kind yet, if you can avoid it – for 'there is many a slip between the cup & the lip' – & I confess that my heart sinks at the idea of this marriage. I think, however, that it will certainly take place & that immediately . . .

On 18 September he sat down to write three letters. In the first, to Maria, he tells her he is to go to Philadelphia and edit Mrs Loud's poetry. That should take a couple of days, and then he hopes to travel back to New York.

My own darling Muddy,
On arriving here last night from Norfolk I received both your letters, including Mrs Lewis's. I cannot tell you the joy they gave me – to learn at least that you are well & hopeful. May God forever bless you, my *dear dear* Muddy – Elmira has just got home from the country. I spent last evening with her. I think she loves me more devotedly than any one I ever knew & I cannot help loving her in return. Nothing is yet definitely settled and it will not do to hurry matters . . . Write immediately in reply & direct to Phila. For fear I should not get the letter, sign no name & address it to E.S.T. Grey Esqre.

If possible I will get married before I start – but there is no telling. Give my dearest love to Mrs L. My poor poor Muddy. I am still unable to send you even one dollar – but keep up heart – I hope that our troubles are nearly over.

God bless & protect you my own darling Muddy. I showed your letter to Elmira and she says it is such a darling precious letter that she loves you for it already.

His second letter was to Stella Lewis, in which he thanks her for her kindness. It is written in a romantic literary style:

My dear, dear Mrs Lewis
My dear sister Anna (for so you have permitted me to call you) – never while I live shall I forget you or your kindness to my mother. If I have not written you in reply to your first cherished letter, think anything of my silence except that I am ungrateful or unmindful of you – or that I do not feel for you the purest and profoundest affection – ah, let me say love. I hope very soon to see you and clasp your dear

hand. In the meantime, may God bless you, my sweet sister.
Yours always,
Edgar.

And finally he wrote to Mrs Loud herself, telling her when to expect him.

That Elmira was serious in her acceptance of Poe's proposal can be seen from the letter she sent to Maria Clemm on 22 September:

> You will no doubt be much surprised to receive a letter from one whom you have never seen, although I feel as if I were writing to one whom I love very devotedly, and whom to know is to love. Mr Poe has been very solicitous that I should write to you, and I do assure you, it is with emotions of pleasure that I now do so. I am fully prepared to love you, and I do sincerely hope that our spirits may be congenial. There shall be nothing wanting on my part to make them so . . .[16]

Poe lectured in Richmond on 24 September and was again well acclaimed. He planned to leave for Philadelphia the next day, but instead he stayed in town, visiting the Talleys. According to Susan Talley, Poe had written to Rufus Griswold asking him to be his literary executor after his death and showed her Griswold's reply, in which he accepted. Susan noticed a meteor in the sky when they said goodbye. That night he slept in Duncan's Lodge with the McKenzies.

On 26 September he met Dr Carter and McKenzie and walked into town. He spent the rest of the day with friends. Later he visited Dr Carter in his office, where he complained of chilliness and exhaustion; he then accidentally took his friend's cane as he went off to dine at Saddler's.

That night he took the boat to Baltimore. Elmira wrote to Maria, saying that he had left Richmond but seemed very unwell:

> Sept 27
> He came up to my house on the evening of the 26th Sept to take leave of me. He was very sad, and complained of being quite sick. I felt his pulse, and found he had considerable fever, and did not think it probable he would be able to start the next morning (Thursday) as he anticipated. I felt so wretched about him all that night, that I went up early the next morning to inquire after him, where, much to my regret, he had left in the boat for Baltimore.

He reached Baltimore the next day, but no one knows what happened over the next six days. A friend, Thomas H. Lane, insisted that he took the train to Philadelphia; he did not see Mrs Loud, but spent some time drinking, and took the Baltimore train instead of the New York train.[17] This may or may not be true. In any event, after six days he reappeared in Baltimore.

On a cold day in Baltimore, on 3 October, Joseph Walker, compositor for the *Baltimore Sun*, was walking through the city. He had had a busy day, as there had been an election for Members of Congress and the House of Delegates; in this part of the city the polling station was Ryan's Fourth Ward Polls, on East Lambert Street, and it was along this street that he was walking. He was passing the Gunner's Hall Tavern, where the ballots had been taken, when he saw a figure lying in a bad way on the ground before him; he at once recognized him as Edgar Allan Poe. He was wearing a shabby thin suit and was grasping Dr Carter's cane in his hand. Seeing that he needed medical attention, Walker sent a note to Poe's old friend Dr Snodgrass, who lived a few blocks away in High Street. 'Oct 3. Dear Sir, there is a gentleman, rather the worse for wear, at Ryan's 4th ward polls, who goes under the cognomen of Edgar A Poe, and who appears in great distress, & he says he is acquainted with you, and I assure you, he is in need of immediate assistance. Yours, in haste, Jos. W. Walker.'[18]

Snodgrass rushed to the scene and found Poe 'intoxicated'. His clothing had obviously been stolen, as well as his boots, and items of an inferior quality put upon him. Snodgrass was alarmed at his condition, and decided he needed to be hospitalized. Henry Herring, the husband of Poe's aunt, was also called to the scene, and together they took him to Washington College Hospital.[19] They arrived there at five in the afternoon.

He was placed in the care of Dr John Moran. According to him, Poe was unconscious until the next day, when delirium took over: he was speaking to spectral images on the walls. Neilson Poe came to visit but was unable to see him. He was quiet the next day, but the delirium then returned and he had to be held down. Among other things, he said he had lost his luggage and that his wife lived in Richmond. On the night of 6 October he started shouting for 'Reynolds', but at three the following morning he became peaceful, said 'Lord help my poor soul' and died.

'Reynolds' would seem to have been William Reynolds, the famous Antarctic explorer, and it has been fancied that Poe was preparing for a voyage of his own – although a voting official in Ryan's shared that name.

There have been many theories about the cause of Poe's death. He may have been mugged. He may have been struck a forceful blow, or fallen, leading to haemorrhage. He may have succumbed to psychosis. He may have died as a result of alcoholism. He may have died from diabetic hypoglycaemia. The idea that he contracted rabies is recent. Certainly, some of his symptoms seem to tally with the classic signs. The incubation period is between ten days and a year, so Poe could have been infected as early as late 1848, before his crazed wooing of Helen and Annie. There may be depression (note Poe's letters to 'Muddy') as well as hallucinations, disorientation (such as described to Sartain) and headaches ('I have had a most distressing headache for the last two weeks'). Death can occur quickly due to respiratory or cardiac distress. On the other hand, it would seem odd that the doctors would miss the symptoms of rabies.

A popular theory was that he had been a victim of 'cooping'. The practice was a notorious one. Unscrupulous agents, wanting to increase the votes for a candidate, would accost a passer-by, drug him, then pull him round from poll to poll as a 'repeater'; votes were registered simply by the counting of hands. The Fourth Ward Coop was a place with a reputation – in 1849 up to 140 false voters had been arrested there. If that had happened to Poe, he had also suffered the mortification of being robbed of his clothes while in a state of total inebriation.

That the cause of Poe's death was somewhat clouded is reflected in the fact that the death certificate read, somewhat doubtfully, 'congestion of the brain'. Snodgrass's diagnosis of 'intoxication' may or may not have been correct, but he was a doctor of many years' standing, and it is unlikely that he would have thought Poe 'beastly drunk' had he not smelt alcohol on him. Again, it is unlikely that any sudden injury would have caused his delirium, as any account of his medical condition must surely take into consideration his past hallucinations and psychiatric condition.

It is not too unreasonable to suppose that Poe's death may have had more than one cause. He may indeed have been drunk, voluntarily or otherwise. Lying, poorly covered, on the cold pavements on a cold October day might well have produced illness. Both of these conditions could have induced his final psychotic attack. But all is speculation.

Maria Clemm heard the news too late to attend the funeral, which took place in Baltimore, at a Presbyterian cemetery in Green Street, on 8 October. The Reverend W.T.D. Clemm officiated.[20] Neilson Poe attended the service with Snodgrass, Henry Herring (who had married General Poe's daughter Elizabeth) and Z.C. Lee, who had known him at university. It was he who confirmed the news to a distraught Maria. There was no headstone, only a marker with the number '80' on it. Later, Neilson did order a headstone for Edgar, but a derailed railway truck smashed it. No epitaph adorned the grave.

16

·:~ 'MY DEAR GRISWOLD . . .' ~:·

After Poe's death Maria Clemm was distraught. Her world had crumbled around her. All her nearest kin were dead, and she was now truly alone. Even when Poe was alive she feared that poverty would crush them, but she had put her trust in him to pull them out of the straits they were in; now she had no means of support or income. Bills were pressing on her, and she was frantic. First of all she wrote to Neilson Poe for confirmation of the terrible tragedy.

> Dear Neilson – I have heard this moment of the death of my dear son Edgar. I have written to you to ascertain the fact and particulars. If it be true, God have mercy on me, for he was the last I had to cling to and love . . . write the instant you receive this, and relieve this dreadful uncertainty. My mind is prepared to bear all – conceal nothing from me. Your afflicted friend, Maria Clemm.[1]

It was Neilson's painful duty to confirm the reports, and Maria had no choice but to face the truth. She resorted to sending impassioned letters to all who were dear to Poe. In return, letters of consolation came to her from Poe's lady friends, who, despite his impetuosity and his many faults, proved to be truly grief-stricken at his loss. Elmira wrote even before she had heard from her: 'Oh! How shall I address you, my dear, and deeply afflicted friend under such heart-rending circumstances? I have no doubt, ere this, you have heard of the death of *our dear Edgar*! Yes, he was the *dearest object* on earth to me; and, well assured am I, that he was the pride of your heart.' Of his death she wrote, 'Oh! My dearest friend! I cannot begin to tell you what my feelings were, as the horrible truth forced itself upon me! It was the most severe trial I have ever had, and God alone knows how I can bear it!'[2]

Annie was more practical. Hearing from Maria of her destitution, and distressed at the news of Poe's death, she wrote a sympathetic letter in return. She also discussed Maria's situation with her husband, who had also felt friendly towards Poe, and the kind couple decided to invite Maria to come and live with them. 'Mr R begs that you will come on here, as soon as you can, and stay with us as long as you please – do, dear mother, gather up all his papers and books, and take them and come to your own Annie who will do everything in her power to make you comfortable. Do not deny me this privilege. God in Heaven bless and sustain you, and bring you safely to your own, faithful, Annie.'[3]

Before Maria had time to reply she was approached by Rufus Wilmot Griswold, whom Poe had chosen as his literary executor. It was an obvious choice; Griswold was reckoned as the country's foremost anthologist, and Poe had believed that any ill-feeling between them had long ago been extinguished. Griswold was a model of pleasantness and urbanity, solicitous for Maria's welfare. Maria dutifully placed Poe's works into his hands and gave him power of attorney for publishing them. She was to have any profits from the sale of the book, which was of significant comfort to her, and which would at least lift from her shoulders many of the financial difficulties she was in. She signed the relevant document, which included the sentence: 'In this edition of my son's works, which is published for my benefit, it is a great pleasure to me to thank Mr Griswold and Mr Willis.'

She then wrote back to Annie:

> I am not deceived in you. You still wish your poor desolate friend to come to you.
>
> They are already making arrangements to publish the works of *my darling lost one*. I have been waited on by several gentlemen, and have finally arranged with Mr Griswold to arrange and bring them out, and he wishes it done immediately. Mr Willis is to share with him this labour of love. They say that I am to have the entire proceeds, so you see, Annie, I will not be entirely destitute.
>
> Never, oh never, will I see those dear lovely eyes. I feel so desolate, so wretched, so friendless and alone.[4]

There were the obligatory notices in various periodicals and newspapers. They were standard, and mentioned Poe's genius as well as commiserating his loss. The *Baltimore Sun* said the announcement of

Poe's death 'will cause poignant regret among all who admire genius',[5] while the *New York Journal of Commerce* stated: 'Few men were his equals. He stands in a position among our poets and prose writers which has made him the envy of many and the admiration of all.'[6] But among the obituaries, one stood out. It appeared in the evening edition of the *New York Tribune* on 9 October, and was penned by someone under the pseudonym 'Ludwig'. It began: 'EDGAR ALLAN POE is dead. He died in Baltimore the day before yesterday. This announcement will startle many, but few will be grieved by it.' This attempt at character-assassination continued:

> Passion, in him, comprehended many of the worst emotions which militate against human happiness. You could not contradict him, but you raised quick choler; you could not speak of wealth, but his cheek paled with gnawing envy. The astonishing natural advantages of this poor boy – his beauty, his readiness, the daring spirit that breathed around him like a fiery atmosphere – had raised his constitutional self-confidence into an arrogance that turned his very claims to admiration into prejudice against him. Irascible, envious – bad enough, but not the worst, for these salient angles were all varnished over with a cold repellent cynicism, his passions vented themselves in sneers. There seemed to him no moral susceptibility; and, what was more remarkable in a proud nature, little or nothing of the true point of honor. He had, to a morbid excess, that desire to rise which is vulgarly called ambition, but no wish for the esteem or love of his species; only the hard wish to succeed – not shine, not serve – succeed, that he might have the right to despise a world which galled his self conceit.[7]

This article fanned the flames of rumour which already raged about Poe's personality, and was very damaging to his memory. The effect was hardly dampened even when articles appeared in Poe's defence by Willis and Henry B. Hirst, among others. Lambert Wilmer wrote a piece entitled 'Edgar A. Poe and His Calumniators', and Wilmer was not one to bandy words:

> There is a spurious biography of Edgar A. Poe which has been extensively published in newspapers and magazines. It is a hypocritical canting document, expressing such commiseration for the follies and 'crimes' of that 'poor outcast'; the writer being evidently just such an one as the Pharisee who thanked God that he was a better fellow than the

publican. But we can tell the slanderous and malicious miscreant who composed the aforesaid biography (we know not and care not who he is) that Edgar A. Poe was infinitely his superior, both in the moral and in the intellectual scale. The writer of this article speaks from his own knowledge when he says that Poe was not the man described by this anonymous scribbler. Some circumstances mentioned by the slanderous hypocrite we *know* to be false, and we have no doubt in the world that nearly all of his statements intended to throw odium and discredit on the character of the deceased are scandalous inventions.[8]

Even the noble Longfellow defended Poe.

I never knew him personally, but have always entertained a high appreciation of his powers as a prose-writer, and a poet. His prose is remarkably vigorous, direct and yet affluent; and his verse has a particular charm of melody, an atmosphere of true poetry about it, which is very winning. The harshness of his criticisms, I have never attributed to anything but the irritation of a sensitive nature, chafed by some indefinite sense of wrong.[9]

The reopening of old wounds exasperated Maria, and she blamed Sarah Helen Whitman for much of the odium, particularly the stories told after the rupture between Poe and herself. She also blamed Helen for much of the latest wounding article and suspected that she had been in communication with a third party about the details of the engagement, to Poe's detriment. Accordingly she wrote to Helen on the subject.

But Helen was also distraught and proved herself one of Poe's staunchest defenders. She realized that of the many rumours spread about Poe during his lifetime, one had indeed concerned the breaking-off of their engagement. Although she had done her best to contradict the dark stories that had been current, she was uncertain how to approach Maria. In the end she hit upon the expedient of writing a few words of sympathy and also writing a long letter to Rufus Griswold, wishing him to confirm that she had never harboured any ill-will towards Poe, or wished to cause him any harm; she gave a full description of the terms of their relationship, stressing that no blame should be apportioned to him for subsequent events. In this way, Helen not only expressed her sympathy, but also gave practical help in rescuing Poe from the calumnies he had faced. To Maria she wrote:

> Every day since I received the heart-rending intelligence of Edgar's death I have been wishing to address you. Not knowing whether a letter directed to you at Fordham would reach you, I, this morning, commenced a letter to Mr Griswold requesting him to assure you of my sympathy in your deep sorrow and of my unalterable affection for one whose memory is still most dear to me. I had not finished my long letter to him when I received your note.
>
> Its contents greatly surprised me because I have written to no one since your son's death, nor have I forwarded or received any communication of the kind to which you allude. I cannot but think there has been some misapprehension in relation to this affair. If I am well enough to write you again while you remain at Lowell I will do so. If not my letter to Mr Griswold will inform you of much that I have been long wishing to communicate to you – in the mean time believe me madam, respectfully and affectionately, your friend, Sarah H. Whitman.[10]

Accordingly she sent the explanatory letter to Griswold, but had she tried to damage Poe further she could not have done better. Unknown to her, and to most of the literary world, the writer of the 'Ludwig' article had been none other than Griswold himself. Griswold had never felt friendly towards Poe, and had indeed harboured an intense hatred of him; and he had decided to do him as much wrong after his death as he could. It is astonishing to witness such malice.[11] The 'Ludwig' article was only a beginning. Griswold had little liking for Maria herself, and had ingratiated himself with her solely to get the rights to Poe's work. Now he need pretend friendship no further.

The rights to profits gained from a publication of Poe's complete works became a matter of litigation. Griswold had promised Maria all the profits, but Rosalie's lawyer made out the case that, as Poe's sister, she herself was next in line to inherit any such income. When Griswold informed Maria of that fact, it is not difficult to imagine Maria's reaction. She still assumed that Griswold had been acting in her interests.

Things were further muddied by the fact that Poe had sold the copyright to his publishers Wiley & Putnam. That seemed to rule out any legacy at all, although the publishers had only purchased rights to a portion of Poe's works. In any case, none of Poe's relatives were to see any money at all from subsequent printing of them. It is hard to believe that Griswold did not profit from the venture, and it is likely that the whole business may have been engineered from the start by himself and the publisher J.S. Redfield.

Griswold had received Helen's letter, and she must have been shocked by his reply. 'I was not his friend, nor was he mine, as I remember to have told you.' He also wrote:

> I cannot refrain from begging you to be *very* careful what you say to, or write to, Mrs Clemm, who is not your friend, or anyone's friend, and who has no element of goodness or kindness in her nature – but whose whole heart and understanding are full of malice and wickedness. I confide to you these sentences for your sake only – for Mrs C appears to be a very warm friend to me.[12]

Griswold had asked Maria to send him all the correspondence between Poe and various women, but instead she burned them, fearing that her poverty may force her to hand them over.

Now Griswold proceeded to edit Poe's complete works, and as a preface he intended to write a memoir of the author's life. For outward appearances he asked Lowell to edit and review his last biographical sketch; but when it came to the writing he wrote much of it himself. It was truly a damning document, calculated to do irrevocable harm to Poe's memory. This infamous memoir blackened Poe's name for many years to come, and proved Griswold to be an unscrupulous as well as a deadly foe. Even now the full extent of his lies and forgeries has not been unravelled. He concentrated on Poe's faults, magnifying them and stressing them; he told or insinuated stories to Poe's detriment; and he forged parts of letters to portray Poe in the worst possible light. At his first school, Griswold says that he was forced to wear a turnip or carrot round his neck for disobeying its rules. At university 'he was known as the wildest and most reckless student of his class', and 'his gambling intemperance, and other vices, induced his expulsion'. He gives Poe's story of why he parted with Allan, but hints at another interpretation which 'throws a dark shade upon the quarrel, and a very ugly light upon Poe's character'. He won the prize for 'MS. Found in a Bottle' because it was the only one the judges opened and found legible. White dismissed Poe because 'for a week he was in a condition of brutish drunkenness'. He was also drunk at Burton's, and Griswold (in the third edition) claims Poe said to him: 'Burton, I am – the editor – of the *Penn* Magazine – and you are – *hiccup* – a fool.' He states that Poe's detective stories were thought to be more ingenious than they really were, and while praising 'Eureka' he regretted its pantheism; he accuses Poe of plagiarism in several of his works. As for the intended marriage to Helen Whitman, 'in his drunkenness he committed at her house such outrages as made necessary a summons of the police'. He ends with the 'Ludwig' piece quoted above. Interweaved with these damning fabrications were pieces of praise and critical insight (which were quite acute) to give the impression of sincerity.

The first two volumes of the *Works* appeared in January 1850, in conjunction with publisher J.D. Redfield, complete with Griswold's memoir; in later editions his attacks would expand on the accusations. Now everyone became aware of who had written the 'Ludwig' article, which was mild stuff compared with the prefatory memoir.

Many people came to Poe's defence, including his old employer, George R. Graham. Graham wrote to Maria that she should 'remain quiet, that he has a host of my Eddie's friends prepared to do him justice, and that he intends to devote nearly half of the December number to the memory and defence of my injured Eddie'. Graham was as good as his word. Incensed at what he plainly saw as a literary 'execution', he wrote a powerful defence, denouncing the introduction to Poe's work as 'unfair and untrue', an 'immortal infamy – a death's head over the entrance to the garden of beauty – a horror that clings to the brow of morning, whispering of murder'.

Courageously, he attacked Griswold himself: 'He is not Mr Poe's peer, and I challenge him before the country . . . His [Poe's] whole nature . . . eludes the grasp of a mind so warped and uncongenial as Mr Griswold's.' As for the assertion that Poe was 'quick to choler', Graham explained that this would only be the case when he was confronted with works of inferior literature; in ordinary life he was quite the reverse. 'Literature with him was a religion; and he, its high-priest, with a whip of scorpions scourged the money-changers from the temple. In all else he had the docility and kind-heartedness of a child.' Graham was also well aware of Poe's motives and the power of the cliques Poe so often defied.

> Could he have stepped down and chronicled small beer, made himself the shifting toady of the hour, and with bow and cringe, hung upon the steps of greatness, sounding the glory of third-rate ability with a penny trumpet, he would have been feted alive, and, perhaps, been praised when dead. But no! His views of the duties of the critic were stern, and he felt that in praising an unworthy writer, he committed dishonour.[13]

Well written as *Graham's* article was, and there were others in the same vein, Griswold's memoir was more widely read and became the reference work for the general public. If dark words had been whispered about Poe while he was alive, when he was dead he became a pariah. Stories about him were expanded and joined the folklore. He became the literary scoundrel, a man who was faithless and thoroughly unprincipled, an immoral charlatan. The efforts of his best friends could not stem the tide.

When Helen read the lies which Griswold had spread about her involvement with Poe, she realized the full extent of his perfidy. She discussed the matter with her neighbour Pabodie, who was so incensed he wrote a strongly worded letter to Griswold (published in the *Tribune*), demanding that he retract all his statements concerning Poe's relationship with Helen Whitman.[14] But he was entering the lion's den, and he must have been shocked when he read the brutality of Griswold's reply.

Griswold was an implacable enemy, and also an extremely powerful man. He replied to Pabodie in a rage, insisting that he publish his letter with a full explanation of his accusations. Should he refuse, Griswold threatened to publish letters in his possession that would damage both Mrs Whitman 'and all concerned'. While expressing admiration for Helen, he judged that 'on this subject . . . she is insane'. Pabodie must have gasped when he read on:

> As to Poe's general conduct towards women, it is illustrated in the fact that he wrote to his mother-in-law (with whom it is commonly understood and believed, in neighbourhoods where they lived, that he had criminal relations), that if he married the woman to whom he was engaged, in Richmond, for her money, he must still manage to live so near a creature whom he loved in Lowell, as to have intercourse to her as his mistress.[15]

Griswold claimed to have proof of his assertions in letters in his possession, although he had none. To his credit, Pabodie was not browbeaten by Griswold's threats. Instead, he wrote of Poe:

> He was still urgently anxious that the marriage should take place before he left the city. That very morning, he wrote a note to Dr Crocker, requesting him to publish the intended marriage, at the earliest opportunity, and intrusted this note to me, with the request that I should

> deliver it in person. The note is still in my possession. I delayed complying with his request, in the hope that the union may yet be prevented. Many of Mrs W's friends deprecated this hasty and imprudent marriage, and it was their urgent solicitations, and certain representations, which were made by them to Mrs W and her family, that led to the postponement of the marriage, and eventually to a dissolution of the engagement. In the evening of that day, Mr Poe left for New York. These are the facts, which I am ready to make oath to, if necessary. You will perceive, therefore, that I did not write inadvisedly, in the documents published in the *Tribune*.[16]

Griswold took the matter no further. His bluff had been called.

Poe was staunchly defended in France by his admirer Baudelaire, who lashed out at Griswold: 'Does there not exist in America an ordinance which forbids to curs an entrance to the cemeteries? Griswold, the most detestable of those animals, has committed an immortal infamy; he is a pedagogue vampire who had defamed his friend.'[17]

Of course, the New York clique jumped on the bandwagon. It is untrue that the cliques had destroyed Poe, as has been universally attested; they pummelled him, beat him and brought him to his knees, but they never destroyed him. Just before his death he had planned to set up a model magazine to contain the best of American literature as well as the sharpest of critiques, something which must have made his enemies quail. Only death had prevented him from once more entering the lists. But even death had not muted the enmity of such as Lewis Gaylord Clark, who wrote his own memoir, accentuating the worst that Griswold had written and adding venom of his own.[18]

In Britain Griswold's words were swallowed whole, without the benefit of more positive seasoning. So cleverly did Griswold fool his audience that a writer in the *Edinburgh Review* called Poe 'a beggar, a vagabond, the slanderer of a woman, the delirious drunken pauper of a common hospital, hated by some, despised by others, and avoided by all respectable men'.[19] The *London Critic* stated that 'Poe was no more a gentleman than he was a saint, and of all the poetic fraternity, Poe was the most worthless and wicked.'[20] Other reviews followed suit, although not all were quite so harsh.

When the dust settled, only the malignant memoir was remembered. When Griswold died from tuberculosis in 1857 he had achieved all he had set out to do: he left Poe's name mangled and an object of disdain.

As for Thomas Holley Chivers, after Poe's death he became convinced that Poe had imitated his own work, even in such a masterpiece as 'The Raven'. If any similarity between their work existed, it was extremely slender, but Chivers wrote several anonymous articles trying to prove his assertion. None the less he, too, was disgusted at the treatment of his old friend and intended to give his own impressions of him; between 1852 and 1854 he approached publishers in an effort to drum up interest in his 'New Life of Edgar Allan Poe', 'a faithful analysis of his genius as a poet, the publication of many golden letters, together with some beautiful elegies on his death'. He was disappointed with the lack of interest – it was not fashionable to praise Poe at that time – and the work was never completed. A long time later his notes were gathered together into *Chivers' Life of Poe*.

To begin with, in his familiar style, Chivers bemoans the treatment Poe's memory has received from his enemies, that 'host of hypocrites, who aspire to embalm their dying names in the Amber of his Immortality':

> . . . far be it from me to wish to disturb their low-minded Eyrie – for very well do I know that Buzzards must have somewhere to roost.
>
> Suppose he did drink. Did he not live – feel, think and love? Did he not have an immortal soul in his body? Was he not tempted like other men? Did he not suffer that which would, perhaps, have been the bitterest death to many men? But independently of all this, was he not, with all his foibles, greater, better, in every sense of the term – infinitely better – than the very best of those who denounced him?[21]

Not that Chivers's work was altogether flattering to Poe. In many ways it was damaging – his coloured report of their first meeting, and the thought that Poe did not love his wife (based on the fact that he took to drink after her death) would have been further ammunition to Poe's critics. Chivers's final section was 'An Analysis of His Genius' in which he apprised Poe's canon; having described the 'seven devils' he was possessed with, he ended by saying: 'I do not know a Man, living or dead, of whom the following might be said with greater propriety than of Edgar A. Poe – *Nihil tetigit quod non ornavit* (he touched nothing which he did not beautify).'

Chivers died in 1858. The failure of the publication of his book, together with the death of Griswold, may have spurred Helen Whitman into action. Her book, *Edgar Poe and His Critics*, was published in New York in 1860. She had finally straightened things with Maria and asked many questions about Poe and his life. To Maria she promised that her work would 'very essentially modify the popular judgment'.

Meanwhile Maria began to hear the dark whispers that Poe had been unfaithful to Virginia and had even beaten her. She was shocked and wrote to Neilson Poe:

> It is utterly false the report of his being faithless or unkind to her. He was devoted to her until the last hour of her death, as all our friends can testify. I enclose you two of Eddie's letters . . . The other was written at the time you generously offered to take my darling Virginia. I wrote Eddie, asking his advice, and this is his answer. Does the affliction then expressed look as if he could ever cease to love her? And he never did.[22]

Helen's book was eventually published. The preface of her work begins:

> Dr Griswold's 'Memoir of Edgar Poe' has been extensively read and circulated; its perverted facts and baseless assumptions have been adopted into every subsequent memoir and notice of the poet, and have been translated into many languages. For ten years this great wrong to the dead has passed unchallenged and unrebuked.[23]

She defended Poe from the accusations of moral taint by accentuating all his good qualities, his bond of love with Virginia, and his own beauty of character as reflected in his works. She omitted all mention of her personal involvement and the rumours which had spread about them. She ended her short monograph with the hope that a new biography would show Poe in his truest light or would at least describe the 'silver lining' to his life.

The critics were by and large patronizing, damning her with faint praise, which was directed rather at her noble intentions than at the truth of her assertions. Nathaniel P. Willis gave a complimentary notice of it in his *Home Journal*, stating that 'in this beautiful volume' she ably defended Poe; while George W. Curtis described it as an 'exquisitely tender, subtle, sympathetic and profoundly appreciative sketch of Poe'.[24, 25] But however critics may have felt about Helen, their attitudes towards Poe changed little, and in terms of winning people over to Poe the project failed. Harper's *New Monthly Magazine* stated: 'Her poetic spirit, her womanly ingenuity of argument, and her affectionate admiration of the genius in whose behalf she has enlisted, have done the utmost to redeem the memory of Edgar Poe; but they will probably have little effect to change his place in public opinion.'[26]

Helen's hope for a new biography sympathetic to Poe was soon realized. In England a Poe fan was seething at the calumnies which had been written and was carefully gathering evidence to refute them. He was a post office clerk called John Henry Ingram; he collected a wealth of material about Poe and corresponded with Helen and Annie. His efforts to overturn Griswold's libel culminated in a memoir in 1874 (introducing his own 'complete works' of Poe) and a biography in 1880, *The Life and Letters of Edgar Allan Poe*, which completely vindicated the poet from the worst slanders of Griswold.[27] Although biased towards Poe, Ingram's work was the most influential after Griswold's and exposed Griswold as a liar and a forger.

Ingram's memoir gave impetus to a project which had been brewing in Baltimore – the erection of a monument to Poe. In 1875 it was completed, an eight-foot marble stone, with a portrait of Poe. The ceremony was attended by Joseph Snodgrass, Neilson Poe and even Poe's old schoolmaster Joseph Clarke; but of poets only Walt Whitman turned up. There had been much discussion over an epitaph, but none seemed appropriate, and so none was etched on the headstone.

The next two biographies, a memoir by Richard Henry Stoddard and a book by George Edward Woodberry, were written by writers antipathetic to Poe, which angered Ingram. Stoddard's memoir was attached to a collected works and published in 1884.[28] Stoddard had begun as a blacksmith and iron-moulder, but had given up his trade to write, becoming a regular correspondent to the New York coterie and contributing to the *Knickerbocker* and the *New York Evening Post*. He was also biased against Poe because the latter had once rejected a poem of his called 'Ode to a Grecian Flute', accusing him of forgery, and saying that some of it was too good while some of it was too bad. Now Stoddard took his revenge.

He attacked every aspect of Poe's literary life. He remarked that the idea of Poe being a critic was 'a delusion which could never have been obtained in any country where the principles of criticism had been studied'. He called 'Annabel Lee' a 'jingling melody' and alleged that the tales were marred by the constant theme of madness.

In 1909 came Woodberry's *The Life of Edgar Allan Poe*.[29] Woodberry was an eminent scholar who had been Professor of Comparative Literature at Columbia University and was then elected to the American Academy of Arts and Letters. He had some experience in the field of biography, having already written books on Nathaniel Hawthorne, Algernon Swinburne and Thomas Edison. At first, he did not take to the theme, and was a Griswoldian; although he wrote a competent biography, he had obviously been taken in by Griswold's forgeries, and this coloured what was otherwise an honest labour.

It was not until 1941 that the full extent of Griswold's lies and forgeries came to light, when Arthur Hobson Quinn published his *Edgar Allan Poe: A Critical Biography*.[30] Quinn hunted out the forgeries and published both forgery and true letter side by side, proving beyond doubt Griswold's perfidy. At last Poe's name became more respected, and his reputation to some degree saved. But not wholly – Griswold's legacy continues, even today, in the dark tales that still surround him.

Poe was anything but a saint. He had drink problems and mental problems, could be spiteful and unreliable, occasionally lied, quickly made enemies, had a morbid turn of mind and was constantly attracted to women. To a considerable degree, these flaws arose from the weight of troubles which haunted his sad history. He could also be said to have been brave, kind, generous, chivalrous, loving and industrious. The wish to serve American letters was always uppermost in his mind, and he pursued his quest despite the forces arrayed against him. He left a legacy of fine literature which still influences writers and critics alike but at a terrible cost. Unstooping and determined, he fought against powerful enemies who constantly battered at his peace and comfort, and he championed American letters to his last breath.

During his lifetime he suffered much and was assaulted with worries and fears. These he gave vent to in his poems and many of his tales – the fear of death, horror, terror. The reader is ill at ease when reading these confrontations with the darkness of the human spirit; and it is precisely this which makes Poe such a popular author. The dreadful terrors resonate with our own hidden fears, and we are drawn towards his madness because we see it mirrored in our own souls. Poe's mental disturbance and his constant need for love pushed him into realms to which we are attracted by a vague familiarity, the awful feeling that but for pure chance these nightmares could be our own. He put his finger on a common sore, and we react to it, attracted and repulsed.

The reader may be thankful not to have endured the torment that was the impetus for Poe's writings.

As for the major characters in this drama – Griswold exchanged fond letters with Frances Sargent Osgood and wrote one other important work, *Republican Court*. He died from tuberculosis. John Henry Ingram died quietly in 1916.

Fanny Osgood only outlived Poe by a year, dying of tuberculosis in 1850. Stella Lewis was divorced in 1858 and had a huge success with her play *Sappho of Lesbos*. She remained on friendly terms with Griswold. She died in 1880. Mrs Locke fell out with Griswold when he found her rifling through a private drawer; she died in 1859. Helen Whitman continued to live in Rhode Island, where she died at the age of seventy-five, leaving money to the Providence Association for the Benefit of Colored Children and the Rhode Island Society for the Prevention of Cruelty to Animals. Annie Richmond's husband died in 1873 and she in her late seventies, in 1898. Elmira Shelton also lived to her late seventies and died in 1888.

Maria Clemm stayed with several of Poe's literary lady friends – Annie Richmond, Stella Lewis and Louisa Shew.[31] She learned how to live by writing begging letters and had no lack of experience in the poor years with Poe. She died in 1871 in Baltimore's Church Home and Infirmary and was buried next to Edgar.

There is a strange addendum to the story of Virginia Poe. A biographer called William Gill found the sexton digging up Virginia's remains, so he gathered them together and kept them in a box under his bed. They were reunited with Edgar in 1885.

Neilson Poe continued his law career with some success, being appointed Chief Judge of the Orphans' Court in 1878. He died in 1884. Rosalie Poe was not so lucky. The McKenzies lost everything after the disaster of the Civil War, and she tried to support herself by selling pictures of Edgar on the street. She died in the Epiphany Church Home, Washington, in 1874.

Poe's literary works fared much better and were in constant demand straight after his death. It was his fate that it should have been so. He had worked so hard to be successful and had achieved only a glimpse of fame after writing 'The Raven'. He would no doubt have been satisfied to see himself today as someone ranking in the top echelons of literary genius, someone whose tales and poems are constantly anthologized and who has never been out of print.

He might have been gratified, but it is unlikely that he would have been happy. The ill stars he was born under, coupled with the tragic occurrences of his life, combined to form a personality so damaged as to constantly need admiration and help. When he spoke his last words he might well have thought:

> Thank Heaven! the crisis –
> The danger is past,
> And the lingering illness
> Is over at last –
> And the fever called 'Living'
> Is conquer'd at last.[32]

NOTES

Note: Most of the Poe letters are contained in Ostrom, John W., The Letters of Edgar Allan Poe, *Harvard University Press, Cambridge, 1948.*

Chapter 1: The Fever Called 'Living'

1. The exact date of the marriage between Charles Tubbs and Elizabeth Arnold is unknown, although reasons of propriety suggest that it took place before the voyage.
2. Little Elizabeth is also sometimes known as 'Eliza'.
3. *Massachusetts Mercury*, Boston, Massachusetts, 5 January 1796.
4. *Eastern Herald and Gazette of Maine*, Portland, Maine, 28 November and 1 December 1796.
5. Timothy Dwight, *An Essay on the Stage*, Sharp, Jones and Co., 1794.
6. The Battle of North Point (1811) was a decisive battle in which the British under General Ross were defeated by the American army near General Poe's home town of Baltimore.
7. An adaptation of *La Payrouse* by German dramatist Baron August Friedrich Ferdinand von Kotzebue. *The Dramatic Works of Baron Kotzebue*, Kessinger Publishing, Whitefish, Montana, 2007.
8. Thomas Morton, *Speed the Plough* (1796), in *Speed the Plough, The Way to Get Married, A Cure for the Heart Ache, The School of Reform, The Dramatist*, Longman, London, *c.* 1840.
9. Letter, David Poe to George Poe, quoted by Arthur H. Quinn, *Edgar Allan Poe: A Critical Biography*, D. Appleton-Century, New York, 1941; reprinted 1969, pp. 32–3 of the 1969 edition.
10. Tyrone Power, 'Impressions of America', Lea & Blanchard, Philadelphia, 1836.
11. For example, the critic of the *Ramblers' Magazine and New York Theatrical Register*, September 1809, pp. 27–9, noted Poe's mispronunciation of 'Dandoli' in *Abaellino, The Great Bandit* and thereafter mocked him as 'Dan Dilly'.
12. *Richmond Enquirer*, Richmond, Virginia, 'To the Humane Heart', 29 November 1811.
13. *Richmond Enquirer*, Richmond, Virginia, 10 December 1811.

Chapter 2: Yours Affectionately

1. The 'Incorporated Trades' were established in 1646.
2. Walter Scott, *The Lay of the Last Minstrel: A Poem*, John Sharpe, London, 1810–11. The poem was written in 1805.

3. The Napoleonic Wars effectively came to an end after the Battle of Waterloo, 18 June 1815.
4. Now swallowed up by the Victoria House complex.
5. The Rev. John Bransby lectured in Stoke Newington between 1805 and 1825.
6. His nanny – possibly called Judith – has been credited (as well as the other servants) with telling Poe ghost stories around the fire in the servants' quarters.
7. Col. J.T. Preston 'Some Reminiscences of Edgar A. Poe as a Schoolboy'; his essay was later published in the *Edgar A. Poe Memorial Edition* (ed. Devora Lovell), Turnbull Brothers, Baltimore, Maryland, 1877.
8. Jane Stanard died, insane, in April 1824, aged twenty-eight years.
9. George Long, Professor of Ancient Languages, and George Blaettermann, Professor of Modern Languages.
10. On the back of the letter Allan wrote: 'Edw'd [Edward] Crump, Mar 25 1827, to E.A. Poe, alias Henri Le Rennet'.

Chapter 3: I Am at Present a Soldier

1. The years 1773 and 1775–6, respectively.
2. Maulana Muhammad Ali, *The Holy Qu'ran*, Ahmadiyya Anjuman Isha'at Islam, Lahore, 1917, p. 326. Ali considers Al A'raaf as the places 'on which stand those righteous servants of Allah who walk perfectly in the ways of truth and goodness'.
3. The exact cause of Frances Allan's death is unknown.
4. *North American*, Baltimore, Maryland, 27 November 1827.
5. Apart from contributing to the American Revolutionary War, Kosciuszko also led the Kosciuszko Rebellion against Imperial Russia (1794).
6. Poe was twenty-one and looked older. His colleagues mocked him by asking if he had taken his son's place.

Chapter 4: A Descent into the Maelstrom

1. Letter, Poe to William Gwynn, 4 May 1831. 'I am almost ashamed to ask any favour at your hands after my foolish conduct on a former occasion.'
2. The original title of 'Silence' was 'Siope'.
3. Delia Bacon (1811–59) was most famous as an early exponent of the belief that Shakespeare's plays were written by others.
4. One tale, devoid of truth, has Poe hunting for his roots in 'Povalley', having an affair with one Anne Savidge and finding the 'Raven Hotel'. Mary E. Phillips, *Edgar Allan Poe – The Man*, John C. Winston, Chicago, Philadelphia and Toronto, 1926, pp. 601–17.
5. Based on a single article by Augustus van Cleef in *Harper's Magazine*, New York, 'Poe's Mary', pp. 634–40, March 1889. In it he claimed to give the reminiscences of an aged Mary Devereaux – 'Baltimore Mary'.

6. The story was written by T.H. Ellis and published in the *Richmond Standard*, Richmond, Virginia, 7 May 1881. In it he clearly states that he heard the tale at second hand.
7. *Southern Literary Messenger*, Richmond, Virginia, 'Berenicë', pp. 331–6, March 1835.
8. *Southern Literary Messenger*, Richmond, Virginia, 'Morella', pp. 448–50, April 1835.

Chapter 5: The Literary Life of Thingum Bob, Esq.

1. *Southern Literary Messenger*, Richmond, Virginia, 'Lionizing: A Tale', May 1835, pp. 515–16.
2. *Southern Literary Messenger*, Richmond, Virginia, 'Review of "Horse-Shoe Robinson"', May 1835, pp. 522–4.
3. *Southern Literary Messenger*, Richmond, Virginia, 'Confessions of a Poet', April 1835.
4. *Southern Literary Messenger*, Richmond, Virginia, 'Hans Phaal: A Tale', June 1835, pp. 565–80.
5. The US Constitution was drawn up on 17 September 1787 by the Constitutional Convention of Philadelphia in Pennsylvania.
6. The line was drawn up between 1763 and 1767 by Charles Mason and Jeremiah Dixon to settle a dispute between American colonies. After the Revolution it eventually took on the significance of the North–South divide.
7. Founded by William Lloyd Garrison, the *Liberator* included several poems by the Quaker abolitionist poet John Greenleaf Whittier.
8. Elijah Parish Lovejoy, the abolitionist minister, was murdered by a mob in Alton, Illinois, 7 November 1837.
9. *Aristidean*, New York, 'Longfellow's Poems', April 1845, pp. 130–42.
10. *Broadway Journal*, New York, April 1845.
11. Letter, Willis Clark to William Stone, 1837, quoted by Sidney P. Moss, *Poe's Literary Battles*, Fefer and Simmons, London and Amsterdam, 1963, p. 75.
12. *Southern Literary Messenger*, Richmond, Virginia, December 1835, pp. 54–7.
13. *Southern Literary Messenger,* Richmond, Virginia, 'Critical Notices: "Paul Ulric"', February 1836, pp. 173–9.
14. *Southern Literary Messenger,* Richmond, Virginia, 'Autography'; August 1836.
15. *New York Mirror,* New York, 'The Successful Novel!!!', 9 April 1836.
16. *Philadelphia Gazette and Commercial Intelligencer,* Philadelphia, Pennsylvania, 8 April 1836.
17. *New York Commercial Advertiser,* New York, 11 April 1836.
18. *Southern Literary Messenger*, Richmond, Virginia, 'Review of the "Culprit Fay" and "Alnwick Castle"', April 1836.

19. *Southern Literary Messenger*, Richmond, Virginia, 'Review of "*Zinzendorff*, etc."', January 1836.
20. *Southern Literary Messenger*, Richmond, Virginia, 'Maelzel's Chess Player', April 1836, pp. 318–26.
21. *Southern Literary Messenger*, Richmond, Virginia, 'Ups and Downs in the Life of a Distressed Gentleman', June 1836.
22. *Southern Literary Messenger*, Richmond, Virginia, January 1837, pp. 13–16, and February 1837, pp. 109–16.

Chapter 6: 'You Speak of Enemies'

1. Edgar Allan Poe, *The Narrative of Arthur Gordon Pym of Nantucket*, Harper and Brothers, New York, 1838.
2. *Knickerbocker*, New York, August 1838, p. 529.
3. Letter, Francis Hawks to Poe, quoted in the *Saturday Museum*, Philadelphia, Pennsylvania, 4 March 1843.
4. In William Gowans's *Catalogue of American Book For Sale*, J. Munsell, New York, 1858
5. Of 850 banks, 343 closed completely.
6. Letter, Poe to Nathan Covington Brookes, 4 September 1838.
7. *American Museum*, Baltimore, Maryland, 'Ligeia', September 1838, pp. 25–37.
8. Baron Georges Léopold Chrétien Frédéric Dagobert Cuvier (1769–1832) was the greatest naturalist and paleontologist of his day.
9. Edgar Allan Poe, *The Conchologist's First Book*, Haswell, Barrington and Haswell, Philadelphia, Pensylvania, 1838.
10. Sartain's engraving would be based on the1845 painting by Samuel Osgood.
11. *Gentleman's Magazine*, Philadelphia, Pennsylvania,'The Fall of the House of Usher', September 1839, pp. 145–52; 'William Wilson', October1839, pp. 205–12; and 'Morella', November 1839, pp. 264–6, respectively.
12. *Gentleman's Magazine,* Philadelphia, Pennsylvania, 'The Conversation of Eiros and Charmion', December 1839, pp. 321–3.
13. *Literary Review and Western Monthly Examiner,* Pittsburgh, Pennsylvania, 'Literary Reviews: "Tortesa, the Usurer", July 1839, pp. 209–13.
14. Christopher North was the *nom de plume* of writer and poet John Wilson, a Scot who had joined Blackwood's *Edinburgh Magazine* in 1817.
15. Edgar Allan Poe, *Tales of the Grotesque and Arabesque*, Lea & Blanchard, Philadelphia, Pennsylvania (2 vols), 1840.
16. 'These volumes are inscribed to Colonel William Drayton, of Philadelphia, with every sentiment of respect, gratitude, and esteem.'
17. *Gentleman's Magazine*, Philadelphia, Pennsylvania, 'Review of "Hyperion"', October 1839.
18. *Gentleman's Magazine*, Philadelphia, Pennsylvania, February 1840.
19. *Philadelphia Gazette*, Philadelphia, Pennsylvania, 4 February 1840.
20. *Gentleman's Magazine*, Philadelphia, Pennsylvania, 'The Philosophy of

Furniture', May 1840, pp. 243–5; *The Journal of Julius Rodman*. Chapter 1, January 1840, pp. 44–7; Chapter 2, February 1840, pp. 80–85; Chapter 3, March 1840, pp. 109–13; Chapter 4, April 1840, pp. 178–83; Chapter 5, May 1840, pp. 206–10; Chapter 6, June 1840, pp. 255–9.

Chapter 7: In Search of Eldorado

1. *Philadelphia Saturday Courier*, Philadelphia, Pennsylvania, 'Prospectus of the Penn Magazine: A Monthly Literary Journal', 13 June 1840.
2. *Knickerbocker*, New York, July 1840, p. 88.
3. Van Buren was born in Old Kinderhook, and during the 1840 campaign his supporters formed the OK Club. It is thought that the term 'OK' was coined at this time.
4. *Saturday Evening Post*, Philadelphia, Pennsylvania, 20 February 1841.

Chapter 8: 'You Must Get Afloat by Yourself, Poe'

1. *Graham's Magazine*, Philadelphia, Pennsylvania, 'A Descent into the Maelstrom', May 1841; 'The Colloquy of Monos and Una', August 1841, pp. 52–3; 'A Chapter on Autography: Part I', November 1841, pp. 224–34; 'A Chapter on Autography: Part II', December 1841, pp. 273–86; 'An Appendix of Autographs', January 1842, pp. 44–9, respectively.
2. *Graham's Magazine*, Philadelphia, Pennsylvania, 'The Murders in the Rue Morgue', April 1841, pp. 166–79.
3. Conan Doyle acknowledged the inspiration Poe had given him at a dinner of the Authors' Club that celebrated Poe's centenary (1 March 1909).
4. Published in *Master Humphrey's Clock*, a weekly published by Chapman and Hall, London, 1841.
5. Rufus Wilmot Griswold, *The Poets and Poetry of America*, Carey and Hart, Philadelphia, Pennsylvania, 1842
6. *Graham's Magazine*, Philadelphia, Pennsylvania, 'Review of "The Quacks of Helicon"', August 1841, pp. 90–93.
7. *Graham's Magazine*, Philadelphia, Pennsylvania, November 1841 – January 1842 (see Ch. 8, note 1 above – the three articles in the 'Autography' series).
8. *Graham's Magazine*, Philadelphia, Pennsylvania, 'A Chapter on Autography: Part II – Theodore Fay', December 1841.
9. *Graham's Magazine*, Philadelphia, Pennsylvania, 'Review of "Wakondah"', February 1842.
10. 'The Pit and the Pendulum' was finally accepted by *The Gift*, New York, for its 1843 publication.

Chapter 9: The Valley of Unrest

1. George Graham, 'The Late Edgar Allan Poe', in *Graham's Magazine*, Philadelphia, Pennsylvania, March 1850, p. 225.
2. 'The Mystery of Marie Rogêt' was eventually sold to the *Ladies' Companion*,

New York, where it was serialized; November 1842 (Part I, pp. 15–20), December 1843 (Part II, pp. 93–9) and January 1843 (Part III, pp. 162–7).
3. *Graham's Magazine*, Philadelphia, Pennsylvania, 'A Chapter on Autography: Part II – Thomas Chivers', December 1841.
4. The 'Landscape Garden' (later 'The Domain of Arnheim') was eventually printed in the *Ladies' Companion*, New York, October 1842
5. 'The Tell-Tale Heart' was published in the *Pioneer*, Boston, Massachusetts, in January 1843, pp. 29–33.
6. Felix Octavius Carr Darley (1821–88) was an eminent illustrator, particularly remembered for his work on Washington Irving's *The Legend of Sleepy Hollow*.
7. *Saturday Museum,* Philadelphia, Pennsylvania, 'Prospectus of the *Stylus*: A Monthly Journal of General Literature', 4 March 1843, p. 3.
8. The *Pioneer* folded in March 1843
9. Letter, Robert Tyler to Poe, 31 March 1843.
10. 'My object in addressing you is to ascertain if the list of "The South: Lit: Messenger" is to be disposed of, and, if so, upon what terms.' The letter was sent to White's son-in-law Peter D. Bernard, 24 March 1843.
11. 'The Gold Bug' was printed in the *Dollar Newspaper,* Philadelphia, Pennsylvania, Part I, 24 June 1843, pp. 1–2; Part II, 28 June 1843, pp.1–4.

Chapter 10: Once Upon a Midnight Dreary

1. Poe's good nature may be glimpsed in part of his reply to Idle's first letter. 'You ask me for my hand in friendship. I give it with the deepest sincerity.'
2. At the end of the letter Poe confesses that he still owes Graham $37.50. The letter was later published in *Graham's Magazine*, Philadelphia, Pennsylvania, 'The Late Edgar Allan Poe', March 1850, p. 225.
3. Poe had published a version of this in a review of *Griswold's American Poetry*, November 1842 edition of the *Boston Miscellany,* Boston, Massachusetts, pp. 218–21.
4. *Graham's Magazine*, Philadelphia, Pennsylvania, 'Review of New Books – "Poems" by James Russell Lowell', March 1844, pp. 142–3.
5. The tortoiseshell cat.
6. *Columbia Spy*, Columbia, Pennsylvania, 'Doings of Gotham – Letter II', 25 May, 1844
7. In fact, Hale published the 'The Oblong Box' in the *Godey's Lady's Book*, Philadelphia, Pennsylvania, September 1844.
8. 'The Purloined Letter' was published in the 1845 edition of *The Gift*, New York, pp. 41–61.
9. Originally published in the *United States Saturday Post*, Philadelphia, Pennsylvania, 19 August 1843, p. 1.
10. 'The Omnibus', or 'A Moving Chapter', *Public Ledger*, Philadelphia, Pennsylvania, 17–18 July, and 'The Premature Burial', *Dollar Newspaper,* Philadelphia, Pennsylvania, 31 July, respectively.

11. *Columbian Magazine*, Columbia, Pennsylvania, 'Mesmeric Revelation', August 1844, pp. 67–70.
12. *Graham's Magazine,* Philadelphia, Pennsylvania, 'Our Contributors', Lowell's life of Edgar Allan Poe, February 1845.
13. *Home Journal*, New York, 'The Death of Edgar A. Poe', 20 October 1849.
14. 'Thou Art the Man' appeared in *Godey's Lady's Book*, Philadelphia, Pennsylvania, November 1844, pp. 219–24, and the first part of Poe's 'Marginalia' appeared in the *Democratic Review,* New York, during the same month (pp. 484–94). However, Poe would continue to write his 'Marginalia' between 1844 and 1849 in various journals – 'Marginalia Part II', *Democratic Review,* December 1844, pp. 580–94, 'Marginalia Part III', *Godey's Lady's Book,* Philadelphia, Pennsylvania, August 1845, pp. 49–51; 'Marginalia Part IV', *Godey's Lady's Book*, September 1845, pp. 120–23; 'Marginalia Part V', *Graham's Magazine,* Philadelphia, Pennsylvania, March 1846; 'Marginalia Part VI', *Democratic Review*, April 1846, 'Marginalia Part VII', *Democratic Review*, July 1846; 'Marginalia Part VIII', *Graham's Magazine*, 1846, pp. 245–7; 'Marginalia Part IX', *Graham's Magazine*, December 1846; 'Marginalia Part X', *Graham's Magazine*, January 1848, 'Marginalia Part XI', *Graham's Magazine*, February 1848; 'Marginalia Part XII', *Graham's Magazine*, , March 1848; 'Marginalia Part XIII', *Southern Literary Messenger*, Richmond, Virginia, April 1849, pp. 217–22; 'Marginalia Part XIV', *Southern Literary Messenger*, May 1849; 'Marginalia Part XV', *Southern Literary Messenger*, June 1849, 'Marginalia Part XVI', *Southern Literary Messenger,* July 1849; 'Marginalia Part XVII', *Southern Literary Messenger*, September 1849.
15. *Southern Literary Messenger*, Richmond, Virginia, 'The Literary Life of Thingum Bob, Esq.', December 1844, pp. 719–29.

Chapter 11: 'At Least the Prospects Are Good'

1. *Knickerbocker*, New York, Review of 'The Raven' by Lewis G. Clark, March 1845, p. 128.
2. The praise is contained in personal letters – Mary Hewitt to Poe, 21 March 1845, and Elizabeth Barrett to Poe, April 1846.
3. *Broadway Journal*, New York, 'The Raven', 8 February, p. 90.
4. All published in the *Broadway Journal,* New York, during 1845. 'Some Words with a Mummy', 1 November, pp. 251–6 (first appeared in the *American Review,* New York, April 1845); 'Magazine Writing', 7 June 1845; the poem 'Lenore', 16 August 1845, p. 81 (it had first appeared in the form 'A Paean' in his *Poems*, Elam Bliss, New York 1831, p. 67) ; 'The Tell-Tale Heart', 23 August, pp. 97–9 (first appeared in the *Pioneer,* Boston, Massachusetts, June 1843, pp. 29–31); 'The Island of the Fay', 1 October, pp. 188–90 (first appeared in *Graham's Magazine,* Philadelphia, Pennsylvania, June 1841, pp. 253–5); and 'The Spectacles' , 22 November (first appeared in the *Dollar Newspaper*, Philadelphia, Pennsylvania, 27 March 1844).

5. Letter, Charles Briggs to James Russell Lowell, 6 January 1845.
6. *Evening Mirror*, New York, 'Longfellow's Waif' January 13–14, pp. 250–51.
7. *Evening Mirror*, New York, 20 January 1845, p. 251.
8. *Buffalo Western Literary Messenger*, New York, 25 January 1845.
9. *Evening Mirror*, New York, letter from Outis, 8 March 1845, pp. 346–7.
10. *Broadway Journal*, New York, 'Imitation – Plagiarism – The Conclusion of Mr Poe's Reply to the letter of Outis', 29 March 1845.
11. *Boston Evening Transcript*, Boston, Massachusetts, 5 March 1845.
12. *Aristidean*, New York, 'Longfellow's Poems', April 1845, pp. 130–42.
13. *Broadway Journal*, New York, 'Plagiarism – Imitation – Postscript', 5 April 1845.
14. *New York Tribune*, New York, 1 March 1845.
15. *Boston Evening Transcript*, Boston, Massachusetts, 5 March 1845.
16. *Southern Literary Messenger*, Richmond, Virginia, Editorial, April 1845.
17. Thomas Chivers, *Chivers' Life of Poe*, E.P. Dutton, New York, 1952, pp. 58–9.
18. Letter, Maria Clemm to James Lowell, 12 March 1850.
19. Chivers's sense of humour; he reorders these adjectives describing Poe in order of importance after one has got to know him.
20. *Ibid.*, pp. 53–7.
21. *Journal of the American Medical Association*, Chicago, Illinois, 26 August 1992.
22. As seen in the Briggs–Lowell correspondence quoted by Woodberry. 'I have never met a person so utterly deficient of high motive.' George E. Woodberry, *The Life of Edgar Allan Poe*, Houghton Mifflin, New York, 1909, p. 145.
23. *Godey's Lady's Book*, Philadelphia, Pennsylvania, 'The Literati of New York City – Frances Sargent Osgood', September 1846, p. 126.
24. *Godey's Lady's Book,* Philadelphia, Pennsylvania, 'Literary Criticism – *A Wreath of Wild Flowers from New England* by Frances Osgood Sargent', March 1846, pp. 134–9.
25. *Broadway Journal*, New York, 'Echo Song', 6 September 1845.
26. *Broadway Journal,* New York, 'To F—', 13 September 1845, p. 148.
27. These comments were passed on to Rufus Griswold by Frances Osgood, and he later incorporated them into his memoir, *The Works of the Late Edgar Allan Poe* (ed. Rufus Griswold), J.S. Redfield, New York, 1850.
28. Edgar Allan Poe, *The Raven and Other Poems*, Wiley & Putnam, London and New York, 1845.
29. *Sunday Times and Messenger*, New York, 26 October 1845.
30. *Boston Evening Transcript,* Boston, Massachusetts, 29 October 1845.
31. *Broadway Journal,* New York, 'Editorial Miscellany', 1 November 1845, pp. 261–4.
32. *Boston Evening Transcript,* Boston, Massachusetts, 30 October 1845.
33. Edgar Allan Poe, *The Raven and Other Poems*, Wiley & Putnam, New York, 1845, p. iii.

34. *Knickerbocker,* New York, January 1846, pp. 69–72.
35. *Broadway Journal,* New York, 'The Facts in the Case of M. Valdemar' December 1845, pp. 561–5.
36. *Broadway Journal,* New York, 3 January 1846'.

Chapter 12: The Man That Was Used Up

1. A letter from Idle to Poe, 26 February 1846, shows that he still is not sure whether to believe Poe's announcement of last December 1845 'Indeed, I know not yet certainly, whether it is dead or no . . .'
2. Letter from Maria Clemm to Neilson Poe, 19 August 1860.
3. *Godey's Lady's Book,* Philadelphia, Pennsylvania, 'The Literati of New York City – Charles F. Briggs', May 1846; reprinted in June, p. 199.
4. *Evening Mirror,* New York, 'A Card', 8 May 1846.
5. *Knickerbocker,* New York, May 1846, p. 461.
6. *Evening Mirror,* New York, 16 May 1846.
7. *Godey's Lady's Book,* Philadelphia, Pennsylvania, 'The Literati of New York City – Thomas Dunn English', July 1846, p. 17.
8. *Evening Mirror,* New York, 'Card', 23 June 1846. The infamous article was known as 'English's Card'. Presumably he already seen the July instalment of the 'Literati' sketches. The 'Card' was also published by the *Morning Telegraph* on the same date.
9. *Spirit of the Times,* New York, 'Mr Poe's Reply to Mr English and Others', 10 July 1846 (although dated 27 June).
10. *Evening Mirror,* New York, 'In Reply to Mr Poe's Rejoinder', 13 July 1846.
11. Thomas Dunn English, *1844, or, The Power of the S.F.*, Burgess, Stringer and Co., New York, 1947. In *1844*, Hammerhead, who has a 'broad low receding and deformed forehead, asks in his cups: "Did you see my re-re-view upon L-L-Longfellow?"'
12. Briggs followed English's example, serializing 'The Trippings of Tom Pepper' in which Poe is caricatured as the inebriate critic Austin Wicks. *Knickerbocker*, New York, 1847–50.
13. *Godey's Lady's Book,* Philadelphia, Pennsylvania, 'The Literati of New York City – Lewis Gaylord Clark', September 1846, p. 132.
14. *Knickerbocker,* New York, October 1846, pp. 368–9.
15. *Godey's Lady's Book,* Philadelphia, Pennsylvania, 'The Literati of New York City – Charles Fenno Hoffman', October 1846, p. 157.
16. Poe also asked Ramsay to check on any members of the Allan family in his neighbourhood. (Letter, 30 December 1846).
17. *New York Morning Express,* New York, 'Illness of Edgar A. Poe', 15 December 1846.
18. *Home Journal,* New York, 30 December 1846. The date is uncertain and quoted by Griswold; this edition cannot be traced.
19. Letter, Maria Clemm to Neilson Poe, 26 August 1860.

Chapter 13: Eureka

1. Letter, Poe to George Eveleth, 4 January 1848.
2. John H. Ingram, *Edgar Allan Poe: His Life, Letters and Opinions*, John Hogg, New York (2 vols), 1880, pp115–16.
3. Published in *Flag of Our Union*, Boston, Massachusetts, as 'Sonnet – To My Mother', 7 July 1849.
4. Whitman, Sarah H., *Edgar Poe and His Critics*, Rudd and Carleton, New York, 1860, pp 47–8.
5. Poe's lawyer, Enoch Fancher, had the merchant , Edward Thomas, retract his forgery statement. English, however, made a deposition that Poe was 'a notorious liar' and a 'common drunkard'.
6. 'The Bells' was printed in *Sartain's Union Magazine,* Philadelphia, Pennsylvania, in December 1849.
7. *American Review,* New York, December 1847, as 'To — Ulalume: A Ballad', pp. 599–600.
8. Laplace argued that the solar system began as a cloud of hot gas which condensed, the centre formed the sun which revolved quickly, heating up and producing a centrifugal force. This force caused a 'ring' of matter to detach itself, and individual groups of 'condensations' became the planets.
9. Kepler's major three laws of planetary motion: the planets orbit in an ellipse; they sweep of equal areas (with a line joining them to the sun) for any given distance of orbit; the ratio of the squares of the orbit periods of two planets is in proportion to the ratio of the cubes of their semi-major axes.
10. Edgar Allan Poe, *Eureka*, Wiley & Putnam, New York, 1848.
11. Olbers' Paradox: why is the night sky black if there is an infinity of stars?
12. *Courier and Enquirer*, Richmond, Virginia, 11 February 1848: 'a nobler effort than any other Mr Poe has yet given to the world.'
13. Edgar Allan Poe, *Eureka*, Wiley & Putnam, New York, 1848

Chapter 14: 'Whose Heart-Strings Are a Lute'

1. Printed in *Home Journal*, New York, 18 March 1848.
2. 'To Helen' was printed in the *Union Magazine*, October 1848, pp. 386–7.
3. Caroline Tickner, *Poe's Helen*, Charles Scribner's Sons , New York, 1916, p. 48.
4. Whitman, Sarah H., *Edgar Poe and His Critics*, Rudd and Carleton, New York, 1860, pp. 42–3.
5. As reported to Ingram.
6. Mrs Power, Helen's mother, was an intimidating, intrusive lady who dominated her daughter. Since the death of her husband, Helen had had any suitors but had to reject most because of her mother's objections.
7. *The Flag of Our Union*, 'Hop-Frog, or The Eight Chained Ourang-Outangs', 17 March 1849, p. 2.

8. *Godey's Lady's Book*, November 1848, pp. 216–18.
9. James R. Lowell, *A Fable for Critics Or, A Glance at a Few of Our Pro-Genies from the Tub of Diogenes*, Putnam, New York, 1848.
10. Printed in the *Flag of Our Union*, 28 April 1849, p. 2.

Chapter 15: A Dream Within a Dream

1. Griswold included 'Annabel Lee' in his anthology. It was also published in the *Richmond Examiner*, Richmond, Virginia, in September 1849. Helen Whitman, Annie Richmond and Elmira Shelton all believed the poem to be written about them; but Fanny Osgood maintained that it was about Virginia.
2. John H. Ingram, *Edgar Allan Poe: His Life, Letters and Opinions*, John Hogg, New York (2 vols), 1880, p. 221.
3. It is obvious that the Ellett–Osgood and Locke–Whitman affairs were preying on his mind.
4. *Lippincott's Magazine*, Philadelphia, Pennsylvania, 'Reminiscences of Poe', March 1889, pp. 411–15.
5. John H. Ingram, *Edgar Allan Poe: His Life, Letters and Opinions*, John Hogg, New York (2 vols), 1880, pp. 222–3.
6. The Swan was close to Duncan Lodge, house of the McKenzies and his sister Rosalie.
7. *Scribner's Monthly*, New York, 'The Last Days of Edgar A. Poe', March 1878, pp. 707–16.
8. Arthur H. Quinn, *Edgar Allan Poe: A Critical Biography*, Cooper-Square, New York, 1941, p. 628 (1969 edition).
9. *Ibid.*
10. The lecture, 'The Poetic Principle', was printed in the *Home Journal*, August 1850, p. 1.
11. The article was published in the *Southern Literary Messenger*, March 1850, pp. 172–87.
12. Letter, William Glenn to E.V. Valentine, 29 June 1899.
13. Scribner's Monthly, New York, 'The Last Days of Edgar A. Poe', March 1878, pp. 707–16.
14. *New York Herald*, New York, 19 February 1905.
15. *Norfolk American Beacon*, Norfolk, Virginia, Editorial, 17 September 1849.
16. Letter, Elmira Shelton to Maria Clemm, 22 September 1849.
17. Arthur H. Quinn, *Edgar Allan Poe: A Critical Biography*, Cooper-Square, New York, 1941, p. 637.
18. William Hand Browne copied this note from the original and sent it to the biographer John Ingram.
19. Henry Herring had married David Poe's sister, Elizabeth.
20. No known relation to Maria Clemm.

Chapter 16: 'My Dear Griswold'

1. Letter, Maria Clemm to Neilson Poe, 10 October 1849.
2. Letter, Elmira Shelton to Maria Clemm, 11 October 1849.
3. Letter, Annie Richmond to Maria Clem, 10 October 1849.
4. Letter, Maria Clem to Annie Richmond, 13 October 1849.
5. *Baltimore Sun*, 8 October 1849, p. 2.
6. *New York Journal of Commerce*, New York, Editorial, 9 October 1849.
7. *New York Tribune*, New York, evening edition, 'Ludwig', 9 October 1849.
8. The magazine in which the article originally appeared has not been ascertained, but it was reprinted in *Our Press Gang* for 1860, p. 385.
9. *Southern Literary Messenger*, Richmond, Virginia, November 1849.
10. Letter, Helen Whitman to Maria Clemm, 28 October 1849.
11. Mrs Oakes Smith, a hostess of literary soirées, would later describe him as 'capricious' and that 'he allowed his personal predilections and prejudices to sway him'; also that 'he could not forgive criticism or forget jealousy'.
12. Letter, Rufus Griswold to Helen Whitman, 17 December 1849.
13. *Graham's Magazine*, Philadelphia, Pennsylvania, March 1850.
14. *New York Tribune*, New York, 2 June 1852.
15. William F. Gill, *The Life of Edgar Allan Poe*, Appleton and Co., New York, Philadelphia and Boston, 1877, p. 222.
16. Letter, William Pabodie to Rufus Griswold, 11 June, 1852.
17. Charles Baudelaire, *Histoires Extraordinaires: Traduit d'Edgar Allan Poe* (introduction), Alphonse Lemerre, Paris 1891.
18. *Knickerbocker*, New York, October 1850.
19. *Edinburgh Review*, Edinburgh, Scotland, April 1858.
20. *The London Critic*, London, 1 March 1854.
21. Thomas Chivers, *Chivers' Life of Poe*, E.P. Dutton, New York, 1952, p. 22.
22. Letter, Maria Clemm to Neilson Poe, 26 August 1860.
23. Whitman, Sarah H., *Edgar Poe and His Critics*, Rudd and Carleton, New York, 1860, p29.
24. *Home Journal*, New York, 3 March 1860.
25. *Harpers' Weekly*, New York, 17 March 1860.
26. *Harper's New Monthly Magazine,* New York, April 1860.
27. John H. Ingram, *Edgar Allan Poe: His Life, Letters and Opinions*, John Hogg, New York, 1880.
28. Richard Henry Stoddard's memoir in *Select Works of Edgar Allan Poe*, W.J. Widdleton, New York, 1880.
29. George E. Woodberry, *The Life of Edgar Allan Poe*, Riverside Press, Boston and New York, 1909.
30. Arthur H. Quinn, *Edgar Allan Poe: A Critical Biography*, Cooper-Square, New York, 1941.
31. Unfortunately each of the ladies regretted their charity and found her unwilling to move; Annie found her untrustworthy.
32. From 'For Annie'.

BIBLIOGRAPHY

Allen, Harvey, *Israfel*, Farrar and Rinehart, New York 1934.

Alterton, Margaret B., *Origins of Poe's Critical Theory*, Russell and Russell, New York, 1965 (originally published University of Iowa Press, Iowa, 1925)

Bittner, William, *Poe: A Biography*, Little Brown and Co., Boston, Massachusetts, 1962

Bonaparte, Marie, *Life and Works of Edgar Allan Poe: A Psychoanalytical Interpretation*, Imago Publishing, London, 1949

Campbell, Killis, *The Mind of Poe and Other Studies*, Harvard University Press, Cambridge, Massachusetts, 1933

Chivers, Thomas H., *Chivers' Life of Poe,* E.P. Dutton, New York, 1952

Davidson, Edward H., *Poe: A Critical Study*, Belknap Press, Cambridge, Massachusetts, 1957

Didier, Eugene L, *The Life and Poems of Edgar Allan Poe,* A.C. Armstrong and Son, New York, 1882

Fagin, N. Bryllion, *The Histrionic Mr Poe,* Johns Hopkins Press, Baltimore, Maryland, 1949

Gill, William F., *The Life of Edgar Allan Poe*, D. Appleton and Co., New York, 1877

Hoffman, Daniel, *Poe Poe Poe Poe Poe*, Anchor Books, New York, 1973

Ingram, John H., *Life and Letters of Edgar Allan Poe*, John Hogg, New York, 1880

Jackson, David K., *Poe and the Southern Literary Messenger*, Dietz, Richmond, Virginia, 1934

Jacobs, Robert D., *Poe: Journalist and Critic*, Louisiana State University Press, Baton Rouge, Louisiana, 1969

Kent, Charles W. and Patton, John S. (eds), *The Book of the Poe Centenary*, University of Virginia, Charlottesville, Louisiana, 1909

Krutch, Joseph W., *Edgar Allan Poe: A Study in Genius,* Alfred A. Knopf, New York, 1926

Lindsay, Philip, *The Haunted Man: A Portrait of Edgar Allan Poe*, Philosophical Library, New York, 1954

Mankowitz, Wolf, *The Extraordinary Mr Poe: A Biography of Edgar Allan Poe*, Weidenfeld and Nicolson, London, 1978

Miller, John C., *Building Poe Biography*, Louisiana State University Press, Baton Rouge, Louisiana, 1977

Moss, Sidney P., *Poe's Literary Battles*, Duke University Press, Durham, North Carolina, 1963

Myers, Jeffrey, *Edgar Allan Poe, His Life and Legacy*, Charles Scribner's Sons, New York, 1992

Ostrom, John W., *The Letters of Edgar Allan Poe*, Harvard University Press, Cambridge, Massachusetts, 1948

Phillips. Mary E, *Edgar Allan Poe: The Man*, John C. Winston, Chicago, 1926

Poe, Edgar Allan, *Al Aaraaf, Tamerlane and Minor Poems*, Hatch & Dunning, Baltimore, Maryland, 1829

Poe, Edgar Allan, *Poems*, Elam Bliss, New York, 1831

Poe, Edgar Allan, *Select Works of Edgar Allan Poe* (with Stoddard's *Life*), W.J. Widdleton, New York, 1880

Poe, Edgar Allan, *Tales*, Wiley & Putnam, New York and London, 1845

Poe, Edgar Allan, *Tales of the Grotesque and Arabesque*, Lea & Blanchard, Philadelphia, Pennsylvania, 1840

Poe, Edgar Allan, *Tamerlane and Other Poems*, Calvin F.S. Thomas, Boston, Massachusetts, 1827

Poe, Edgar Allan, *The Narrative of Arthur Gordon Pym*, Harper and Bros, New York, 1838

Poe, Edgar Allan, *The Raven and Other Poems*, Wiley & Putnam, New York, 1845

Poe, Edgar Allan, *Works*, ed. James A. Harrison, T. Crowell, New York, 1902

Poe, Edgar Allan, *The Works of the Late Edgar Allan Poe* (with Griswold memoir), J.S. Redfield, New York, 1850

Pollin, Burton R., *Discoveries in Poe*, University of Notre Dame Press, Notre Dame, Indiana, 1970.

Pope-Hennessy, Una, *Edgar Allan Poe: A Critical Biography*, Macmillan, London, 1934

Powell, Thomas, *The Living Writers of America*, Stringer and Townsend, New York, 1850

Quinn, Arthur H., *Edgar Allan Poe: A Critical Biography*, D. Appleton-Century, New York, 1941

Quinn, Patrick F., *The French Face of Edgar Poe*, Southern Illinois University Press, Carbondale, Illinois, 1957

Robertson, John W., *Edgar A. Poe: A Psychopathic Study*, Putnam, New York, 1923

Shanks, Edward, *Edgar Allan Poe*, Macmillan, New York, 1937

Silverman, Kenneth, *Mournful and Never-Ending Remembrance,* Weidenfeld and Nicolson, London, 1992
Sinclair, David, *Edgar Allan Poe*, J.M. Dent and Sons, London, 1977
Stedman, Edmund C., *Edgar Allan Poe*, Houghton Mifflin, Boston, Massachusetts, 1881
Stovall, Floyd, *Edgar Poe the Poet*, Charlottesville University Press, Virginia, 1969
Symons, Julian, *The Tell-Tale Heart*, Faber and Faber, London, 1978
Thomas, Dwight and Jackson, David K., *The Poe Log: A Documentary Life of Edgar Allan Poe*, G.K. Hall and Co., Boston, Massachusetts, 1987
Thompson, G.R., *Poe's Fiction: Romantic Irony in the Gothic Tales*, University of Wisconsin Press, Madison, Wisconsin, 1973
Ticknor, Caroline, *Poe's Helen*, Charles Scribner's Sons, New York, 1916
Wagenknecht, Edward, *Edgar Allan Poe: The Man Behind the Legend*, Oxford University Press, New York, 1963
Walker, Ian M., *Edgar Allan Poe: The Critical Heritage*, Routledge and Kegan Paul, London, 1986
Walsh, John E., *Poe the Detective*, Rutgers University Press, New Brunswick, New Jersey, 1968
Walter, Georges, *Edgar Allan Poe*, Flammarion, Paris, 1991
Weiss, Susan A., *The Home Life of Poe*, Broadway Publishing, New York, 1907
Whittier, Eugene, *The Life and Poems of Edgar Allan Poe, With Additional Poems*, W.J. Widdleton, New York, 1877
Whitman, Sarah H., *Edgar Poe and His Critics*, Rudd and Carleton, New York, 1860
Winwar, Frances, *The Haunted Palace: The Life of Edgar Allan Poe*, Harper, New York, 1959
Woodberry, George E., *The Life of Edgar Allan Poe*, Houghton Mifflin, New York. 1909

APPENDIX I

TRANSCRIPTS OF POE'S LETTERS AND VERSE

'The Haunted Palace'

Excerpt (verses 4–5)

(First published April 1839 in the *American Museum*)

And all with pearl and ruby glowing,
  Was the fair palace door;
Through which came flowing, flowing, flowing,
  And sparkling evermore,
A troop of Echoes, whose sweet duty
  Was but to sing,
In voices of surpassing beauty,
  The wit and wisdom of their king.

But evil things, in robes of sorrow,
  Assailed the monarch's high estate.
(Ah, let us mourn — for never morrow
  Shall dawn upon him, desolate!)
And round about his home the glory,
  That blushed and bloomed,
Is but a dim-remembered story
  Of the old-time entombed.

Extract from a letter from Edgar Allan Poe to Maria Clemm, 28 August 1835

I am blinded with tears while writing this letter – I have no wish to live another hour. Amid sorrow, and the deepest anxiety your letter reached – and you well know how little I am able to bear up under the pressure of grief. My bitterest enemy would pity me could he now read my heart. My last my last my only hold on life is cruelly torn away – I have no desire to live and *will not*. But let my duty be done. I love, *you know* I love Virginia passionately devotedly. I cannot express in words the fervent devotion I feel towards my dear little cousin – my own darling. But what can I say? Oh think for me for I am incapable of thinking. All [my thoughts are occupied with the supposition that both you & she will prefer to go with N. [Neilson] Poe. I do sincerely believe that your *comforts* will for the present be secured – I cannot speak as regards your peace – your happiness. You have both tender hearts – and you will always have the reflection that my agony is more than I can bear – that you have driven me to the grave – for love like mine can never be gotten over. It is useless to disguise the truth that when Virginia goes with N. P. that I shall never behold her again – that is absolutely sure. Pity me, my dear Aunty, pity me. I have no one now to fly to. I am among strangers, and my wretchedness is more than I can bear. It is useless to expect advice from me – what can I say? – Can I, in honour & in truth say – Virginia! do not go! – do not go where you can be comfortable & perhaps happy – and on the other hand can I calmly resign my – life itself. If she had truly loved me would she not have rejected the offer with scorn? Oh God have mercy on me!

Postscript to the same letter; note for Virginia Clemm

Kiss her for me – a million times.

For Virginia,

My love, my own sweetest Sissy, my darling little wifey, think well before you break the heart of your Cousin, Eddy.

Letter from Edgar Allan Poe to Marie Louise Shew, 29 January 1847

Kindest – dearest friend – My poor Virginia still lives, although failing fast and now suffering much pain. May God grant her life until she sees you and thanks you once again! Her bosom is full to overflowing – like my own – with a boundless – inexpressible gratitude to you. Lest she may never see you more – she bids me say that she sends you her sweetest kiss of love and will die blessing you. But come – oh come tomorrow! Yes, I will be calm – everything you so nobly wish to see me. My mother sends you, also, her 'warmest love and thanks'. She begs me to ask you, if possible, to make arrangements at home so that you may stay with us tomorrow night. I enclose the order to the Postmaster.

Heaven bless you and farewell

Edgar A. Poe

Fordham,

Jan. 29. 47

Extract from a letter to George Washington Eveleth, 4 January 1848

[Note: Poe is answering some of Eveleth's former queries one by one, hence the numbers in the extract. The excerpt begins with an attack on the feminist and author Margaret Fuller, who had become involved (against Poe) in the Frances Osgood – Elizabeth Ellett scandal.]

[page 2:] . . . [critic]izing an author you must imitate him, ape him, out-Herod Herod. She is grossly dishonest. She abuses Lowell, for example, (the best of our poets, perhaps) on account of a personal quarrel with him. She has omitted all mention of me for the same reason – although, a short time before the issue of her book, she praised me highly in the Tribune. I enclose you her criticism that you may judge for yourself. She praised 'Witchcraft' because Mathews (who toadies her) wrote it. In a word, she is an ill-tempered and very inconsistent old maid – avoid her. 7 – Nothing was omitted in 'Marie Roget' but what I omitted myself: – all *that* is mystification. The story was originally published in Snowden's 'Lady's Companion'. The 'naval officer' who committed the murder (or rather the accidental death arising from an attempt at abortion) *confessed* it; and the whole matter is now well understood – but, for the sake of relatives, his is a topic on which I must not speak further. 8 – 'The Gold Bug' was originally sent to Graham, but he not liking it, I got him to take some critical papers instead, and sent it to The Dollar Newspaper which had offered $100 for the best story. It obtained the premium and made a great noise. 9 – The 'necessities' were pecuniary ones. I referred to a sneer at my poverty on the part of the Mirror. 10 –You say – 'Can you *hint* to me what was the terrible evil which caused the irregularities so profoundly lamented?' Yes; I can do more than hint. This 'evil' was the greatest which can befall a man. Six years ago, a wife, whom I loved as no man ever loved before, ruptured a blood-vessel in singing. Her life was despaired of. I took leave of her forever & underwent all the agonies of her death. She recovered partially and I again hoped. At the end of a year the vessel broke again – I went through precisely the same scene. Again in about a year afterward. Then again – again – again & even once again at varying intervals. Each time I felt all the agonies of her death – and at each accession of the disorder I loved her more dearly & clung to her life with more desperate pertinacity. But I am constitutionally sensitive – nervous to a very unusual degree. I became insane, with long intervals of horrible sanity. During these fits of absolute unconsciousness I drank, God only knows how often or how much. As a matter of course, my enemies referred the insanity to the drink rather than the drink to the insanity. I had indeed, nearly abandoned all hope of a permanent cure when I found one in the *death* of my wife. This I can & do endure as becomes a man – it was the horrible never-ending oscillation between hope & despair which I could *not* longer have endured without the total loss of reason. In the death of what was my life, then, I receive a new but – oh God! how melancholy an existence.

And now, having replied to all your queries let me refer to The Stylus. I am resolved to be my own publisher. To be controlled is to be ruined. My ambition is great. If I succeed, I put myself (within 2 years) in possession of a fortune & infinitely more. My plan is to go through the South & West & endeavor to interest my friends so as *to commence with a list of at least 500 subscribers*. With this list I can take the matter into my own hands. There are some few of my friends who have sufficient confidence in me to advance their subscriptions – but at all events succeed *I will*. Can you or will you help me? I have room to say no more.

Truly Yours – E. A. Poe.

APPENDIX 2

CHRONOLOGICAL TABLE OF POE'S WRITINGS

Note: This list contains first publication dates and titles. Later title revisions are indicated in square brackets. Articles and criticisms are not signed in the journals, making attribution difficult. Those of doubtful origin have been omitted. In the case of posthumous publication the year of composition has been given in parentheses. A question-mark indicates that the year is uncertain. It should be noted that *Burton's Magazine* was more properly entitled *Burton's Gentleman's Magazine*. Abbreviations: LC (literary criticism), M (miscellaneous), P (poem), T (tale).

Year	Date	Title	Publication	Genre
1827		'Dreams'	*Tamerlane and Other Poems*	P
1827		'Evening Star'	*Tamerlane and Other Poems*	P
1827		'Imitation'	*Tamerlane and Other Poems*	P
1827		'Tamerlane'	*Tamerlane and Other Poems*	P
1827		'The Lake' ['The Lake – To ——']	*Tamerlane and Other Poems*	P
1827		'To ——' ('I saw thee on thy bridal day')	*Tamerlane and Other Poems*	P
1827		Untitled ['A Dream']	*Tamerlane and Other Poems*	P
1827		Untitled ['Stanzas']	*Tamerlane and Other Poems*	P
1827		Untitled ['The Happiest Day']	*Tamerlane and Other Poems*	P
1827		'Visit of the Dead' ['Spirits of the Dead']	*Tamerlane and Other Poems*	P
1829		'Al Aaraaf'	*Al Aaraaf, Tamerlane and Minor Poems*	P
1829		'Fairyland'	*Al Aaraaf, Tamerlane and Minor Poems*	P
1829		'Preface' ['Introduction', 'Romance']	*Al Aaraaf, Tamerlane and Minor Poems*	P
1829		'Spirits of the Dead'	*Al Aaraaf, Tamerlane and Minor Poems*	P
1829		'To ——' ('Should my early life seem')	*Al Aaraaf, Tamerlane and Minor Poems*	P
1829		'To —— (The bowers whereat)'	*Al Aaraaf, Tamerlane and Minor Poems*	P
1829		'To M——' ['To ——']	*Al Aaraaf, Tamerlane and Minor Poems*	P
1829		'To the River'	*Al Aaraaf, Tamerlane and Minor Poems*	P
1829		Untitled ['Sonnet to Science']	*Al Aaraaf, Tamerlane and Minor Poems*	P
1831		'A Paean' ['Lenore']	*Poems*	P
1831		Introduction	*Poems*	P

Year	Date	Title	Publication	Genre
1831		'Irene'	*Poems*	P
1831		'Israfel'	*Poems*	P
1831		'Letter to B——'	*Poems*	M
1831		'The Doomed City' ['The City of Sin', 'The City in the Sea']	*Poems*	P
1831		'To Helen' ('Helen, thy beauty is to me . . .')	*Poems*	P
1832	14 January	'Metzengestein' ['The Horse-Shade']	*Saturday Courier*	T
1832	3 March	'The Duke d'Omelette' ['The Duc d'Omelette']	*Saturday Courier*	T
1832	9 June	'A Tale of Jerusalem'	*Saturday Courier*	T
1832	10 November	'A Decided Loss' ['Loss of Breath']	*Saturday Courier*	T
1832	1 December	'The Bargain Lost' ['Bob-Bon']	*Saturday Courier*	T
1833	2 February	'Enigma'	*Baltimore Saturday Visitor*	P
1833	20 April	'Serenade'	*Baltimore Saturday Visitor*	P
1833	4 May	'Epimanes' ['The Homo-Cameleopard', 'Four Beasts in One']	*Southern Literary Messenger*	T
1833	11 May	'To ——' ('Sleep on, sleep on')	*Baltimore Saturday Visitor*	P
1833	19 October	'MS Found in a Bottle'	*Baltimore Saturday Visitor*	T
1833	26 October	'The Coliseum'	*Baltimore Saturday Visitor*	P
1834	January	'The Visionary' ['The Assignation']	*The Lady's Book*	T
1835	March	'Berenicë – A Tale' ['Berenicë']	*Southern Literary Messenger*	T
1835	April	'Morella'	*Southern Literary Messenger*	T
1835	April	Review of *Confessions of a Poet* (Laughton Osborn)	*Southern Literary Messenger*	LC
1835	May	Review of *Horse-Shoe Robinson* (John P. Kennedy)	*Southern Literary Messenger*	LC

Year	Date	Title	Publication	Genre
1835	May	Review of *Journal* (Frances A. Butler)	*Southern Literary Messenger*	LC
1835	May	'Lionizing: A Tale' ['Lionizing', 'Some Passages in the Life of a Lion']	*Southern Literary Messenger*	T
1835	14 May	Notice of the 8th Number of the *Southern Literary Messenger*	*Baltimore Republican and Commercial Advertiser*	M
1835	June	'Hans Phaal – A Tale' ['Hans Phaal', 'The Unparalleled Adventure of One Hans Pfaal']	*Southern Literary Messenger*	T
1835	June	Review of *A History of Ireland* (Thomas Moore)	*Southern Literary Messenger*	LC
1835	June	Review of *Blackbeard*	*Southern Literary Messenger*	LC
1835	June	Review of *Outre-Mer* (H.W. Longfellow)	*Southern Literary Messenger*	LC
1835	June	Review of *Pencil Sketches* (Eliza Leslie)	*Southern Literary Messenger*	LC
1835	June	Review of *The American Quarterly Magazine*	*Southern Literary Messenger*	LC
1835	June	Review of *The Infidel* (Robert M. Bird)	*Southern Literary Messenger*	LC
1835	June	Review of *Voyage of the US Frigate Potomac* (Jeremiah N. Reynolds)	*Southern Literary Messenger*	LC
1835	13 June	Notice of the 9th Number of the *Southern Literary Messenger*	*Baltimore Republican and Commercial Advertiser*	M
1835	16 June	Review of *The Italian Sketch-Book* (Henry T. Tuckerman)	*Baltimore American*	LC
1835	July	'To Mary'	*Southern Literary Messenger*	P
1835	10 July	Notice of the 10th Number of the *Southern Literary Messenger*	*Baltimore Republican and Commercial Advertiser*	M
1835	11 July	Notice of *The Student* (Edward L. Bulwer)	*Baltimore American*	LC
1835	August	'Critical Notices and Literary Intelligence'	*Southern Literary Messenger*	M
1835	August	Notice of *Magpie Castle* (Theodore Hook)	*Southern Literary Messenger*	LC
1835	August	Notice of *Visit to the American Churches* (Andrew Reed, James Matheson)	*Southern Literary Messenger*	LC

YEAR	DATE	TITLE	PUBLICATION	GENRE
1835	September	'King Pest the First: A Tale Containing an Allegory' ['King Pest: A Tale Containing an Allegory']	*Southern Literary Messenger*	T
1835	September	'Lines Written in an Album' ['To F—— O——']	*Southern Literary Messenger*	P
1835	September	Review of *Mephistopheles in England* (Robert F. Williams)	*Southern Literary Messenger*	LC
1835	September	Review of *The Early Naval History of England* (Robert Southey)	*Southern Literary Messenger*	LC
1835	September	Review of *The Classical Family Library: Euripides*	*Southern Literary Messenger*	LC
1835	September	Review of *The Gift*	*Southern Literary Messenger*	LC
		Review of *The New England Magazine*	*Southern Literary Messenger*	LC
1835	September	'Shadow – A Fable' ['Shadow – A Parable']	*Southern Literary Messenger*	T
1835	December	Review of *A Memoir of the Rev. John H. Rice* (William Maxwell)	*Southern Literary Messenger*	LC
1835	December	Review of *An Address on Education* (Lucian Minor)	*Southern Literary Messenger*	LC
1835	December	Review of *Clinton Bradshaw* (Frederick W. Thomas)	*Southern Literary Messenger*	LC
1835	December	Review of *Lives of the Necromancers* (William Godwin)	*Southern Literary Messenger*	LC
1835	December	Review of *Norman Leslie* (Theodore S. Fay)	*Southern Literary Messenger*	LC
1835	December	Review of *Nuts to Crack* (Richard Gooch)	*Southern Literary Messenger*	LC
1835	December	Review of *On the Life and Character of the Rev. Joseph Caldwell, DD* (Walker Anderson)	*Southern Literary Messenger*	LC
1835	December	Review of *Tales of the Peerage and the Peasantry* (Lady Dacre)	*Southern Literary Messenger*	LC
1835	December	Review of *The American Almanac*	*Southern Literary Messenger*	LC
1835	December	Review of *The Crayon Miscellany* (Washington Irving)	*Southern Literary Messenger*	LC

YEAR	DATE	TITLE	PUBLICATION	GENRE
1835	December	Review of *The Edinburgh Review*	*Southern Literary Messenger*	LC
1835	December	Review of *The English Annals*	*Southern Literary Messenger*	LC
1835	December	Review of *The Heroine* (Eaton S. Barrett)	*Southern Literary Messenger*	LC
1835	December	Review of *The Hawks of Hawk-Hollow* (Robert M. Bird)	*Southern Literary Messenger*	LC
1835	December	Review of *The Linwoods* (Catherine M. Sedgwick)	*Southern Literary Messenger*	LC
1835	December	Review of *The London Quarterly Review*	*Southern Literary Messenger*	LC
1835	December	Review of *The North American Review*	*Southern Literary Messenger*	LC
1835	December	Review of *The Westminster Review*	*Southern Literary Messenger*	LC
1835	December	Review of *Traits of American Life* (Sarah J. Hale)	*Southern Literary Messenger*	LC
1835	December	Review of *Washington Vita* (Francis Glass)	*Southern Literary Messenger*	LC
1835-1836	December–January	'Scenes from an Unfinished Drama' ('Politian')	*Southern Literary Messenger*	P
1836	January	Review of *Poems* (Hannah F. Gould)	*Southern Literary Messenger*	LC
1836	January	Review of *Poems: Translated and Original* (Elizabeth F. Ellett)	*Southern Literary Messenger*	LC
1836	January	Review of *Reminiscences of an Intercourse with Mr Niebuhr* (Francis Lieber)	*Southern Literary Messenger*	LC
1836	January	Review of *Robinson Crusoe* (Daniel Defoe)	*Southern Literary Messenger*	LC
1836	January	Review of *The Partisan* (William G. Simms)	*Southern Literary Messenger*	LC
1836	January	Review of *The Poetry of Life* (Sarah Stickney)	*Southern Literary Messenger*	LC
1836	January	Review of *Zinzendorff and Other Poems* (Lydia H. Sigourney)	*Southern Literary Messenger*	LC
1836	February	'Autography I'	*Southern Literary Messenger*	M
1836	February	Notice of *Rose Hill*	*Southern Literary Messenger*	LC

Year	Date	Title	Publication	Genre
1836	February	Notice of *Noble Deeds of Women*	*Southern Literary Messenger*	LC
1836	February	'On Palaestine'	*Southern Literary Messenger*	M
1836	February	Review of *A New and Comprehensive Gazetteer of Virginia* (Joseph Martin)	*Southern Literary Messenger*	LC
1836	February	Review of *Animal and Vegetable Physiology* (Peter M. Roget)	*Southern Literary Messenger*	LC
1836	February	Review of Carey's *Autobiography*	*Southern Literary Messenger*	LC
1836	February	Review of *Conti the Discarded* (Henry F. Chorley)	*Southern Literary Messenger*	LC
1836	February	Review of *Paul Ulric* (Morris Mattson)	*Southern Literary Messenger*	LC
1836	February	Review of *Rienzi, the Last of the Tribunes* (Edward L. Bulwer)	*Southern Literary Messenger*	LC
1836	February	Review of *The American in England* (Alexander Slidell)	*Southern Literary Messenger*	LC
1826	February	Review of *The Confessions of Emilia Harrington* (Lambert A. Wilmer)	*Southern Literary Messenger*	LC
1836	March	'Latin Hymn'	*Southern Literary Messenger*	P
1836	March	Review of *Contributions to the Ecclesiastical History of the USA* (Francis L. Hawks)	*Southern Literary Messenger*	LC
1836	March	Review of *Georgia Scenes, Characters, Incidents, &c.* (Augustus B. Longstreet)	*Southern Literary Messenger*	LC
1836	March	Review of *Phrenology* (L. Miles)	*Southern Literary Messenger*	LC
1836	April	'Maelzel's Chess Player'	*Southern Literary Messenger*	M
1836	April	Review of *The Culprit Fay* (Joseph R. Drake) and *Alnwick Castle* (Fitz-Greene Halleck)	*Southern Literary Messenger*	LC
1836	May	Review of *A Life of Washington* (James K. Paulding)	*Southern Literary Messenger*	LC
1836	May	Review of *Didactics* (Robert Walsh)	*Southern Literary Messenger*	LC

YEAR	DATE	TITLE	PUBLICATION	GENRE
1836	June	Review of *Letters, Conversations and Reflections of S.T. Coleridge*	*Southern Literary Messenger*	LC
1836	June	Review of *Ups and Downs in the Life of a Distressed Gentleman* (William L. Stone)	*Southern Literary Messenger*	LC
1836	June	Review of *Watkins Tottle* (Charles Dickens)	*Southern Literary Messenger*	LC
1836	July	Review of *The Doctor &c.* (Robert Southey)	*Southern Literary Messenger*	LC
1836	August	'Autography II'	*Southern Literary Messenger*	M
1836	August	'Pinakidia'	*Southern Literary Messenger*	M
1836	August	Review of *Lafitte* (Joseph H. Ingraham)	*Southern Literary Messenger*	LC
1836	August	Review of *The Book of Gems* (Samuel C. Hall)	*Southern Literary Messenger*	LC
1836	September	Review of *Sheppard Lee* (Robert M. Bird)	*Southern Literary Messenger*	LC
1836	October	Review of *Memorials of Mrs Hemans* (Henry F. Chorley)	*Southern Literary Messenger*	LC
1836	October	Review of *The Swiss Heiress* (Susan R. Morgan)	*Southern Literary Messenger*	LC
1836	November	Notice of *The Posthumous Papers of the Pickwick Club* (Charles Dickens)	*Southern Literary Messenger*	LC
1837	January	'Bridal Ballad'	*Southern Literary Messenger*	P
1837	January	Review of *Address on the Subject of . . . Expedition to the Pacific Ocean and South Seas* (Charles Wilkes)	*Southern Literary Messenger*	LC
1837	January	Review of *Astoria* (Washington Irving)	*Southern Literary Messenger*	LC
1837	January	Review of *George Balcombe* (Beverley Tucker)	*Southern Literary Messenger*	LC
1837	January	Review of *Poems* (William C. Bryant)	*Southern Literary Messenger*	LC
1837	January	Review of *Select Orations of Cicero* (Charles Anthon)	*Southern Literary Messenger*	LC
1837	January	Review of *South-Sea Expedition* (Jeremiah N. Reynolds)	*Southern Literary Messenger*	LC

Year	Date	Title	Publication	Genre
1837	January	'Sonnet: To Zante' ['To Zante']	*Southern Literary Messenger*	P
1837	January–February	'Arthur Gordon Pym' (first chapters)	*Southern Literary Messenger*	T
1837	June	'Von Jung, the Mystific' ['Mystification']	*American Monthly Magazine*	T
1837	October	Review of *Arabia Petraea* (John L. Stephens)	*New York Review*	LC
1838		'Silence – A Fable' [originally 'Siope']	*The Baltimore Book, 1838*	T
1838		*The Narrative of Arthur Gordon Pym*	Harper Brothers	T
1838	September	'Ligeia'	*American Museum*	T
1838	November	'The Psyche Zenobia' (with 'The Scythe of Time')	*American Museum*	T
1839		'Intemperance'	*Southern First Class Book, 1839*	M
1839		*The Conchologist's First Book*	Haswell, Barrington, Haswell	M
1839	January–February	'Literary Small Talk'	*American Museum*	M
1839	April	'The Haunted Palace'	*American Museum*	P
1839	18 May	'The Devil in the Belfry: An Extravaganza' ['The Devil in the Belfry']	*Saturday Chronicle*	T
1839	July	Review of *Synopsis of Natural History* (Thomas Wyatt)	*Burton's Magazine*	LC
1839	July	Review of *Francia's Reign of Terror* (J.P. and W.P. Robinson)	*Burton's Magazine*	LC
1839	July	Review of *Isabel* (H.T. Tuckerman)	*Burton's Magazine*	LC
1839	July	Review of *Memoirs of Celebrated Women* (G.P.R. James)	*Burton's Magazine*	LC
1839	July	Review of *Sketches of Public Characters* (Henry L. Brougham)	*Burton's Magazine*	LC
1839	July	Review of *The History of the Navy* (James F. Cooper)	*Burton's Magazine*	LC
1839	July	Review of *Tortesa the Usurer* (Nathaniel P. Willis)	*Literary Examiner and Western Monthly Review*	LC

Year	Date	Title	Publication	Genre
1839	July	'To Ianthe in Heaven'	*Burton's Magazine*	P
1839	July–February 1840	'A Chapter on Field Sports and Manly Pastimes'	*Burton's Magazine*	M
1839	August	'American Novel Writing'	*Literary Examiner and Western Monthly Review*	M
1839	August	'An Opinion on Dreams'	*Burton's Magazine*	M
1839	August	Review of *A Defense of Female Education* (John S. Lewis)	*Burton's Magazine*	LC
1839	August	Review of *Popular Lectures on Geology* (H.C. von Leonhard)	*Burton's Magazine*	LC
1839	August	Review of *Precaution* (James F. Cooper)	*Burton's Magazine*	LC
1839	August	Review of *Sketches of London* (James Grant)	*Burton's Magazine*	LC
1839	August	Review of *The Gentleman of the Old School* (G.P.R. James)	*Burton's Magazine*	LC
1839	August	Review of *The Pocket Lacon* (John Taylor)	*Burton's Magazine*	LC
1839	August	Review of *The Triumphs of Science* (William Wallace)	*Burton's Magazine*	LC
1839	August	'The Man That Was Used Up'	*Burton's Magazine*	T
1839	August	'To ——' ('Fair Maiden . . .')	*Burton's Magazine*	P
1839	September	Review of *A Voice to the South* (J.M. Austin)	*Burton's Magazine*	LC
1839	September	Review of *Algeic Researches* (H.R. Schoolcraft)	*Burton's Magazine*	LC
1839	September	Review of *Birds and Flowers and Other Country Things* (Mary Howitt)	*Burton's Magazine*	LC
1839	September	Review of *Charles Hartland* (William A. Alcott)	*Burton's Magazine*	LC
1839	September	Review of *Continuation of the Diary* (James Galt)	*Burton's Magazine*	LC
1839	September	Review of *Historical Sketches of Statesmen* (Henry L. Brougham)	*Burton's Magazine*	LC

Year	Date	Title	Publication	Genre
1839	September	Review of *Letters During the Invasion and Possession of Charleston* (Eliza Wilkinson)	*Burton's Magazine*	LC
1839	September	Review of *Practical Lessons in Flower Painting* (James Ackerman)	*Burton's Magazine*	LC
1839	September	Review of *Solomon Seesaw* (J.P. Robertson)	*Burton's Magazine*	LC
1839	September	Review of *Tales of Shipwrecks and Other Disasters at Sea* (Thomas Bingley)	*Burton's Magazine*	LC
1839	September	Review of *The American Flower Garden Companion* (Edward Sayers)	*Burton's Magazine*	LC
1839	September	Review of *The American Fruit Garden Companion* (Edward Sayers)	*Burton's Magazine*	LC
1839	September	Review of *The Bride of Fort Edward* (Delia Bacon)	*Burton's Magazine*	LC
1839	September	Review of *The Thugs or Phansigars of India* (W.H. Sleeman)	*Burton's Magazine*	LC
1839	September	Review of *Undine* (Friedrich Fouqué)	*Burton's Magazine*	LC
1839	September	'The Fall of the House of Usher'	*Burton's Magazine*	T
1839	October	Review of *A System of Modern Geography* (S. Augustustus Mitchell)	*Burton's Magazine*	LC
1839	October	Review of *Fair Rosamond* (Thomas Miller)	*Burton's Magazine*	LC
1839	October	Review of *Flora's Lexicon*	*Burton's Magazine*	LC
1839	October	Review of *Hamilton King*	*Burton's Magazine*	LC
1839	October	Review of *Hyperion* (H.W. Longfellow)	*Burton's Magazine*	LC
1839	October	Review of *Opinions of Lord Brougham*	*Burton's Magazine*	LC
1839	October	Review of *The Man About Town* (Cornelius Webbe)	*Burton's Magazine*	LC
1839	October	Review of The *Poems of Ossian* (James McPherson)	*Burton's Magazine*	LC

YEAR	DATE	TITLE	PUBLICATION	GENRE
1839	October	Review of *Travels in North America* (Charles A. Murray)	*Burton's Magazine*	LC
1839	October	'William Wilson'	*Burton's Magazine*	T
1839	November	Review of *Father Butler and the Lough Deary Pilgrim* (W.H. Carleton)	*Burton's Magazine*	LC
1839	November	Review of *Nan Darrell*	*Burton's Magazine*	LC
1839	November	Review of *The Canons of Good Breeding*	*Burton's Magazine*	LC
1839	November	Review of *The Damsel of Darien* (William G. Simms)	*Burton's Magazine*	LC
1839	November	Review of *The Literary Souvenir, 1840*	*Burton's Magazine*	LC
1839	November	Review of *The Violet, 1840*	*Burton's Magazine*	LC
1839	November	'The Capitol at Washington'	*Burton's Magazine*	M
1839	December	Review of *An Address* (Joseph R. Chandler)	*Burton's Magazine*	LC
1839	December	Review of *Memoirs of His Own Time* (Mathieu Dumas)	*Burton's Magazine*	LC
1839	December	Review of *National Melodies of America* (George P. Morris)	*Burton's Magazine*	LC
1839	December	Review of *Nicholas Nickleby* (Charles Dickens)	*Burton's Magazine*	LC
1839	December	Review of *Nix's Exile* (Rufus Dawes)	*Burton's Magazine*	LC
1839	December	Review of *The Good Housekeeper* (Sarah J. Hale)	*Burton's Magazine*	LC
1839	December	*Review of The Most Important Parts of Blackwood's Commentaries* (Asa Kinne)	*Burton's Magazine*	LC
1839	December	Review of *The United States Military Magazine*	*Burton's Magazine*	LC
1839	December	Review of *Walks and Wanderings in the World of Literature* (James Grant)	*Burton's Magazine*	LC
1839	December	'The Conversation of Eiros and Charmion'	*Burton's Magazine*	T

Year	Date	Title	Publication	Genre
1839	18 December	'Enigmatical and Conundrumical'	*Alexander's Weekly Magazine*	M
1840	January	Review of *Alciphron* (Thomas Moore)	*Burton's Magazine*	LC
1840	January	Review of *The Governess* (Marguerite Power)	*Burton's Magazine*	LC
1840	1 January	Notice of *New York Mirror*	*Alexander's Weekly Magazine*	LC
1840	4 January	'Silence – A Sonnet'	*Saturday Courier*	P
1840	15 January	'Enigmatical'	*Alexander's Weekly Magazine*	M
1840	15 January	'The Daguerreotype'	*Alexander's Weekly Magazine*	M
1840	22 January	'Another Poser, and Yet Another'	*Alexander's Weekly Magazine*	M
1840	29 January	'Instinct vs Reason – A Black Cat'	*Alexander's Weekly Magazine*	M
1840	29 January	Notice of *Burton's Gentleman's Magazine*	*Alexander's Weekly Magazine*	LC
1840	29 January	'The Bloodhound Story'	*Alexander's Weekly Magazine*	M
1840	January–June	'The Journal of Julius Rodman'	*Burton's Magazine*	T
1840	February	Notice of *The United States Military Magazine*	*Burton's Magazine*	LC
1840	February	'Peter Pendulum, the Business Man' ['The Business Man']	*Burton's Magazine*	T
1840	February	Review of *A Monograph of the Limniades* (Samuel S. Haldeman)	*Burton's Magazine*	LC
1840	February	Review of *Pictures of Early Life* (Emma C. Embury)	*Burton's Magazine*	LC
1840	February	Review of *Sacred Philosophy of the Seasons, Part ¾* (Henry Duncan)	*Burton's Magazine*	LC
1840	February	Review of *The Fright* (Ellen Pickering)	*Burton's Magazine*	LC
1840	February	Review of *The Philosophy of Human Life* (Amos Dean)	*Burton's Magazine*	LC
1840	February	Review of *Voices of the Night* (W.H. Longfellow)	*Burton's Magazine*	LC

Year	Date	Title	Publication	Genre
1840	February	Review of *Where Hudson's Wave, Ida* (George P. Morris)	*Burton's Magazine*	LC
1840	5 February	'Still Another Poser'	*Alexander's Weekly Magazine*	M
1840	12 February	'Our Late Puzzles'	*Alexander's Weekly Magazine*	M
1840	12 February	'Swimming'	*Alexander's Weekly Magazine*	M
1840	12 February	'Tennyson vs Longfellow'	*Alexander's Weekly Magazine*	M
1840	19 February	'Our Puzzles – Again'	*Alexander's Weekly Magazine*	M
1840	26 February	'Advertising Oddities'	*Alexander's Weekly Magazine*	M
1840	26 February	'More of Our Puzzles'	*Alexander's Weekly Magazine*	M
1840	26 February	'Our Puzzles Once More'	*Alexander's Weekly Magazine*	M
1840	February–March	Review of *Sacred Philosophy of the Seasons* (Henry Duncan)	*Burton's Magazine*	LC
1840	February–July	'A Chapter on Science and Art'	*Burton's Magazine*	M
1840	March	Review of *Memoirs and Reminiscences* (Madame Tussaud)	*Burton's Magazine*	LC
1840	March	Review of *Rambles in the Footsteps of Don Quixote* (H.D. Inglis)	*Burton's Magazine*	LC
1840	March	Review of *Romance of Travel* (Nathaniel P. Willis)	*Burton's Magazine*	LC
1840	March	Review of *The Letter Bad of the Great Western* (T.C. Haliburton)	*Burton's Magazine*	LC
1840	March	Review of *Trials of the Heart* (Mrs Bray)	*Burton's Magazine*	LC
1840	4 March	'More of the Puzzles'	*Alexander's Weekly Magazine*	M
1840	4 March	'Revivals'	*Alexander's Weekly Magazine*	M
1840	4 March	'Solution to a Cypher'	*Alexander's Weekly Magazine*	M
1840	11 March	'Puzzles Again!'	*Alexander's Weekly Magazine*	M

Year	Date	Title	Publication	Genre
1840	18 March	Notice of *The Virginia Star*	*Alexander's Weekly Magazine*	M
1840	18 March	Notice of *The Young Gardener's Assistant* (Thomas Bridgeman)	*Alexander's Weekly Magazine*	LC
1840	18 March	'The Rail-Road War'	*Alexander's Weekly Magazine*	M
1840	25 March	'Puzzles Again!'	*Alexander's Weekly Magazine*	M
1840	March–July	'A Chapter on Science and Art'	*Burton's Magazine*	M
1840	April	'A Word or Two on the Copy-Right Question'	*Burton's Magazine*	M
1840	1 April	'Cabs'	*Alexander's Weekly Magazine*	M
1840	1 April	'Disinterment'	*Alexander's Weekly Magazine*	M
1840	1 April	Notice of *Burton's Gentleman's Magazine*	*Alexander's Weekly Magazine*	LC
1840	1 April	'The Trial of James Wood'	*Alexander's Weekly Magazine*	M
1840	8 April	'Cyphers'	*Alexander's Weekly Magazine*	M
1840	15 April	'Revivals'	*Alexander's Weekly Magazine*	M
1840	15 April	'The Worm'	*Alexander's Weekly Magazine*	M
1840	22 April	'A Long Leap'	*Alexander's Weekly Magazine*	M
1840	22 April	'Changing Seats'	*Alexander's Weekly Magazine*	M
1840	22 April	'Cyphers Again'	*Alexander's Weekly Magazine*	M
1840	29 April	'A Charlatan!'	*Alexander's Weekly Magazine*	M
1840	29 April	'Cyphers'	*Alexander's Weekly Magazine*	M
1840	April–August	'Omniana'	*Burton's Magazine*	M
1840	May	Notice of William Cullen Bryant	*Burton's Magazine*	LC

Year	Date	Title	Publication	Genre
1840	May	Review of *Frank* (James Pedder)	*Burton's Magazine*	LC
1840	May	Review of *Memoirs and Letters of Madame Malibran* (Maria F. Malibran)	*Burton's Magazine*	LC
1840	May	Review of *The Duke* (Mrs Grey)	*Burton's Magazine*	LC
1840	May	Review of *The Florist's Guide*	*Burton's Magazine*	LC
1840	May	Review of *The Uncertainty of Literary Fame* (Charles W. Thompson)	*Burton's Magazine*	LC
1840	May	Review of *The Utility of Classical Studies* (N.C. Brooks)	*Burton's Magazine*	LC
1840	6 May	'Best Conundrum Yet'	*Alexander's Weekly Magazine*	M
1840	6 May	'Bulwer Used Up'	*Alexander's Weekly Magazine*	LC
1840	6 May	'Credulity'	*Alexander's Weekly Magazine*	M
1840	19 May	Notice of *F.W. Thomas*	*Daily Chronicle*	LC
1840	19 May	Notice of *J.E. Dow*	*Daily Chronicle*	LC
1840	June	Review of *High-Ways and By-Ways* (Thomas C. Grattan)	*Burton's Magazine*	LC
1840	June	Review of *The Proud Ladye* (Spencer W. Cone)	*Burton's Magazine*	LC
1840	June	'Some Account of Stonehenge'	*Burton's Magazine*	M
1840	December	'The Man of the Crowd'	*Burton's Magazine / The Casket*	T
1841	April	'The Murders in the Rue Morgue'	*Graham's Magazine*	T
1841	April	Review of *Heads of the People* (Kenny Meadows)	*Graham's Magazine*	LC
1841	April	Review of *Night and Morning* (Edward L. Bulwer)	*Graham's Magazine*	LC

YEAR	DATE	TITLE	PUBLICATION	GENRE
1841	April	Review of *Patchwork* (Basil Hall)	*Graham's Magazine*	LC
1841	April	*Review of Sketches of Conspicuous Living Characters of France* (Robert M. Walsh)	*Graham's Magazine*	LC
1841	May	'A Descent into the Maelstrom'	*Graham's Magazine*	T
1841	May	Review of *The Old Curiosity Shop* (Charles Dickens)	*Graham's Magazine*	LC
1841	May	Review of *The Sovereignty of Mind* (John N. McJilton)	*Graham's Magazine*	LC
1841	1 May	Review of *Barnaby Rudge* (Charles Dickens)	*Graham's Magazine*	LC
1841	June	Review of *Critical and Miscellaneous Essays* (Thomas B. Macaulay)	*Graham's Magazine*	LC
1841	June	Review of *Selections from the Poetical Literature of the West* (William D. Gallagher)	*Graham's Magazine*	LC
1841	June	Review of *The Quadroone* (Joseph H. Ingraham)	*Graham's Magazine*	LC
1841	June	'The Island of the Fay'	*Graham's Magazine*	T
1841	July	'A Few Words on Secret Writing'	*Graham's Magazine*	M
1841	July	Review of *A Memoir of the Very Reverend Theobald Mathew* (James Bermingham)	*Graham's Magazine*	LC
1841	July	Review of *Carleton* (John R. Willis)	*Graham's Magazine*	LC
1841	July	Review of *English Grammar* (Hugh A. Pue)	*Graham's Magazine*	LC
1841	July	Review of *Lives of the Queens of England* (Agnes Strickland)	*Graham's Magazine*	LC
1841	July	Review of *Miscellanies of Literature* (Isaac D'Israeli)	*Graham's Magazine*	LC
1841	July	Review of *Outlines of Geography* (Frederick Emerson)	*Graham's Magazine*	LC
1841	July	Review of *Powhatan* (Seba Smith)	*Graham's Magazine*	LC

Year	Date	Title	Publication	Genre
1841	July	Review of *The History of a Flirt* (Charlotte Campbell Bury)	*Graham's Magazine*	LC
1841	July	Review of *The Life and Land of Burns* (Allan Cunningham)	*Graham's Magazine*	LC
1841	August	Review of *Incidents of Travel in Central America* (John L. Stephens)	*Graham's Magazine*	LC
1841	August	Review of *The Quacks of Helicon* (Lambert A. Wilmer)	*Graham's Magazine*	LC
1841	August	'Secret Writing – Addendum'	*Graham's Magazine*	M
1841	August	'The Colloquy of Monos and Una'	*Graham's Magazine*	T
1841	September	'Never Bet Your Head: A Moral Tale' ['Never Bet the Devil Your Head']	*Graham's Magazine*	T
1841	September	Review of *Joseph Rushbrook* (Francis Marryatt)	*Graham's Magazine*	LC
1841	September	Review of *The Idler in France* ('Countess Blessington')	*Graham's Magazine*	LC
1841	October	'Secret Writing – Addendum II'	*Graham's Magazine*	M
1841	November	'A Chapter on Autography I'	*Graham's Magazine*	M
1841	November	Notice of *A Token of Friendship*	*Graham's Magazine*	LC
1841	November	Notice of *Dr Clifford* (R.P. Ward)	*Graham's Magazine*	LC
1841	November	Notice of *Incidents of a Whaling Voyage* (Francis A. Olmstead)	*Graham's Magazine*	LC
1841	November	Notice of *The Book of the Seasons* (William Hewitt)	*Graham's Magazine*	LC
1841	November	Notice of *The History of the Church* (Nathan C. Brooks)	*Graham's Magazine*	LC
1841	November	Notice of *The Life of Gilbert Motier de Lafayette* (Ebenezer Mack)	*Graham's Magazine*	LC
1841	November	Review of *Amenities of Literature* (Isaac D'Israeli)	*Graham's Magazine*	LC

YEAR	DATE	TITLE	PUBLICATION	GENRE
1841	November	Review of *Guy Fawkes* (W.H. Ainsworth)	*Graham's Magazine*	LC
1841	November	Review of *History of the War in the Peninsula* (W.F. Napier)	*Graham's Magazine*	LC
1841	November	Review of *Ten Thousand a Year* (Samuel Warren)	*Graham's Magazine*	LC
1841	November	Review of *The Critical and Miscellaneous Writings of Sir* Edward Lytton Bulwer	*Graham's Magazine*	LC
1841	November	Review of *The Pic-Nic Papers* (ed. Charles Dickens)	*Graham's Magazine*	LC
1841	27 November	'A Succession of Sundays' ['Three Sundays in a Week']	*Sunday Evening Post*	T
1841	December	'A Chapter on Autography II'	*Graham's Magazine*	M
1841	December	Review of *Cecil* (Catherine Gore)	*Graham's Magazine*	LC
1841	December	Review of *Confessions* W.G. Simms)	*Graham's Magazine*	LC
1841	December	Review of *Fragments from German Prose Writers* (Sarah Austin)	*Graham's Magazine*	LC
1841	December	Review of *Poetical Remains* (Lucretia M. Davidson)	*Graham's Magazine*	LC
1841	December	*Review of The Miser* (William Carleton)	*Graham's Magazine*	LC
1841	December	Review of *The Seaman's Friend* (R.H. Dana)	*Graham's Magazine*	LC
1841	December	'Secret Writing – Addendum III'	*Graham's Magazine*	M
1842		'Eleonora'	*The Gift* 1842	T
1842	January	'An Appendix of Autographs'	*Graham's Magazine*	M
1842	January	'Exordium'	*Graham's Magazine*	M
1842	January	Review of *Critical and Miscellaneous Essays* (Christopher North)	*Graham's Magazine*	LC
1842	January	Review of *Pocahontas* (Lydia H. Sigourney)	*Graham's Magazine*	LC

Year	Date	Title	Publication	Genre
1842	January	Review of *Poetical Works* (Reginald Heber)	*Graham's Magazine*	LC
1842	January	Review of *Stanley Thorn* (Henry Cockton)	*Graham's Magazine*	LC
1842	January	Review of *Tales and Souvenirs* (Mrs Rives)	*Graham's Magazine*	LC
1842	January	Review of *The Poetical Works* (Byron)	*Graham's Magazine*	LC
1842	February	'A Few Words About Brainard'	*Graham's Magazine*	LC
1842	February	'Harpers Ferry'	*Graham's Magazine*	M
1842	February	Notice of *The Lady's Musical Library* (Charles Jarvis)	*Graham's Magazine*	LC
1842	February	Notice of *The Ruins of Athens, Titania's Banquet, A Mask and Other Poems* (G. Hill)	*Graham's Magazine*	LC
1842	February	Notice of *Wealth and Worth* (Maria Sedgwick)	*Graham's Magazine*	LC
1842	February	Review of *Barnaby Rudge* (Charles Dickens)	*Graham's Magazine*	LC
1842	February	Review of *Wakondah* (Cornelius Mathews)	*Graham's Magazine*	LC
1842	March	Review of *Ballads and Other Poems I* (H.W. Longfellow)	*Graham's Magazine*	LC
1842	March	Review of *Charles O'Malley* (Charles J. Lever)	*Graham's Magazine*	LC
1842	March	Review of *Pantalogy* (Roswell Park)	*Graham's Magazine*	LC
1842	March	Review of *The Critical and Miscellaneous Writings* (Henry P.L. Brougham)	*Graham's Magazine*	LC
1842	April	'Life in Death' ['The Oval Portrait']	*Graham's Magazine*	T
1842	April	Review of *Ballads and Other Poems II* (H.W. Longfellow)	*Graham's Magazine*	LC
1842	April	Review of *Ideals* (Algernon)	*Graham's Magazine*	LC
1842	May	Review of *Beauchampe* (W.G. Simms)	*Graham's Magazine*	LC
1842	May	Review of *The Vigil of Faith* (C.F. Hoffman)	*Graham's Magazine*	LC

Year	Date	Title	Publication	Genre
1842	May	Review of *Twice-Told Tales* (Nathaniel Hawthorne)	*Graham's Magazine*	LC
1842	May	'The Mask of the Red Death' ['The Masque of the Red Death']	*Graham's Magazine*	T
1842	June	Review of *Poets and Poetry of America* (Rufus W. Griswold)	*Graham's Magazine*	LC
1842	October	'The Landscape-Garden' ['The Domain of Arnheim']	*The Ladies' Companion*	T
1842	October	'The Poetry of Rufus Dawes'	*Graham's Magazine*	LC
1842	November	Griswold's *American Poetry*	*Boston Miscellany*	LC
1842–1843	November–February	'The Mystery of Marie Rogêt'	*The Ladies' Companion*	T
1843		'The Pit and the Pendulum'	*The Gift 1843*	T
1843	January	Notice of *The Pioneer*	*Saturday Museum*	LC
1843	January	'The Conqueror Worm'	*Graham's Magazine*	P
1843	January	'The Tell-Tale Heart'	*The Pioneer*	T
1843	February	'Lenore'	*The Pioneer*	P
1843	March	'Notes Upon English Verse'	*The Pioneer*	LC
1843	March	'Our Amateur Poets – Flaccus'	*Graham's Magazine*	LC
1843	4 March	'Lines on Joe Locke'	*Saturday Museum*	P
1843	4 March	'The Sleeper'	*Saturday Museum*	P
1843	4 March	'To One in Paradise'	*Saturday Museum*	P
1843	25 March	'Original Conundrums'	*Saturday Museum*	M
1843	13 May	'Souvenirs of Youth' (translation)	*New Mirror*	T
1843	1 April	'Original Conundrums II'	*Saturday Museum*	M

Year	Date	Title	Publication	Genre
1843	June	'The Gold Bug'	*Dollar Newspaper*	T
1843	17 June	'The Head of St John the Baptist' (translation)	*New Mirror*	M
1843	August	'Our Amateur Poets – William Ellery Channing'	*Graham's Magazine*	LC
1843	19 August	'The Black Cat'	*United States Saturday Post*	T
1843	September	'Our Contributors – Fitz-Greene Halleck'	*Graham's Magazine*	LC
1843	September	Review of *A Brief Account of the Discoveries and Results of the US Exploring Expedition* (Jeremiah N. Reynolds)	*Graham's Magazine*	LC
1843	14 October	'Raising the Wind, or, Diddling Considered as One of the Exact Sciences'	*Saturday Courier*	M
1843	November	Review of *Wyandotte* (James F. Cooper)	*Graham's Magazine*	LC
1844		'A Chapter of Suggestions'	*The Opal 1844*	M
1844		'Morning on the Wissahiccon' ['The Elk']	*The Opal 1844*	M
1844	January	Review of *Ned Myer* (James F. Cooper)	*Graham's Magazine*	LC
1844	January	Review of *Orion* (Richard H. Horne)	*Graham's Magazine*	LC
1844	March	Review of *Poems* (James R. Lowell)	*Graham's Magazine*	LC
1844	27 March	'The Spectacles'	*Dollar Newspaper*	T
1844	April	'A Tale of the Ragged Mountains'	*Godey's Lady's Book*	T
1844	13 April	'The Balloon Hoax'	*New York Sun (extra)*	T
1844	May–June	'Doings of Gotham: Letters I–VII'	*Columbia Spy*	M
1844	June	'Dream-Land'	*Graham's Magazine*	P
1844	June	'Our Contributors – Robert T. Conrad'	*Graham's Magazine*	LC

YEAR	DATE	TITLE	PUBLICATION	GENRE
1844	June	Review of *The Light-House* (Epes Sargent)	*Graham's Magazine*	LC
1844	17–18 July	'A Moving Chapter'	*Public Ledger*	M
1844	19 July	'Desultory Notes on Cats'	*Public Ledger*	M
1844	31 July	'The Premature Burial'	*Dollar Newspaper*	T
1844	August	'Mesmeric Revelation'	*Columbian Magazine*	T
1844	September	'The Literary Life of Thingum Bob, Esq.'	*Southern Literary Messenger*	T
1844	September	'The Oblong Box'	*Godey's Lady's Book*	T
1844	October	'The Angel of the Odd – An Extravaganza'	*Columbian Magazine*	T
1844	10 October	'Author's Pay in America'	*Evening Mirror*	M
1844	10 October	'The Swiss Bell-Ringers'	*Evening Mirror*	M
1844	12 October	'Pay for Periodical Writing'	*Evening Mirror*	M
1844	21 October	'An Old Fire Bursting Out Afresh'	*Evening Mirror*	M
1844	November	'Thou Art the Man'	*Godey's Lady's Book*	T
1844	19 November	Notice of *The Linden Tree* (Frederick W. Thomas)	*Evening Mirror*	LC
1844	November–December	'Marginalia I–II'	*US Magazine and Democratic Review*	M
1844	December	'Byron and Miss Chaworth'	*Columbian Magazine*	M
1844	December	Review of *Death* (Robert Tyler)	*Graham's Magazine*	LC
1845		'The Purloined Letter'	*The Gift 1845*	T
1845		'To F—— O—— [Frances Osgood]'	*The Raven and Other Poems*	P
1845	4 January	Review of *The Drama of Exile* (Elizabeth Barrett)	*Broadway Journal*	LC
1845	9 January	'Does the Drama of the Day Deserve Support?'	*Evening Mirror*	M

Year	Date	Title	Publication	Genre
1845	11 January	'Lines After Elizabeth Barrett'	*Broadway Journal*	LC
1845	11 January	*Review of Conversations* (James R. Lowell)	*Evening Mirror*	LC
1845	11 January	'The Alphadelphia Tocsin'	*Evening Mirror*	M
1845	13 January	Review of *The Waif* (H.W. Longfellow)	*Evening Mirror*	LC
1845	17 January	Criticism: 'The Tribune of Tuesday . . .'	*Evening Mirror*	LC
1845	17 January	'Nature and Art'	*Evening Mirror*	LC
1845	17 January	'The Branded Hand'	*Evening Mirror*	LC
1845	18 January	Review of *The Drama of Exile* (Elizabeth Barrett)	*Broadway Journal*	LC
1845	20 January	'Post Notes by a Critic'	*Evening Mirror*	LC
1845	22 January	'American Diffuseness – Objectionable Concision'	*Evening Mirror*	LC
1845	23 January	'Epigram for Wall Street'	*Evening Mirror*	P
1845	23 January	'Four Hundred Miles of Grasshoppers!'	*Evening Mirror*	M
1845	24–31 January	'Pay of American Authors I–IV'	*Evening Mirror*	M
1845	25 January	Review of *The Waif* (H.W. Longfellow)	*Weekly Mirror*	LC
1845	29 January	'The Raven'	*Evening Mirror*	P
1845	31 January	'Wood Pavements'	*Evening Mirror*	M
1845	February	'The Thousand and Second Tale of Scheherazade'	*Godey's Lady's Book*	T
1845	3 February	'Increase of the Poetical Heresy – Didactism'	*Evening Mirror*	LC
1845	8 February	Review of *Poems* (Edward L. Bulwer)	*Broadway Journal*	LC
1845	8 February	'Why Not Try a Mineralized Pavement?'	*Evening Mirror*	M
1845	12 February	'Magazine Literature'	*Evening Mirror*	LC

YEAR	DATE	TITLE	PUBLICATION	GENRE
1845	15 February	'Some Secrets of the Magazine Prison-House'	*Broadway Journal*	M
1845	17 February	'Plagiarism'	*Evening Mirror*	LC
1845	March	Review of *Ancient America* (George Jones)	*Aristidean*	LC
1845	8 March	'Imitation – Plagiarism – Mr Poe's Reply to the Letter of Outis' (1 March)	*Broadway Journal*	M
1845	8 March	'Portrait of a Distinguished Authoress' (Margaret Fuller)	*Broadway Journal*	LC
1845	15 March	'A Continuation of the Voluminous History of the Longfellow War'	*Broadway Journal*	M
1845	15 March	Review of *Infatuation* (Benjamin Park)	*Broadway Journal*	LC
1845	15 March	'Satirical *Poems*'	*Broadway Journal*	LC
1845	22 March	'More of the Voluminous History of the Longfellow War'	*Broadway Journal*	M
1845	22 March	'Mrs R.S. Nichols . . .'	*Broadway Journal*	LC
1845	29 March	Review of *Fashion* (Anna C. Mowatt)	*Broadway Journal*	LC
1845	29 March	'Imitation – Plagiarism – the Conclusion of Mr Poe's Reply to the Letter of Outis'	*Broadway Journal*	M
1845	April	'Longfellow's *Poems*'	*Aristidean*	LC
1845	April	Notice of *Phreno-Mnemotechny* (Francis Fauvel-Gouraud)	*Broadway Journal*	LC
1845	April	'Some Words with a Mummy'	*American Review*	T
1845	April	'The Valley of Unrest'	*American Review*	P
1845	5 April	'Imitation – Plagiarism – Postscript'	*Broadway Journal*	M
1845	5 April	Review of *Human Magnetism* (W. Newman)	*Broadway Journal*	LC
1845	12 April	'Anastatic Writing'	*Broadway Journal*	M

YEAR	DATE	TITLE	PUBLICATION	GENRE
1845	19 April	'Achilles' Wrath'	*Broadway Journal*	M
1845	19 April	'Street Paving'	*Broadway Journal*	M
1845	26 April	'Impromptu to Kate Carol'	*Broadway Journal*	M
1845	May	Review of *A Dictionary of Roman and Greek Antiquities* (Charles Anthon)	*Southern Literary Messenger*	LC
1845	May	Review of Titian's *Venus*	*Broadway Journal*	LC
1845	24 May	'To ——' [Violet Vane – the pseudonym of Frances Osgood]	*Broadway Journal*	P
1845	24 May	Review of *Poems* (William W. Lord)	*Broadway Journal*	LC
1845	June	'The Power of Words'	*Democratic Review*	T
1845	7 June	'Magazine-Writing – Peter Snook'	*Broadway Journal*	T
1845	14 June	Review of *An Explanatory and Phonographic Dictionary of the English Language* (William Bolles)	*Broadway Journal*	LC
1845	21 June	Review of *Plato Contra Atheos* (Tayler Lewis)	*Broadway Journal*	LC
1845	July	'Eulalie'	*American Review*	P
1845	July	'The Imp of the Perverse'	*Graham's Magazine*	T
1845	12 July	'How to Write a Blackwood Article' (with 'A Predicament')	*Broadway Journal*	M
1845	12 July	Review of *The Coming of the Mammoth* (Henry B. Hirst)	*Broadway Journal*	LC
1845	19 July	Alfred Tennyson	*Broadway Journal*	LC
1845	26 July	Review of *A Chaunt of Life* (Ralph Hoyt)	*Broadway Journal*	LC
1845	August	'The American Drama'	*American Whig Review*	LC
1845	2 August	Review of *The Fortune-Hunter* (Anna C. Mowatt)	*Broadway Journal*	LC

Year	Date	Title	Publication	Genre
1845	9 August	Review of *Ettore Fieramosca* (tr. C. Edwards Lester)	*Broadway Journal*	LC
1845	9 August	Review of *Prose and Verse* (Thomas Hood)	*Broadway Journal*	LC
1845	16 August	'Catholic Hymn' (from 'Morella')	*Broadway Journal*	P
1845	16 August	Review of *The Characters of Shakespeare* (William Hazlitt)	*Broadway Journal*	LC
1845	23 August	Review of *Dashes at Life with a Free Pencil* (Nathaniel P. Willis)	*Broadway Journal*	LC
1845	30 August	Review of *The Indicator and Companion* (Leigh Hunt)	*Broadway Journal*	LC
1845	30 August	'Romance'	*Broadway Journal*	P
1845	August–September	'Marginalia III–IV'	*Godey's Lady's Book*	M
1845	September	'Stanzas' [to Frances Osgood]	*Graham's Magazine*	P
1845	6 September	Review of 'Festus: A Poem' (Philip J. Bailey)	*Broadway Journal*	LC
1845	6 September	Review of *Genius and Character of Burns* (Christopher North)	*Broadway Journal*	LC
1845	6 September	'Why the Little Frenchman Wears His Hand in a Sling'	*Broadway Journal*	T
1845	13 September	'To F——' [Frances Osgood]	*Broadway Journal*	P
1845	27 September	Review of *The Prose Works of John Milton*	*Broadway Journal*	LC
1845	October	'The Divine Right of Kings'	*Graham's Magazine*	M
1845	4 October	Notice of *Simm's Monthly Magazine*	*Broadway Journal*	LC
1845	11 October	Review of *The Broken Vow* (Amanda M. Edwards)	*Broadway Journal*	LC
1845	11 October	Review of *Historical Sketch of the Second War Between the USA and Great Britain* (Charles J. Ingersoll)	*Broadway Journal*	LC
1845	November	Review of *The Wigwam and the Cabin* (William G. Simms)	*Broadway Journal*	LC
1845	November	'The System of Dr Tarr and Prof. Fether'	*Graham's Magazine*	T

Year	Date	Title	Publication	Genre
1845	1 November	Review of *Alice Ray* (Sarah J. Hale)	*Broadway Journal*	LC
1845	1 November	'The Fine Arts'	*Broadway Journal*	LC
1845	29 November	Notice of Alfred Tennyson	*Broadway Journal*	LC
1845	December	Review of *The Poetical Writings* (Elizabeth O. Smith)	*Godey's Lady's Book*	LC
1845	December	'The Facts in the Case of M. Valdemar'	*American Review*	T
1846	January	'The Sphinx'	*Arthur's Ladies' Magazine*	T
1846	February	Review of *The Songs of Our Land* (Mary E. Hewitt)	*Godey's Lady's Book*	LC
1846	21 February	'To Her Whose Name Is Written Below'	*Evening Mirror*	P
1846	March	'Marginalia V'	*Graham's Magazine*	M
1846	March	Review of *A Wreath of Flowers from New England* (Frances S. Osgood)	*Godey's Lady's Book*	LC
1846	April	'Marginalia VI'	*Democratic Review*	M
1846	April	Review of *The Complete Poetical Works* (William C. Bryant)	*Godey's Lady's Book*	LC
1846	April	'The Philosophy of Composition'	*Graham's Magazine*	M
1846	May–October	'The Literati of New York City'	*Godey's Lady's Book*	LC
1846	July	'Marginalia VII'	*Democratic Review*	M
1846	10 July	'Mr Poe's Reply to Mr English and Others'	*Spirit of the Times*	M
1846	August	'A Few Words on Etiquette'	*Godey's Lady's Book*	M
1846	November	'The Cask of Amontillado'	*Godey's Lady's Book*	T
1846	November–December	'Marginalia VIII–IX'	*Graham's Magazine*	M
1847	13 March	'To M.L.S.' [Marie Louise Shew]	*Home Journal*	P
1847	May	Review of *The Froissart Ballads* (Phillip P. Cooke)	*Graham's Magazine*	LC

YEAR	DATE	TITLE	PUBLICATION	GENRE
1847	November	'Tale-Writing – Nathaniel Hawthorne'	*Godey's Lady's Book*	LC
1847	December	'To ——. Ulalume: A Ballad' ['Ulalume']	*American Review*	P
1848		Eureka	G.P. Putnam	M
1848		'George Bush'	*Literary America*	LC
1848		'Richard Adams Locke'	*Literary America*	LC
1848	January–March	'Marginalia X–XII'	*Graham's Magazine*	M
1848	March	'Sonnet' [acrostic – Sarah Anna Lewis]	*Union Magazine*	P
1848	March	'To —— [Marie Shew]' ['An Enigma']	*Columbian Magazine*	P
1848	August	'The Literati of New York – S. Anna Lewis'	*United States Magazine and Democratic Review*	LC
1848	September	Review of *The Child of the Sea* (Sarah A. Lewis)	*Southern Literary Messenger*	LC
1848	October–November	'The Rationale of Verse'	*Southern Literary Messenger*	M
1848	November	'To ——' [Helen Whitman]	*Union Magazine*	P
1849	February	'Mellonta Tauta'	*Godey's Lady's Book*	T
1849	February	Review of *The Female Poets of America* (Rufus W. Griswold)	*Southern Literary Messenger*	LC
1849	March	Review of *A Fable for Critics* (James R. Lowell)	*Southern Literary Messenger*	LC
1849	3 March	'A Valentine'	*Flag of Our Union*	P
1849	17 March	'Hop-Frog'	*Flag of Our Union*	T
1849	31 March	'A Dream Within a Dream'	*Flag of Our Union*	P
1849	April	'Notice of Bayard Taylor'	*Southern Literary Messenger*	LC
1849	14 April	'Von Kempelen and His Discovery'	*Flag of Our Union*	T
1849	21 April	'Eldorado'	*Flag of Our Union*	P

Year	Date	Title	Publication	Genre
1849	28 April	'For Annie'	*Flag of Our Union*	P
1849	April–July	'Marginalia XIII–XVI'	*Southern Literary Messenger*	M
1849	12 May	'X-ing a Paragrab'	*Flag of Our Union*	T
1849	May–June	'Fifty Suggestions'	*Graham's Magazine*	M
1849	9 June	'Landor's Cottage'	*Flag of Our Union*	T
1849	7 July	'Sonnet: To My Mother'	*Flag of Our Union*	P
1849	August	'Notice of Frances Sargent Osgood'	*Southern Literary Messenger*	LC
1849	September	'Marginalia XCII'	*Southern Literary Messenger*	M
1849	9 October	'Annabel Lee'	*New York Tribune*	P
1849	22 October	'William Ross Wallace'	*New York Tribune*	LC
1849	December	'The Bells' (1848)	*Sartain's Magazine*	P
1850	January	'About Critics and Criticism' (?1849)	*Graham's Magazine*	M
1850	31 August	'The Poetic Principle' (1848)	*Home Journal*	M
1868	7 March	'O Tempora! O Mores!' (?1825)	*Southern Opinion*	P
1875	September	'Alone' (?1829)	*Scribner's Monthly Magazine*	P
1899	4 March	'A Campaign Song' (?1844)	*New York Times Saturday Review*	P
1909	January	'Beloved Physician' (?1847)	*The Bookman*	P
1914	December	'Deep in Earth' (?1847)	*Bulletin of the New York Public Library*	P
1917		'An Acrostic' ('Elizabeth') (?1829)	*The Complete Poems of Edgar Allan Poe*, ed. J.H. Whitty	P
1917		'Queen of May Ode' (?1836)	*The Complete Poems of Edgar Allan Poe*, ed. J.H. Whitty	P

YEAR	DATE	TITLE	PUBLICATION	GENRE
1931	28 November	'To Margaret' (?1827)	*Notes and Queries*	P
1932	21 February	'To Miss Louise Olivia Butler' (1847)	*Notes and Queries*	P
1939	29 July	'Lines on Ale' (?1848)	*Notes and Queries*	P
1941		'To Octavia'	Introduction. Facsimile of *Tamerlane and Other Poems*	P
1942	25 April	'The Light-House'	*Notes and Queries*	T

INDEX

All works by Poe are listed under Poe, Edgar Allan, Works